MAGNA CARTA
AND
MEDIEVAL GOVERNMENT

STUDIES PRESENTED TO THE
INTERNATIONAL COMMISSION
FOR THE HISTORY OF
REPRESENTATIVE AND
PARLIAMENTARY OPINION

LXVIII

ÉTUDES PRÉSENTÉES À LA
COMMISSION INTERNATIONALE
POUR L'HISTOIRE DES
ASSEMBLÉES D'ÉTATS

MAGNA CARTA
AND
MEDIEVAL GOVERNMENT

J. C. HOLT

THE HAMBLEDON PRESS

LONDON   AND   RONCEVERTE

Published by The Hambledon Press 1985

35 Gloucester Avenue,
London NW1 7AX (U.K.)

309 Greenbrier Avenue,
Ronceverte, West Virginia (U.S.A.)

ISBN 0 907628 38 9

British Library Cataloguing in Publication Data

Holt, J.C.
    Magna Carta and Medieval government. —
    (History series; 38)
    1. Great Britain — History — John, 1199-1216
    2. Great Britain — Politics and government —
    1154-1399
    I. Title
    942.03'3   DA208

Library of Congress Cataloging in Publication Data

Holt, James Clarke
    Magna Carta and Medieval government.

    Includes bibliographical references and index.
    1. Magna Carta — Addresses, essays, lectures.
    2. Great Britain — History — John, 1199-1216 —
    Addresses, essays, lectures. I Title.
    JN147.H642   1985   942.03'3   85-5542
    ISBN 0 907628 38 9

Printed and bound in Great Britain
by Robert Hartnoll Ltd., Bodmin, Cornwall

CONTENTS

ACKNOWLEDGEMENTS

The articles reprinted here appeared first in the following places and are reprinted by the kind permission of the original publishers.

1   The Hinkley Lecture, Johns Hopkins University, 31 March 1983; this appears in print here for the first time.

2   The Raleigh Lecture on History, 1975. *Proceedings of the British Academy*, lxi (1975), 3-45.

3   *Accademia Nazionale dei Lincei*, 253 (1981), 17-33.

4   *Historical Association General Series*, 53 (1963).

5   *Nottingham Medieval Studies*, v (1961), 75-86.

6   Published by the University Press of Virginia (1965) under the title, 'The Making of Magna Carta'.

7   *English Historical Review*, lx (1955), 1-24.

8   *Album Helen Maud Cam* (Nauwelarts, Louvain, 1960), i. 57-69.

9   *English Historical Review*, lxii (1957), 401-22.

10   *English Historical Review*, lxxxix (1974), 346-64.

11   *The Hatcher Review*, 2 (1982), 147-52, 191.

12   *Transactions of the Royal Historical Society*, 5th series, 14 (1964), 67-88.

13   *Studia Gratiana*, xv (1972), 487-508.

PREFACE

The studies collected in this book are drawn from a widely scattered range of periodical and other literature. The first has not been published previously; the rest represent work extending over thirty years. Extensive renovation of these has not been necessary and would in any case have been impossible. I have taken the opportunity to correct some slips and have added a few notes drawing attention to subsequent literature where appropriate. The index is exhaustive for persons and places, but more selective as regards subject-matter.

To reflect at any length on such a prolonged period of work would be neither inspiring for the reader nor remedial for the author. Yet the act of assembling and re-reading cannot but provoke a response which involves both retrospect and prospect. Looking back, these studies now seem to me to depend in one way or another on two distinct lines of thought. The first is that the political ideas and motives of men of action in the Middle Ages are best traced, not in academic theory, whether of schoolmen or lawyers, but in the fragmentary indications which can be pieced together from the records of their actions. The second is that the documents, their production and their function, matter so decisively that no time spent in their study and elucidation is ever wasted. The first line took hold in my mind when I presented a preliminary version of the essay on the barons and the Great Charter to the Stubbs Society in Oxford in 1949. The second owed much to *Stubbs's Charters* and to my tutor, J.O. Prestwich, but the work which led to the paper on the making of Magna Carta owed even more to V.H. Galbraith, who listened and debated with relish as the argument took shape. Galbraith's 'nose' for a document was incomparable. I have been the happier in preparing this volume in knowing that I was bringing together a number of essays which are a small individual tribute to his memory.

Looking forward, the main compensation for errors of commission and omission is that they point to work still to be done. Much more can be said about the law and about justice and judgment, and I hope to deal with these in a second edition of *Magna Carta*, now in preparation. The essay on the government of Richard I is a preliminary study of matters which must await the collection of *acta* of the Angevin kings. This too, I hope to be able to complete. No such hope can be expressed about the first study which I include as a medievalist's contribution to the great debate about the seventeenth century.

J.C. Holt

Fitzwilliam College
Cambridge
1 January, 1985

THE ORIGINS OF THE
CONSTITUTIONAL TRADITION IN ENGLAND[1]

'Constitutions should be short and preferably obscure', said Napoleon. If the length of a written constitution is taken in evidence then the English constitution is the shortest of all: it is non-existent. And even if we fabricate a constitution from statutory bits and pieces — Magna Carta, the Bill of Rights, *Habeas Corpus* — it would all be conditional on parliamentary sovereignty and subject at times to urgent necessity, whether in the form of the special pleadings of medieval monarchs or of the Defence of the Realm Act of the present century. The constitution, such as it is, has certainly been obscure, not simply because it has always left much room for interpretation, but also because it has always been very difficult to see why in this assemblage of statutory provision, legal precedent and administrative convention, one piece should seem more important than another. What had led us in short to attach enduring significance to some of these bits and pieces and to dismiss others as merely transitory?

Perhaps part of the answer is obvious enough: some documents have such intrinsic worth, so much political heat has gone into their forging, that they are bound to stand out from the everyday base material. Yet that explanation is not wholly satisfactory. Pre-eminence is not always so obvious. Each of our common law writs in origin was a practical workaday document of no obvious world-shaking importance. Taken together, however, they constituted a system of law which is fundamental to our understanding of English history. Equally, we have not all been agreed on what constitutes pre-eminence. Compare for example any one of our collection of 'const. docs.' (as they used to be called when they reigned as a compulsory part of the Oxford History School), from Stubbs onward, with the selection made by the anonymous author of Huntington Library MS, Ellesmere 1169. This is a modest volume, dating probably from the reign of James I:

A collection of notes out of the Records in the Tower Not purposlie nor perfectlie gathered in due order of years,

---

1   The following was delivered as the Hinkley Lecture in Johns Hopkins University on 31 March 1983. It is printed with minimal amendments.

But skatteringlie and by occasion gleaned as they came to hand, shewinge as a taste to understand rather what, than howe muche maie there be further funde, and to nothinge such matters as is therein contayned, Beinge of sundry natures and sume in sundry sort to contayne...[2]

The chapter headings whet the appetite, for the writer begins with 'the Kinge, his oath, office, authorytie Royall and prerogatyve' and then moves on to sundry other headings — 'The King's authorytie lymited and restrayned; Auncient laws and customes of this land for the most parte either not used or not knowen; Subsidies of sundrie sortes pertayning to the king either by grante or auncient Righte, Matters apperteyninge to the Church and specially against the Pope's usurpacions.'[3] The author was of Royalist bent and almost certainly in royal employment. So his opening section illustrated that the King 'governethe, comandeth and ordayneth, forbiddethe and restraynethe, priviledgethe, dispenseth, assureth and secureth.'[4] Only once in his collection of the limits and restraints on royal authority does he mention Magna Carta and then only in quoting Edward III's reversal of his father's process against Roger Mortimer as being 'erronious and injuriouse to the Common Lawe and liberte of Magna Carta' in that it was done without arraignment or trial by peers.[5] That and a writ assessing the ancient custom of 1275 and some material concerning subsidies and the resumption of Crown lands, are the only matters in which this selection overlaps our standard collections.[6] This was very much a minority report, on the fringe of the antiquarian activity, idiosyncratic, even quaint. The author was still interested in the right of royal tallage of the Jews, a right which had fallen into disuse with the official expulsion of the Jews in 1290.[7]

Such concoctions may be dismissed too perfunctorily. Ellesmere MS 1169, as the author admitted, was collected but 'skatteringlie and by occasion gleaned'. But it contained in it the seeds of those ideas which were to emphasise the Crown's prerogative in the later seventeenth century. Moreover, it stands as a warning against our identifying the ultimately predominant voice of Coke as the only one and against our failing to recognise that the tone set by Coke and others was to some degree determined by the need to contend with the weaker

2   Huntington Library, San Marino, Ellesmere MS 1169, title page.
3   Ellesmere MS 1169, fos. 16, 35, 87, 97.
4   Ellesmere MS 1169, fos. 1-13.
5   Ellesmere MS 1169, fo. 16. Compare *C.P.R. 1327-30*, 141-3.
6   Ellesmere MS 1169, fos. 16-17, 87-88.
7   Ellesmere MS 1169, fo. 88.

voices, many now suppressed and lost, which argued for a different conclusion. But when all that is said, the weakness of Ellesmere 1169 is still apparent. It was never published; it would have made an indigestible book. It therefore seems insipid beside the printed works of Lambarde, Selden, Prynne and Coke. Moreover, in its method it was simply part of the antiquarian stream. For the author, as for Coke, the antiquarian method was everything. Legal right was to be founded in the past. Precedent was nine-tenths of the argument. It was a lawyer's, indeed a common lawyer's world. The case for the prerogative called on much greater skill, a much deeper historical awareness than this searcher could provide. But his heart was in the right place. He ended his table of contents with an apologia which would have delighted V.H. Galbraith:

> The faultes herein committed through hast or lack of heade namlye in Relateinge, in Reportinge, alledginge of matters impertinent or superfluous, doe all desire pardon [and] maie at more leasure be reformed by Better Judgement: But specially by vewe of the Records themselves, unto which as there is particular reference every wheare made, So is it required that the same be only credited and not this reporte beinge sometymes over shorte and subject to misconceite.[8]

If only Coke had shown such modesty.

Of the ancient constitution as it was proclaimed by Coke, Selden and Prynne, I shall say little; it has been illuminated by Professor Pocock and others,[9] and I am less concerned with the logic and importance of the antiquarian argument of the seventeenth century which he has so skillfully delineated, than with its origins. How did it happen that men came to believe, and believe deeply, that the standing and even the structure of Parliament, the limitation of the prerogative in taxation, the protection of the individual by the common law, trial by jury, due process, were all part of an ancient structure which royal power had overlain but only partly impaired? That Coke and his fellows claimed an antiquity for their vision of the constitution which was quite spurious in terms of modern historical scholarship is plain. Indeed it was becoming plain by the end of the seventeenth century through the challenge of Robert Brady and others. But how far back did Coke's

---

9   J.G.A. Pocock, *The Ancient Constitution and the Feudal Law* (Cambridge, 1957); Herbert Butterfield, *Magna Carta in the Historiography of the sixteenth and seventeenth centuries* (Reading, 1969).

impression go? Did it go sufficiently far back in time for it to be difficult for Coke and like minded men to distinguish fact from fiction? What in any case was the borderline between the two?

My first text in pursuit of an answer is taken from the *De Laudibus Legum Angliae* of Sir John Fortescue, chief Justice of the King's Bench of Henry VI. The *De Laudibus* was written 1468-71 during Fortescue's exile in France and was strongly influenced by his French experience which led him to produce one of the first coherent exercises in comparative law. It is as one part of a comparison that the following must be understood:

> In the realm of England, no one billets himself in another's house against its master's will, unless in public hostelries, where even so he will pay in full for all that he has expended there, before his departure thence; nor does anyone take with impunity the goods of another without the permission of the proprietor of them; nor, in that realm, is anyone hindered from providing himself with salt or any goods whatever, at his own pleasure and of any vendor. The king, indeed, may, by his officers, take necessaries for his household, at a reasonable price to be assessed at the discretion of the constables of the villages, without the owners' permission. But none the less he is obliged by his own laws to pay this price out of hand or at a day fixed by the greater officers of his household, because by those laws he cannot despoil any of his subjects of their goods without due satisfaction for them. Nor does the king there, by himself or by his ministers, impose tallages, subsidies, or any other burdens whatever on his subjects, nor change their laws, nor make new ones, without the concession or assent of his whole realm expressed in his parliament.
>
> Hence every inhabitant of that realm uses at his own pleasure the fruits which his land yields, the increase of his flock, and all the emoluments which he gains, whether by his own industry or that of others, from land and sea, hindered by the injuries and rapine of none without obtaining at least due amends. Hence the inhabitants of that land are rich, abounding in gold and silver and all the necessaries of life. They do not drink water, except those who sometimes abstain from other drinks by way of devotional or penitential zeal. They eat every kind of flesh and fish in abundance, with which their land is not meanly stocked. They are clothed with good woollens throughout their garments; they have abundant bedding,

woollen like the rest of their furnishings, in all their houses, and are rich in all household goods and agricultural equipment, and in all that is requisite for a quiet and happy life, according to their estate. They are not brought to trial except before the ordinary judges, where they are treated justly according to the law of the land. Nor are they examined or impleaded in respect of their chattels, or possessions, nor arrested for crime of whatever magnitude and enormity, except according to the laws of that land and before the aforesaid judges.[10]

That passage has a threefold significance for my present purpose. First, already it embodies some of the important elements of the ancient constitution as it was understood in the seventeenth century: the limitation of purveyance, perhaps given more emphasis here than it might receive later; the legislative and financial power of parliament as representing the whole realm; common law procedures of arrest and trial, here still summarised, not as due process, but by the older term, *lex terrae* the law of the land. Secondly, Fortescue was a direct influence on the constitutional thinkers of the seventeenth century; Selden edited him in 1616 and Coke gave him the accolade that the chapters in the *De Laudibus* on trial by jury were 'worthy to be written in letters of gold for the weight and worthiness thereof'.[11] Thirdly, Fortescue takes us further back in time, for in an earlier passage in the *De Laudibus* he asserted:

The kingdom of England was first inhabited by Britons; then ruled by Romans, again by Britons, then possessed by Saxons, but finally by Normans, whose posterity hold the realm at the present time. And throughout the period of these nations and their kings, the realm has been continuously ruled by the same customs as it is now, customs which, if they had not been the best, some of those kings would have changed for the sake of justice or by the impulse of caprice, and totally abolished them, especially the Romans, who judged almost the whole of the rest of the world by their laws. Indeed, neither the civil laws of the Romans, so deeply rooted by usage of so many ages, nor the laws of the Venetians, which are renowned above others for their antiquity — though their island was uninhabited and Rome

10   Sir John Fortescue, *De Laudibus Legum Angliae*, ed. S.B. Chrimes (Cambridge, 1942), 86-9.
11   Coke continued — 'I will not abridge any part of the same, but refer the learned reader to the fountain itself'. See *Eight Part of the Reports of Sir Edward Coke* (London, 1738), xiv.

unbuilt at the time of the origin of the Britons — nor the laws of any Christian kingdom are so rooted in antiquity. Hence there is no gainsaying nor legitimate doubt but that the customs of the English are not only good but the best.[12]

That may lead you to think that it is not only English law which has deep roots. There is a certain self-satisfaction in the passage which has a modern ring to it: 'Buy British', as the advertising slogan runs. But apart from that, the passage is an ample demonstration that the notion of an ancient constitution was already axiomatic within the legal establishment in the second half of the fifteenth century. One of the greatest lawyers of his age, certainly the one who brought himself to think politically about the law, envisaged it as antedating all the powers and principalities to which the land had subsequently been subjected.

In time this was rendered down into a more concentrated form. Fortescue's successors in the seventeenth century argued more precisely that the ancient constitution was Anglo-Saxon and that in so far as it had been challenged or overlain it was by the brute fact of the Norman Conquest rather than by any succession of invasions or by the subtler attack of Roman Law. Royal prerogative was seen as the residue of the right of conquest which Duke William had won in 1066. Resistance to the royal prerogative since that time had been nothing more than a reassertion of the ancient law and the ancient liberty of the English people. In short the theory of the Norman yoke.[13]

Yet this analysis too was itself old. We do not know how old and we certainly cannot treat its earlier history continuously. But we can come fairly close to its point of origin. The evidence comes from the Staffordshire monastery of Burton on Trent, where, at the end of the thirteenth century, a monastic annalist was curiously active and adept at collecting and assembling historical records and related information. This included what claimed to be a verbatim account of the negotiations between King John of England and Pope Innocent III's nuncio, Pandulf, in 1211, over the affair of the disputed election to the archbishopric of Canterbury. The Burton annalist was writing seventy years or so after the event; the verisimilitude of his account, itself suspicious, is reduced by a number of historical inaccuracies; quite apart from that it is a good rule to be wary of any medieval chronicler, and of most modern historians too for that matter, as soon as they break out into direct speech.

12   *De Laudibus*, ed. Chrimes, 40-1.
13   For a general discussion of the theory see Christopher Hill, *Puritanism and Revolution* (London, 1958), 50-122.

To set the scene: in 1205-6 Pope Innocent and King John had boxed themselves and each other in over the Canterbury election, the Pope being committed to the election at Rome of Stephen Langton, the King equally committed to its rejection; as a result of the King's intransigence an Interdict was laid on England in 1208 and he himself was excommunicated in 1209; at the point at which we take up the story the dispute was coming to a final crisis; the Pope was threatening to absolve John's subjects from their allegiance.[14] These are some of the words which, in the Burton annalist's story, King John now used to justify his stance. He is addressing the papal nuncio:

> Moreover I can demonstrate to you that all my predecessors conferred archbishoprics, bishoprics and abbeys in their chambers. You can read in the holy record how the holy and glorious king St Edward in his time conferred the bishopric of Worcester on St Wulfstan. Then William the Bastard, conqueror of England, wanted to take his bishopric away from him because he did not know any French, but St Wulfstan answered him saying: 'You did not confer on me my staff nor will I surrender it to you', and thereupon he went to the tomb of St Edward and said in his native language: 'Edward, you gave me my staff; I cannot hold it by virtue of this king and so I commit it to you; defend it as best you can'. So he embedded the staff in the carved stone of the tomb and miraculously the staff remained immovable in the tomb of St Edward, so that no-one could withdraw it except St Wulfstan.[15]

That was a tall story, rendered taller by the obvious analogy between Wulfstan's staff and Arthur's Excalibur. Whether King John had his tongue in his cheek we cannot know. But he is presented here as a cool customer still with some shots in his locker for he then apparently continued with a claim for moral support even from the history of Thomas Becket:

> Furthermore in our own times my father Henry conferred the archbishopric of Canterbury on St Thomas. And now the Pope wishes to withdraw from me at his behest, all the liberties which my predecessors held. He does me wrong.[16]

---

14   For a detailed study see C.R. Cheney, 'The alleged deposition of King John' in *Studies in Medieval History presented to F.M. Powicke*, ed. R.W. Hunt, W.A. Pantin, R.W. Southern (Oxford, 1948), 100-16.

15   *Annales Monastici*, ed. H.R. Luard, 5 vols (Rolls Series, 1864-9), i. 211.

16   *Annales Monastici*, i. 211-12.

Fact or fiction? The tale cannot be totally dismissed for the Burton annalist shared his knowledge of the dialogue, although not of the crucial section which I have quoted, with another annalist, at Waverley, who was probably writing within a decade of the event.[17] There is a ring of truth perhaps in the motive attributed to William for Wulfstan's removal – that he did not know any French. Moreover, it is well known that King John was especially devoted to the Church of Worcester. His tomb still stands there with Worcester's two bishop-saints, Wulfstan and Oswald, carved in miniature either side of the King's own effigy, and that was done within ten or twenty years of the king's death.[18] This tale helps to explain why he was so devoted. However, the interest of the story for my present purpose lies not so much in the King's argument as in Pandulf's reply:

> You adduce St Edward and William the Bastard. To this I answer that you are not the successor of St Edward nor are you worthy to be compared with him. For he was the protector of holy Church and you offend and ruin it. But we well allow that you are the successor of William the Bastard since at the beginning he assaulted Holy Church in that he wished to deprive the blessed Wulfstan of the church of Worcester and therefore you are his successor and not St Edward's. And in this you have not changed your spots because you and all your predecessors have sought the destruction of the holy Church. Moreover you enjoy and enforce the evil laws of William the Bastard, even the worst; and you spurn as worthless the laws of St Edward, even the best.[19]

That leaves no real doubt the theory of the Norman yoke was already in vogue in the thirteenth century, certainly by the last decade, probably very much earlier, possibly even in the reign of John. One thing is plain. The theory was not newly invented in the antiquarian movement of the seventeenth century. It first arose from an earlier antiquarian movement in the late twelfth century when all kinds of men, kings, scholars, bishops and barons, were ceasing to regard the Anglo-Saxon past as barbaric and potentially hostile, and monks were developing a new interest in the English past to replace the wary hostility with which they had regarded the traditions of the conquered English hitherto. The theory of good and ancient law is of a piece with

17   *Annales Monastici*, ii. 268-71.
18   Lawrence Stone, *Sculpture in Britain in the Middle Ages* (Harmondsworth, 1955), 105.
19   *Annales Monastici* i. 213.

interest in Anglo-Saxon saints, with the canonisation of Edward the Confessor and with the royal and aristocratic patronage of the matter of England, namely the Arthurian legend.

It is not possible to point to a source of Pandulf's statement. However there was certainly an analogue, for the thirteenth-century annals of St Augustine's, Canterbury, ending in 1220, which were attributed to or copied by Thomas Sprott, and later repeated by William Thorne, preserved another story of considerable interest:

> In [the year of our Lord 1066] Duke William on the 14th October landed at Pevensey, and having fought with Harold — who himself was killed — and accepted the surrender of the city of London into his power, the said William directed his way to the castle of Dover that he might bring it with the rest of the county under his power. When he learnt of this, Archbishop Stigand and Abbot Egelsin, and the elders of the whole of Kent, seeing the whole kingdom in evil state, and whereas, before the coming of the said William there were no slaves amongst the English, now all, indiscriminately, both nobles and plebeians, were brought down into everlasting slavery to the Normans, used the dangers of their neighbours to fashion a structure of salvation for themselves and their county. So they got together the whole population of the whole of Kent and explained to them the dangers threatening them, the misery of their neighbours, the arrogance of the Normans and the hardships of a condition of slavery, by unanimous vote decided to oppose Duke William, and fight with him for their ancestral rights. But the aforesaid archbishop and abbot, preferring to die in battle rather than see these evils come upon their nation, and animated by the example of the holy Maccabees, became the leaders of the army. And on the appointed day the whole population met at Swanscombe and hiding in ambushes in the woods awaited the arrival of the said duke: and because abundance of caution is useful they arranged among themselves that, as the duke approached, all fords were to be closed so that he should have no means of escape on any side, and each and all, both horse and foot were to carry a bough as a protection. The duke, therefore, when he arrived on the following day, found with astonishment that in the fields close to the above-mentioned place the whole country was ranged around him in a circle, like a moveable wood, and approaching him at a slow pace. He saw this not without consternation, but when the

leaders of the Kentish people perceived William in their midst completely hemmed in, the signal was given with the trumpet, their standards were raised aloft, they threw down their boughs, and drawing their bows and unsheathing their swords with spears and other kinds of weapons at the charge, they showed themselves ready for battle. The duke, however, and those who were with him — and no wonder — stood astounded, and he who thought he held the whole of England in the hollow of his hand was now anxious about his own life. Then, on the part of the Kentish folk, the archbishop and abbot aforesaid were sent to King William, bringing him a message as follows: 'Lord duke, here are the people of Kent coming out to meet you, prepared to receive you as their liege lord, asking for peace on this condition, that the whole people of Kent shall enjoy the liberty they have always had and use their ancestral laws and customs: otherwise they, being ready, declare war upon you and yours, here and now, being willing to die here rather than give up their ancestral laws and customs in any way, or submit to unwonted slavery.' But the duke, seeing himself in a tight spot, having held a council with his men, wisely understanding that if he should suffer a repulse or any loss from this people which was the key of England, the whole undertaking which he had so far carried out would be nugatory and all his hope and security be turned to danger, granted, though more prudently than willingly, what the people of Kent requested. When the treaty had been duly sealed and hostages given on both sides, the people of Kent, in joy, conveyed the Normans, also joyful, to Rochester. They also gave up to the duke the county of Kent with the famous castle of Dover into his power, and thus the ancient liberty of the English and their ancestral laws and customs which, before the arrival of Duke William, were in force equally throughout the whole of England, have remained inviolable up to the present time in the county of Kent only, and that too through the agency of Archbishop Stigand and Abbot Egelsin.[20]

20   Roger Twysden, *Historiae Anglicanae scriptores decem* (London, 1652), 1786-7. I have largely followed the translation in *William Thorne's Chronicle of Saint Augustine's Abbey Canterbury*, trans. A.H. Davis (Oxford, 1934), 47-9. The attribution to Thomas Sprott is uncertain as indeed is the precise relationship of this early chronicle, whether written by Sprott or another, to the later chronicle of William Thorne. See A.H. Davis, xx-xxxiii and Eric John, 'The litigation of an exempt house, St. Augustine's Canterbury, 1182-1237', *Bulletin of the John Rylands Library*, xxxix (1956-7), 390-415, especially 391n.

The tale is all plainly fictitious. The Conqueror's itinerary is wrong: the men of Kent submitted before, not after, his entry into London; there was no Abbot Egelsin, merely a distorted memory of Aethelsige, the last English abbot of St. Augustine's. But it preserves the notion of the Norman Yoke in explicit form: all were brought down in everlasting slavery to the Normans; what the men of Kent resisted was 'the yoke of slavery'. Furthermore, there can be little doubt that this story had a purpose, namely to provide at one and the same time a historical explanation and a justification of the customs of Kent, of the privileges of gavelkind and the gavelkinders, which were such a marked feature of Kentish society by the thirteenth century. These were well known. They comprised not only the practice of partition and ultimogeniture, but also sundry jurisdictional and tenurial privileges and the claim that all Kentishmen were free, that there was no serfdom in the eyre in Kent in 1293, headed by John of Berwick, and in this too, the ancient, pre-Norman origin of Kentish custom was accepted, for it concludes – 'Here end the customs and liberties of gavelkind and of the gavelkinders in Kent, as they were before the Conquest, and at the Conquest, and ever since till now.'[21] So the men of Kent believed in the antiquity of their privileges and that belief was accepted by royal justices. All apparently were gullible.

Whether such tales contributed to the source on which Pandulf drew it is impossible to say. But his altercation with King John concerned the archbishopric of Canterbury and took place at Dover. The monks of St Augustine's had not apparently been expelled from their house during the Interdict.[22] Those of Christchurch were in exile in France at S. Bertin.[23] Pandulf may have picked up something from either house.

It is more certain and more interesting that the story preserved at St. Augustine's was intended to explain the peculiar liberties of the men of Kent, which, as they were summarised in 1293, certainly embodied Old English proverbs – 'The father to the bough, the son to the plough'[24] – and in its insistence on partible inheritance preserved the old English pattern of succession. Here, genuinely, there was an ancient law traceable to the Old England before the Norman Conquest and one

21   *Statutes of the Realm*, i. 223-5. The final phrases are derived from Lambarde's alleged original. For further comments on the text see F.R.H. Du Boulay, *The Lordship of Canterbury* (London, 1966), 144.

22   Twysden, 1864. On the whole question see C.R. Cheney, 'King John's reaction to the Interdict on England', *Trans. Royal Historical Society*, 4th ser., xxxi (1949), 129-150.

23   *The historical works of Gervase of Canterbury*, ed. W. Stubbs (Rolls Series, 1879-80), ii. 100.

24   *Statutes of the Realm*, i. 223.

which emphasised freedom. Moreover, both the St. Augustine's story and the statement of 1293 take us in one massive leap from the theory of the Norman Yoke at or near its origin to the antiquarian movement of the 16th and 17th centuries, for the tale of Swanscombe Down was repeated by Holinshed[25] and was then taken up and published by William Lambarde, historian of Kent, author of the prime textbook on Justices of the Peace, Keeper of the Records at the Rolls Chapel in 1597, and of the Records of the Tower in 1601, the year of his death. Lambarde included a summary of the story, along with a well-documented discussion of Kentish custom, which included the record of 1293 of which he claimed to have a contemporary text, in his *Perambulation of Kent* written in 1570 and published in 1576.[26] The text was seen both by Archbishop Parker and Lord Burleigh before publication. Lambarde himself corresponded with Camden. His papers went to Cotton. *The Perambulation of Kent*, which became the model for all subsequent county histories, went through four further editions between 1596 and 1656. Quite unpredictably, therefore, Thomas Sprott and William Thorne got a good press for their tale of the moving forest of Swanscombe. It was injected directly into the main stream of the antiquarian movement of the sixteenth and seventeenth centuries.

So much for the origin of the theory of the Norman Yoke. Two points are worth reiterating. In that origin there was an element of pure phantasy, the moving forest of Swanscombe Down and the tale of Wulfstan's tomb. But there was also something plausible which sought to explain known facts: namely the notion that the freer tenure of gavelkind was an Anglo-Saxon survival which the Normans had failed to override. At the core of the fiction there was a material point. Lawyers will note it was a matter of terms of tenure, a practical question. Historians will note that the explanation still stands. Maitland, very wary of myth, doubted it.[27] Modern opinion is tending more and more to accept it.[28]

What otherwise was the ancient law? Gavelkind and the theory of the Norman yoke might embody the essence of the argument, but politically they were side issues. No-one in medieval England ever demanded the restoration of gavelkind to the rest of the realm. It

25   Raphael Holinshed, *The Chronicles of England, Scotland and Irelande* (London, 1577), ii. 292-3.

26   William Lambarde, *Perambulation of Kent* (London, 1576), 388-427.

27   *History of English Law*, i. 186-8.

28   Du Boulay, 145-59; K.P. Witney, 'The economic position of husbandmen at the time of Domesday Book: a Kentish perspective', *Economic History Review*, 2nd ser., xxxvii (1984), 23-34, especially 30.

always had the flavour of an intriguing, antique survival. The answer to the main question of what was this ancient law, is relatively straightforward. Ancient law was embodied in the Laws of Edward the Confessor and the Laws of Henry I, both of which in origin go back to recensions of the second quarter of the twelfth century. But the text to which the answer would direct us at the end of the twelfth century, would rather be to a further recension, first surviving at London and probably originating there within ten years of the turn of the century. This included a number of apocryphal sections which embodied the constitutional tradition of the late twelfth century concocted from a number of scholastic political principles, distinguishing kingship from tyranny, and an extended version of the coronation oath of the English kings.[29] The texts have a familiar ring. The king is to provide just judgement with the advice of the magnates. He is to take nothing except by right of reason, by the law of the land and the judgement of a court. Officials are to maintain the just and ancient constitutions of the realm. It is all of a piece with Fortescue. The text, or its source, was known to Bracton. Sections of it were regurgitated by London lawyers in the Kings Bench in the early fifteenth century. William Lambarde again played an important part in its later history for this was the text of the laws of Edward the Confessor and Henry I which he brought together in his *Archaionomia* published in 1568,[30] which in turn was Coke's main source of information on Anglo-Saxon law.[31]

This is well enough known. I want to develop it only at one particular point. If there was any single reason why men turned to express their legal objectives in terms of ancient law it was because the kings themselves had called this down upon their own heads. It was the very essence of William the Conqueror's formal claim to the throne that he was the lawful successor of Edward the Confessor. Henry I, in his coronation charter confirmed the law of King Edward with the amendments which his father had made with the counsel of his barons. Stephen in his turn granted to his subjects the good laws of both King Henry and King Edward, and Henry II, to complete the series of coronation charters, granted all his subjects the liberties which they had

29   F. Liebermann, *Über die Leges Anglorum saeculo xiii ineunte Londonii collectae*, (Halle, 1894); 'A contemporary manuscript of the 'Leges Anglorum Londoniis Collectae', *English Historical Review*, xxviii (1913), 732-745; *Gesetze der Angelsachsen*, 3 vols (Halle, 1898-1916), i. 655-7; J.C. Holt, *Magna Carta* (Cambridge, 1965), 79-80.

30   William Lambarde, *Archaionomia* (London, 1568), 130v-131.

31   Pocock, 42-4.

held in the days of his grandfather Henry I.[32] It may be best to regard these promises not so much as grants in perpetuity as shabby election programmes, shabbily honoured by the grantors. Nevertheless they were reiterated, and in practical terms that meant that there were copies available throughout the realm, some easy to get at, some more difficult.[33] They provoked two straightforward questions. What were these liberties which had been promised and confirmed so consistently? It was that question which the London version of the texts sought to answer. And what was to be done about securing these promises and putting them into proper effect? It was that question which culminated at Runnymede in 1215 in Magna Carta. It is at this point that it is possible to add something to the story.

It has long been recognised that the demand for Magna Carta was preceded by a demand for the confirmation of the coronation charter of Henry I. This is recounted in several narrative sources, and Henry's charter is associated in one document with informal notes of preliminary demands or concessions which preceded the great charter itself.[34] One document, which has been bypassed by scholars, indicates that what we have known hitherto represents only the tip of the iceberg. This is Harleian MS 458 in the British Library. It was known to Liebermann, but it has escaped notice since.[35] Liebermann dated it to the early thirteenth century and in all probability it comes from the years in which the Great Charter itself was being forged. As manuscripts go it is an enigma, a mere bifolium, carefully and indeed handsomely written in a business hand, or probably more than one. All we know of it is that it passed through the hands of the antiquary Peter Le Neve in the seventeenth century. It opens with a copy of the Coronation charter of Henry I. That is no occasion for surprise. But this is then followed by the coronation charter of King Stephen of 1135, which in turn is followed by the coronation charter of Henry II. So the first

32   The sequence of charters carrying through the law of King Edward to the accession of Henry II and thence to Magna Carta was fully exploited by Coke in *Eighth Report*, iv-xi.

33   For the many copies of Henry I's charter see F. Liebermann, 'The text of Henry I's Coronation Charter', *Trans. Royal Historical Society*, new ser., viii (1894), 21-48, supplemented by *Regesta Regum Anglo-Normannorum*, ii. ed. Charles Johnson and H.A. Cronne (Oxford, 1956), no. 488 and *Councils and Synods*, I. ed. D. Whitelock, M. Brett and C.N.L. Brooke (Oxford, 1981), pt. ii. no. 108. See also Ludwig Riess, 'The reissue of Henry I's coronation charter', *English Historical Review*, xli (1926), 321-31. For Stephen's two charters of liberties see *Regesta Regum Anglo-Normannorum*, iii. ed. H.A. Cronne and R.H.C Davis (Oxford, 1968), 270, 271. For the charter of Henry II see *Statutes of the Realm*, i. Charters of Liberties, 4, and note 39 below.

34   The so-called 'unknown' charter; see Holt (1965), 296-303.

35   Liebermann (1894), 37. I am indebted to Dr. Martin Brett for drawing my attention to this manuscript.

importance of the document is that someone was collecting coronation charters, trying them on for size as it were, and for the first time we have clear evidence that Stephen and Henry II were reviewed as well as Henry I. But that is only half the story, literally so, for the scribes, after giving the Latin texts of all these documents on folio 1, proceeded to render them into French on folio 2.[36] The importance of this is signalled by the fact that the first important official document known hitherto to have been translated into the French was Magna Carta itself and one of the accompanying writs.[37]

Those familiar with the length of Henry I's charter will agree that the translation in Harleian 458 was not done for fun. It cannot have been done simply as a linguistic exercise, for bringing the texts together must have been no easy task (this is only the second copy of Henry II's charter which has come down to us). It cannot have been done for clerks who would understand the relatively simple Latin of the originals. It cannot even have been done for those laymen who were ready to put up with the off-the-cuff translations which clerks must have provided in reading Latin documents in court. It must in all probability have been done for laymen who wanted something better than an off-the-cuff rendering, a precise text for serious consideration and debate. So far logic and common sense seem to carry us. It is possible to go a little further. The text of Henry I's charter was derived immediately or otherwise from Westminster for it contained an apocryphal section peculiar to that abbey.[38] The other texts are good, that of Henry II better than the other surviving version.[39] One other tantalising reference should be noted. Before the disastrous fire of 1731 the Cottonian collection included a version of the coronation charter of Henry I *Latine et Saxonice*,[40] whether this bilingual version was

---

36 Liebermann was the source of some confusion in that he allotted the Latin text of Henry I's charter on fo.1 to the early 13th century and the French text on fo.2 to the mid-thirteenth century (1894, 37). The handwriting scarcely allows for this since the same scribe was responsible for the Latin versions of Stephen and Henry II on fo.1 and for the translation of Henry II on fo.2. In assessing the script I have benefited from the advice of the late N.R. Ker and of Dr. Pierre Chaplais and Dr. Malcolm Parkes. There has been some difference of opinion about the number of scribes involved, but all have taken the view that the handwriting is consistent with a date of c.1215.

37 J.C. Holt, 'A vernacular-French version of Magna Carta 1215', *English Historical Review*, lxxxix (1974), 346-64. See below, 239-57.

38 Liebermann (1894), 26-7, 37.

39 The version in Harleian 458 lacks the inappropriate *dei gratia* of Cotton MS, Claudius D. ii, fo. 79. Interestingly, like the Cottonian text, it has Richard de Lucy as sole witness.

40 Thomas Smith's catalogue of the Cottonian charters refers to 'Charta R. Henrici primi de terris et privilegiis episcopis et comitibus suis aliisque concessis et de servandis integris consuetudinibus quas pater eius et rex Edwardus concesserunt. Latine et Saxonice' (Bodleian, MS Smith 90, p. 19). I am again indebted to Dr. Martin Brett for bringing this to my notice.

produced in 1100 or was coeval with the renewed interest in the charter at the beginning of the thirteenth century is a matter of guesswork; the former is probably more likely. At all events an English version of the Charter of Henry I survived to the eighteenth century.

This has a double significance. First we must take the search for precedent in royal charters as much more widespread and serious than has been imagined hitherto. Secondly, we have to imagine it as involving a wider band of lay society than we have guessed at. The possibility that an English version of the charter of Henry I was in circulation affects how we look at the free man of Magna Carta. Somehow he looks less baronial, even less knightly or gentle, if we imagine that he might have had access to an English translation of the essential preparatory document.[41]

I verge on the speculative. Perhaps I may continue to do so to the extent of pulling together, with a little imagination, all the trends which came to a head in the summer of 1215, creating a photographic still, if you like, of the movements which I have sketched. Such a picture is focused almost entirely on London. Somewhere in the city there were manuscripts of the laws of King Edward and King Henry which embodied the constitutional doctrine of the apocryphal additions. Perhaps their author was still alive there, ready to admit the barons through the walls on 17 May. Someone, perhaps a royal clerk or a custodian of the records in the Treasury, had gained access to a copy of the charter of Henry I at Westminster or to a Westminster copy available in the city. The same person had access to copies of the charters of King Stephen and King Henry II. At least a small group was at work collecting and translating some of the critical preparatory texts. To none of these men can we give a name, but we can name another small group, churchmen, some of them canons of St Paul's Cathedral, who had been associated with the incipient baronial rebellion as far back as 1212 or were to stand out against papal prohibitions in support of the baronial cause in the civil war against King John in 1216.[42] One of these was Simon Langton, brother of Stephen, archbishop of Canterbury, who was to become Chancellor to Prince Louis in 1216 during his invasion in support of the barons. Simon had only to cross the Thames to Lambeth to meet his brother's steward, Elyas of

---

41   Some scholars have gone further in supposing that English translations of Magna Carta may have been available in 1215. See J.R. Maddicott 'Magna Carta and the local community 1217-1259', (*Past and Present*, 102 (1984), 30 and M.T. Clanchy, *From memory to Written Record* (London, 1979), 170-1. There seems to be no direct evidence or compelling logic that this was so.

42   Holt (1965), 189-90.

Dereham, who played a more immediate role than any other single individual in the preliminaries and execution of the settlement of 1215.[43] Rebellion probably blighted the careers of these relatively young men. None of them attained the bishopric to which their career and intelligence would normally have entitled them. To use an establishment phrase they had shown themselves 'unsound'.

So our photographic shot will give us the men and delineate the ideas. It does not allow us to bring the two together. Nevertheless it is firm enough in outline to show that the rebellion of 1215, like the rebellion of 1642, was prefaced by an antiquarian movement which sought restraint of the Crown. Between the two, across four centuries, there were differences. Feudal rebellion was licensed in 1215, not in 1642; there were religious issues which seared mens' souls in 1642 which were totally absent in 1215, but the constitutional argument, the argument about the relationship of the royal power to law, was closely similar in each case, all the more so in that the antiquarians of the second occasion drew on the antiquarians of the first in mounting their case against what they would call the royal prerogative and what their predecessors described more plainly as the will of the king, which carried with it the implied, even the explicit, charge of tyranny.

So much for a sketch of origins, or at least of a point much nearer the origins than the seventeenth century. What are we to make of it historiographically? Our first reaction perhaps is to note how history was distorted, in particular how the myth or tradition of an ancient constitution was used to belabour the Stuart monarchy. But although that is true it is barely adequate, for what are we to make of a myth or tradition which already embodied some notable apocrypha even before matters came to a head in 1215? Moreover, it is plain that, once embodied in texts, these myths or traditions had an independent existence quite apart from immediate political requirements. What mattered in the seventeenth century was not so much that Coke regarded the common law as ancient, but that he buttressed his view with tales and texts which already embodied the myth in a parent myth of their own. And it is easy enough to see how the core of the myth or tradition was transmitted, through the Great Charter, through Bracton and the *Mirror of Justices* to Fortescue, Lambarde and Coke. Faced with this, the model of the recurrent figment in which a doctrine of ancient law happened, as it were, to be deployed in successive crises, will not suffice. The history of the antiquarian tradition is also a history of texts and a history of an autonomous body of doctrine with its own internal logic. The tradition, in short, brings us to historiographical ground which is familiar to all intellectual historians. How far does a coherent body of knowledge develop through its own internal and external logic? How far is it determined by immediate political or social circumstances? In weighing that, such objective truth as it embodies may be of minor importance.

The medieval end of this tradition contributed something quite specific, something more than the simple fact that it came first. Consider how intelligent men in the thirteenth century reacted to a document. They were sharp enough in asserting and stating their legal rights and some of them were relatively skilled in detecting forgery. But the concessions in the royal charters of the twelfth century were often couched in wide terms and so also was Magna Carta. The learned man confronted with the statement that 'To no-one will be sell, to no one will be deny or delay right or justice' knew very well that he was dealing with a principle well enough known to canonists.[44] He tended therefore to bring his scholarly techniques to bear so that he treated the successive versions of the charter as he might successive glosses. If in the process he attributed a Charter of the Forest to King John, or presented the charter of 1225 as if it were the charter of 1215, or added bits of pieces of the 1215 text to the 1225 versions, that perhaps was a shabby performance and in our eyes gross incompetence and distortion, but it was no more than what contemporary methods were likely to encourage, and that is what the St Albans chronicler, Roger of Wendover, did. Moreover, his greater successor, Matthew Paris, on obtaining a correct text of the 1215 document, did no more than follow suit. He added the correct text in the margin and at the foot of the incorrect text as if it were a gloss.[45] So scholastic method contributed to the myth. It treated the terms of the Great Charter, which had a more or less precise significance in the context of 1215, as if they were comments on eternal truth to be glossed, commented on and reinterpreted by each successive generation.[46]

The same conclusion could be reached by another route. By the end of the thirteenth century there was sufficient legislation for lawyers and landowners to require their own collections of statutes. These survive today in considerable numbers; how many no one has counted, certainly a hundred or more. They vary from lavish, handsome,

---

44   C.R. Cheney, *From Becket to Langton* (Manchester, 1956), 153; *Councils and Synods*, I, pt. ii, 1050; II, pt. 1, ed. F.M. Powicke and C.R. Cheney (Oxford, 1965), 34.

45   J.C. Holt, 'The St. Albans Chroniclers and Magna Carta', *Trans. Royal Historical Society*, 5th ser., xiv (1964) 67-88. See below, 265-87.

46   Compare Pocock, 8-10, where the Bartolist treatment of Roman Law is discussed.

illuminated volumes designed for the library shelves, to well-thumbed everyday copies which the working lawyer used for reference. They almost always include a text of Magna Carta, but where so, it is almost inevitably the first enrolled version which Edward I confirmed in 1297. Despite that, practically every compiler took it upon himself to place the Charter at the beginning of his collection, in front of all the Edwardian legislation, in front of the Statute of Marlborough of 1267, in front of the Statute or Provisions of Merton of 1236. The charter was seen in short as a founding statute and that by the working lawyers of ninety years or so later. And indeed that is what it had proved to be. But consider the logical consequences. The whole structure of statute law went back to a document which was not a statute at all but a grant of privileges. It conveyed rights and liberties and what is more it conveyed them in perpetuity. That amounted to an open invitation to gloss and reinterpret. Indeed certain sections, most obviously the famous *nullus liber homo* were so open and loosely defined initially that they did more than allow reinterpretation; they almost demanded it.[47] So the tradition which went down to the seventeenth century was not accidental, it was not primarily a fabrication, it was part of the inherent logic built into the Charter in 1215. It was this intermingling of liberties in a practical everyday document to which men turned in the courts of law which formed the essential opening chapter of the tradition, which in the end embodied the rights of the freeborn Englishman.

Can we go even further back? Beyond the generation of the Charter of 1215? I have already said a little of the earlier royal charters and the first recension of the laws of Edward the Confessor and Henry I and I shall revert to them in a moment. I want first to suggest the kind of ground on which the events of 1215 were slowly being prepared. Consider first a purely linguistic point, the sense, or rather senses, of our word 'custom'. Perhaps only the English could manage for eight centuries with a word which at one and the same time means usages and imposts. The French resolved these matters long ago with refinement, *coutumes* on the one hand and *douanes* on the other. We are stuck with a confusion which goes back in its origin to our period and our problem. For in origin the word *coutume*, or in Latin *consuetudo*, simply meant those rights and charges which a lord could demand from his vassals. Very broadly speaking customs were imposts of one kind or another. That is the prime sense of the word in Carolingian documents and it remained in use in this sense throughout the middle ages; in

47   Holt (1965), 9, 226-9. See below, 265-87.

England in the thirteenth century estates were granted, bought and sold with their appurtenances and customs as they had been earlier.[48] But by then this was not the only sense of the word. Customs of this kind embraced not simply imposts but legitimate imposts. They referred to past practice as a kind of datum line and that datum line set a standard, indeed acquired almost a moral quality. So that through a kind of elision custom in the sense of impost became custom in the sense of long standing practice. This is apparent in our most elementary documents. When William Rufus and Duke Robert came together to define the rights of the Norman dukes in 1091 in the document known as the *Consuetudines et Justicie* they were using custom in its prime sense.[49] For them customs were feudal rights. Henry I used the word in the same sense when in his coronation charter he abandoned the evil customs with which the realm of England had been oppressed under William Rufus. Then it began to change in sense and moral quality; for Stephen in 1135 confirmed all liberties and good laws which Henry I had given his peoples and all good laws and good customs which they had enjoyed in the time of King Edward. This new tone is stronger still in Henry II's charter of 1154: he promised the destruction of evil customs and then confirmed all gifts, concessions, liberties and free customs which his grandfather Henry I had provided. That presents the change in atmosphere very crudely. Much more could be said. But it has the virtue of presenting it in documents all emanating from the ruling house and from similar sets of circumstances. The change which took place, the notion that custom might be good, that it constituted not a privilege for a lord but a protection for a subject, is not something which can be attributed to any one person or occasion, or to any single document or treatise. It was simply spreading gradually through men's minds by the middle years of the twelfth century.

It was a semantic point, but one with immediate practical implications. For example it was a very common, indeed the habitual practice in the first half of the twelfth century, for a landlord to lease out estates to farm.[50] This meant a kind of trade-off in which the tenant usually paid less than the real yield of the estate and the lord received an assured income without incurring any of the burden of direct management. The method was used not only by great nobles but by churches and monasteries and above all by the Crown. Many demesne estates were held at farm. All sheriffs held their counties at

---

48   J-F Lemarignier, 'La dislocation du "pagus" et le problème des "consuetudines" (xe-xie siècles)', *Mélanges Louis Halphen* (Paris, 1951), 401-410.

49   C.H. Haskins, *Norman Institutions* (Cambridge, Mass., 1918), 281-4.

50   Reginald Lennard, *Rural England 1086-1135* (Oxford, 1959), 105-212.

farm. Now the importance of this to our story is that by the middle of the twelfth century these farms of the counties had become stable, fixed, increasingly protected by antiquity. The Crown was never able to revise them. It added increments to them, it took profits over and above them, but the ancient farms always remained as the base-line; hence Magna Carta 1215, cap.25 — 'all shires, hundreds, wapentakes and ridings shall be at the ancient farms without any increment, except our demesne manors'. All this took place in a period of increasing profitability which culminated in a threefold increase in prices, partly inflationary, in the forty years between 1180 and 1220.[51] In these circumstances the insistence that certain renders were ancient and customary, the one because of the other and no matter which came first, was of immediate practical consequence. It was probably in that kind of situation, multiplied over and over again throughout the country, as relevant to the relations between the sheriff and the king as it was to the relations between the manorial tenant and his lord, that custom became both good and ancient at one and the same time. It embodied the tenant's success over the rentier. And the King was the chief rentier.

That leaves a final question. Why did England play so prominent a part in these matters? That is a large question for another occasion, but I cannot leave the topic without saying something about it. Part of the answer of course is that the developments which I have described were not at this stage peculiar to England. Other countries also, from Spain to Hungary, had their charters of liberties. Others experienced the definition of custom which I have illustrated.[52] The conflict between farming and rising productivity and rising prices was general throughout much of western Europe. But it may well be that development was more intense in England. Certainly no other country in the twelfth century can produce such a series of royal coronation charters, and in no other country in western Europe was there the kind of interest in the immediate past which is revealed in the early twelfth century laws of Edward the Confessor and the Laws of Henry I. So in some ways England was unique. And the reason is not hard to find. It has always astonished me that American scholars of medieval England have never really emphasised that England was a colonial country. Somehow they, like English historians, have found it difficult to escape from the tradition which centres the Norman and Angevin realms on London rather than Rouen, Caen, Le Mans or Tours. Perhaps it all has to do with those maps in which these dominions are all coloured in the

51   P.D.A. Harvey, 'The English Inflation of 1180-1220', *Past and Present*, 61 (1973), 3-30.

52   Holt (1965), 20-4, 63-4.

traditional red. Yet England was a colony and that fact accounted for a lot. It gave the Normans in England something of a *tabula rasa* for governmental, tenurial and legal experiment. It forced them into a position where precedent, right and practice, had to be ascertained in Domesday Book, and, less exactly, in the *Leges Henrici* and the *Leges Edwardi*. It forced their rulers into recurrent definitions of their rights or customs, which depended in turn on what they knew of the practice before the Conquest. The ultimate source of the constitutional tradition, if you like, lay in the Norman Conquest, its circumstances and its consequences. And if that is right the tradition which was emerging by the time of John did the Normans less than justice. In the end it has to be conceded that Coke got it wrong. He saw the liberties of England deriving from the Anglo-Saxon past. In reality it was to the earlier Norman colonization of England that the colonists in America owed their political traditions and their liberties.

2

THE END OF THE ANGLO-NORMAN REALM

HISTORY is easiest recalled as a series of noteworthy dates: 1066, 1215, 1789, 1914, and so on. 1204 belongs perhaps to a minor calendar. It was the year in which the Anglo-Norman realm, established by William the Conqueror, collapsed: the year of the loss of Normandy for the English, the conquest of Normandy for the French. Thirty years after the event a scribe entered a list of dates in the cartulary of the lepers' hospital of St. Giles at Pont-Audemer in Normandy.[1] He was writing, he stated, on the feast of St. Calixtus in the year 1234. Then he computed the passage of time from a series of events. In addition to the Incarnation these were in order: the conquest of Jerusalem by the Crusaders which he placed incorrectly in 1097, the loss of Jerusalem and the Holy Cross to Saladin in 1187, the Norman Conquest of England in 1066, the battle of Val-ès-Dunes of 1047, the battle of Tinchebrai of 1106, and the deaths of the Norman Henry I, the English archbishop Thomas Becket, the Angevins, Henry II, Richard and John, and the Capetians, Philip II and Louis VIII. By the side of the great events of Christendom he placed the stages in the establishment of the Norman duchy and the Anglo-Norman realm. He named the great martyr of the Anglo-Norman Church. He listed the rulers of the duchy, Norman, Angevin, and Capetian, indiscrimnately except that he gave Philip his territorial style. He gave no hint of any enforced break in the succession in 1204. He made no mention of the loss or conquest of Normandy or of King John's attempt at recovery which ended at Bouvines ten years later. He envisaged only one single line of Norman rulers; for him

---

[1] Rouen, Bibliothèque Municipale, MS. Y 200, fol. 78.

King Philip's son was not Louis VIII, but Louis I.[1] It was as if the events of 1204 had not mattered.

That was a Norman view of history. It would be easy to attribute the omissions in this list of dates to embarrassment or simple forgetfulness. Nevertheless, it is odd that one who could remember Val-ès-Dunes did not recall Bouvines, and the contrast is all the odder in that he wrote at a house founded by the Beaumont Counts of Meulan, who suffered dispossession as a result of the débâcle of 1204, a house where other scribes were avid collectors of documents of Anglo-Norman and English history.[2] At all events his list of dates contained little hint of a great dynastic dispute and none at all of a prolonged Anglo-French conflict.

The events which he failed to describe were the subject of a great book by Sir Maurice Powicke—*The Loss of Normandy*.[3] To award praise to this would now be superfluous: still after sixty-two years it provides the base for all subsequent discussion. Yet Powicke published his book in 1913. He began work with the Boer War scarcely over and he completed it while the Balkan wars were fought. Inevitably, for all his subtle insight into the

[1] The text is as follows:

Anno ab Incarnatione domini m^{o}cc^o xxx^o quarto factum fuit hoc scriptum in festo sancti Kalixti pape hoc modo:

Annus ab Incarnatione domini m^{us} cc^{us} xxx^{us} quartus
A conquisitione Jerusalem c^{us} xxx^{us} vij^{us}
A captivitate Jerusalem et raptu crucis per Salahadinum xlvij^{us}
A subjugatione Anglie per regem Willelmi c^{us} lx^{us} viij^{us}
A bello Vall' dunarum c^{us}lxxx^{us} vij^{us}
A bello Tenchebrai c^{us} xx^{us} octavus
A decessu regis Henrici primi xc^{us} ix^{us}
A martirio sancti Thomae lx^{us} quartus
A decessu regis Henrici secundi xl^{us} vj^{us}
A decessu regis Ricardi xxx^{us} vj^{us}
A decessu regis Johannis xviij^{us}
A decessu regis Philippi Francie xj^{us}
A decessu regis Ludovici primi ix^{us}

The scribe not only miscalculated the date of the capture of Jerusalem of 1099, but also erred in placing the deaths of Henry II and Richard I in 1188 and 1198 respectively. The remaining dates are correct. No known reckoning of the beginning of the year would allow him to place 6 July, when Henry II died, a year earlier than 14 July when Philip II died.

[2] J. C. Holt, 'A Vernacular-French Text of Magna Carta', *English Historical Review*, lxxxix (1974), 352–6. See below, pp. 239-57

[3] Manchester, 1913; 2nd edn., Manchester, 1961. All references below, except where noted, are taken from the second edition.

medieval mind, he wrote in an age of national and imperial conflicts and annexations. And in his book he envisaged a great international event, a clash of states. 'I wish to study the Norman state during the crisis which led to its union with France'.[1] That, his opening sentence, was matched by the conclusion: 'For the first time in the modern world one highly organised state had annexed another'. 'When the Normans became French they did a great deal more than bring their national epic to a close. They permitted the English once more to become a nation, and they established the French state for all time.'[2] French scholars likewise have seen the history of the Plantagenet lands as part of a national epic. Professor Boussard, for example, maintains that 'Henry II, despite appearances and scholastic interpretations which present him as an alien and an enemy, is really one of the architects of a unified France'.[3] Yet it is possible to tell the story in a plainer context of governmental and feudal relations. In 1204 the Normans were in many senses French; so indeed were the kings and nobles of England. Normandy and all the other continental possessions of the Plantagenet house, except Gascony, were fiefs held of the French Crown. In feudal terms the loss or conquest of these provinces amounted to the reversion of the lordship of the Duke of Normandy and Count of Anjou to his superior the King of France. In formal terms it executed a judgement in King Philip's court. Once complete the kings of France based their rights in those areas on those previously exercised by the Plantagenets. It was not annexation but supercession.[4] That may be why the change went unnoticed by the scribe of Pont-Audemer.

---

[1] Powicke, op. cit., p. 7.

[2] Ibid., pp. 306, 307.

[3] 'Henri II, malgré les apparences et les schémas scolaires qui font de lui un étranger et un ennemi, est en réalité l'un des artisans de l'unité française' (J. Boussard, 'L'Empire Plantagenêt' in F. Lot and R. Fawtier, *Histoire des institutions françaises au moyen âge*, i. 69). Cf. 'Pour une grande part la France de saint Louis et l'Angleterre d'Édouard Ier sont le prolongement de l'œuvre d'Henri II' (*Le Gouvernement d'Henri II Plantagenêt*, Paris, 1956, p. 582).

[4] It is striking that among the large number of *querimonia* of 1247 only a very few adduced the ancient customs of Normandy *ante conquestum* against new impositions which had arisen under the Capetians. See *Recueil des historiens des Gaules et de la France*, xxiv, pt. i, nos. 261, 262, 355, 369, 480, 504, 551. The point may be illustrated on a smaller scale: at Verneuil King John ordered the construction of a tanning mill which King Philip subsequently completed, both to the damage of a citizen of the town (ibid., no. 250).

Up to 1154 this realm was held together not only by the energy of its rulers, but also by the interest of the great Anglo-Norman families. They indeed had helped to build it. Some were contentious and rebellious, prone on occasion to exploit, even initiate, violence and anarchy. But when the kingdom was separated from the duchy in 1087 and 1100, and when the invasion of Geoffrey of Anjou detached Normandy from allegiance to Stephen after 1138, families with estates on both sides of the Channel on the whole sought to repair such a division of the realm. In 1153–4 they excluded Stephen's heirs from the succession and accepted Henry of Anjou. Fifty years later their descendants reacted very differently. There was no prolonged resistance or disturbance like that which marked the earlier divisions. In 1204 the Anglo-Norman realm simply fell apart. Soon the collapse was total and the defeat complete. Within ten years of the loss of Normandy English barons banded together to resist military service on the Continent. They opposed King John not in order to achieve the reunification of England and Normandy, but to resist all that followed from his own insistent ambition towards that end.

At one important point this contrast is inexact. The old Anglo-Norman realm was self-contained. There were outlying interests in Maine and Brittany, but it was nevertheless compact and by contemporary standards well governed. However, from 1154 it formed only a part of a larger dominion stretching south through the Angevin patrimony to the vast possessions acquired through Henry's marriage to Eleanor of Aquitaine. The old realm and the new dominion were distinct. No new tenurial bond was established like that which stretched across the Channel. Within the new dominion England and Normandy shared closer administrative ties than those which bound the rest. Nevertheless when the break came in 1204 the line of fracture was not between the old Norman and the newer Angevin lands but between Normandy, Anjou, and Brittany on the one hand, and England and Gascony on the other; Poitou for the moment remained debatable. Hence the break between England and Normandy was part of the collapse of the Plantagenet dominion and it is in the history and structure of that dominion that an explanation of the end of the Anglo-Norman realm must start.

The study of the government of the Plantagenet lands involves more than ordinary difficulties in selecting and interpreting the evidence. For Professor Boussard 'the Angevin Empire was conceived as an extremely strong state within the structure of the feudal system'.[1] Professor Warren, in contrast, has maintained that 'Henry II conceived the future of the Angevin dominions not as an *empire* but as a *federation*'.[2] Somewhere between these two extremes Professor Le Patourel describes it both as a 'feudal empire' and a 'family assemblage' of lands.[3] The Angevin kings encouraged the development of strong centralized systems of government within provinces of their dominions, especially in Normandy and England. But that does not establish that they sought to impose a similar centralization on their dominions as a whole. True, there are examples of what may fairly be described as imperial acts. They are worth listing. The first probable example is provided by the Norman edict of 1159 which seems to follow an earlier English *constitutio* concerning the jurisdiction of the courts of deans and archdeacons.[4] A second is provided by the Norman inquest of 1171 which bore some similarity to the English Inquest of Sheriffs of 1170.[5] A third such act is an edict of 1177 concerning sureties for debt which, according to the *Gesta Henrici*, was directed to Normandy, Anjou, Aquitaine, and Brittany.[6] Thereafter there is the English Assize of Arms of 1181 which was preceded by similar measures on the Continent.[7] None of these acts survive in the original; some are known only from summaries or references by chroniclers.[8] The list may be supplemented by other less certain

---

[1] 'L'empire angevin était donc conçu comme un État très fort, mais dans le cadre du système féodale' (*Le Gouvernement d'Henri II Plantagenêt*, p. 569).

[2] *Henry II* (London, 1973), p. 561.

[3] 'The Plantagenet Dominions', *History*, l (1965), 299, 301, 302.

[4] C. H. Haskins, *Norman Institutions* (Harvard, 1918), pp. 329–33.

[5] Ibid., pp. 337–43; L. Delisle and E. Berger, *Recueil des actes de Henri II* (Paris, 1909–27), *Introduction*, pp. 345–7.

[6] *Gesta regis Henrici secundi Benedicti Abbatis*, ed. W. Stubbs (Rolls Series, 1867), i. 194.

[7] Ibid. i. 269–70. The text of the assize is conveniently accessible in W. Stubbs, *Select Charters*, 9th edn. (Oxford, 1921), pp. 183–4. For arguments that Howden misdated this assize and that it could be attributed more reasonably to 1176 see H. G. Richardson and G. O. Sayles, *The Governance of Medieval England* (Edinburgh, 1963), p. 439 n., and their *Law and Legislation from Aethelberht to Magna Carta* (Edinburgh, 1966), pp. 99–100. Compare J. C. Holt, 'The Assizes of Henry II: the Texts', in *The Study of Medieval Records*, ed. D. A. Bullough and R. L. Storey (Oxford, 1971), pp. 90–1.

[8] For an attempt to exploit another source by tracing 'legislation' underlying the earliest Norman custumal see J. Yver, 'Le "Très Ancien Coutumier" de Normandie, miroir de la législation ducale?', *Revue d'Histoire du Droit*, xxxix (1971), 333–74. This does not add to the 'imperial acts'.

examples. The assize of Count Geoffrey, establishing primogeniture in Brittany, may be based on a *constitutio* of Normandy attributable to Henry II.[1] It is possible that the English eyre of 1194 was accompanied by a similar measure in Normandy,[2] and there were common measures imposed by common extraneous needs, like the Saladin tithe and King Richard's ransom.[3] But even when extended thus the list is not long. It looks even less long if set against the measures imposed on England, for example, which were *not* extended to other parts of the Empire. It almost disappears if those measures shared by the old Anglo-Norman realm are excluded. The edict of 1177 and perhaps the Assize of Arms alone remain. The case may be supported by vaguer evidence. Powicke, for example, argued that Henry II introduced tenure in *parage* from Anjou into Normandy and that he exercised a strong influence throughout his lands in favour of impartibility in the inheritance of feudal estates. But this is not entirely convincing.[4]

[1] The Norman *constitutio* is in the *Très Ancien Coutumier*, cap. viii, *Coutumiers de Normandie*, ed. E. J. Tardif (Société de l'histoire de Normandie, 1881), i. 8–9. For Count Geoffrey's assize see G. Planiol, 'L'Assise au Comte Geffroi', *Nouvelle Revue historique de droit*, xi (1887), 117–62, 652–708, and for a better presentation of the text his *La Très Ancienne Coutume de Bretagne* (Rennes, 1896), pp. 319–23. Planiol attributed the Assize to Anglo-Norman influences ('L'Assise', p. 135) and this has been followed by others. See R. Génestal, *Le Parage normand* (Bibliothèque d'histoire du droit normand, 2nd ser., études i, fasc. 2, Caen, 1911), 1–2; F. M. Powicke, 'The Angevin Administration of Normandy', *English Historical Review*, xxii (1907), 38; J. Yver, 'Les Caractères Originaux du Groupe de Coutumes de l'Ouest de la France', *Revue historique de droit français et étranger*, 4th ser., xxx (1952), 46 n. 2; and J. Boussard, op. cit., p. 571. However, there is no certainty about the attribution of the *constitutio* to Henry. Moreover the Assize of Count Geoffrey reveals no trace of any direct intervention on his part. It was granted *petitioni episcoporum et baronum omnium Britanniae satisfaciens . . . communi assensu eorum*, and was sealed with the seals of Geoffrey and his wife Constance. Cap. 4, which establishes primogeniture among heiresses, is inconsistent with any English precedent.

[2] F. M. Powicke, *The Loss of Normandy*, pp. 52 n., 77.

[3] For the effect of such demands on Normandy see L. Delisle, 'Des Revenus Publics en Normandie', *Bibliothèque de l'École des Chartes*, 3rd ser., iii (1852), 119–31, and F. M. Powicke, op. cit., p. 233.

[4] F. M. Powicke, 'The Angevin Administration of Normandy', *English Historical Review*, xxii (1907), 38; *The Loss of Normandy*, pp. 34 n., 50–1. Powicke relied in the main here on Guilhiermoz, *Essai sur l'origine de la noblesse en France au moyen âge* (Paris, 1902), pp. 203–51, 214, but it now seems certain that this form of tenure in Normandy emerged well before the reign of Henry II. See J. C. Holt, 'Politics and Property in Early Medieval England', *Past and Present*, lvii (1972), 44–5.

However, if the extent of 'imperial legislation' was negligible, that was very far from true of the activities of the king and his itinerant court, of his great officials, supporters and advisers: clerks, *magistri*, literate laymen, and magnates lay and ecclesiastical, who dealt with matters arising throughout the Plantagenet dominions. This 'top tier' of government, as Professor Le Patourel describes it,[1] gave central direction to the management of the 'empire', and it would be hard to exaggerate the amount of work which the Angevin kings and the men around them achieved. Nevertheless, it calls for some cautionary comment. First, the circle in and around the *curia* was made up of men who might be called upon to serve the king in important office now in one province, now in another. They were all interested in secular office and ecclesiastical preferment, in matters in which the king's rule seemed truly imperial. Regularly they experienced manifestations of the extent of Plantagenet government, assisting with business from, or executing mandates for, the most far-flung of the king's dominions. Two such men, 'Glanville' and Richard Fitz Neal, wrote commentaries on their own sectors of government. Others in, or on the fringes of, the court, Peter of Blois, Walter Map, and Gerald of Wales, wrote in a more gossipy style about its life and work. It was perhaps inevitable that even the more professional of them resorted to adulatory exaggeration:

For although this king (Henry II) was 'sprung from ancient kings' and extended his empire far and wide by his triumphs, it is his even greater glory that his actions exceeded his extravagant reputation.[2]

These men were commenting on government from within, from a standpoint which could only exaggerate the control, the capacity to devise and enforce policy, which the Plantagenet kings and the men around them exercised.

Secondly, there were practical limits to what an itinerant king could do. Henry II, Richard, and for a time, John, had to cover far more ground than their Norman predecessors, and this without any technical improvement in the means of transport. It is a commonplace of English history that Richard I was an absentee and that Henry II spent long periods away from his kingdom. But the same may be said of any one of the Plantagenet domains. Henry II spent roughly 13 years in England,

---

[1] 'The Plantagenet Dominions', p. 298.
[2] *Dialogus de Scaccario*, ed. Charles Johnson (London, 1950), pp. 27–8.

only a little more, roughly 14½ years in total, in Normandy, and far less, only 7 years in total, in Anjou/Touraine and Aquitaine.[1] If he was an absentee in England he was an absentee everywhere. It is customary to commend the Angevin kings for their hard travelling. But it is well to question what travelling involved, whether indeed a horse was the most effective seat of regular orderly government. 'He was always on the move', wrote Walter Map of Henry II, 'travelling in unbelievably long stages, like a post, and in this respect merciless beyond measure to the household that accompanied him'.[2] Peter of Blois also painted a picture of uncertain starts and unscheduled stops, a court moving at the whim of a man who apparently delighted in creating uncertainty.[3] Much of the quality of Angevin government could be summed up in the single word 'restless'. One of these kings received his death wound in the saddle, the other two died from illness brought on or exacerbated by travel. None of them could afford repose.

Thirdly, the view that such an itinerant monarch positively directed the affairs of his widespread dominions does not square entirely with the surviving acts of government. At first sight the work of the Chancellor and the clerks of the writing office suggests that they were the hub around which the wheel of state revolved. But this impression is faulty. Much of the documentary material which survives arose from the initiative of subjects. Many royal acts make it perfectly clear that they are drawn up at the request of the beneficiary or some other party. Some were prepared when the beneficiary or a friend or agent was at court. Still under Henry II some were drafted by the beneficiary.[4] Just occasionally a letter requesting a royal confirmation still survives, an occasional example of what must have formed an extensive class of correspondence.[5] Frequently too, a royal act simply marked a stage in prolonged litigation or

---

[1] See Doris M. Stenton in *Cambridge Medieval History*, v. 554, and J. Le Patourel 'The Plantagenet Dominions', p. 295. As Professor Le Patourel notes, these figures provide only a rough guide. R. W. Eyton, *The Court, Household and Itinerary of Henry II* (London, 1878), on which the calculations are based, is far from reliable, especially in its use of information drawn from the Pipe Rolls.

[2] *De Nugis Curialum*, trans. M. R. James, ed. E. S. Harland (Cymmrodorion Record Series, ix, 1923), p. 261.

[3] J. P. Migne, *Patrologia Latina*, ccvii. 48–9.

[4] T. A. M. Bishop, *Scriptores Regis* (Oxford, 1961), pp. 9–10.

[5] *Actes de Henri II*, no. DLIII.

negotiation between parties.[1] All this is quite apart from routine operations of the courts which necessarily reflected the requirements of litigants. Hence, at any one point in time, the actions of the king seem random. In February or March 1158, for example, Henry II lay at Brockenhurst in the New Forest. At least five *acta* survive from that period. Two concern English monasteries—Plympton and Lenton priories;[2] one sought to ensure the return of escaped serfs to the Norman abbey of Jumièges;[3] two concerned the privileges of the monastery of S. Florent-Lès-Saumur in Anjou and arose from actions settled in Henry's court before Jocelin of Tours, seneschal of Anjou.[4] Such day-to-day activity, attending to widely scattered, unconnected business, made up a great deal of the king's contribution to the government of the Plantagenet lands.[5] It might embody policy and political attitudes, but it was not itself a policy or even a programme of work. It was simply a response to demand; the provision of protection, assurance, and confirmation, by an ultimate feudal superior. Procedure in these matters was primitive and near chaotic. The petitioner might suffer interminable delay before gaining satisfaction: the king, on the other hand, was pestered:

Now the aforesaid King Henry II was distinguished by many good traits and blemished by some few faults. . . . He is wasteful of time over the affairs of his people, and so it comes about that many die before they get their matters settled, or leave the court depressed and penniless, driven by hunger. . . . Whatever way he goes out he is seized upon by the crowds and pulled hither and thither, pushed whither he would not, and, surprising to say, listens to each man with patience, and

[1] See in particular ibid., nos. CCXXVI, CCLX (confirming CCXXIV), CCLXXV, CCLXXXIII, DIII, all concerned with the privileges of Angevin monasteries. Compare no. CC, an act of Stephen de Marçay, seneschal of Anjou.

[2] *Monasticon Anglicanum*, v. 112; vi, pt. i, 53–4.

[3] *Actes de Henri II*, no. XCII.

[4] Ibid., nos. XC, XCI.

[5] Henry II's charters rarely carry a time-date. The fact that Richard I's are dated makes it possible in his case to illustrate a similar wide scatter of attention within the confines of a single day. On 12 November 1189 charters or letters were dated for the monks of Christ Church, Canterbury, the cathedral church of Rouen, the hospital of St. Mary Magdalen, Rouen, the cathedral church of Lichfield, the Bishop of Agen in Aquitaine, the monasteries of Cirencester and Bury St. Edmund and the citizens of Bedford and Worcester (L. Landon, *Itinerary of Richard I*, Pipe Roll Society, new ser., xiii. 14–15).

though assaulted by all with shouts and pullings and rough pushings, does not challenge anyone for it, nor show any appearance of anger, and when he is hustled beyond bearing silently retreats to some place of quiet.

That picture of Walter Map's is one of a badly overworked monarch.[1]

Of course this is not the whole story. There were important sessions of magnates and advisers, who gave their counsel, meetings where, on occasion, 'great acts of state' were decided and promulgated. More important still, there was the regular and continuing work of government in each of the Plantagenet lands: the enforcement of law, the provision of justice, the collection of revenue, the management of the demesne, the upkeep of castles, the maintenance of the royal forest. At this point surviving royal *acta* are themselves misleading, for charters sought as a warrant for privilege have survived far better than the much more numerous writs concerned with the donkey work of day-to-day government. If therefore it were possible to study all the letters issuing from the writing office over a period of a few months, it is very likely that the government's activities would look much more methodical than the surviving *acta* indicate. The English and Norman Pipe Rolls bear witness to these administrative ephemera in the very large number of *brevia regis* which were vouched as authority during the annual audit. But these present their own problems, for they can be set in three quite different contexts. Either they were issued while the king was in the country concerned; in that case the itinerant household overlapped provincial government, the one reinforcing the other. Alternatively, the writs were issued in the absence of the king on the authority of a deputed royal seal; this was done in the English Exchequer. Or again, writs might be issued at long range, appearing in England, for example, as *brevia de ultra mare*; this was appropriate for special instructions, but would have been inordinately inefficient for routine matters. Under King John, in the years after 1204, the system became compact and efficient, even inventive; by then the itinerant household was largely confined to one single province, the realm of England. But this was not so earlier. Henry II and Richard were faced with a harsh choice between delegation and inefficiency. Centralization of routine government was impossible. They could but try to hold delegated authority

[1] *De Nugis Curialium*, p. 265.

together by supervision from afar and personal visitation. These were to prove inadequate.

The Pipe Rolls of the English Exchequer are the only source to provide a continuous record of the relations between the king and the government of one of his dominions. They reveal that there were close links between the Exchequer and the household, that the work and personnel might overlap when the king was in the realm. But they also demonstrate that the Exchequer was already perfectly capable of functioning almost on its own during the long periods of royal absence, for example from 1158 to 1163 and 1166 to 1170. It did so on the authority of royal writs sealed with the Exchequer seal or on the authority of the Justiciar's writ under his personal seal.[1] Occasionally the king intervened; the Justiciar acted on the warrant of a royal writ *de ultra mare*, or a royal pardon was produced by a debtor, or payment was directed to the king's chamber, or a royal writ ordered a delay in account, or special protection was provided for a litigant. But in the absence of the king the Exchequer was an authoritative and effective organ of government. The king might initiate the Assize of Clarendon but the justices and barons of the Exchequer executed and developed it in the years after 1166. The king could descend on England and provide for the overhaul of local government in the Inquest of Sheriffs, but he departed within a few months and left the Justiciar and Exchequer to get on with it. In 1173 he was content to leave the Justiciar to contend with the rebellion of the earls and the resulting fortification, provisioning, and garrisoning of castles and the muster of troops for dispatch to the Continent. Sometimes the king's intervention was occasional and casual, a brief

---

[1] The rules governing the use of the Exchequer seal are described by Richard fitz Neal. See *Dialogus*, pp. 16, 19, 33, 62. The question is discussed by H. G. Richardson, *Memoranda Roll I John* (Pipe Roll Society, new ser., xxi), pp. lxiii–lxxxvii. Richardson emphasized that the enormous increase in the number of instruments of public administration during the reign of Henry II was the chief reason for the increased use of the Exchequer seal and the Justiciar's seal. Between 1158 and 1164 Richard of Anstey sought all but one of the writs for his famous legal action from the king overseas, either himself or through an agent (ibid., pp. lxxviii–lxxix). The first certain example of a writ issued under the Exchequer seal seems to be a writ of *perdono* in favour of the Knights Hospitaller of 1174–9 (*Actes de Henri II*, no. DXLII). On this and for further discussion of the whole question see P. Chaplais, *English Royal Documents King John–Henry VI, 1199–1461* (Oxford, 1971), pp. 45–7, where it is suggested that the Exchequer may have been provided with a seal before the accession of Henry II.

instruction from Normandy or Anjou. Sometimes it was dramatic, even catastrophic, as in the Inquest of Sheriffs or the punitive investigations into the royal forest in 1175. It was always predatory.

Although the Pipe Rolls reveal a methodical system of government in England, they also raise an important doubt. Sometimes, in the early years of Henry II, they give the impression that the main results of the king's presence in the country lay in the improvement of his castles and hunting lodges, the maintenance of his hounds and falcons, and the provision of luxuries for the court. Much more seriously, it seems plain that in many years the resources available to the Angevin kings were far less than those which the Normans had enjoyed. On the whole historians have fought shy of the annual totals of the accounts which Sir James Ramsay provided in 1926.[1] His work was received with stringent and justified criticism.[2] Nevertheless the critics agreed that the figures were useful as a 'general guide' to royal resources.[3] These figures are telling. The sole surviving Pipe Roll of Henry I of 1130 records an audit of over £24,500.[4] That was not surpassed by his grandson's exchequer until 1177. The audit in 1157 and 1163 amounted to less than £10,000. It only exceeded £20,000 on four occasions before 1176; after 1176 it only exceeded the figure for 1130 on three occasions, in 1177, 1185, and 1187.[5] Now admittedly the calculation of these totals is hazardous and their significance has perhaps become even more debatable since the publication of Ramsay's book. In certain years, special measures, tallages on the Jews, or the ransom for King Richard, or the Thirteenth of 1207, raised revenue far above the normal. Some major items might

---

[1] *A History of the Revenues of the Kings of England 1066–1399* (Oxford, 1925).

[2] See *The Times Literary Supplement*, 11 March 1926; R. Fawtier, 'L'Histoire Financière de l'Angleterre', *Le Moyen Âge*, 2nd ser., xxix (1928), 48–67; Mabel Mills in *English Historical Review*, xli (1926), 429–31. Fawtier attributed the review in *T.L.S.* to Tout. There were two main criticisms of Ramsay's book: first that he failed to take note of financial business which lay outside the Exchequer account and secondly that he tended to treat the figures on the rolls as representing revenue and expenditure rather than an audit of account of writs and tallies as well as cash.

[3] 'Le chiffre d'affaires est un miroir assez fidèle de l'état d'une entreprise' (R. Fawtier, op. cit., p. 63). Cf. Mabel M. Mills: 'These statistics furnish a basis of comparison' (op. cit., p. 431).

[4] J. H. Ramsay, op. cit., p. 60. I have excluded Ramsay's guess for the missing counties from this figure.

[5] Ibid., p. 191.

be handled by special exchequers and by-pass the main account,[1] or the Chamber might collect revenue to the same effect.[2] But the Chamber did this already under Henry I.[3] Moreover, these arguments scarcely fill the enormous gap in regular revenue which the Pipe Rolls reveal, especially since the figures take no account of the fact that prices rose between 100 and 200 per cent between 1130 and the end of the century.[4] Allowing for that, and discounting special measures, it seems likely that the audit of 1130 was not matched in real terms with any regularity until the reign of John in the years after 1204. By then the king's energies were concentrated once again within a compact manageable unit of government. That may seem a hazardous assessment. To substantiate the point more work still needs to be done on the administration of Hubert Walter in particular, and on the effectiveness of royal taxation and the extent and consequences of inflation. But it is worth stating in a preliminary fashion for two main reasons. First, the Pipe Roll totals provide no ground at all for assuming that Henry II brought a new efficiency to English government in 1154. The improvement in the king's resources came later, in the main after 1170, when he was already under increasing pressure to maintain and defend his continental holdings. Secondly, the figures give no support at all to the argument that John was incompetent, slack, or improvident in the management of financial affairs.

There are no equivalent records for Maine, Anjou, and the provinces further south.[5] For Normandy occasional totals are

[1] See in particular S. K. Mitchell, *Taxation in Medieval England* (New Haven, 1951), pp. 12–17, 22–33.

[2] See in particular J. E. A. Jolliffe 'The *Camera Regis* under Henry II', *English Historical Review*, lxviii (1953), 1–21, 337–62, and the important criticism thereof by H. G. Richardson, 'The Chamber under Henry II', *English Historical Review*, lxix (1954), 596–611. It should be remembered that when an account was rendered in the Chamber for debts in charge at the Exchequer it would subsequently be cleared on the Pipe Roll. Some of the accounts rendered in the Chamber are therefore included in the Pipe Roll totals.

[3] *Pipe Roll 31 Henry I*, p. 134; H. G. Richardson and G. O. Sayles, *Governance of Medieval England*, pp. 230–1.

[4] The main increase came in the last quarter of the twelfth century. See P. D. A. Harvey, 'The English Inflation of 1180–1220', *Past and Present*, no. 61 (1973), 3–30.

[5] Some attempt was made by Lot and Fawtier to calculate the revenues of these provinces from later records, but it is obviously very insecurely based. They concluded that at the end of the Angevin period they must have yielded far less than Normandy. See F. Lot and R. Fawtier, *Le Premier Budget de la*

possible. In 1198, for example, the receipts from the duchy amounted to 98,000 l. *angevin* (£24,500).[1] But since complete, or nearly complete, rolls have survived only for 1180, 1195, and 1198, any continuous analysis of the Norman accounts is impossible. However, Powicke demonstrated very clearly that Norman revenues were quite inadequate for the demands imposed upon them from 1194 onwards;[2] the recorded expenditure on the construction of Château Gaillard alone, for example, exceeded 46,000 l. *angevin* (£11,500).[3] Moreover, as time passed the Duchy was wasted and reduced by the French. Ultimately the defence of Normandy depended on English treasure.[4] Indeed in the final years of the war money was also sent from England in an attempt to buttress Plantagenet fortunes in Anjou and Gascony.[5] There is nothing in the history of any of these lands to suggest that they were administered more efficiently or exploited more profitably than England. Indeed in 1177 Richard of Ilchester was dispatched from England to remodel the Norman Exchequer.[6] Further south the Plantagenets were content with the development of provincial government around members of the royal family, Queen Eleanor and Richard in Poitou, Count Geoffrey in Brittany, or around the seneschals of the various provinces.[7] They seem to have ensured that the seneschals of

monarchie Française: le compte général de 1202–1203 (Bibliothèque de l'École des Hautes Études, Paris, 1932), pp. 138–9.

[1] Lot and Fawtier, op. cit., p. 138.

[2] *The Loss of Normandy*, pp. 233–5.

[3] Ibid., pp. 194, 204–6.

[4] Between October 1202 and October 1203 at least £14,733. 6s. 8d. was transferred from the English Exchequer to Normandy (*Pipe Roll 5 John*, p. xi). See also F. M. Powicke, op. cit., pp. 160–1. Compare the receipts of English treasure recorded on the Norman roll for 1198 (*Rot. Scacc. Norm.* ii. 301–2).

[5] *Rot. Norm.*, p. 89. *Rot. Litt. Pat.*, p. 22. For the transfer of funds to the southern provinces from the Norman Exchequer see below pp. 23–4.

[6] *Gesta Henrici*, i. 124; *The Historical Works of Ralph of Diceto*, ed. W. Stubbs (Rolls Series, 1876), i. 415. On Richard see Delisle, *Actes de Henri II, Introduction*, pp. 431–4; C. H. Haskins, op. cit., pp. 174–6; F. M. Powicke, op. cit. (1907), 23–4; C. Duggan, 'Richard of Ilchester, Royal Servant and Bishop,' *Transactions of the Royal Historical Society*, 5th ser., xvi (1966), 1–21.

[7] On Anjou see J. Boussard, *Le Comté d'Anjou sous Henri Plantagenêt et ses fils (1151–1204)* (Bibliothèque de l'École des Hautes Études, 1938), especially pp. 113–28. Boussard printed a number of administrative acts of the seneschals of Anjou, ibid., pp. 171 ff. See also *Actes de Henri II*, nos. CC, CCXXIV. On Poitou and Aquitaine see A. Richard, *Histoire des comtes de Poitou 778–1204* (Paris, 1903), ii. 260–325.

Anjou and Poitou held office under similar conditions,[1] but there was little in this to compare with the complex machinery of the English or Norman Exchequers.[2]

At the time men were impressed by the apparently enormous wealth which the Angevin kings enjoyed. The anonymous chronicler of Béthune noted with awe that King Richard was:

extremely rich in land and resources, much more so than the King of France. He could raise a very large army from his vassals and mercenaries, for he could summon English, Normans, Bretons, Manceaux, Angevins, and Poitevins. He also had numerous *routiers* who did much damage to the King of France.[3]

Others told a different story. Gerald of Wales reported a conversation with Ranulf Glanville, who in comparing Normandy with France had simply said that France had been weak at the time of Normandy's rise to power.[4] In the old Justiciar's view it was a question of resources. Already at the time of which the anonymous of Béthune was writing, the reopening of the wars after Richard's return from captivity in Germany, the balance had swung strongly to the side of the Capetians. The most important changes occurred outside the Plantagenet lands, in Amiennois and Artois which came into Philip's hands after the death of Philip of Alsace in 1191. These acquisitions outflanked Normandy, greatly increased the territorial and feudal resources of the French Crown, and advanced the commerce between France and Flanders.[5] By 1202–3, the year of the first chance

[1] See the statements of August 1204 on the powers and perquisites of William des Roches as seneschal of Anjou, Maine, and Touraine, and of Guy, Vicomte of Thouars as seneschal of Poitou and the duchy of Aquitaine (A. Teulet, *Layettes du trésor des Chartes*, Paris, 1863, i, nos. 723, 724, 725). These documents are identical. They must therefore reflect a consciously imposed uniformity, but whether one of the Plantagenets or Philip Augustus was responsible for this is open to question.

[2] Powicke argued that there were 'exchequers' both in Anjou and Poitou (op. cit., pp. 31, 236 n.). He seems to have based this on the following enrolled letter: 'Rex . . . Senescallo Pictavie etc. Mandamus vobis quod faciatis habere Savarico de Malo Leone ducentas libras Andegavensium ad scaccarium nostrum de feodo suo quod ei dedimus' (*Rot. Norm.*, p. 28). This certainly does not imply that there was an exchequer of Anjou and does not refer specifically to an exchequer of Poitou.

[3] *Recueil des historiens de Gaule et de la France*, xxiv, pt. 2, 758.

[4] *Giraldi Cambrensis, Opera*, ed. G. F. Warner (Rolls Series, 1891), viii. 258.

[5] L. L. Borrelli de Serres, *La Réunion des provinces septentrionales à la Couronne par Philippe Auguste* (Paris, 1899).

survival of the royal accounts, the revenues of the French king amounted to 197,000 l. *parisis*, roughly equivalent to £73,000.[1] The English total for that year is very speculative, but may have been not much more than £30,000.[2] By that time the Exchequer was involved in hand-to-mouth measures exporting revenues and treasure urgently to Normandy.[3] In Normandy itself the receipts of the Exchequer were totally committed to fortification and the payment of troops.[4] The rest of the Plantagenet lands could not help. In the end the Angevin kings failed to meet the costs of defence.

Like Sir James Ramsay's totals of the audit of the English Exchequer, the French 'budget' of 1202–3 has been sadly neglected by English historians. The text was published by Brussel in 1727,[5] and the original was destroyed in the fire at the Chambre des Comptes in 1737. It may be that Powicke was influenced by the criticism which Delisle and Borrelli de Serres brought against Brussel's edition.[6] At all events he paid no attention to it in the first edition of *The Loss of Normandy*. He also wrote without the benefit of the printed texts of the English Pipe Rolls for the reigns of Richard and John, and without the more hazardous advantage of Ramsay's totals. His summary was roughly this: that Henry II managed his income carefully

[1] F. Lot and R. Fawtier, op. cit., pp. 28–51.

[2] Ramsay calculated a figure of £24,000 for 1203 before estimating for the levy of the Seventh on moveables. This was collected separately and does not figure on the Pipe Roll. Ramsay's suggested total of £110,000 is a simple arithmetical computation from the known yield of the Thirteenth of 1207. That is quite unacceptable. There is no evidence of widespread resistance to the Seventh, as there was to the Thirteenth. In the case of the carrucage of 1198 and 1200 quick returns were accepted instead of accurate assessment. Of the four writs which refer to the Seventh two excuse payment. Finally the assessment of the Seventh may have been restricted to those who had failed to help the king in Normandy. See J. C. Holt, *The Northerners* (Oxford, 1961), pp. 146–7, and F. Lot and R. Fawtier, op. cit., p. 137. Lot and Fawtier were inclined to place the total of 1203 somewhere between that of 1202 (£24,000) and 1204 (£42,000). That is simply a guess, but it does match the almost complete lack of any evidence that the Seventh was a serious imposition.

[3] *Pipe Roll 4 John*, pp. xiii, xviii–xix; *Pipe Roll 5 John*, p. xi.

[4] F. M. Powicke, op. cit., pp. 160–1.

[5] *Nouvel Examen de l'usage général des fiefs en France* (Paris, 1727), ii. cxxxix–ccx. Brussel's version was reproduced in facsimile by Lot and Fawtier, op. cit. following p. 298.

[6] L. L. Borrelli de Serres, *Recherches sur divers services publics* (Paris, 1895–1909), i. 12; L. Delisle, 'Revenus publics en Normandie au XIIe siècle', *Bibliothèque de l'École des Chartes*, 2nd ser., v (1848–9), 176.

and doubled his revenues from England;[1] that the resources of
Henry II and Richard were perhaps greater than those of Philip
Augustus; that in so far as Philip Augustus's 'financial system
was less developed, he suffered by contrast with John';[2] but
that 'by mismanagement John brought chaos. . . . The Chamber
was a centre of intrigue and recklessness. . . . Treasure poured
in and was poured out with heedless confusion'.[3] In 1961
Powicke still held these views.[4] It is now possible to advance an
alternative hypothesis: that initially the Plantagenet dominions
were not exploited very effectively; that from 1170 Henry II,
Richard, John, and their servants did a great deal to increase
their means; but that it was perhaps only in England after 1204
that the improvement was sufficient to overtake the consequences of inflation, and that it failed to match the extraordinary
advance in Capetian resources revealed in the account of 1202–3.
Both these hypotheses emphasize the strain placed on Normandy
and England after 1194. But that is the only point where they
coincide.

One of the causes of Philip Augustus's success in 1204 was
de bonnes finances.[5] Equally, one of the reasons for the Plantagenet
failure was that their resources were inadequate for the task.
A full investigation of this would raise large questions about the
wealth of France, about the extent of the demesne of the rival
houses within their various lordships, and about the optimum
size for a feudal monarchy. But there is also a simple and immediate explanation. The Plantagenet dominions were not designed as an 'empire', as a great centralized administrative
structure, which was ultimately broken down by rebellion and
French attack. On the contrary these lands were simply cobbled
together. They were founded, and continued to survive, on an

---

[1] *The Loss of Normandy*, 1st edn. (1913), p. 350.
[2] Ibid., pp. 436–7, 366.
[3] Ibid., p. 350.
[4] He noted the edition of the budget by Lot and Fawtier in *The Loss of
Normandy*, 2nd edn. (1961), p. 249 n., but did not comment on their assessment of Brussel's work as an *édition soignée* published *avec scrupule* (op. cit.,
p. 2), or on their comparison of Plantagenet and Capetian resources (ibid.,
pp. 135–9). Powicke also noted the work of J. E. A. Jolliffe on the royal
household under John, but decided to stick to his original views (op. cit.,
2nd edn., p. 237 n.). It is fair to say that it would have been difficult to
readjust his arguments without an extensive reconstruction of the book.
[5] F. Lot and R. Fawtier, op. cit., p. 139. They add—'en dépit de l'exiguïté
du domaine royal de France', but that may not allow enough to the advances
made in the 1190s or to the variety of the Crown's interests.

unholy combination of princely greed and genealogical accident. Henry II and his sons imposed some centralized control, some kind of common pattern, but they did so by improvisation rather than premeditated design, for none of the Plantagenets intended their dominions to continue as a single estate. When the ruling house tried to provide for the succession, it simply turned to the ordinary rules of feudal descent which distinguished between inherited and acquired lands.[1] Both Geoffrey of Anjou and Henry planned to partition their lands within these guidelines.[2] Richard also envisaged division.[3] In fact, none

---

[1] For a discussion of these rules which embodies much of the recent literature see J. C. Holt, 'Politics and Property in Early Medieval England', *Past and Present*, no. 57 (1972), 3–52.

[2] The arrangements made by Geoffrey before his death in 1151 were complicated by the fact that at the time Henry had not yet acquired the succession to England. However, he had already succeeded his father as Duke of Normandy in 1150. There were two peculiarities in the succession as Geoffrey planned it:

(i) He decided that his eldest son should succeed to the lands he had acquired by marriage. This followed inevitably from the fact that Henry was already embroiled in the war against Stephen.

(ii) Since Henry had not yet succeeded in England he allowed him to retain Anjou and Maine until he had fully recovered his mother's inheritance. Once that was secured, he was to restore Anjou and Maine to his younger brother, Geoffrey.

This complicated story depends on William of Newburgh (*Chronicles of the reigns of Stephen, Henry II, and Richard I*, ed. R. Howlett, Rolls Series, 1884–90, i. 112–14). It gains some support from the fragmentary Angevin chronicle in *Chroniques des Comtes d'Anjou*, ed. L. Halphen and R. Poupardin (Paris, 1913), pp. 251–2. It was accepted by Professor Boussard in *Le Comté d'Anjou* (1938), pp. 68 ff. and *Le Gouvernement d'Henri II* (1956), pp. 8–11, 408–10, as indeed it has been by most authorities, most recently by C. Warren Hollister and T. K. Keefe, 'The Making of the Angevin Empire', *Journal of British Studies*, xii (1973), 17–21. It has been challenged by Professor Warren who would dismiss it as a manifestation of a fraudulent attempt by Geoffrey, Henry's younger brother, to stake a claim to part of the inheritance (*Henry II*, pp. 46–7, 64). I have not been convinced by his argument which is examined critically and in detail in T. K. Keefe, 'Geoffrey Plantagenet's Will and the Angevin Succession', *Albion*, vi (1974), 266–74. This convincingly restates the generally accepted view.

Henry's own arrangements were straightforward. He provided that his eldest surviving son, Henry, should succeed to the lands which his father, Geoffrey, and mother, Matilda, had held and to which he claimed to have succeeded by inheritance. He arranged that Richard should succeed to Aquitaine, which he had acquired by marriage with Eleanor, and he provided for Geoffrey by marrying him to Constance heiress of Brittany. This was confirmed in 1169 when it was approved by Louis VII. It remained in

of these schemes ever took full effect. Henry rejected Geoffrey's settlement,[1] and when, after the death of the Young King in 1183, Henry revised his own arrangements to make a provision for John as Count of Poitou, Richard in turn rejected Henry's arrangements.[2] Neither Henry nor Richard was inspired by a concept of a single united dominion. Each grabbed the whole for himself. Each was ready to divide it subsequently. Accident played a big part. Henry was able to override his father's provision because Geoffrey happened to die before Henry conquered England. Richard would have been restricted to Aquitaine if his elder brother had survived. Any reasonable prediction of the state of these dominions in 1170 would have been that they would descend in three collateral lines: England, Normandy, Maine, and Anjou through the Young King, Aquitaine through Richard, and Brittany through Geoffrey. Any prediction in 1183 would have been that Richard would step into the Young King's shoes and John into Richard's. Even near the end they were no wiser in providing for the succession. In 1199 there was a real difficulty: the claim of a younger son, John, against that of his nephew Arthur, the representative heir of the senior line. Men tried to meet it by arguing the point on political convenience, or by turning to rules of private law which were themselves a product of the chicanery of the moment.[3] The nearest approximation to a theory of sovereign succession was provided by Hubert Walter, Archbishop of Canterbury, who turned to the biblical examples of Saul and

force until the death of the Young King in 1183. Thereafter, Henry intended to transfer Aquitaine to John. In the face of Richard's intransigence he seems to have considered completely new arrangements. In 1187, according to Gerald of Wales, he proposed that John should hold all the continental estates except Normandy which would remain with England as the heritage of the eldest son (*Opera*, viii. 232).

[3] The treaty concluded between Richard and Philip at Messina in March 1191 provided that if Richard had two or more sons, the second should hold either Normandy, or Anjou and Maine, or Aquitaine and Poitou, in chief of the French Crown (*Recueil des actes de Philippe Auguste*, ed. M. H.-F. Delaborde (Paris, 1916, i, no. 376).

The agreement between Philip Augustus and John of January 1194 also provided that if John had two sons or more, each would hold his barony directly of the King of France (*Layettes du trésor des Chartes*, i, no. 412).

[1] C. Warren Hollister and T. K. Keefe, op. cit., pp. 22–5.
[2] *Gesta Henrici*, i. 308, 311; *Diceto*, ii. 18–19.
[3] I have dealt with this matter in a forthcoming paper entitled 'The Plantagenet succession of 1199 and the *casus regis*'.

David to justify a theory of election from the royal line.[1] But that was antiquated and came too late.

These schemes for division will not allow any but the most elementary conception of an Angevin empire. It was adventitious. At any moment the accident of death might lead to division or the revision of a division. Indeed, Henry's sons were not prepared to wait for that and wanted division before their father died. John too, tried to grab a portion while Richard was still king.[2] This family squabble always stood in the way of effective exploitation. More than that, it meant that valuable resources were frittered away. The risks were not just financial. Already in 1156 Henry II performed homage to Louis VII for the succession to Normandy, Maine and Anjou which overrode his father's will.[3] He was the first of the royal line to do so as king.[4] His sons followed suit in seeking Capetian support: the young Henry and Richard in 1173, Richard in 1183, John in 1192. The process was repeated in the next generation when Arthur turned to Philip in 1199. Each one of these appeals put the Angevin dominions at grave risk. Each one encouraged Capetian intrusion. John in 1194 agreed to abandon vital provinces on the Norman frontier.[5] Arthur in 1199 abandoned Normandy *in toto*.[6] Not one of these princes seemed aware that he was rocking the boat.

---

[1] *Mathaei Parisiensis, chronica majora*, ed. H. R. Luard (Rolls Series, 1872–83), ii. 454–6.

[2] *Layettes du trésor des Chartes*, i, no. 412. John sought to get his hand on all the continental dominions apart from extensive concessions to Philip Augustus. The agreement provided that in any peace with Richard, John would continue to hold directly of the King of France. If that proved impossible, he was to answer to Richard by attorney and never personally.

[3] *Chronica Rogeri de Hoveden*, ed. W. Stubbs (Rolls Series, 1868–71), i. 215.

[4] Henry came to take a serious view of such an homage. At the reconciliation with his sons in 1174 he refused to accept homage from the young Henry 'because he was a king' (*Actes de Henri II*, no. CCCCLXVIII). Compare *Draco Normannicus*, below, p. 44.

[5] Vaudreuil, Évreux, and Verneuil and further withdrawals in Anjou and the Touraine (*Layettes du trésor des Chartes*, i, no. 412). The agreement also confirmed Philip's possession of Loches, Châtillon-sur-Indre, Drincourt, and Arques, which had been surrendered to him as guarantees by Richard's emissaries at Mantes in July 1193. Philip placed John in charge of Arques, Drincourt, and Évreux. See Powicke, op. cit., pp. 97–8. For the date of John's agreement with Philip see Landon, *Itinerary of Richard I*, p. 205 n.

[6] In 1202 Philip Augustus received homage from Arthur for Brittany, Anjou, Maine, and Touraine. Normandy was to remain at Philip's disposal (*Actes de Philippe Auguste*, no. 723).

It was in such an uncertain political climate that the Plantagenet dominions were governed. The effects were curiously contradictory. On the one hand, the family squabble and the increasing insistent Capetian challenge always threatened to erode or divide the dominions. On the other, the king's response to this and the urgent need to provide resources for war demanded more effective financial exploitation and tighter control through the household and the local organs of government. At one and the same time, therefore, centrifugal and centripetal tendencies were at work. This affected the relationships between the different components of the Plantagenets' lands. New links were forged, old links were weakened. In this complex process England and Normandy began to drift apart.

The governance of the 'empire' depended on separate provincial administrations held together by the itinerant monarch and his household. But in practice these provincial administrations were of unequal weight. On the Continent the real centre lay in Normandy. It was there that Henry II spent the greater part of his time when in France, and the same was true of Richard, despite his southern upbringing. In part this arose from their concentration on the defence of the Norman frontier; in part it recognized that Normandy was the strategic link between England and the south. It meant that the Norman Exchequer at Caen acted as a central base, concentrating the revenues of Normandy, receiving the king's treasure from England through Barfleur, and dispensing funds not only for expenditure on the Norman defences, but also for the king's needs as he travelled south to Chinon or Loches. Treasure went from Caen into Anjou in 1180.[1] Payments were made to the king's knights going to Issoudun and treasure was sent to the king himself at Chinon in 1195.[2] Further treasure went south into Anjou in 1198 and 1201.[3] Under John, the king's receipts from English treasure in Gascony and disbursements therefrom to William des Roches, seneschal of Anjou, were notified to Samson, Abbot of St. Stephen, Caen, and Ralph l'Abbé, who were directing the day-to-day work of the Exchequer at Caen.[4] By all appearances the Norman Exchequer had all the capacity for independent action of its counterpart in England.[5] By com-

---

[1] *Rot. Scacc. Norm.* i. 56. [2] Ibid. i. 136, 171, 225.
[3] Ibid. ii. 351, 501. [4] *Rot. Norm.*, p. 36.
[5] I have not found any direct evidence that there was an Exchequer seal in the Norman Exchequer. The matter has not been raised by those who have discussed the seal in England (see above p. 33, n. 1) or by the authorities on

parison the seneschalsies of the southern provinces were primitive and fragile. In Anjou, the seneschal's powers of jurisdiction as the local agent of the duke were not fully established until 1174.[1] In Poitou and Gascony the seneschalsies were still subject to rearrangement under Richard and John.[2] In the crisis following 1203 the men in charge came to depend on loans and letters of credence from the king to bolster their weakening authority and supplement the meagre resources which John was able to advance to them.[3]

It was not only in financial matters that Normandy played a leading role. Rouen was the nearest approach to a capital city that the Plantagenet kings had on the Continent. The agreement concluded between Henry and Louis VII in 1177 in anticipation of the Crusade provided that Henry's officers would protect and defend Louis's lands as vigorously as if the city of Rouen were under attack, and that Louis's officers would protect Henry's land as vigorously as if the city of Paris were the one to suffer.[4] Rouen and Paris were thus placed on a par. And it was Étienne of Rouen, monk of Bec, who in *Draco Normannicus* maintained that the two kings were on a par. That one should perform homage to the other was shameful. They were 'equal in virtue, equal in honour, equal in their realms'.[5] Indeed, more

Norman institutions. There are numerous *brevia regis* recorded in the Norman Pipe Rolls. This may indicate that there was an Exchequer seal but unfortunately all the surviving Pipe Rolls come from years when the king spent some time in Normandy.

[1] J. Boussard, *Le Comté d'Anjou*, pp. 121–5; *Gouvernement d'Henri II*, p. 287.

[2] See the fluctuations in which Gascony and Poitou were established as a single or separate seneschalseas (F. M. Powicke, op. cit., p. 30). John also established Gerard d'Athée as seneschal of the Touraine in August 1202 (*Rot. Litt. Pat.*, p. 17).

[3] See the letters of 12 December 1201 requiring the Gascon bishops to supply their service to Robert of Thornham as if to the king in person (*Rot. Litt. Pat.*, p. 3b) and letters to the citizens of Bordeaux seeking an aid in February 1202 (ibid., p. 5b). Letters of 19 February 1203, authorizing Robert of Thornham to contract two separate loans of 1,000 m. sterling on behalf of the king on the king's guarantee as principal surety, reflect the deepening crisis (ibid., p. 25b).

[4] *Actes de Henri II*, no. DVI. The phrases were repeated in the renewal of the agreement with Philip Augustus in 1180 (ibid., no. DL).

[5] See the words attributed to the Emperor:

'Mandat ne regi Francorum subiciatur
Cum sibi par virtus, par honor atque thronus'

(*Chron. Stephen, Henry II, and Richard I*, ii. 720).

than that, it was right that the 'indomitable lion' should refuse
the yoke, for had not Pepin replaced Childeric, and was not
the kingdom of France but a petty remnant of the realm of the
Carolingians?[1] Henry II himself played a part in blending
Plantagenet rule with the genius of the great Norman dukes.
In 1162 the bodies of Richard I and Richard II were raised
and translated to Fécamp in his presence; he issued a special
protection for those who attended the ceremony.[2] Henry,
Eleanor of Aquitaine and Richard Cœur de Lion were all
buried at Fontevrault, but Richard bequeathed his heart to
the Church of Rouen and it was there too that his elder brother,
the Young King, had been buried. For John the Church of
Rouen was *mater* and *magistra* to all the Norman churches, the
burial place of his brothers and friends, where flourished the
deeds of saints whose merits augmented the prosperity of his
realm and honour.[3]

The government of the Plantagenets, in changing the role of
Normandy in France, also changed her relationship to England.
England and Normandy had the closest of ties. Great officials
in Church and State: Richard of Ilchester, Walter of Coutances,
William fitz Ralph, and great magnates: William de Mandeville Earl of Essex, Ranulph Earl of Chester, Robert fitz Parnel
Earl of Leicester, were equally at home on both sides of the
Channel. The two Exchequers may, in Richard fitz Neal's
words, have differed in important respects[4] but they continued
to work hand in hand until the final disaster of 1204. It was not
simply that the Norman Exchequer received and accounted
for treasure dispatched from England. Debtors holding land on

[1]   'Temnit Francigenis audacia subdere colla
        Indomitusque leo, respuit omne jugum'   (ibid. ii. 675).
For Childeric and Pepin see ibid. ii. 665–71, and for the comments on the
Carolingian Empire ibid. ii. 674.

[2] *Actes de Henri II*, nos. CCXXI–CCXXIII.

[3] *Rot. Litt. Pat.*, p. 19.

[4] 'Verum in plurimis et pene maioribus dissident' (*Dialogus de Scaccario*,
p. 14). Fitz Neal did not explain this cryptic remark, but he was concerned
at this point with the origins of the English Exchequer. Stapleton emphasized
the similarities of the two institutions (*Rot. Scacc. Norm.* i. ix–xiii). Haskins
discussed the divergences in *Norman Institutions*, pp. 176–8. Perhaps the most
important was in the structure of local government where the superimposi-
tion of *bailliages* on the older *vicomtés* and *prepositurae* produced complications
of which England was largely free until the establishment of special administrative units based on escheats and quasi-military commands in the reign of
John. The Norman developments are very fully discussed by F. M. Powicke,
op. cit., pp. 45–56, 68–78.

both sides of the Channel found it convenient to pay into one Exchequer and present writs on account in the other.[1] Moreover, even in the last years of Angevin rule the king's officials saw no difficulty in making complex arrangements which required action in both England and Normandy. Typical of these transactions is the proffer whereby Richard de Soliis fined 600 l. *angevin* for his land in Normandy and England, and to marry as he wished. The Abbot of Caen and Ralph l'Abbé were instructed to take sureties for the payment and give him seisin in Normandy. They were also to notify the English Justiciar, Geoffrey fitz Peter. If they did not get sureties for the full amount they were to inform Geoffrey of the deficit, for which he would then seek sureties. Geoffrey was instructed separately to enrol only that portion of the debt for which Richard would be responsible in England. In short he was given an instruction which was conditional on the actions of the officials of the Norman Exchequer.[2] Such an arrangement suggests that the closest contact between the two institutions lasted right to the end of the Anglo-Norman realm. But this was not the whole story. Among the enrolments which appeared in the early years of John's reign, the Norman rolls clearly reveal the newer links between Normandy and the other Plantagenet lands on the Continent. One, a roll of charters and cyrographs recorded in the Exchequer at Caen, is somewhat similar to the English *cartae antiquae* rolls.[3] One is a Fine Roll[4] and three are rolls of *contrabrevia*,[5] mainly of the types which, within a year or so, were being described officially as letters close. All these last four rolls include Angevin and Poitevin business as well as Norman. Normandy, Anjou, and Poitou appear as related administrative units, separate from England. An item relating to Ireland which appeared accidentally was annotated—*debuit scribi in rotulo Angliae*.[6] The separation was not unilateral. Items of Norman

---

[1] This goes back as far as the Exchequer records. See *Pipe Roll 31 Henry I*, pp. 7, 13, 38–9. For later examples see *Pipe Roll 32 Henry II*, p. 60; *Rot. Scacc. Norm.* ii. 364, 443, 496.

[2] *Rot. Norm.*, p. 38. Compare the arrangements for Queen Berengaria's dower (*Rot. Litt. Pat.*, pp. 2b–3). For a loan advanced by the king in Gascony and put in charge at the English Exchequer see ibid., p. 24b. For money advanced to the king in Normandy and treated likewise see *Rot. Lib.* p. 76.

[3] For 2 John (*Rot. Norm.*, pp. 1–22).   [4] For 2 John (ibid., pp. 37–44).

[5] For 2, 4, and 5 John (ibid., pp. 22–37, 45–98, 98–122).

[6] Ibid., p. 77. However, one writ dated at Westminster and addressed to William the Treasurer and the Chamberlains of the Exchequer (of England) was included in error (ibid., p. 34).

business appearing on the English rolls at this time were annotated—*debent inrotulari in rotulo Normanniae*.[1] Many of the writs
on these rolls are concerned with issues, receipts, or accounts.
It is in the enrolments most closely associated with Exchequer
business that the separation of England from Normandy first
became apparent.

There were other signs that Normandy and England were
beginning to go their separate ways. There is no doubt that
much of the unique quality of Norman law in France in the
thirteenth century derived from its association with England
in the twelfth. In the Norman courts the jury played as important a role as in England. The writs of the possessory actions
were in regular use, most of them in a closely similar form.
Justices held assizes. Litigants made final concords in the courts.
However, the duchy developed its own variants of this system.
For example, although the writs of petty assize stemmed from
a common stock the time-limit applied to such actions was quite
different from that in England. Moreover in Normandy there
was no writ of naifty, no *praecipe quod reddat*, no general rule of
nemo tenetur and nothing similar to the English writ of right.[2]
Even more important was that the law of inheritance and succession was slowly settling into different patterns. In England
by Glanville's day all land held by military service was indi-
visible and descended by primogeniture; provision was made
for younger sons by enfeoffments held of the senior line.[3]
In Normandy in contrast estates might still be divided if there
was more than one feof; provision was made for younger sons
by the practice of *parage*.[4] These rules were still debated both
in England and Normandy, but no one apparently pointed to
the virtues of a common pattern or suggested that different
rules might prove awkward to families holding on both sides
of the Channel. It is probable that it did not seem to matter,

[1] *Rot. Lib.*, p. 68.
[2] For a convenient summary of this see R. C. van Caenegem, *The Birth of
the English Common Law* (Cambridge, 1971), pp. 57–9. For the jury see C. H.
Haskins, op. cit., pp. 196–238. For examples of writs and further comment
on differences of procedure between England, Normandy, and the Channel
Isles see *Early Register of Writs*, ed. Elsa de Haas and G. D. G. Hall (Selden
Society, lxxxvii, 1970), pp. xcix–civ. There are further examples of writs
earlier than 1219 in the cartulary of S. Giles of Pont-Audemer (Rouen,
Bibliothèque Municipale, MS. Y 200 fols. 44ᵛ–45ᵛ).
[3] Glanvill, *De Legibus*, ed. G. D. G. Hall (London, 1965), p. 75.
[4] *Coutumiers de Normandie*, ed. E. J. Tardif, i. 8–9; iii. 79–83. R. Génestal,
Le Parage normand, pp. 16–30.

that these variants were seen as further pieces in the jigsaw of local customs and procedures over which the courts presided. No one could have been wary of these changes on the ground that they contributed to an imminent separation of the kingdom from the duchy, for that could not be foreseen. But once the separation had taken place, these differences in law and government could but help to perpetuate it.

However, some matters were obvious, especially war and the costs of war. In these, probably more than in any other matter, the accession of the Plantagenets marked a turning-point, for these kings assumed that the resources of the Anglo-Norman realm were available to them in all parts of the new dominion. Hitherto there had been no precise definition of the limits within which the tenants-in-chief provided military service. They accepted in a rough and ready way that they might be called upon to fight or provide service or aid anywhere in England or Normandy, that they might be involved in war with Brittany or against the French in the Vexin or elsewhere over the Norman border, and that those with lands in England might serve against the Welsh or Scots. But campaigns further afield had never arisen. Now, suddenly, their responsibilities were vastly extended. In 1158 Henry II mustered the Norman host against Brittany and then, after a diplomatic success over Conan Count of Brittany, led it south into Anjou and Poitou, where he seized Thouars.[1] In 1159 the great scutage of Toulouse established the precedent that the service due from both Normandy and England might be extended to the furthest provinces which the Plantagenets could claim. The last great demand of this kind in Normandy was made in 1202 when service and aid was sought *pro exercitu Gasconiae* and numerous prests were paid to the barons and knights who served on the campaign.[2] Thereafter England continued to bear the burden alone in the Poitevin expeditions of 1206 and 1214.

In England the imposition of these demands led to isolated protests and then finally to the outcry against overseas service

[1] Robert de Torigni, *Chronique*, ed. L. Delisle (Société de l'histoire de Normandie, 1872–3), i. 311–13.

[2] For service and the aid see *Rot. Scacc. Norm.* ii. 530, 545, 551, 566, and *Rot. Norm.* p. 92. For the prests see *Rot. Scacc. Norm.* ii. 510, 536–7, 545, 557, and S. R. Packard, *Miscellaneous Records of the Norman Exchequer 1199–1204* (Smith College Studies in History, Northampton, Mass., 1927), pp. 17, 22, 38. It should be noted that the prests were advances paid to knights who attended the campaign, not forced loans raised by the king, as they are interpreted by Powicke (op. cit., p. 154 n.).

of 1213 and 1214. The objectors had a case. They were bound to serve in England; by custom they served in Normandy; but on what ground could they be required to serve in lands which had not been part of the realm when their fiefs were established? On the Continent the arguments were apparently less vociferous, but by the thirteenth century and probably earlier provincial custom resolved into a compromise that service outside the province should be at the prince's cost.[1] In England all the pressures, military, financial, administrative, led ultimately to the crisis of 1215 and Magna Carta. On the Continent also similar pressures produced similar results. In February 1214, Thomas Count of le Perche, who was to die in battle beneath the walls of Lincoln castle three years later, granted to his knights of the castlery of Bellême that he would not levy impositions on them and their men except on four occasions: his first military campaign, his first ransom in war, the knighting of his eldest son, and the marriage of his eldest daughter.[2] But on the whole the effects of the war were different on each side of the Channel. England suffered mainly in money and other resources and she responded ultimately in Magna Carta. Normandy suffered war and destruction and responded by defecting. Those holding land on both sides of the Channel were torn one way or the other.

[1] Professor Boussard has suggested that Norman military tenants could not be required to serve outside the duchy except at the king's expense (*Gouvernement d'Henri II*, p. 416; 'L'Enquête de 1172' *Recueil de travaux offert à M. Clovis Brunel*, Paris, 1955, i. 204–208). This is not borne out by the evidence of the Gascon expedition of 1202. Those who served were military tenants of the duchy; they received prests, but prests were accountable at the Exchequer. See the comments on the Praestita Roll of 14–18 John in *Pipe Roll 17 John*, pp. 71–80. On the limitation of military service in other provinces of the dominions see P. Chaplais, 'Le duché-pairie de Guyenne', *Annales du Midi*, lxix (1957), 14–15.

[2] 'Thomas comes Pertici, omnibus ad quos praesentes litterae pervenerint salutem in Domino. Ad universorum notitiam volumus pervenire quod milites nostri de castellario Beilimensi talliam de feodis suis et hominibus suis nobis debent tantummodo feodaliter pro his quatuor rebus quae sequuntur. Pro prima militia nostra, pro prima captione nostra de guerra, pro militia filii nostri primogeniti viventis, et pro prima filia nostra maritanda. Praeter has tallias nec a militum feodis, nec ab eorum hominibus, tallias possumus feodaliter extorquere. Et ne hujusmodi libertas ab aliquo heredum nostrorum in posterum infringatur, eam sigilli caractere fecimus communiri. Actum, anno gratiae MCCXIIII mense Februario' (E. Martène and V. Durand, *Veterum Scriptorum et Monumentorum amplissima collectio*, Paris, 1724, i, col. 1117). It seems necessary to read 'militia' in two different senses, both of which are permissible.

The Normans were accustomed to war with the French over the Vexin and other debatable frontiers. From 1154 they had to face in addition war in Normandy brought on by events in distant parts of France over which they had no control. In 1159 Henry II attacked Toulouse; as a result, war broke out along the Norman border.[1] In 1167 there was a dispute between the two kings over their respective suzerainty in the Auvergne, followed in the same year by a rebellion of the Lusignans in Poitou; Louis devastated the land around Pacy and raided the Vexin.[2] In 1173, when Normandy was the last province to break out into rebellion, the Count of Boulogne attacked Aumale and Neufmarché, and Louis VII invaded the Vexin and burned Verneuil; the next year Louis and the Young King attacked Rouen.[3] True, there were occasions when the Normans derived some benefit from the provinces further south. In May 1194 an Angevin contingent was in the army which relieved Verneuil,[4] and at Vaudreuil in May 1195 Richard was able to muster a host from England, Brittany, Poitou, Maine, Anjou, and Gascony.[5] But these multiple resources were at the king's service and convenience. When the Archbishop of Rouen and the king's officers concluded a truce with Philip in 1194, Richard insisted that it did not apply to the barons of Poitou. He maintained that it would infringe the law and custom of Poitou if Poitevin magnates were prevented from settling differences by the sword.[6] The war went on.

In the end Normandy was ravaged: her towns, Évreux, Dieppe, Verneuil sacked and burned, her churches so devastated that both Philip and Richard suffered interdicts on their lands for the damage they had caused, her commerce interrupted and her monetary system shattered.[7] England, in contrast, only

[1] Torigni, i. 325; 'Continuatio Beccensis', ibid. ii. 174.

[2] Torigni, i. 363–6.

[3] Torigni, ii. 39–42; *Gesta Henrici*, i. 47–8, 53–6, 73–4.

[4] Diceto, ii. 116–17; F. M. Powicke, op. cit., p. 102.

[5] *Histoire de Guillaume le Maréchal*, ed. P. Meyer (Société de l'histoire de France, 1891–1901), lines 10560–3.

[6] *Hoveden*, iii. 253–5.

[7] The currency of Normandy was the *livre angevin*. It was replaced under the Capetians by the *livre tournois*. At the time of the collapse and in the immediately subsequent years payment was often arranged *usualis monete currentis per Normanniam*, or *communis monete*, or some such phrase which indicates the general uncertainty. There is a good run of charters illustrating this in the cartulary of S. Giles of Pont-Audemer (Rouen, Bibliothèque Municipale, MS. Y 200).

suffered war during the rebellion of 1173–4 and in John's
abortive rising of 1194. The comparative calm at home, the
long absences of the king abroad, the relative independence of
English government in the absence of the king, could foster a
comfortable sense of detachment from events across the Channel.
After Gervase of Canterbury, a nearly contemporary witness,
had commented on the disasters in Normandy in 1203 he added:
'England meanwhile, by the grace of God and under the
guidance of Hubert Archbishop of Canterbury and Geoffrey
fitz Peter, enjoyed tranquillity and peace'.[1] This was not simply
the insular smugness of a cloistered monk. Some time before
1205 Roger Bigod Earl of Norfolk, confirmed a lease made by
one of his knights to Wymondham Abbey which ran for twelve
years 'from the Christmas after Hubert Walter, Archbishop and
Justiciar, first came to Norwich'.[2] Roger Bigod himself in 1198
confirmed to the prior of St. Felix of Walton   all the grants
made by his ancestors and tenants 'up to the feast of St. Egidius
following the transfer of the Justiciarship of England from
Hubert Walter to Geoffrey fitz Peter'.[3] Those provisions reflected
the regular government of the Justiciars which provided the
peace and tranquility of which Gervase wrote.

Gervase's reaction was simply one among many. For some
the rule of the Angevins was a great enterprise, which for a time
opened wide horizons and provided splendid opportunities for
advancement. Walter of Coutances, a Cornish clerk, became
Archbishop of Rouen and for a time Justiciar of England.[4]
William Marshal, a landless knight became lord of Longueville
and Earl of Pembroke. Others like Hubert de Burgh the defender
of Chinon, Gerard d'Athée the castellan of Loches, Robert of
Thornham seneschal of Poitou and Gascony, were all climbing
towards landed prosperity through administrative and military
service to the Crown, even as Normandy collapsed. Some like
Bertrand de Born revelled in the struggle and indulged in
extravagant glorifications of war.[5] Others, like Waleran 4th

[1] *Historical Works of Gervase of Canterbury*, ed. W. Stubbs (Rolls Series,
1879–80), ii. 95.
[2] B.M. Cotton MS., Titus C viii, fol. 67ᵛ. I am obliged for this and the
following reference to Miss Susan Atkin.
[3] B.M. Cotton MS., Domitian A x, fol. 197ᵛ.
[4] On Walter's early career see L. Delisle, *Actes de Henri II, Introduction*,
pp. 106–13.
[5] Bertrand's best known passage is accessible in Marc Bloch, *Feudal
Society* (London, 1961), p. 293.

Earl of Warwick, fined with the king that they might be allowed
to go home.[1] The Anglo-Norman nobles were still apt for war.
They would still cross half Christendom for adventure and
spiritual reward in the Holy Land.[2] In Ireland they could still
revive the old buccaneering enthusiasm which had brought
their ancestors to mastery in England.[3] But by these standards
the French conflict was the wrong war in the wrong place. It
was too expensive. It put the homeland at risk and it brought
no profit except to those who used it to seek advancement
within the polity.

In imaginative words, Powicke attributed to the collapse of
Normandy 'the inexplicable character which attaches to some
men's moral downfall. With no apparent failure, maintaining
to the end the exercise of their peculiar virtues, they lose their
hold on life'.[4] He believed that the Norman power of resistance
had been sapped by the autocratic rule of the Plantagenet
kings.[5] Few would now accept such a conclusion, even of King
John. But it is certainly true that Anglo-Norman resistance
lacked moral fibre. Sir Richard Southern has shown how men's
minds were dominated by the prestige of France and by the
literary conventions of *douce France* stemming from the *Chanson
de Roland*.[6] There was nothing equivalent on the Plantagenet
side. Some in England and Normandy, especially perhaps those
subject to the influence of the Schools, shared in the respect for
Paris and things French. But below that level among the annalists and chroniclers who recorded the story of the war, there was
a different impression, one of growing provincial suspicion and
prejudice. In Poitou Henry II came to be regarded as an arbitrary tyrant fittingly dubbed the King of the North as a mark
of his barbarity. Aquitaine and Poitou were urged to rejoice at

---

[1] *Chancellor's Roll 8 Richard I*, p. 58.

[2] Among those who planned to embark on a crusade or pilgrimage to the
Holy Land in 1202–4 were Gerard de Furneval, Henry du Puiset, Hugh
count of S. Paul, and Henry de Longchamp. Geoffrey fitz Peter, the Justiciar
of England, William de Stuteville, Hugh Bardolf, and William Briwerre all
took vows but withdrew because of their duties at home (F. M. Powicke,
op. cit., pp. 245–7).

[3] Both William de Briouze and William Marshal were present in the
defence of Normandy. They were also of great importance in the occupation
of Ireland.

[4] Op. cit., 249.

[5] Ibid., pp. 248–9.

[6] R. W. Southern, 'England's First Entry into Europe', in *Medieval
Humanism and other Studies* (Oxford, 1970), pp. 135–57.

his discomfiture; England and Neustria were threatened with desolation.[1] To the Normans, on the other hand, the Poitevins seemed treacherous.[2] In England William de Longchamps, a Norman, was attacked as a foreigner who ignored English ways,[3] and at Canterbury Richard's Norman ministers were regarded as untrustworthy and capable of treason.[4] In Normandy, conversely, the surrender of Vaudreuil by Saer de Quenci and Robert fitz Walter gave rise to the view that the English surrendered castles which they should have guarded as the Normans did: this a comment on two barons of unquestionable continental stock.[5] There was no common ethos; no great tradition to set against the French. In the *Roman des Franceis*, André of Coutances preserved the tale, derived from Wace, that Arthur had conquered the French, but in the crude form of a burlesque which also poked fun at the English under their mythical king Arflet of Northumberland.[6] There was nothing in this to inspire loyalty throughout the Plantagenet lands.[7] Indeed, the Arthurian story itself was now divisive. In England the Barnwell chronicler asserted that the Bretons, in pressing the claims of the young prince Arthur, were seeking to revive the glories of the ancient Arthur and were thereby plotting to destroy the English race.[8] Here a great legend, which might have been developed

---

[1] The continuator of Richard of Poitou in *Recueil des historiens des Gaules et de la France*, xii. 419–20.

[2] *Histoire de Guillaume le Maréchal*, lines 12545–50; *Histoire des ducs de Normandie et des rois d'Angleterre*, ed. F. Michel (Société de l'histoire de France, 1859), p. 96.

[3] *Hoveden*, iii. 142–3; discussed by R. W. Southern, op. cit., pp. 141–2.

[4] Gervase of Canterbury, i. 515.

[5] *Histoire des ducs de Normandie*, p. 130.

[6] This has now been given a scholarly edition by A. J. Holden in *Études de langue et de littérature du moyen âge offertes à Félix Lecoy* (Paris, 1973), pp. 213–33. I am obliged to Professor Wolfgang Van Emden for drawing my attention to it.

[7] Apart from its tone, which would scarcely inspire anyone, the *Roman* is entirely Anglo-Norman in its material and context. André concludes:

> Que Englais, Breton, Angevin,
> Mansel, Gascoign at Peitevin
> Tienent Andreu a bon devin
> Quer partot dit veir. C'est la fin
>   (ibid., p. 225)

That is the solitary hint of a wider background. André also called on Flemings, Burgundians, and Lorrainers to warrant the truth of his tale (ibid.).

[8] *Memoriale fratris Walteri de Coventria*, ed. W. Stubbs (Rolls Series, 1872–3), ii. 196.

to rival the powerful French tradition of the *Roland*, was turned instead to separate and divide the countries which had fostered it. At the last count staunch men on the Plantagenet side, like William Marshal or Baldwin of Béthune, honourable within the conventions of the day, found their strength and justification in a code of feudal loyalty. It allowed William to perform homage to both Philip Augustus and John.

These conditions, material and moral, look like symptoms of collapse, as Powicke suggested. That represents an Anglo-Norman or Plantagenet point of view. The Capetian attitude was different and straightforward. It was simply that the Plantagenet dominions, with the exception of England, were part of the realm of France. In 1184–5, on the occasion of renewed attempts by Henry II to get archiepiscopal status for the Breton bishopric of Dol, Philip Augustus wrote to Pope Lucius III defending the rights of the Archbishop of Tours whose authority, he wrote, extended throughout Lower Brittany 'to the furthest corners of our realm as far as the ocean'.[1] In his agreement with King Richard at Messina in 1191 Philip made the same point in another fashion: he referred to the major divisions of the Plantagenet lands simply as baronies.[2] Similar terms were used in the agreement with John of 1194.[3] Once there was reasonable parity in resources, the main weakness of the Plantagenets and the main strength of the Capetians lay in the feudal suzerainty of the kings of France. Using that they undermined the structure of the Plantagenet dominion, sapping the feudal loyalties which bound it together. In the end the two provinces to survive the attack, England and Gascony, were those not subject to the Crown of France.

One such story begins at Tours, where both the archbishopric and the great abbey of St. Martin enjoyed special privileges under the French Crown. They were demesne churches of the king, both in Tours and in their surrounding properties. As a result the Plantagenets could never make the town a major Angevin centre of government like Angers or Le Mans. Louis VII and Philip II were particularly attentive to these churches' needs, confirming their privileges and helping them to resist the nascent commune in the town.[4] There was another side to

[1] *Actes de Philippe Auguste*, i, no. 136.
[2] Ibid. i, no. 316.
[3] *Layettes du trésor des Chartes*, I, no. 412.
[4] A. Luchaire, *Études sur les actes de Louis VII* (Paris, 1885), nos. 75, 117, 120, 121, 397, 752; *Actes de Philippe Auguste*, i, nos. 122, 331.

this manifest concern. Sometime in 1167, when Louis was at war with Henry, he wrote as follows to Bartholomew, Dean of the church of St. Martin:

We wish to be informed about the King of England's intentions. Will he be 'advancing into Poitou or returning to the Norman sea-coast? If you are certain about this send us the information by letter to be returned with our sergeants. If the matter is uncertain, send such rumours as you have through one of them and retain the other until you are able to give us further information.[1]

An identical message was sent to William, Treasurer of St. Martin.[2] It is surely not surprising that the Plantagenets became impatient. One of Richard's first acts was to try to reach a settlement. In July 1189, before going to England for his coronation, he and King Philip met in the chapter house of the abbey. After a full inquiry they agreed on a long, detailed definition of the respective rights of the abbey and the count of Anjou. This laid down that the count could not ask for military service against the king of France or tax the men of the abbey, or seize its estates, possessions or property. The agreement also embarked on a long complaint that the count's men had disturbed these and other rights in the past and in particular that the count had demanded homage from twelve representatives on behalf of the men of Châteauneuf, saving the fealty due to the king of France and the Church, as safeguard for their property during his war with the king. The agreement was confirmed by the two kings in July 1190.[3] By then Richard had also settled with the archbishop on detailed arrangements for the partition of customary renders and jurisdictional rights between the officers of the archbishop and the count. This also Philip confirmed, emphasizing as he did so that all these rights were of his fee.[4] The agreement was of no avail. Its advantages to Richard are not obvious. In June 1194 he ejected the canons of St. Martin and confiscated their revenues.[5] Philip replied on the instant by confiscating all the property, revenues, and chattels of the churches and abbeys of the province of Rouen on which he could lay his hands.[6] It was not until November, that the two kings restored the ejected clergy.[7]

---

[1] *Recueil des historiens des Gaules et de la France*, xvi. 141–2.   [2] Ibid.
[3] *Actes de Philippe Auguste*, i, no. 361.   [4] Ibid., no. 357.
[5] *Recueil des historiens des Gaules et de la France*, xviii. 293.
[6] *Œuvres de Rigord et de Guillaume le Breton*, ed. H. F. Delaborde(Société de l'Histoire de France, 1882–5), i. 128–9.
[7] *Actes de Philippe Auguste*, i, no. 483; Diceto, ii. 122.

This is of interest not simply because the seizure of the property of the Normans was triggered by events outside the duchy,
but also because of the light it throws on what was in fact a
border conflict. In Tours the counts of Anjou were hedged
about by rights of property and jurisdiction which were alms of
the Crown of France. The count and the Church shared customs,
jurisdiction, and administrative responsibilities in the town, the
suburbs, and the surrounding estates and forests. Neither the
count's nor the archbishop's reeve could rent the pannage
without the consent of the other; nor could the agents of either
party settle the tolls on ships coming up the Loire except in
consort. Here the demarcation between Capetian and Plantagenet France was defined in terms, not of frontiers, but of
feudal rights.

That was true in general and on a larger scale. For example,
the older Norman monastic foundations all held property and
rights in the Île-de-France, some of it since Carolingian days.
One of Louis VII's first acts of 1137 was to issue instructions
giving the monks of Bec protection and freedom from custom
at the tolls of Poissy and Mantes Gassicourt.[1] This order was
repeated in 1176.[2] In 1152–3 he confirmed and extended rights
of assart at Genainville, near Mantes, which Louis the Fat had
granted to the monks of Jumièges and in 1168 he confirmed their
possession of rights of tithe in the church of St. Martin of Bouafle
near Meulan.[3] In 1165 he confirmed gifts which Aubrey his
chamberlain had made to the house of Villers St. Paul, a priory
of the abbey of Fécamp.[4] In 1169 he confirmed the manor of
Pecq in the Oise valley to the monks of St. Wandrille and in
1177 issued a general confirmation to St. Wandrille of its rights
of free passage on the Seine and its property in the dioceses of
Amiens, Beauvais, Paris, and Chartres.[5] In these matters Philip
Augustus followed the example of his father in confirming and
extending the privileges of the Norman Church in his own
dominions. Jumièges, Bec, St. Ouen, and Foucarmont all
benefited.[6] As the war progressed so royal patronage was

[1] *Actes de Louis VII*, no. 5.
[2] Ibid., no. 713.
[3] Ibid., nos. 282, 557.
[4] Ibid., no. 515.
[5] Ibid., nos. 572, 729.
[6] *Actes de Philippe Auguste*, i, nos. 172, 243 for Jumièges; i, no. 283, ii,
nos. 646, 674, for Bec; i, nos. 366, 381 for St. Ouen; ii, no. 541 for Foucarmont.

extended, confirming revenues at Pacy to the monks of Ivry,[1]
and at Évreux all the gifts made to the cathedral church by
William de Vernon, William de Pacy, and Robert Earl of
Leicester.[2] Philip was particularly attentive to Walter of
Coutances Archbishop of Rouen, offering him protection, safe
conduct and hospitality when the campaign of 1196 laid waste
the archbishop's lands in the Vexin and provoked him into
imposing an Interdict and protesting in exile at Cambrai.[3]
Royal benevolence did not go unacknowledged. In 1185 Henry
Abbot of Fécamp wrote to Philip Augustus asking him to take
into his custody and protection the abbey's property and men
at Boissy-Mauvoisin, which lay just beyond the border of the
Norman Vexin. His letter ended—*Bene semper valeat dominus
noster rex*.[4] In 1204 the Norman church stood aside and then
made its peace as the duchy fell to Philip.[5]

Laymen were subject to similar influences. In 1157 Louis VII
entered on an agreement with Waleran, Count of Meulan, lord
of Beaumont-le-Roger, Brionne, and Pont-Audemer, and of
considerable properties in England. The agreement concerned
his honour of Gournay centred on the Marne above Paris. It
allowed the King of France to call upon the military service
of the men of the honour for a day, and more only if they wished.
It provided that Gournay should be at peace if the king did evil
in the comté of Meulan, but allowed them to support Waleran
if the king sought to deprive him of the comté. It made royal
justice available to all those men of Gournay who wished to
appeal to it.[6] That was not quite an imposition of sovereignty;
both parties had something to bargain with; but it was the thin
end of the wedge. Louis's superiority was acknowledged im-
plicitly in the same year in a confirmation of the properties of
the church of Notre Dame de Gournay.[7] The agreement may have
had wider political repercussions. Henry II seems to have got
wind of something he did not like. In 1161 he seized the castles
of Count Waleran and other Norman barons and entrusted them
to faithful officers.[8] Waleran lived on to die as a monk of Préaux

---

[1] Ibid. ii, no. 511.
[2] Ibid. ii, no. 528.
[3] Ibid. ii, nos. 520–2.
[4] *Layettes du trésor des Chartes*, i, no. 351.
[5] F. M. Powicke, 'The Angevin administration of Normandy', *English
Historical Review*, xxi (1906), 639–40.
[6] *Recueil des historiens des Gaules et de la France*, xvi. 15–16.
[7] *Actes de Louis VII*, no. 386.
[8] Torigni, i. 331.

in 1166. He had been a great Trimmer.[1] The same Norman poet who celebrated Henry II as the successor of the Norman dukes presented Waleran of Meulan as the flower of the Norman nobility.[2]

The arrangements between Louis and Waleran were part of a shift in the feudal balance from the Plantagenets to the Capetians which began slowly under Louis VII and then became precipitous as Philip II acquired authority and influence. Its progress is apparent in the treaties concluded between the two royal houses. In 1160 the balance favoured Henry II. In the border province of the Vexin, the fees of the Archbishop of Rouen, the Earl of Leicester, and the Count of Évreux were used to define the political boundary; their loyalties were thus firmly placed on the Norman side. Not only that but Henry was able to obtain the restoration in the Vexin of two lords who had sided with him, Jocelin Crispin and Joel de Baudemont; Louis was to act towards them with the advice of the King of England. Louis also agreed to accept the full reinstatement of Simon Count of Évreux, another of Henry's allies; he abandoned the homage which he had received from some of Simon's tenants and agreed to a reasonable adjudication on rights in dispute between him and the count.[3] By 1177 the two kings were roughly on a par. In their agreement drawn up as a preliminary to a Crusade they simply provided that such differences as arose between them would be subject to the arbitration of twelve barons and bishops, six chosen by each side.[4] That was repeated in 1180.[5] The balance between the two changed markedly thereafter. In 1189 Philip was able to insist that all those who had deserted Henry and supported Richard's rebellion need not return to Henry's allegiance until a month before Richard's departure on the Crusade. Henry's barons and knights were to swear that if he withdrew from the settlement they would aid Philip and Richard against him.[6] Philip never lost this capacity to impose feudal conditions. In the negotiations of 1193 he provided that Hugh de Gournay could continue in his allegiance to the King of France unless he wished to return

---

[1] For his earlier career in Stephen's reign see G. H. White, 'The Career of Waleran, Count of Meulan and Earl of Worcester (1104–66)', *Transactions of the Royal Historical Society*, 4th ser. xvii (1934), 19–48.

[2] *Chron. Stephen, Henry II and Richard*, ii. 766–70.

[3] *Actes de Henri II*, i, no. CXLI.

[4] Ibid. ii, no. DVI.   [5] Ibid. ii, no. DL.

[6] *Gesta Henrici*, ii. 70; *Hoveden*, ii. 365; Diceto, ii. 63–4.

to the allegiance of King Richard, that Robert Count of Meulan who had fought on his side should recover the lands which he held of Richard, that Geoffrey Count of Le Perche should recover his rents in England and that Richard should assign lands to Louis Count of Blois.[1] In 1160 Henry II was able to provide for the restoration of his followers in the French demesne. In 1193 Philip II was able to provide for his followers within the Plantagenet dominion. At that point Richard was in prison in Germany but his return made little difference. At the truce of Tillières of 1194 a much longer list of those who had gone over to Philip were included in its terms.[2] Richard made only a slight recovery in the Treaty of Louviers of 1196. He was able to provide that Stephen de Longchamps should hold Baudemont of Philip and that the men of Hugh de Gournay who had fought on his side should be restored, but he now had to guarantee to Philip the good behaviour of the Earl of Leicester and Richard de Vernon, both of whom lost heavily under the agreement.[3] By 1198 the balance had tilted further. When Richard asked that the Count of Flanders and others who had recently joined him should be included in the agreement, Philip refused and negotiations broke down.[4]

The effect of this was to undermine the Norman frontier. Administratively it depended on the Exchequer; that was still functioning in 1203. Militarily it depended on the great castles of the border provinces; some of the most crucial of these were abandoned by Richard at Louviers in 1196 and by John at Le Goulet in 1200. Politically it depended on the great families of the Norman March. Many of these were also feudal dependents of the King of France outside Normandy, or close relatives of such dependents, or dependents of close allies of the king. Ralph of Exoudun, Count of Eu *iure uxoris* held land around St. Valery-sur-Somme and Abbeville where he had control of the mint. Here he was dependent on the Count of Ponthieu, a direct vassal of the French Crown. His own patrimony lay in Poitou. He was the brother of Hugh de Lusignan and was one of the leaders of the rebellion against John in 1201.[5] Hugh de

---

[1] *Hoveden*, iii. 217–20.
[2] *Hoveden*, iii. 257–60; F. M. Powicke, op. cit., p. 108.
[3] *Layettes du trésor des Chartes*, i, no. 431. Robert Earl of Leicester surrendered Pacy and Richard de Vernon, Vernon. See ibid., nos. 433–41; *Actes de Philippe Auguste*, ii, no. 519.   [4] *Hoveden*, iv. 61.
[5] J. Boussard, *Gouvernement d'Henri II*, p. 88; F. M. Powicke, op. cit., pp. 141, 143–4, 147 n.

Gournay, who acquired an evil reputation as a traitor for his tergiversations, held lands over the Norman border in Amienois and Beauvaisis. He owed his tenure of the county of Aumale to Philip and as Count of Aumale was a tenant of the Count of Flanders.[1] The counts of Évreux had tried to resolve their loyalties by separating French and Norman estates between two collateral lines.[2] Amaury Count of Évreux was drawn to the side of England by his possession of the part of the honour of William Earl of Gloucester. Even so, for a time in 1203, he followed his father-in-law, Hugh de Gournay, into the French camp.[3] Further west Robert Count of Sées was cousin to William Count of Ponthieu brother-in-law of Philip Augustus. He married his daughter to Theobald VI Count of Blois.[4] His defection in 1203 was decisive since it carried the great border fortress of Alençon.[5] Meanwhile, further into the Norman interior, Peter, son of Robert Count of Meulan, surrendered Beaumont-le-Roger to the French. In trying to balance along a knife-edge of divided loyalties Count Robert lost his lands and ended his days as King John's pensioner.[6] This group of families had a long history of rebellion and defection. Their ancestors had joined in rebellion with the Young Henry in 1173.[7] But they were only the tip of the iceberg. When Richard I captured Philip's baggage in the flight from Vendôme in 1194, he is said to have discovered numerous charters in which Normans pledged themselves to the French king.[8] When John tried to relieve Alençon in 1203, he was apparently deterred from pressing his action by false rumours, spread within his army, that the French king was at hand with a relieving force.[9]

---

[1] *Rot. Scacc. Norm.* i, pp. clxxix–clxxx; J. Boussard, op. cit., pp. 88–9; F. M. Powicke, op. cit., pp. 108, 340–1.

[2] See below p. 62.

[3] *Rot. Norm.*, p. 92; F. M. Powicke, op. cit., pp. 175–6.

[4] This apparently distant relationship hides a close link between the counts of Sées and Ponthieu, which arose from the division of the lands of William Talvas, Count of Sées (d. 1171). See below p. 61. For the marriage of Robert's daughter see *L'Art de vérifier les dates* (Paris, 1783–7), ii. 884.

[5] F. M. Powicke, op. cit., pp. 156–60. Count Robert was apparently assisted at Alençon by Juhel de Mayenne, one of the greatest barons of Maine and Brittany, and a staunch supporter of Arthur. See *Diplomatic Documents*, ed. P. Chaplais (London, 1964), i, no. 206.

[6] F. M. Powicke, op. cit., pp. 161, 344–5.

[7] J. Boussard, op. cit., pp. 477–8 n.

[8] *Hoveden*, iii. 256.

[9] *Diplomatic Documents*, p. 140.

The final collapse came suddenly. Men were singularly ill prepared for it. It is probable that no one in 1199, not even King Philip, intended or expected what had happened by 1204. The final conflict did not begin as a fight to the death for Normandy but as a dispute about the Plantagenet succession. The competing claims of John and his nephew Arthur involved a real debate about representative succession. John and his supporters settled the matter rapidly without reference to Philip. In so doing they deprived him of the opportunity to divide the Plantagenet lands. If the matter had come to him for judgement he would have had at least one precedent in mind. When William Talvas Count of Sées died in 1171, he was succeeded in Normandy, Maine, and England by John his younger son.[1] In 1126-9 he had already arranged for his eldest son, Guy, to succeed him in the county of Ponthieu. In 1147 Ponthieu descended to Guy's son, John, with whom it remained in 1171. Hence on William Talvas's death there was a division between a younger son and a grandson who were in the same relationship as John and Arthur in 1199.[2] All this must have been known to Philip for he married his sister Alice to the grandson's successor, William Count of Ponthieu.[3] That he had some such solution in mind seems clear both from the Treaty of Le Goulet, which made no formal statement on John's position in Anjou,[4] and from the agreement of July 1202 with Arthur which reserved Normandy to Philip.[5] By then Philip clearly intended to retain Normandy for the Crown. The capture of Arthur at Mirebeau and his subsequent murder made that certain.

Feudal relationships could not be adjusted at all easily to such life-and-death conflict. The customs governing succession

---

[1] Torigni, ii. 28.

[2] The details are given in *L'Art de vérifier les dates*, ii. 753-4, 883-4. Both branches of the family agreed to William Talvas's cession of Alençon and Roche Mabile to Henry II in 1166 (Torigni, i. 360). The descent is of interest in that Ponthieu, which was the inheritance of William Talvas's mother, descended in the elder line, and Alençon, William's patrimony, in the junior line. See also *Recueil des Actes des Comtes de Pontieu (1026-1279)*, ed. Clovis Brunel (Paris, 1930), pp. v-vi, 38-133.

[3] *Actes de Philippe Auguste*, ii, no. 508.

[4] Ibid., no. 633. However, it did allow John to receive homage from the Count of Angoulême and the Vicomte of Limoges. It also allowed that Arthur should hold Brittany of John. The formal agreement on Anjou seems to have been made on John's subsequent visit to Paris (*Recueil des historiens des Gaules et de la France*, xviii. 295).

[5] *Actes de Philippe Auguste*, ii, no. 723.

allowed for the division of estates among heirs as part of family law. It did not permit any separation of Norman and French, or Norman and English estates on grounds of political convenience. There are some examples where this apparently occurred, either by exchange or at a succession. In the Pipe Roll of 1130 Arnold de Bosco offered 100 m. for land in Thorpe in return for surrendering Pailly in the castlery of Verneuil to the king.[1] In the late 1160s Henry II confirmed an agreement whereby Robert le Calceis conceded all the fee which he held of William of Roumare in England in return for William's demesne in Le Bourg-Dun and elsewhere.[2] In 1181–2 a division was made between the sons of Simon Count of Évreux whereby Amaury succeeded in Évreux and Simon in the lordship of Rochefort and other lands directly dependent on the King of France.[3] But such instances are on the whole unusual. Moreover, Norman families went on acquiring lands in France and English families land in Normandy. William de Mandeville Earl of Essex extended his Norman holdings by purchase.[4] So did Hugh de Lacy who was enfeoffed in the barony of Le Pin by Robert Count of Meulan.[5] When Richard I bestowed the lands of the Giffard inheritance on Richard de Clare Earl of Hertford, and William Marshal in 1189, he divided both the Norman and the English estates between them with the proviso that the earl was to have the seniority in Normandy and the Marshal the seniority in England.[6] As late as 1200 a dispute between Henry de Tilly and William, his brother, on the partition of their inheritance led to a division of lands between them, both in England and in Normandy.[7] None of this revealed any serious lack of confidence in the future. Indeed there were examples where the consequences of war had been mitigated for landowners. When under the terms of the Treaty of Louviers of 1196 Richard de Vernon was forced to surrender Vernon to the French he was compensated by land in England and by the grant of a barony from the King of France.[8] The experience of generations was also a source of comfort. Many of these families

---

[1] *Pipe Roll 31 Henry I*, p. 88.
[2] *Actes de Henri II*, no. CCCCXXIX.
[3] Torigni, ii. 103.
[4] *Actes de Henri II*, no. DXLVII.
[5] Ibid., no. DCCVIII.
[6] *Cartae Antiquae Rolls 11–20* (Pipe Roll Society, N.S. xxxiii, 1957), no. 564.
[7] *Rot. Norm.*, pp. 7, 8, 41, 42.
[8] *Layettes du trésor des Chartes*, i, nos. 431, 441.

had lived with a dual fealty, to the French king for their French holdings and to the English king for their English and Norman holdings. Why should the transfer of the immediate lordship of Normandy alter this? It was easy to assume that the loss of Normandy to King John would not be a loss to them. That was one of the main reasons for the collapse. Normandy was not properly defended because there seemed to be no real need to do so. It was an assumption which Philip encouraged. After the victory he was ready to accept liege homage for Norman fiefs from those resident in England. It was John who dropped the barrier. When his men sought permission to perform homage to Philip for their Norman lands he refused. The scene provided one of the good stories of the day. John wished to take advice in the matter and consulted Baldwin of Béthune Count of Aumale. Baldwin was one of the few heroic figures of the war. Staunchly loyal to the Angevin cause he had served as a hostage for Richard in Germany. He had gained the Comté of Aumale by marriage as a reward, only to lose it when Aumale fell to the French in 1196. Now, crippled by arthritis, held up between two servants, he gave his view. The petitioners had told John that although their bodies might be with the King of France their hearts would be with him. 'Were I in your place', said Baldwin, 'if their bodies were against me and their hearts for me, if the hearts of those whose bodies were against me came into my hands I would throw them into the privy'.[1]

That seems to represent a turning-point, an acceptance that feudal loyalty could no longer be divided, that men had to choose between England and Normandy. But the story was recorded nearly twenty years later, after the battle of Bouvines and the civil war in England in which Prince Louis of France had claimed the English throne. Moreover, it came from a milieu where men were sensitively aware of conflicts of feudal loyalty. It was the same author who pilloried the tergiversations of Hugh de Gournay.[2] The biographer of William Marshal showed the same concern for loyalty and disdain for turncoats— the *tornés*.[3] Yet his hero was the outstanding example of those who sought to retain their interests on both sides of the Channel. He did it successfully and still became regent of England in 1216. It is not very easy to manufacture the birth of either the English

[1] *Histoire des ducs de Normandie*, p. 100.
[2] Ibid., p. 92.
[3] *Histoire de Guillaume le Maréchal*, lines 12552–84.

or the French nation from the events of 1204. Afterwards, as
before, Anglo-Norman monasteries held land on both sides of
the Channel; so did some lay landowners; Rouen merchants
still came to London, English scholars still went to Paris; and
English magnates still went on the Crusade.[1] For some 1204
was just a stage and not even an irrevocable one. Some of those
who had defected to Philip later returned to John's allegiance.[2]

In 1227 a citizen of Caen, R. Gaudin, sent a long, badly
written intelligence report to Henry III of England. He had
been listening to conversations between the son of the castellan
of Caen and a clerk, Master Nicholas.[3] These two had gossiped
at length about relations between the kings of England and
France and the reasons for the loss of Normandy. They had
then turned to the schemes which were afoot under the direction of the dowager Queen, Blanche of Castille, granddaughter
of Henry II.

She has it in mind to do what her lord wished to do and acquire
England . . . and she intends to instruct the barons of Normandy to
accompany her. If she succeeds she wishes them to have all their
hereditary properties. She will tell the Earl of Chester and the Earl
Bigod and the Earl Ferrers and lord Philip of Albini and lord William

[1] These matters have been discussed by Wendy B. Stevenson, 'England
and Normandy 1204–1259', Ph.D. thesis, University of Leeds, 1974.

[2] Amaury, Count of Évreux returned to John's allegiance later in 1203
(*Rot. Norm.*, p. 110). Hugh de Gournay rejoined John in 1206 (*Rot. Litt. Pat.*,
p. 57b). Ralph of Exoudun returned to John's favour in 1214 (ibid., p. 116).

[3] *Diplomatic Documents*, no. 206. This letter deserves more attention than
it has received since its publication in England in 1964. Its information on the
fall of Normandy seems authentic. It lists as John's errors the appointment
of William le Gros as the last seneschal, the appointment of Louvrecaire to the
custody of Falaise, and the consequent appearance of mercenaries in the
interior rather than in the March, and finally the conduct of those mercenaries towards the Normans. This is all supported from other sources.
The conversation of the two Frenchmen is of some general interest. They
commended the King of France for taking advice from a restricted group of
members of the royal household—*two* only. The King of England, on the
other hand, took advice and counsel from a large number, and thereby
revealed his intentions. When the King of France sent to the papal curia he
used a member of his household and got what he wanted. The King of
England sent letters by the hand of a bishop, and the King of France would
know all about it before he arrived in Rome.
Admittedly this seems to refer to the early years of Henry III, but it is in
sharp contrast to the view stated by Gerald of Wales that the conflict was
one between *libertatis hilaritas* (in France) and *servitutis oppressio* (in England)
(*Opera*, viii. 258). These men saw it as a conflict, not between good and bad,
but between the more and the less effective.

of St. John and all those who have claims to land in Normandy that they should join her and remain at her side on landing, and she will then persuade her son to restore their estates in Normandy. If the lord Louis had done this when he was in England he would have got control of the realm without opposition, because he had the aid and counsel of the best men of England.

The burgess went on to give his own advice to Henry: he was not to repeat his father's errors in Normandy in employing mercenary troops; if he wanted to reconquer Normandy then he was to inform all those Normans who had claims to land in England that their property would be restored. Indeed he was to retort in kind to the intentions of the French. It was now envisaged that those pressures which had earlier been applied across the Norman border should now be applied across the Channel. Apart from that, nothing had changed. The policies intended by Blanche and recommended to Henry III would not have seemed strange to Philip Augustus or Henry II.

NOTE

The evidence and arguments advanced above, pp.34-9, on Angevin and Capetian financial resources have been challenged in John Gillingham, *Richard the Lionheart* (London, 1978), pp.303-4. I have not been persuaded by his criticism. See J.C. Holt, 'The Loss of Normandy and royal finances' in *War and Government in the Middle Ages: Essays in honour of J.O. Prestwich*, ed. John Gillingham and J.C. Holt (Woodbridge, 1984), pp.92-105, which presents fresh calculations of the relevant Norman and English accounts. There is some further comment on the administrative structure of the Plantagenet dominions in J.C. Holt, 'Eléanore d'Aquitaine, Jean-sans-terre et la succession de onze cent quatre-vingt dix-neuf', forthcoming in *Cahiers de Civilization Médiévale*.

The two seals of Richard I, equestrian side. *(British Library)*

3

RICARDUS REX ANGLORUM ET DUX NORMANNORUM

I intend to investigate the relationship between monarchy and what a king actually did in the late twelfth century. Of the concept of monarchy I shall say little, for much has already been written of theories about royal authority, of the majesty and symbolism of the crown, and of the sacring of the king. The reign of Richard Lion-Heart had some part in this. His is the first coronation of which detailed descriptions survive, one written by Ralph of Diss, Dean of St, Paul's who, on behalf of his bishop, passed the *ampula* to the Archbishop of Canterbury for Richard's anointing. We know that he was anointed on head, chest and hands, that he himself took the Crown from the altar and handed it to the Archbishop for his crowning, and that he then sat robed and enthroned, as he appears in majesty on his Great Seal, to hear his first Mass as king [1]. How much in the ceremony was new cannot be determined. It is, however, certain that notions touching the sovereignty of the king were beginning to take a clearer shape in Richard's day. He was the first English king to use the plural of majesty [2]. His justices confronted by a sentence of excommunication laid on a royal sheriff asserted that it was done *contra regalen dingnitatem [sic] et excelenciam* [3]. Men's minds were moving from the *consuetudines et dignitates regni* and the *consuetudines et dignitates regia*, the phrases of the Constitutions of Clarendon of 1164, to the *iura coronae* of the London version of the *Leges Edwardi Confessoris* of c. 1205 [4]. Already in 1194 a pleading in the *curia regis* contains the assertion that a disseisin had been *in lesionem coronae domini Regis Ricardi* [5]. All this involved an increasingly clear distinction between the Crown and the person of the King.

---

(1) The chief source is the *ordo* preserved by Roger of Howden, printed in *Gesta Regis Henrici Secundi Benedicti Abbatis*, ed. W. Stubbs (Roll Series, 1867), ii. 80–3 and in *Chronica Magistri Rogeri de Hovedene*, ed. W. Stubbs (Roll Series, 1870) iii. 9–12. For Ralph of Diss see *The Historical Works of Master Ralph de Diceto*, ed. W. Stubbs (Rolls Series, 1876), ii. 68–9.

(2) PIERRE CHAPLAIS, *English Royal Documents King John–Henry VI* (Oxford, 1971), p. 13. For the origins of the practice in papal and episcopal chanceries see C. R. Cheney, *English Bishops' Chanceries 1100–1250* (Manchester, 1950), pp. 58–9.

(3) *Three Rolls of the King's Court*, ed. F. W. Maitland (Pipe Roll Society, xiv, 1891), p. 50.

(4) F. LIEBERMANN, *Gesetze der Angelsachsen* (Halle, 1903–16), i. 635.

(5) *Rotuli Curiae Regis*, ed. F. Palgrave (Record Commission, London, 1835), i. 31.

This distinction was drawn gradually. It was not until 1272, for example, that the perpetuation of the Crown despite the death of its wearer was recognized by dating the accession of the new king from the death of his predecessor and not from his own coronation. The reality of the king was never wholly replaced by the concept of the Crown. The monarchy of King Alfred or of William the Conqueror was more than personal, that of Henry VIII or Queen Victoria was very far from impersonal. It drew on many sources, from Old English law on the King's peace, to the Canon Law of the Church and the Roman Law which was beginning to percolate through to England in the second half of the twelfth century. But one element in it was purely practical. This was the capacity of the king's officials to act in his name in his absence, and in this England was the centre of precocious development in the course of the twelfth century.

Some form of delegation of authority was necessary for the joint government of the realm of England and the duchy of Normandy. The king duke could not be on both sides of the Channel at one and the same time. To this twin dominion Henry of Anjou added not only his own patrimony in Anjou and the Touraine, but also the dominions of his wife which stretched south through Poitou and Aquitaine to the Pyrenees and the county of Toulouse. The reigns of the Angevin kings are therefore of particular importance in studying this development, and that of Richard I especially so for two reasons. First, he accentuated the problem; he was the great absentee among English kings; he spent four months in England in 1189 and two months in 1194, and that was all. Secondly, for technical reasons, it is easier to examine the problem under Richard than under Henry II. Richard's *acta*, unlike those of his father, were dated both in place and time; the King's movements and the surviving acts of his government can therefore be placed in a far more exact chronological relationship than is possible for an earlier date. For the present purpose King John may be left out of the count. With the loss of Normandy, Anjou and the Touraine in the years following 1204 the problem changed. Furthermore John was cast in a different mould. King Henry II was Angevin; Richard Lion-Heart was Poitevin; both were to some extent imbued with the traditions of the Norman ducal house. By comparison John was English, insular.

Yet one comparison of Richard and John provides a useful starting point. Writing probably c. 1225, Ralph, abbot of the Cistercian house of Coggeshall, ended a well informed and dramatic account of the death of King John by saying that he had reigned for seventeen years and five months *satis laboriose*. Whatever construction is put upon these words [6], one thing is

---

(6) V. H. Galbraith proposed 'indefatigably' (*Studies in the Public Records*, London, 1948, p. 126). An alternative is 'with reasonable industry' (J. C. HOLT, *King John*, Historical Association, 1963: below, p. 97). Mr. J. O. Prestwich has suggested that a better translation would be 'with difficulty'. See also DuCange, *Glossarium*.

striking: Abbot Ralph made exactly the same comment on Richard Lion-Heart. In short he bracketed Richard and John together in contrast to their father, Henry II, who reigned *strenuissime* [7]. True he went far from identifying the two in all respects; Richard was the valiant Christian knight, protector of the Church, while John was a suspicious tyrant who persecuted the Cistercian order. But there can be no doubt that Coggeshall took Richard seriously as a king. He drew on sources near the King, and he concluded his account of the reign with a long, edifying discussion of the character of Richard's rule, which has coloured many subsequent narratives [8]. In his view Richard was not merely a soldier-poet. Most contemporaries shared this attitude. Indeed writers commented on the administrative difficulties created by the King's prolonged absences from the realm. The problem is not one invented by the modern historian. It was appreciated and discussed at the time.

Apart from the commentaries of contemporaries and near-contemporaries, there are three major sources for the study of Richard's conduct of government. First, as for all other monarchs of the period, there are the King's surviving *acta*. Of these there was as yet no register, for the full enrolment of copies of documents emanating from the Chancery only began with the reign of John, but some rudimentary record of charters was already kept in the *Cartae Antiquae* Rolls [9]. The historian therefore has to depend on the laborious collection of original *acta* from scattered repositories and of copies from cartularies and private registers. The results are highly selective. Such a collection, by definition, excludes all ephemera, since it can only include items which were thought to be worth preserving. It is made up almost entirely of charters and *privilegia* of various kinds. At present it is incomplete. The assembling of the *acta* in continental sources is well advanced, but work on the English sources still has a long way to go. Interim conclusions therefore have to be based on the collection made by Lionel Landon for his *Itinerary of Richard I* published in 1935. He noted over 650 items, 66 of which were re-issues under Richard's second seal, of earlier *acta* [10].

The second source is to be found in the fines and *oblata* which were proffered as feudal incidents, or as bids for privileges, or as amercements for breaches of the law or for offences against the King. Some formal record

---

(7) *Radulphi de Coggeshall Chronicon Anglicanum*, ed. J. Stevenson (Rolls Series, 1875) pp. 25, 96, 184.

(8) *Ibid.*, pp. 89–98. For comment on Ralph's historical works see ANTONIA GRANSDEN, *Historical Writing in England* (London, 1974), pp. 322–31.

(9) *Cartae Antiquae Rolls 1–10*, ed. Lionel Landon (Pipe Roll Society, new series xvii, 1939); *Cartae Antiquae Rolls 11–20*, ed. J. Conway Davies (Pipe Roll Society, new series, xxxiii, 1957).

(10) L. LANDON, *Itinerary of Richard I* (Pipe Roll Society, new series, xiii, 1935), pp. 146–72, 181–2.

of these was certainly kept in Richard's reign, but only a solitary fragment now survives [11]. Practically all such arrangements, however, were accountable at the Exchequer, and were entered on the annual account in the Pipe Roll, sometimes in extended, sometimes in summary form. Hence a systematic examination of this aspect of government is possible.

The third source also derives from the Pipe Rolls and the supervisory role of the Exchequer. The ephemera of Richard's Chancery may not have been preserved as originals or transcripts in private archives, but many, indeed most, were mandates to officials. Such instructions, wherever they involved expenditure by a royal officer accountable to the Exchequer for his office, were presented at the annual account. The accounts of sheriffs and *custodes* are therefore bestrewn with references to expenditure *per breve regis*. Through them it is possible to reconstruct the transfer of treasure from England to Normandy for the war against Philip of France, or work on the repair of royal castles or the King's galley, or the transport of venison, chickens and wine for the King's feasts, or the purchase of costly cloth for him and his household. This information is not as complete as that on fines and *oblata*. The references to *brevia regis* are not entirely systematic. Moreover, it does not include the large number of administrative instructions which had no financial consequences. Here one other source is of value. From 1194 onwards the judicial records of the *curia regis* survive in increasing abundance. From these it is possible to gain some impression of Richard's supervision of and interventions in the ordinary processes of litigation in his court.

What then does this evidence reveal about Richard's rule? First the surviving *acta*. How do they compare with those of his father or of his successor, King John? Landon's list of charters plainly reveals an easily expected result, that immediately following his coronation, Richard's Chancery was busy providing royal confirmations of existing privileges and liberties. This occurred at every accession, 1154 and 1199 as well as 1189. But that is not the whole story. If the *acta* are viewed, not as a compilation, but as the collector has to approach them, as items in the cartularies of secular churches and religious houses, then an important point at once becomes apparent. In British sources grants and confirmations by Richard I are far fewer than grants and confirmations by Henry II or King John. The difference is not to be explained by the fact that Henry II reigned for more thirty four years, John for more than seventeen and Richard for less than ten. It is not uncommon to find cartularies which contain charters of Henry II and John and none at all of Richard. I have found none so far where Richard's acts outnumber either his father's or his brother's. The case is presented at its extreme in Ireland. Grants and confirmations of

(11) Originalia Roll 7 Richard I, printed in *Memoranda Roll 1 John*, ed. H.G. Richardson (Pipe Roll Society, new series, xxi, 1943), pp. 85–8.

land and privileges in Ireland by Henry II are not uncommon. John also was responsible for a considerable number, both as Lord of Ireland and as King. In contrast, Landon lists only one such act of Richard I and that was a confirmation in favour of Walter de Lacy who joined the King at the seige of Nottingham in 1194 [12]. That solitary document can be supplemented by one other action: Richard certainly intervened to ensure that William Marshal, the newly wedded husband of Isabel de Clare, was enfeoffed by Count John in his wife's lordship in Leinster [13]. But that seems to be all. Seen from Westminster, Rouen or Chinon, even more from Messina or Acre, it may not seem surprising. It is not surprising either that one modern Irish historian condemns Richard for his ' almost complete neglect of Irish affairs ' [14].

Whether such comparisons of Richard with his father and brother also hold good for Normandy is still a matter for conjecture; they will necessarily reflect John's loss of the Duchy in 1204. In any case they must be used with care. This is best illustrated by a simpler calculation. During the few months when Richard was in England in 1189 and 1194 surviving *acta* in favour of English beneficiaries outnumber those in favour of Norman beneficiaries by roughly 6:1. But the converse is not true when the King was in Normandy. *Acta* in favour of Norman beneficiaries are marginally more numerous for 1190-1 and 1195-6, but for 1197-9 *acta* for England and Wales, excluding re-issues under the second seal, outnumber those for Normandy by roughly 3-2. It would be wrong to conclude from this that the King was more attentive to English than to Norman affairs, or that he neglected Normandy more when he was in England than he did England when he was in Normandy. For the figures reflect, not so much the concern of the King, as the disposition of his subjects to seek his intervention. To this end Richard's English subjects were apparently readier to travel more frequently and further than his Norman, and there were in any case more of them. This sets the Irish evidence, too, in its proper context. The reason why Richard neglected Ireland is that Ireland neglected him. The two solitary actions mentioned above were initiated not by the King but by his vassals [15]. The whole matter is presented in a nutshell by the re-issue of *privilegia* under the Kings's second seal. The surviving examples of these are all dated May 1198 to April 1199. They were all issued in Normandy, most of them at Château-Gaillard. The English outnumber the Norman privileges by 7:1. English cathedral churches and religious houses were

(12) LANDON, pp. 86–7.

(13) *Histoire de Guillaume le Maréchal*, ed. P. Meyer (Société de l'Histoire de France, 1891–1901), ll. 9581–618.

(14) MICHAEL DOLLEY, *Anglo–Norman Ireland* (Dublin, 1972), p. 94.

(15) For the circumstances which led to Walter de Lacy's performance of homage to Richard see *ibid.*, pp. 96–7 and, more fully, A. J. OTWAY–RUTHVEN, *A History of Medieval Ireland* (Dublin, 1980), pp. 70–3.

preponderant among the beneficiaries. They had been informed that their charters under the old seal would be treated as void. If the level of protest is an accurate measure, this financial extorsion was not applied so rigorously in Normandy as it was in England where it must have been introduced as one of the last acts of Hubert Walter, Richard's great Justiciar [16]. Here the structure and relative efficiency of the two Exchequers of Normandy and England, the competence of those who directed affairs in the King Duke's absence, and the relationship of litigants and recipients of *privilegia* to the royal and ducal courts of law, have to be brought into the count.

All this throws light on what kings and their officials did with their time. Kings are said to make policy. Indeed the young historian in England learns from his text books that the temper of a reign was set by the character of the king. And, to be sure, on particular occasions Richard Lion-Heart did indeed make policy: at his great council at Nonancourt in March 1190, for example, when arrangements were made for the government of England and Normandy during his absence on the crusade, or again at Nottingham in 1194, where between 30 March and 2 April he punished his brother John's rebellion, settled the government of the northern counties, tried to arrange the affairs of his turbulent half-brother, Geoffrey, archbishop of York, and arranged financial and military resources for his coming campaign against King Philip of France [17]. On such occasions Richard behaved, and can be seen to have behaved, very much like the medieval monarch of the textbook. On some lesser occasions also an administrative logic seems to underlie his actions. *Privilegia* for a particular class of recipients seem at times to have been grouped together in the business of a single day. But more often the sequence of *acta* reveals no trace at all of administrative coherence. They follow each other as a jumble. Hence, for example, on 12 November 1189, when royal acts were attested at Westminster, the business of the day included letters or charters for the monks of Christchurch, Canterbury, the cathedral church of Rouen, the hospital of St. Mary Magdalen, Rouen, the abbey of Bury St. Edmunds, the canons of St. Mary of Cirencester, the cathedral church of Lichfield and the burgesses of Bedford and Worcester [18]. Such variety carries a clear implication: business could be determined not so much by the King, carving out large schemes of policy, as by his subjects, approaching him with the intent of securing grants and confirmations, rulings and arbitrations, and in the hope of achieving all those benefits which loyal subjects might expect from a feudal monarch. They approached him in no prearranged or predictable order, unless driven to it by some royal measure such as the voiding of charters under the King's first seal. It is only thus that the apparent lack of administrative logic in the sequence of the

---

(16) LANDON, pp. 179–80.

(17) *Ibid.*, pp. 26, 86–7.

(18) *Ibid.*, p. 14. The sequence in which I have listed these items in the day's work, is of course entirely arbitrary.

acta can be understood. On many, indeed on most occasions, the King did not originate; he responded.

This leads from the surviving *acta* of the King to the record in the Pipe Rolls of fines, *oblata* and *promissa*, the means whereby *privilegia* were obtained, and to the fashionable topic of royal patronage. Since the publication of Sir Richard Southern's Raleigh Lecture on ' The Place of Henry I's reign in English History ' in 1962 patronage has been all the rage [19]. Richard Lion-Heart's reign demonstrates that it was a much more complex administrative matter than has often been supposed. It took two to agree to a proffer. Just as the King could not determine which of his subjects would seek his intervention and when, so also he had little control over what a petitioner might be seeking. He could say ' no ', or course, and no doubt those who sought him out had a shrewd notion of what he would be ready to concede and at what price. But the King was not the sole determinant of the market. *Oblata* and *promissa* were not the simple result of unilateral exercise of royal patronage responding to political and financial pressure. They also reflected genealogical accident, legal necessity, social ambition and the manifold circumstances which led his vassals to approach the King.

There is a further complication. Sometimes the King concluded these arrangements in person, but he was not the sole broker. When Richard first came to England in 1189 he set about financing the Crusade through the sale of office and privilege and the imposition of payments for his *benevolencia* on the old King's servants [20]. Again on his return to England in 1194 he took a hand, naturally enough, in settling his realm after Count John's rebellion [21]. Contemporaries caught a personal flavour in these proceedings, for on both occasions they commented that Richard was ready to sell both privilege and office to the highest bidder [22]; in the celebrated phrase of William of Newburgh he would have sold London if he could have found a buyer [23].

To some extent the record in the Pipe Rolls of these transactions confirms such an interpretation. The proffers of 1189 all appear on the Roll of Michaelmas 1190 under the heading *Nova Placita et Nove conventiones de novis promissis* or some similar title. They give the impression of a single unique effort. No doubt Richard himself provided the urgency. How far as a new king, largely ignorant of English circumstances, he had to call on the old hands of the Exchequer in assessing the payments demanded, the record does not reveal. If, as is likely, he took local advice, that does not detract from his effort, for the fact remains that these fines represent the

(19) *Proceedings of the British Academy*, xlviii (1962), 127–69.

(20) KATE NORGATE, *Richard the Lionheart* (London, 1924), pp. 100–4; J. GILLINGHAM, *Richard the Lionheart* (London, 1978), pp. 133–4; *Pipe Roll 2 Richard I* (Pipe Roll Society, new series, i), pp. xxi–ii.

(21) LANDON, pp. 86–7.

(22) WILLIAM OF NEWBURGH in *Chronicles of Stephen, Henry II and Richard I*, ed. R. Howlett (Rolls Series, 1884), i. 304–6; Hoveden, iii. 13; *Gesta Henrici*, ii. 90–1.

(23) *Chronicles of Stephen, Henry II and Richard I*, i. 306.

most determined and single minded exercise of royal patronage recorded at any time in the reigns of the Norman and Angevin kings. The tide was in Richard's favour. The sale or confirmation of privileges was expected of a new king, and he was a crusader in urgent need of money.

The record of 1194 is much less clear. It presents a picture of fragmented activity and this in turn may reflect Richard's haste to cross to Normandy as soon as possible in time for the best of the campaigning season. While he was at Nottingham in March he dealt whith some of John's supporters, and satisfied some other claims [24]. Then at Winchester on 20 April he made arrangements for the ransoming of those of John's party who had been taken prisoner [25]. Many of the Count's supporters in Nottinghamshire, Derbyshire and Lancashire made fine for restoration, perhaps through the respective sheriffs [26]. But these constituted only a small proportion of the fines and offerings entered on the roll. These appear either under the heading *De finibus factis post redditum domini Regis ab Alemannia* or something similar, or under the heading *Nova oblata per Hubertum Archiepiscopum Cantuariensem* or something similar. It would be tempting to conclude that the first group comprised fines made with the King and the second fines made with the Archbishop acting as Justiciar, were it not that in a few instances the titles were combined [27]. But that the second group at least were accepted by Hubert on behalf of the King and submitted by him for account at the Exchequer seems to be beyond doubt, for at least two exceptions were noted. Hubert's list included 500 m. which had been promised by John, bishop of Norwich, to the King at Nottingham. The Bishop had indeed received a charter from Richard there on 28 March. He paid his proffer at Winchester before the King left for Normandy and it was subsequently noted on the Pipe Roll that the Exchequer had received the King's writ to that effect [28]. Something similar occured in the case of William Longchamp, bishop of Ely, who promised 500 m. to the King some time after his return from Germany. This was subsequently pardoned by the King [29]. Now the attribution of the agreement to the King in these two cases would have been pointless if the other fines on the list were also made with him. It follows that the heading in these cases, *Nova oblata per Hubertum archiepiscopum* must be read literally. The Justiciar was indeed accepting proffers and agreeing fines. The King's exercise of patronage was delegated [30].

(24) LANDON, pp. 86–7.

(25) *Hoveden*, iii. 249.

(26) *Pipe Roll 6 Richard I*, pp. 84, 124–5.

(27) Devon, London and Middlesex, Gloucestershire and Kent (*ibid.*, pp. 169, 182, 238, 249).

(28) *Ibid.*, p. 64; LANDON, p. 86.

(29) *Pipe Roll 6 Richard I*, p. 79.

(30) On the whole question see H. G. Richardson in *Memoranda Roll 1 John* (Pipe Roll Society, new series, xxi), pp. xxi–xxxiii.

The interest of this, occurring as it did in 1194, is that for part of that year Richard was in England. In other years, when he was much more of an absentee, the capacity of the Justiciar to accept fines and proffers of all kinds is even more apparent. In theory the fines were made with the King because it was over his feudal and royal rights that the bargains were struck, but in practice they were concluded with the Justiciar or whomsoever enjoyed vice-regal authority. *Oblata per cancellarium* appear in 1191. *Oblata per Walterum Archiepiscopum Rothomagensem et alios* in 1192 and 1193. Fines agreed with Hubert Walter were entered on the rolls from 1194 to the end of his Justiciarship in 1198. That such was the system is confirmed by the fragment of the Originalia Roll, the copy of the Fine Roll sent to the Exchequer, for 1195-6. This lists twenty-two fines, only one of which was concluded with the King; this was in fact a severe penalty of 1,000 m. imposed on Simon of Kime, sheriff of Lincolnshire, for allowing the departure of foreign ships from Boston fair [31]. Now and then the work of one Justiciar might be subsequently revised by another. In 1193 Hervey Bagot offered 200 m. to Walter, archbishop of Rouen, for the succession to the barony of Robert of Stafford. There was some doubt about the proffer for although it was entered on the Pipe Roll it was not put in charge [32]. In the following year it was listed among the *Finibus factis post redditum Regis ab Alemannia*, where it was raised to 300 m. and put in charge at once [33]. It is pleasant, and not entirely inapposite, to suppose that an Archbishop of Canterbury knew better than an Archbishop of Rouen what the going rate should be for an English barony. Occasionally, too, there are signs that the King played an overriding role. On the Originalia Roll of 1195-6 it was noted that Roger Bigod, earl of Norfolk, offered 100 m. that he should not be disseised except by judgment of the King's court of lands in Norfolk to which his half-brother was laying claim. But Roger served with the King in Normandy in 1196 and Richard himself then took a hand. Roger now had to proffer 700 m. to the King for the identical protection. The Exchequer was notified of the new arrangement *per breve Regis de ultra mare* and by the end of the Michaelmas account Roger had paid in full [34]. Hubert Walter might strike a hard bargain by the side of Walter of Rouen. Richard Lion-Heart struck one even harder.

In these matters it is impossible to compare England and Normandy. For Richard's reign there are only two surviving Norman Pipe Rolls, for 1195 and 1198. There is nothing, therefore, to show whether his accession was followed in the Duchy as it was in England by a deliberately exploitative sale of office and privilege. It would be surprising if this did not happen. The two surviving rolls come from a time when Richard was in Nor-

(31) *Ibid.*, pp. 85-8.
(32) *Pipe Roll 5 Richard I*, p. 85.
(33) *Pipe Roll 6 Richard I*, p. 41.
(34) *Memoranda Roll 1 John*, p. 86; *Chancellor's Roll 8 Richard I*, p. 138.

mandy. Moreover they were drafted differently from the rolls of the English Exchequer for *oblata* were not collected together under a heading indicating who had authorized them. The Norman rolls apparently reflect a simpler system in which fines and proffers were agreed in the sessions of the Exchequer itself. How far Richard himself intervened cannot be déternined. Sometimes he did so in order to acquit rather than originate a debt [35].

In one respect, however, Exchequer procedures in the kingdom and the Duchy were closely similar, perhaps identical. In both, accounting officials presented *brevia regis* as authorisations of expenditure. The English and Norman Pipe Rolls are littered with them, and these, which constitute my third category of evidence, reveal a complex story.

Not all fines proffered to the King were in fact concluded with him. Similarly not all *brevia regis* came from the royal Chancery. Many of those which subsequently figured on the Pipe Rolls must have been issued from the Exchequer under the Exchequer seal. In England this was a well established procedure. The rules governing the use of the Exchequer seal were discussed in Richard fitz Neal's *Dialogus de Scaccario* [36]. William Longchamp, Richard's Chancellor, was criticized for his arrogance when, as vice-regent in 1191, he preferred to use his own seal. His successor, Walter of Rouen, did not repeat the error, and this was welcomed as a sign of modesty [37]. Hubert Walter, who unlike his predecessors used the official title of Justiciar, issued many administrative instructions in his own name which were presumably under his own seal. It was impossible for him, or Longchamp before him, always to use the Exchequer seal, if only because they were not always operating from the Exchequer, where the seal was available.

It is easy, therefore to identify those actions for which the vice-regent of Justiciar took personal responsibility. But the writs issued in the King's name are a different kettle of fish, for these may have originated either with the King or with the vice-regent using the Exchequer seal. Some guidance is provided when writs were entered as *brevia regis de ultra mare*. Such writs were frequently sent to the vice-regent or Justiciar so that a note *per breve cancellarii per breve regis de ultra mare*, or *per breve Huberti archiepiscopi Cantuaruensis per breve regis de ultra mare* is a common enough item on the rolls. It should not be thought, however, that these entries necessarily provide an insight into the arcana of Richard's government. A large proportion of such writs were concerned with the grant of privileges agreed with the King in Normandy, or the receipt of money in the King's Chamber in Normandy, or the quittance of debt obtained from the King or

(35) See for example his writ of quittance for Richard de Montigny (*Magni Rotuli Scaccarii Normanniae*, ed. T. Stapleton, London, 1840, i. 167).

(36) Ed. Charles Johnson (London, 1950), p. 19.

(37) *The Historical Works of Gervase of Canterbury*, ed. W. Stubbs (Rolls Series, 1879), i. 509; Giraldus Cambrensis *Opera*, ed. J. S. Brewer (Rolls Series, 1873), iv. 408, 426.

the Norman Exchequer [38], Hence, for example, Eustace, the elect of Ely, accounted on the Roll of 1196 for revenues of his see totalling more than 400 m.   He paid nothing into the Treasury but he was quit because he had paid what was due into the King's Chamber by the hand of Richard of Kirkham who produced a *breve regis de ultra mare* to this effect before the Archbishop and the barons of the Exchequer, which writ was filed in the Marshal's forel under Cambridgeshire [39].   *Brevia regis de ultra mare*, in short, were primarily concerned with correlating the decisions and actions of the King and the government machinery in Normandy with the accounting procedures of the Exchequer in England.

The remaining *brevia* are more difficult to analyse.   Very frequently it is impossible to determine how they were authorized.   But the application of common sense and of logic which may seem somewhat circular to a jaundiced eye, suggests some criteria.   To take a practical example, on 3 March 1195 Hugh du Puiset died at his manor of Howden and during the subsequent vacancy his great see of Durham came in to the hands of royal custodians of whom the chief was Gilbert fitz Reinfrey, lord of Kendal.   Now Richard Lion-Heart was keenly interested in the affairs of the border counties.   Never having been there he probably imagined that they were analogous to the Gascon lordships in the foothills of the Pyrenees, and during the course of the reign he made a number of arrangements, none of them very satisfactory, concerning the earldom of Northumberland.   He now took a close interest in the affairs of the bishopric of Durham and it is not too difficult to distinguish between his instructions and those authorized by the Justiciar.   Much of the routine expenditure on the upkeep of the manors and the necessities of the prior and monks was authorized *per breve Huberti Cantuariensis Archiepiscopi*.   Careful arrangements were also made for the purchase of seed for the sowing of the bishop's arable; these were authorized *per breve Huberti Cantuariensis archiepiscopi per breve Regis de ultra mare*.   It may seen surprising that Richard should take the trouble to instruct the Archbishop to take such an obvious step for the maintenance of the estate. But there is a simple explanation.   Hugh du Puiset's successor, elected between November 1195 and January 1196, was Philip de Poitiers, Richard's most important and most favoured personal clerk.   No-one could have been better placed to ensure that the King intervened to prevent any possible wasting of a newly acquired honour.   Philip, who got control of the temporalities of his see at the beginning of 1196, may also have had a hand in another expression of royal interest.   The dead Bishop had been sorely indebted to the King; he had speculated with aristocratic self-indulgence in a number of expensive proffers.   At the account of 1196 part of this debt was charg-

(38) See, for example, *Pipe Roll 7 Richard I*, pp. 25, 176, 200; *Chancellor's Roll 8 Richard I*, pp. 16, 32, 82, 137, 160, 173, 280; *Pipe Roll 9 Richard I*, pp. 61, 69, 72, 76, 82, 117, 132, 178, 183, 238.

(39) *Chancellor's Roll 8 Richard I*, p. 280.

ed to the tenants of the bishopric. The authority, a unique entry on the rolls, was *per rotulum Regis* [40]. This must have come to the Exchequer direct from the King.

Three items on the account were authorized simply *per breve regis.* Two of these, £ 29 6 s. 8 d. for the custody of Norham castle and £ 91 1 s. 2½ d. payment to manorial officials, probably refer to standing authorizations emanating from the King, either from the letters of appointment of the custodians or from administrative instructions coeval with them directed to the Exchequer. The third item, £ 31 16 s. 1 d. expenses incurred in the carting of £ 3050 to London, is more difficult. A mandate to transfer available cash to London for forwarding to Normandy could have come direct from the King, for it is clear that he was intervening personally in the affairs of the bishopric. It could also have been authorized by the Justiciar, in the King's name and under the Exchequer seal, for he was responsible to Richard for the collection of English revenues and their despatch to Normandy. Between the two there is not much to choose.

There are many similar examples elsewhere on the Pipe Rolls. An account presented two years later from the other end of the realm concerned the Cornish tin mines, which were by now a highly profitable resource to the Crown. The custodian, William of Wrotham, accounted in 1198 for over £ 1,100. Set against this were large amounts of tin which had been despatched to two merchants of Bayonne and to others who received it against credits in *livres Angevins.* All these transactions originated on the continent; to complete the picture William of Wrotham was also allowed the costs of the ships which exported the tin to La Rochelle. The whole operation was authorized *per brevia Regis.* In this context to have said that they were *brevia Regis de ultra mare* would have been otiose. The writs must have been obtained by the merchants on the continent. It was they who presented them to William of Wrotham in order to obtain their tin. There was no need to say that they were *de ultra mare.* That was obvious to all concerned but was quite irrelevant to the transaction [41].

Between these two geographic extremes lay the administrative heart of England. Richard required cloth for his household and for despatch to the continent. He bought it in London. He needed ships for the transport of troops and munitions across the Channel. He got them from the ports of the southern counties. He depended on England for the financial sinews of war. As each campaigning season, approached the treasure was hauled from Westminster, the Tower of London and other centres to Winchester, thence to Portsmouth or Southampton, and thence shipped across the Channel to the King, or to the treasuries at Rouen and Caen. All this activity was authorized by *brevia Regis,* most of which must have originated with

(40) *Ibid.,* pp. 253–4. For Hugh du Puiset's debts see *Pipe Roll 7 Richard I,* pp. 24–5, 81, 82.

(41) *Pipe Roll 10 Richard I,* pp. 181–2.

the King. The accounts for London and Middlesex, Hampshire, Winchester and Southampton are full of them. They mark a treasure route, as essential to the fortunes of the Angevin house as the bullion fleets from America were to the cause of the Hapsburg Kings of Spain in the 16th and 17th centuries. To take but one example, Hugh de Bosco, as sheriff of Hampshire, accounted in 1196 for the embarking of 500 Welsh footsoldiers accompanied by two mounted sergeants and a knight, for the despatch of treasure on eight different occasions, for the passage of the King's falconers, with their hawks and cages, for the passage of another 500 Welsh foot-soldiers accompanied by a knight, Roger de la Haye, and three sergeants with two horses, and for a number of officials who passed through on various occasions and for men taking horses to the King. All this activity was authorized *per breve Regis*. Only one item on the account, concerning construction work in the forest of Porchester, was authorized by writ of the Archbishop [42].

These considerations cannot provide more than a very rough guide to where, within this mass of business, Richard concentrated his personal attention. For this there is only one test, and that a not very satisfactory one, for it can be applied only to the surviving *acta*. This is the formula *teste me ipso*. This appears in nine acts of Henry II, usually in a form which associates the King with other witnesses [43]. Most of these nine acts are of dubious authenticity [44], but two of them in which *teste me ipso* stands by itself, seem to be authentic mandates: one a writ of seisin addressed to the Constable of Cherbourg on behalf of the canons of Équeurdreville, and the other a writ of protection directed to the bailiffs of Falaise on behalf of Robert Marmion [45]. Four of Richard's *acta* drawn up before his accession under his style of Count of Poitou, were attested *teste me ipso*; one, unfortunately surviving only in transcript, has no other witnesses [46].

From 1190 royal acts attested *teste me ipso* appeared in considerable numbers, over 60 out of roughly 600. In the thirteenth century the formula became stereotyped, but in Richard's day it was still subject to variation. *Teste nobis, testibus nobis, testibus nobis met ipsis*, all appear as well as *teste me ipso*. It has been plausibly argued that documents so attested were read to the King in final draft before they were sealed [47]. If so the formula provides some kind of register of Richard's personal interest and intervention.

The King's attention was not casual. It seems likely that from a very early stage the formula could be attached to a particular category of document. Most of the early examples coming from February to July 1190 are

(42) *Chancellor's Roll 8 Richard I*, pp. 60–1.

(43) *Recueil des Actes de Henri II*, ed. L. Delisle and E. Berger (Paris, 1909–27), Introduction, pp, 225–7.

(44) *Ibid.*

(45) *Ibid.*, nos. CCCXL, DCCI.

(46) HILDA PRESCOTT, « The Early Use of ' Teste Me Ipso ' », *English Historical Review*, XXXV (1920), 214–7.

(47) P. CHAPLAIS, *Op. cit.*, p. 16.

writs of various kinds, many of them writs of protection, issued to French and English monasteries before Richard's departure on the Crusade [48]. During this period, except for a short interval from 14 March to 2 April when the Chancellor was in Normandy, the seal was in the custody of John of Alençon, Vice-Chancellor, and it may have been he who decided that the formula gave additional weight to documents which reinforced exemptions or stayed legal procedures in the royal and ducal courts [49]. This could be how the formula came to be stereotyped. But this transition to a formal usage was only in its initial stages. These writs of prohibition apart, there is little if any difficulty in accepting *teste me ipso* as an indication of Richard's direct personal responsibility. Sometimes the formula seems to have been brought in as a form of surety, as in seeking a loan from the men of St. Macaire [50], or in guaranteeing the good behaviour of the citizens of Rouen [51]. Sometimes it seems to have been used to flatter the recipients, as in the letters of protection granted to the commune of Eu [52]. It was deployed in great ecclesiastical causes: elections to bishoprics [53], disputes about monastic property [54], or the quarrel between Hubert Walter and the monks of Canterbury over the proposed collegiate church at Lambeth [55]. Some letters of major diplomatic importance, to Pope Clement III concerning Richard's treaty with Tancred of Sicily [56], to the Genoese concerning the proposed attack on Egypt [57], and to Pope Innocent III, seeking his support for Otto of Brunswick [58], went *teste me ipso, testibus nobis met ipsis* or *testibus nobis*. The letters sent home to Queen Eleanor and others from Germany in 1193 [59] and the letters in which the King accepted the resignation of Hubert Walter from the Justiciarship in 1198 [60], were *teste me ipso*. The formula was largely reserved for the important, the intimate or the confidential occasion. It appeared in matters touching the King's prerogative, in letters of November 1194 concerning the fraudulent use of the seal of

(48) LANDON nos. 221, 266, 270, 280, 282, 285, 293, 296, 305, 307, 309, 315, 332, 334, 339.

(49) It should be noted that although the formula was used before the Chancellor's visit to Normandy the main flow of letters of protection attested *teste me ipso* came subsequently. One letter on behalf of Peterborough (*ibid.*, no. 266) was dated during the visit.

(50) *Ibid.*, no. 224.

(51) *Ibid.*, no. 393.

(52) *Ibid.*, no. 475.

(53) *Ibid.*, nos. 536, 537.

(54) *Ibid.*, no. 455.

(55) *Ibid.*, nos. 497, 498, 506, 507.

(56) *Ibid.*, no. 345.

(57) *Ibid.*, nos. 363 (*Testibus nobis met ipsis*) 364 (*Testibus nobis*). On these see Hans Eberhard Mayer, 'Die Kanzlei Richards I von England auf dem Dritten Kreuzzug', *Mitteilungen des Instituts für Osterreichische Geschichtsforschung*, LXXXV (1977), 22, 30.

(58) LANDON, no. 514; MIGNE, *Patrologia Latina*, ccxvi, 1001-2.

(59) LANDON, nos. 368, 369, 370, 371, 372, 374, 384, 385, 389.

(60) *Ibid.*, no. 504; *Foedera*, i. pt. 1.71.

Henry II [61]. It figured again in administrative instructions of major importance in which Richard took a personal and expert interest: the disciplinary ordinances drafted for the fleet in June 1190 [62], the instructions of August 1194 concerning the holding of tournaments [63]; and the writ of 15 April 1196, addressed to Hubert Walter, which combined a summons of military service assessed on novel principles with a characteristic demand that Hubert should send as soon as possible all the money which he had to hand [64]. Last, but not least, *teste me ipso, teste nobis met ipsis* or *testibus nobis ipsis* were used in all the reports on the King's campaigns: the account of events in Cyprus sent to the Justiciar [65]; the two accounts of events up to and including the battle of Arsuf, one sent to the Abbot of Clairvaux [66]; the report sent to Hubert Walter of the French campaign of 1194 [67], and the letter sent to the King's erstwhile clerk, Philip, now bishop of Durham, which related the campaign of 1198 and King Philip's defeat and flight to Gisor [68]. These carry the reader closer than anything else to the real Richard, the last perhaps best of all, for here the soldier-poet seems to break through the formalities of epistolary composition. ' We so pressed them to the gate of Gisors ', the letter says, ' that the bridge broke beneath them and the King of France, so we hear, drank of the river. Up to twenty other knights were drowned. With our own lance we laid low Matthew de Montmorenci and Alan de Rusci and Fulk de Gilerval and held them captive. Over one hundred of his men were taken. We send you the names of the most important and will forward the rest when we have seen them. Mercadier also took thirty knights whom we have not seen. Mounted and foot-sergeants were also captured, but these are not yet counted, and two hundred chargers were seized of which 140 were armoured. It was thus that we defeated the French King at Gisors; it was not our might but God's and the justice of our cause which triumphed, for in this deed, beyond the advice of all our men, we placed at hazard both our head and our realm. We tell you of these things that your may rejoice along with us. Witness ourselves at Dangu, 30 September '. There seems to speak the true Richard, the *preux chevalier* with a canny eye for the profits of war.

This brief examination of the administrative record of Richard Lion-Heart suggests two conclusions. First, the contrast which has frequently

(61) *Ibid.*, no. 436.
(62) *Hoveden*, iii. 36.
(63) *Diceto*, ii. lxxx-lxxxi.
(64) LANDON, no. 464.
(65) *Ibid.*, no. 360.
(66) *Ibid.*, nos. 361, 362 (*teste nobis met ipsis*).
(67) *Ibid.*, no. 431.
(68) *Hoveden*, iv. 58–9 (*testibus nobis ipsis*). Howden not only obtained a copy of the letter directly or indirectly from Philip, bishop of Durham, but also the list of prisoners to which the letter refers (*ibid.*, iv. 56–7). There is another version addressed to the Chancellor, Eustace, bishop of Ely, in *Coggeshall*, pp. 84–5. This has *teste me ipso*.

been drawn between the absentee warrior King on the one hand, and the government of England on the other, seems too sharp. Certainly Hubert Walter was the ablest and most effective of all the Chief Justiciars and one of the greatest royal ministers of all time. But even during his Justiciarship the stream of *brevia regis* reveals that Richard intervened frequently and persistently in the control of English affairs. Secondly, that intervention, where it was initiated by the King, was concerned with one object: war and the organization of war. That was natural enough. Quite apart from his bellicose instincts, Richard had a war on his hands. This coloured both his own view of his role in government and the attitude of his subjects towards him.

Compare him, finally, in one respect with King John. John took a keen interest in the courts of justice. He conducted royal eyres. He gave judgments in person and he intervened through his writ in the course of civil actions. Judges deferred to him, and litigants sought his arbitration. Some of this is also true of Richard. As king, he was the fount of justice to whom litigants turned. Richard responded. One, who went on the Crusade, was able to get a writ of seisin, apparently a *mort d'ancestor*, from a busy king at Messina [69]. Another sought out Richard in Germany and obtained a stay pending the King's return to England [70]. In another well known case concerning dower in the honour of Mowbray, the parties confronted each other, the one reinforced by a royal writ that she should have her dower, the other relying on general royal letters protecting the lands and men of William de Mowbray from legal action as long as he was a prisoner in Germany, where he was a hostage for the payment of the King's ransom [71]. The royal justices also acknowledged Richard's role. A plea of Michaelmas 1194 which involved the Bishop of Norwich and lay on the borderline between secular and ecclesiastical jurisdiction, was noted; *Interim consulendus Rex super hac loquela* [72]. Another, arising from the dispute between Hugh de Nonant, bishop of Coventry, and the monks expelled from the cathedral convent, which culminated in an unseemly fracas in which the monks drew blood from the Bishop by beating him on the head with a Cross, was recorded with the note: *Et pro hoc lite et contencione voluntatem domini Regis consideratum est consulere.* The case involved royal charters both of Richard and his father [73]. The King's word carried weight. When one of the rebels of 1194 sought seisin in Nottinghamshire on the basis of a royal writ admitting him to the peace, and his seisin was challenged by a claimant who alleged that he had been deprived of lawful possession during the rebellion, Hubert Walter stated that he had it by word of mouth from the King that all those who had been disseised by Count John were to be reinstat-

(69) *Curia Regis Rolls*, i. 285.
(70) *Three Rolls of the King's Court*, p. 121.
(71) *Ibid.*, p. 8.
(72) *Ibid.*, p. 18.
(73) *Rotuli Curiae Regis*, i. 67.

ed. The royal writ of restitution was ignored. The King's verbal instruction was obeyed — *Consideratum est quod magis ratum habetur quod dominus Rex ore precepit quam quod per litteras mandavit* [74].

None of this however, matches the record of King John's persistent intervention. In retrospect this has added to John's reputation and detracted from Richard's. In the Middle Ages men took a different view.

(74) *Ibid.*, i. 47.

King John's treatment of his people as portrayed by Matthew Paris.

4

KING JOHN

IN the opinion of Stubbs King John was totally, not even competently, bad:

> What marks out John personally from the long list of our sovereigns, good and bad, is this – that there is nothing in him which for a single moment calls out for our better sentiments; in his prosperity there is nothing we can admire, and in his adversity nothing we can pity. . . . He looked neither before him nor behind him, drew as little from experience as he sacrificed to expediency. . . . He had neither energy, nor capacity nor honesty. . . .[1]

Stubbs was the predominant, but not the sole voice of his generation. J. R. Green was already claiming that John was 'the ablest and most ruthless of the Angevins. . . . In the rapidity and breadth of his political combinations he far surpassed the statesmen of his time.'[2] It is from Green, who saw the King as a paradox of viciousness and ability, rather than from Stubbs, that the modern view of John descends. In Dr. A. L. Poole's words,

> He was cruel and ruthless, violent and passionate, greedy and self-indulgent, genial and repellent, arbitrary and judicious, clever and capable, original and inquisitive. He is made up of inconsistencies.[3]

The key-word here is inconsistency. No student of King John would wish to exclude it; it is appropriate, but it is wonderfully convenient, too, for it permits and demands contradiction and paradox. It also leaves room for variants, and although few historians today would dissent much from Dr. Poole's judgment, they would undoubtedly wish to adjust the balance by adding comment of their own. Lady Stenton, for example, has emphasized John's ability as a hard-working administrator and as an expert, sometimes merciful, judge;[4] Professor Painter

1. *Historical Introductions to the Rolls Series*, ed. A. Hassall (London, 1902), pp. 439, 487. From *Memoriale Fratris Walteri de Coventria* (Rolls Series, 1873), II, xi, lxxix.
2. *A Short History of the English People* (London, 1888), pp. 122–3.
3. *From Domesday Book to Magna Carta* (Oxford, 1951), p. 425.
4. See her introductions to the pipe rolls of the reign (*Pipe Roll Society, passim*) and especially 'King John and the Courts of Justice', *Proceedings of the British Academy*, XLIV (1958).

placed more weight than most recent scholars on the suspicious side of John's character;[1] and Mr. Jolliffe has pointed to the arbitrary, extra-legal features of his government.[2] But these and other scholars have found common ground in the real and alleged paradoxes in John's personality, and a student could easily imagine that experts were now largely agreed about his character and government, that most of the problems were delineated and understood, if not finally settled. Such unanimity would be surprising in view of the difficulty of the evidence, of the ferocity of contemporary criticisms of John and of the widely varying opinions of him held in different ages. In fact the unanimity is sometimes apparent rather than real.

Modern scholars have followed three main lines of work:

1. They have reinforced from record evidence the contemporary picture of John as ruthless, violent, grasping and arbitrary. Here there has been no real break with Stubbs and his age.

2. They have established that John was an extremely able administrator, the master of a government in which judicial, administrative and financial procedures were developing along new courses. This has depended on record information not readily available to Stubbs' generation.

3. They have devalued the contemporary narrative evidence, partly by direct criticism and partly by comparing it with the record sources. Hence they have dismissed the charge of irreligion, for example, and reduced to limited, human, proportions the sloth, the grotesque lack of dignity and the outbursts of insane rage of the contemporary picture. Here they have parted company not only from the chroniclers but also from Stubbs who largely accepted the contemporary verdict.

I shall examine these three trends in turn.

I

Stubbs and his contemporaries relied mainly on the chroniclers; modern writers rely mainly on the records. However, this difference in approach only partly explains the contrasting con-

1. S. Painter, *The Reign of King John* (Baltimore, 1952).
2. J. E. A. Jolliffe, *Angevin Kingship* (London, 1955), pp. 131–6.

clusions. The antithesis of chronicle and record is not wholly valid, since parts of the record evidence, especially the Chancery and household enrolments, can be used to support a critical assessment of the King. For example, they are essential to any discussion of his treatment of his great vassals, his exaction of hostages, his disseisin and imprisonment of baronial debtors, his seizure of land and castles, his financial harrying of the Jews or his use of mercenary troops. Moreover, these records were almost all published by the Record Commission between 1833 and 1844 and hence were readily available to nineteenth-century scholars. Stubbs included some writs in his *Select Charters* and used others in his *Constitutional History*; but he scarcely exploited them fully, and it was not until the publication of Kate Norgate's great biography, *John Lackland*, in 1902, that a synthesis of royal writ and contemporary narrative was seriously attempted.

It was a synthesis in which the chronicler was very much the chief element. Today this is no longer so. Dr. W. L. Warren, John's latest biographer, tells us that 'we can get closer' to the King in the records 'than through the pages of any chronicle.'[1] Dr. H. G. Richardson, in discussing the events which followed Magna Carta, has asserted that

Nothing is lost by ignoring [the chroniclers], and it is possible to reconstruct a coherent and convincing picture of the principle events of 1215 upon the basis of records of unimpugnable veracity.[2]

These are extreme views, but they represent the fact that the record evidence is now the main force and the narrative simply reinforcement; where the two conflict the contemporary narrative is normally rejected; chronicle evidence unsupported by record is viewed with suspicion. The modern canon is clearly stated by Lady Stenton:

No chronicler should be believed who is not strictly contemporary, and is not supported by record evidence when he makes extravagant statements about the King's evil deeds.[3]

1. W. L. Warren, *King John* (London, 1961), p. 126.
2. 'The Morrow of the Great Charter', *Bulletin of the John Rylands Library*, XXVIII (1944), p. 422.
3. *English Society in the Early Middle Ages* (Pelican Books, 1951), p. 46.

This change in attitude, when reasonably applied, has yielded valuable results. Nevertheless, it has also created problems. It is one thing to use the record evidence for the history of the administration of which it was a direct product; it is quite another matter to use it as comment on the personality of the King, of which it cannot in the nature of things be anything better than a reflection. It is not necessarily invalid to use it in this way, but it requires a degree of imaginative reconstruction which may be far less solid in itself than the documentary evidence on which it is based. Writs are tangible, the conclusions drawn from them are not; and record entries can be marvellously enigmatic. Consider a famous proffer to the King entered on the Fine Roll of 1204–5:

> The wife of Hugh de Neville gives the lord King 200 chickens that she may lie with her husband for one night. Thomas de Sanford stands surety for 100 chickens, and her husband, Hugh, for 100.[1]

From David Hume onwards historians have naturally been curious about this entry. Most have gallantly assumed that it was inspired by John and not by the lady; it has therefore been interpreted as a compulsory payment not a voluntary proffer, and as such it has necessarily come to reflect on the King's character. Some have suggested that Hugh de Neville was the King's prisoner, which is incorrect; others that his wife was the King's mistress, for which there is no evidence; some depict the entry as an extreme example of John's tyranny, others suggest that the King's cronies or his clerks were a little drunk, or that it demonstrates a streak of bawdy nastiness in his humour. One of these interpretations may be the right one, but there is not the slightest foundation for any of them. Moreover, it is easy to imagine several explanations of the entry which would not seriously affect our assessment of the King; it may even have been that Joan de Neville had a nice line in chickens; is not Matilda de Braose said to have boasted of the number and quality of her cheeses? In fact, the entry, as the *Complet Peerage* wisely says, is still unexplained. Its only certain contribution to the understanding of John's character lies in its fina sentence for which no modern authority has yet found space

---

1. *Rotuli de Oblatis et Finibus*, ed. T. Duffus Hardy (Record Commission, 1835) p. 275.

The chickens are to be handed over before the beginning of Lent; any then outstanding are to be delivered at the following Easter.

John wouldn't have his chickens during Lent.[1]

The records give rise to frequently recurring problems of interpretation of this kind; this entry is bizarre but not otherwise exceptional. It belongs to a distinct type of record evidence in which the King's participation is certain, and which comprises fines made with the King, amercements by the King, judgments *coram rege* and the like. Such entries imply that the King took specific actions; the problems emerge in reconstructing his motives. They are often big problems reaching far into the King's character. For example, eight days before he died John permitted Margaret de Lacy, daughter of William de Braose, to clear forest land to found a religious house for the salvation of the souls of her father and mother and brother. Was John showing remorse for his treatment of the Braose family? If so, is it significant that he never apparently showed similar remorse for the fate of Arthur of Brittany? Or again, were the guarantees of Peter de Maulay's good behaviour which the King exacted in 1212 and which included Henry fitz Count's agreement to submit, if necessary, to a whipping, a product of the King's 'grim humour', as Professor Painter suggested,[2] or worse still, of a sadistic appetite? Was it morbid interest or something else which led the King in 1200 to order his justices to defer two judicial duels to his presence? None of these questions has a certain answer; indeed, tentative answers are only possible when made in the light of other evidence or conclusions about John's character. In doing this it is salutary to remember the ease with which a legend of King John was created in the thirteenth century and preserved in the nineteenth. It is just as easy to create one now.

This type of evidence far from exhausts the record sources. Recently, in fact, some historians have drawn much more heavily on less specialized information, particularly on the enrolled writs of the Chancery. Here the reconstruction of motive is sometimes apparently unnecessary; royal letters may state what the King's motives were; but this simplicity is usually only superficial. Moreover, this kind of evidence raises further problems:

1. However, he did not always observe the dietary regulations prescribed by the Church. Compare A. L. Poole, *op. cit.*, p. 428.
2. *Op. cit.*, p. 231.

1. How far do the phrases of royal letters represent the King's own views?

2. How far do such views reflect the application of pre-conceived principles of government? How far, in contrast, are they the product of particular situations in which men drew convenient texts from a common stock of political ideas?

No firm answer is yet possible to the first question. More than twenty years ago Professor Galbraith pointed to the linguistic vigour of the writs of John's chancery.[1] They clearly reflect individual personality and when, for example, John's letters assert that his peace is to be preserved, 'even if we have granted it to a dog',[2] or declare that he has been greatly moved by the complaints against his sheriffs, or render effusive thanks for military and financial aid received or still to come, it is possible that the personality is the King's own. But there were also other influences. The English Chancery, like other chanceries, sometimes drew on the practices of the papal Curia. Those same letters in which John so brusquely emphasized the pervasiveness of the King's peace, contain a preamble which is unmistakably pontifical in tone;[3] so also do letters of May 1207 in which John opened a reprimand to the Irish barons with the words *miramur plurimum*.[4] The tone of the letters also varied with the subject matter and the audience; sheriffs were addressed in direct, simple, sometimes menacing language, but letters recommending candidates for election to high ecclesiastical office could be couched in more florid phrases suitable to the learning and cloth of the addressees. Now it is true that the writs were not yet bound by the red tape of common form; there

1. V. H. Galbraith, *Studies in the Public Records* (London, 1948), p. 125.

2. *Rotuli Litterarum Patentium*, ed. T. Duffus Hardy (Record Commission, 1835), p. 33, quoted by V. H. Galbraith, *loc. cit.*

3. 'The King, etc., to the Mayor and Barons of London, etc. Since we have always held you in great esteem and have had your rights and liberties well respected, we trust that you have special esteem for us and that you wish to bring about those things which will add to our honour and to the peace and tranquillity of our land. But, since you know that the Jews enjoy our special protection, we are astonished that you have allowed the Jews of London to be harmed, since this is manifestly contrary to the peace of our realm and the tranquillity of our land. Indeed we are all the more astonished and disturbed since other Jews throughout England dwell in peace except those in your town'. *Rotuli Litterarum Patentium*, p. 33.

4. *Rotuli Litterarum Patentium*, p. 72.

was room for expressive licence. It is also true that John was a cultivated man who owned and borrowed books, some of which we may charitably presume he read, and that he lived in a period of rapidly developing literary and philosophic sophistication. Nevertheless, if he was not tied by red tape neither were others; and others, too, were men of their time in education and literary tastes. Hence it is possible that the expressive qualities of the King's letters may derive not from him, but from his advisers, officers and clerks. As yet there are insufficient studies of the diplomatic practice of John's Chancery to establish the respective rôles of the King and his officials. We could know much more than we do of the extent to which the language of royal writs changed as the officials changed, and whether John, King of England, spoke with a different voice from that of John, Count of Mortain, or John, Duke of Normandy, or John, Duke of Aquitaine. There are obvious difficulties; a comparison of John's reign with earlier and later periods is never going to be easy, in the first case because of the comparative dearth of Chancery evidence, in the second because of the minority of Henry III. But there is at least one significant indication in the Close Roll of Peter des Roches, the Justiciar, drawn up while John was in Poitou in 1214. This demonstrates that Chancery routine already determined the form of letters and the general arrangement of the roll, whatever the originating authority. It also shows that the Justiciar could adopt tones just as menacing as the King's. In summoning Earl David of Huntingdon to a council at London he wrote:

> Know that we have many things to say to you concerning the business of the lord King and of his kingdom, wherefore we order you, as you love his honour and yourself and your hostages and whatsoever you hold of him, that, without delay or excuse, you shall be in the neighbourhood of London, wherever you hear we are, about the octave of the Assumption of the Blessed Mary to treat concerning his aforesaid business.[1]

This blunt instrument was sent to an earl, indeed to the brother of a king, and to a man old enough to be the Justiciar's father. Peter's unpopularity as Justiciar need cause no wonder. How

---

1. *Rotuli Litterarum Clausarum*, ed. T. Duffus Hardy (Record Commission, 1833), I, p. 213. There are diplomatic grounds for thinking that this letter was a personal one. To the usual greeting of *salutem* it adds *et sinceram in Domino dilectionem*. It ends with the informal *Valete* rather than the formal *Teste* or *Testibus*; and it is entered on the dorse of the roll.

much did he learn from the King? How much did John learn from Peter and his colleagues? How far is the vigour or arbitrariness of some Chancery writs simply the work of clerks with educated minds who had been instructed to take a strong line? How far does it represent policy, how far the conventional political language of the time?

These questions of diplomatic detail involve much wider considerations; in fact, they raise doubts about several recent and important re-interpretations of John's reign which have relied heavily on the authoritarian language sometimes used in the records, particularly in the Chancery writs, and especially on references to the king's will, to his ill-will, wrath, or benevolence. In J. E. A. Jolliffe's opinion, John's view of the exercise of his powers came 'near to conceiving a new foundation for the state'. England in this period was moving 'towards a new monarchy', albeit one in which the obvious absolutist interpretation of Roman law was not yet fully exploited. Even so Mr. Jolliffe believes that 'John's premature death may well have diverted the course of history',[1] and a similar view has recently been reinforced by Dr. Ullmann, who has argued that John's tyranny provoked a reaction which determined the divergent courses of France and England in the thirteenth century, the one moving towards an absolute, the other towards a feudal, constitutional monarchy.[2] Hence, in terms which have been criticized by Professor Galbraith, a 'bad king' is made into a 'good thing'.[3] It is apparent that such interpretations must remain ill-founded until much more is known of who exactly was speaking when royal writs announce, for example, that the King has never heard 'that a new regulation could be introduced into any land without the assent of its ruler, either now or in times past,'[4] or when they assume that custom should give way before a special royal order.

However, whatever conclusions are ultimately reached about the drafting of royal letters, it is both highly selective and anachronistic to attribute uniformity of opinion or consistency of action to the King and his government. That John some-

1. J. E. A. Jolliffe, *op. cit.*, especially pp. 131–6.
2. W. Ullmann, *Principles of Government and Politics in the Middle Ages* (London 1961), pp. 190, 193.
3. 'Good and Bad Kings in Medieval English History', *History* XXX (1945) p. 121.
4. *Rotuli Litterarum Patentium*, p. 72.

times asserted his will does not mean that he conceived of himself as deliberately expanding the royal will at the expense of custom and law. In fact his writs suggest that theories were exploited in a fine eclectic spirit. Against the evidence on which Mr. Jolliffe and Dr. Ullmann rely must be set a much larger number of writs in which the King asserted the importance of custom, gave precedence to custom over his will, agreed that special uncustomary concessions to the Crown would not be used as precedents, or announced the consent of the great men of the land to taxation or other general measures. On some occasions an appeal to custom helped; on some occasions an assertion of will was necessary. The arguments were adjusted to the audience and the situation; if will and custom were contradictory, it was as poles of political theory not as immediately applicable rules of government. Indeed, as Lady Stenton has shown, each had its place in practice; John, in her view, was endeavouring 'to tread the narrow course between the letter of the rigid law and formless equity'.[1]

Much depends on the contemporary attitude to the authoritarian phrases and actions on which modern writers have placed so much weight. It is significant, of course, that they were used. They were understood; indeed, they were used so that theory might give respectability to policy. Nevertheless, the political split between King and opposition did not coincide with a theoretical division of will and theocratic power, on the one side, and of custom and the rights of a community, on the other. John was as ready to appeal to custom as were his subjects; he did it effectively and often justifiably in defending his position both against ecclesiastical claims and against the demands of the rebels in 1215. On the other hand, his baronial subjects were willing enough to pay for the privilege of royal arbitration in their legal disputes.

Hence, although many contemporary writers thought that John was harsh, unjust and arbitrary, they did not conclude that he was a dangerous and tyrannous innovator who was altering the framework of society. In their view, he was not initiating an absolutist pattern of government; he was simply behaving as a bad lord. Some writers introduced terms drawn from contemporary political thinking by contrasting the King's

1. Doris M. Stenton, 'King John and the Courts of Justice', *Proceedings of the British Academy*, XLIV (1958), pp. 104–8.

will with custom and by opposing tyranny to lawful government. There is Gerald of Wales' hysterical portrait of the King:
'tyrannous whelp, who issued from the most bloody tyrants and
was the most tyrannous of them all'.[1] But Gerald was making a
thoroughly unreal contrast between a tyrannous race of Norman and Angevin kings and the allegedly devout, law-abiding
Capetians. Others used similar terms less emphatically: the
Waverley annalist asserted that John's tyrannical will was his
law and stated that Peter des Roches was made Justiciar in 1214
in order to bend the magnates of the land to the King's will;
the Margam annalist frequently referred to John's tyranny;
some writers told of royal counsellors who gave advice according to will rather than reason, others of the King's enemies
complaining of his tyranny. But the theoretical implications of
these phrases were rarely indicated clearly. Moreover, such
terms are chiefly characteristic of the chronicles written after
John's death; the main charge of tyranny was not strictly
contemporary. It might be argued that many monastic
chroniclers were out of touch and failed to understand the
significance of an emphasis on the royal will. But this could not
be said of Richard de Mores, prior of Dunstable, to whom the
annals of Dunstable were attributed, for he was a canonist of
some distinction and had taught at Bologna. He more than any
other known writer was likely to recognize an attempted
assertion of a more authoritarian and theocratic type of monarchy. Yet the Dunstable annals show not the slightest trace
of such an interpretation of John's actions, even though the
writer was critical of his behaviour as king.

II

In these directions the exploitation of the record evidence has
led to provoking but highly debatable conclusions. Elsewhere
however it has yielded real gains, especially in the study of the
development of the royal administration undertaken by Lady

1. 'De principis instructione', *Giraldi Cambrensis Opera*, ed. G. F. Warner (Rolls
series, 1891), VIII, p. 328.

Stenton, Sir Cyril Flower, Sir Hilary Jenkinson[1] and others. Their work has been the main influence in dismissing the old charges against the King of incompetence and irresponsibility. It is now recognized that John took a thoroughly intelligent and immensely energetic interest in the running of the country. He intervened frequently in the business of the Exchequer and sometimes attended its meetings. He sat with his barons and judges to try legal actions; his justices deferred cases to him; suitors paid for the privilege of his arbitration, and, although this was sometimes doubly to their cost, the rolls also record that the King could be moved by compassion. Above all John travelled about his kingdom as no other monarch has done before or since; he and his household covered ground with remarkable speed. As King he only once stayed in one place for more than a month, and that was in 1215 when he and his army laid siege to Rochester Castle. Even a stay of a week's duration was uncommon. Usually after two or three nights, or frequently only one, he was off again, sometimes covering as much as thirty miles a day, penetrating to the farthest corners of the land. It is important to grasp exactly what this meant at the time. When John first visited York in 1200, no English king had been there probably since 1181, certainly since 1186. Those under twenty would not have seen a king, unless they had travelled or caught a glimpse of William the Lion of Scotland on one of his journeys south. John's visit to Newcastle in 1201, was the first recorded visit of an English king since 1158. Here only a few would remember Henry II. Indeed, throughout the north men would be more familiar with the Scottish than the English royal house. And John's journeys in the northern counties were not made for pleasure. Of his seventeen visits to York, eight were made in December, January, February or the first week in March. In March 1205 he journeyed there at the end of one of the longest and hardest winters of the century. Not even a hard-bitten northerner would claim that this would be done from choice. Sometimes John came north to suppress rebellion or deal with the Scots, sometimes he came in the winter because he was fighting in France in the summer. But he

1. See Lady Stenton's introductions to the pipe rolls of the reign, Pipe Roll Society, new series, vols. X ff.; C. T. Flower, *Introduction to the Curia Regis Rolls* (Selden Society, LXII, 1943); Hilary Jenkinson, 'The Financial Records of John's reign', *Magna Carta Commemoration Essays*, ed. H. E. Malden (Royal Historical Society, 1917), pp. 244–300.

came. Richard I never got beyond Clipstone. John's journeys signalized government by the King in person in a manner never experienced before by those whom he was governing. Richard I was only in England as king on two occasions; Henry II spent long periods abroad. And wherever John went he ferreted out infringements of his rights, vigorously imposed the law, castigated and disciplined his officials, and impressed the local inhabitants with the dignity of a King. In 1200–1 the men of York and Newcastle, so long without a royal visit, were quickly reminded of what it entailed by amercements which John imposed on them because they had failed to give his party the right kind of welcome.

John's activity, of course, was conceived very much in his own interests; his main objective was to replenish his treasure. This aim was common to the severe enforcement of justice, the efficient exploitation of the royal demesne, the development of new methods of taxation on land revenues and trade, the exaction from the sheriffs of higher renders from the shires, the imposition of heavy monetary penalties for misdemeanours, the demand for enormous proffers for privileges or as the usual feudal incidents. But his administrative interest and activity had far wider results than this. His reign produced or extended administrative experiments and developments which set the course for the rest of the century: the emergence and specialization of the offices of the Household, the use of a privy seal, the incipient division between what was to be a King's Bench and a Court of Common Pleas, the first known summons of knights of the shire to a national assembly, the first national customs system, the first organized navy since the tenth century, the first experiment in nationalization in the reorganization of the tin mines of Cornwall initiated in 1198 and confirmed by royal charter in 1201. All this was done efficiently – even the nationalization. It was well based on a secure grasp of the economic trends of the period – the expanding wealth and rising prices, the increasing importance of trade, industry and credit transactions – and of the social trends which enabled the government to rely increasingly on the knighthood and gentry as administrative agents. The total achievement was enormous, fit to stand alongside that of Henry II or Edward I. Together, these two and John represent a standard which was never again equalled in the medieval period.

So much is well enough agreed. Its importance to the general assessment of John is not. To be an efficient civil servant or an inventive administrator was only part of the job of being a great king. These standards are essentially those of the twentieth rather than the thirteenth century. All that contemporaries demanded was that the King should maintain good laws, destroy evil customs, judge justly and keep the peace; to do more than that was to do too much. Furthermore, contemporaries had other tests – success in war, ability to lead, geniality towards the great men in both church and state – and by these standards no one could rate John high. Thus to exaggerate the importance of his administrative achievement is to resort to an anachronistic standard. Abbot Ralph of Coggeshall summed up the contemporary assessment when he ended his long and hostile account of John by adding rather casually that he ruled his kingdom for seventeen and a half years 'with reasonable industry – *satis laboriose*'.[1] This was indeed to damn with faint praise – two words to lay beside the volumes of the Record Commission, the Stationery Office, and the Selden and Pipe Roll Societies.

Where the chroniclers said more than this, their first concern was to complain of the harshness of John's government. For them his efficiency was equivalent to oppression; when the King progressed through the land, hearing pleas, enforcing royal rights and selling privileges to ready buyers, they wrote of a ruler holding his subjects to ransom. Times were changing; justice could now be obtained with comparative readiness through the routine use of writs and the regular sessions of the courts; the personal intervention and supervision of the King were no longer necessary; a king who supervised matters closely in his own interests was making a nuisance of himself. Hence contemporaries differentiated between Henry II and his sons much more easily than do modern writers; Coggeshall's bare reference to John's industry stands in sharp contrast to the fulsome praise he gave Henry II for his exercise of justice and maintenance of the peace. John ruled much as his father had done, yet he had to face a different reaction. His maintenance

---

1. *Radulphi de Coggeshall chronicon Anglicanum*, ed. J. Stevenson (Rolls Series, 1875), p. 184. To translate these words as 'indefatigably' seems too generous to John. Coggeshall was awarding a moderate, not a high mark. In any case, the phrase was a formal one which he also applied to Richard I – with considerably less justification (*ibid.*, p. 96). Compare V. H. Galbraith, *Studies in the Public Records*, p. 126, and W. L. Warren, *King John*, p. 133. See also above, p. 68 n. 6.

of the forest law attracted awed comment from the author of the *Histoire des Ducs de Normandie*, who compared his rule with that of the legendary Arthur.[1] Otherwise he earned praise, not for the enforcement of his rule, but for its relaxation in the months of crisis which followed the plot against his life in August 1212.[2] John had not been ineffective. He had been far too effective.

III

The argument has now been carried to the chronicles from two separate discussions of the record sources. This involves moving to less certain ground, for while the records have been splendidly edited, some of the chronicles are still only available in inadequate editions. Moreover in recent years the pattern of criticism, which was set in 1944 by Professor Galbraith's devastating analysis of the St. Albans chroniclers, Roger of Wendover and Matthew Paris, has been largely destructive.[3] The chronicles do not now pull much weight. Indeed, in some respects the St. Albans chroniclers have been as influential in defeat as they were in victory, for it has been easy to take their inaccuracy and bias as representative of the narrative sources as a whole. In fact chronicle opinion on King John varied very considerably. None thought him admirable, still less lovable; the general assessment varied from nondescript to very bad; but different writers saw different qualities of badness and it is in this kind of variation that the chief interest of the chronicle evidence lies.

Most of the surviving narratives of the reign are the work of monastic chroniclers who were understandably prejudiced against the King because of his quarrel with Rome and consequent treatment of the monastic order. However, their evidence cannot be discounted as the outcome of bitter and disillusioned monkish selfishness, for the non-monastic narratives are often

1. *Histoire des Ducs de Normandie*, ed. F. Michel (Société de l'histoire de France, 1840), p. 109.

2. J. C. Holt, *The Northerners* (Oxford, 1961), p. 85, and, more recently, Miss Patricia M. Barnes' introduction to *Pipe Roll 16 John* (Pipe Roll Society, new series, XXXV), pp. xix–xxiii.

3. *Roger of Wendover and Matthew Paris* (Glasgow, 1944).

equally hostile. The biographer of William Marshal, for example, portrays a resentful, suspicious, monarch, whose achievements were always blighted by his pride.[1] This writer, it is true, was concerned to explain William Marshal's differences with the King, but the author of the *Histoire des Ducs de Normandie*, who came to England with John's Flemish allies in 1215, had no such axe to grind and he was even more critical. In his view John was cruel, vicious and lecherous, a king who committed many shameful acts against the nobles of the land; he was not only wicked but petty, a man who could be upbraided by his wife and openly contradicted and challenged by his barons.[2] Bertrand de Born the younger was even more stinging:

> No man may ever trust him
> For his heart is soft and cowardly.[3]

The condemnation of John was not limited to any particular order in society; indeed, the most balanced surviving account of the King, the Barnwell chronicle, was monastic, not secular or lay.

The near unanimity of surviving contemporary opinion is the main difficulty in interpreting John's activities as King and the chief obstacle to any reassessment of his character. The contemporary condemnation is too varied and widely based to be dismissed as prejudice, nor can it be explained entirely by pointing to the differences between medieval and modern standards of judgment. Sometimes this helps. As I have already suggested, the thirteenth and twentieth centuries take different views of administrative efficiency. Modern writers, too, would be much readier than contemporaries to recognize an element of inevitability in the loss of Normandy, for example, or the extent to which price inflation added to the King's financial difficulties and demands. But such considerations sometimes widen the gap between the modern and contemporary view of the King. For example, some modern writers have vigorously condemned him for the murder of Arthur of Brittany; in Professor Painter's view this was John's 'most frightful crime'.[4] Yet contemporaries were far less certain about it. Arthur's

---

1. *Histoire de Guillaume le Maréchal*, ed. P. Meyer (Société de l'histoire de France, 1891–1901), lines 12105–10.
2. *Histoire des Ducs de Normandie*, pp. 104–5, 116–19.
3. *The Political Songs of England*, ed. T. Wright (Camden Society, 1839), p. 6.
4. *Op. cit.*, p. 54.

murder appears as the chief charge against the King in the Margam annals and as an important element in his condemnation in some French chronicles which depend on Margam or on a common source.[1] But the Barnwell chronicler, in contrast, chose to reflect that the anonymity of Arthur's grave was a just reward for his pride,[2] while Wendover quoted what he took to be Innocent III's comments on the matter in 1216:

> The chronicles tell us of the murder of innocent persons by many emperors and princes, the Kings of France as well as others, but we do not read that the murderers were ever condemned to death. Arthur was no innocent victim. He was captured at Mirebeau, a traitor to his lord and uncle to whom he had sworn homage and allegiance, and he could rightly be condemned without judgment to die even the most shameful of deaths.[3]

Thus, apparently, spoke the keeper of the conscience of Christendom.

How was it that men who could stomach Arthur's end should yet condemn King John so violently? Or, to restate the question more generally, why was John so vehemently damned and yet given sufficient political support to fight a civil war in 1215–16? Part of the answer is that opinion about John fluctuated with his changing fortunes, ambitions and policies. Part of the answer lies not so much in John's reign or in anything he did, as in the years which followed, especially in the minority of Henry III. The most elaborate condemnations of the King were retrospective.

The contemporary historians of John may be conveniently divided into three groups:

    1. Those who completed their work before or just after John's accession. The most important of these were Richard of Devizes who ended his chronicle in 1192, William of Newburgh who ended his and died in 1198, and Roger of Howden and Ralph of Diceto, whose histories end in 1201 and 1202 respectively. This group provides the main narrative sources for John's activities before he became king.

    2. Those who completed their work by the time of John's death. This group consists largely of anonymous monastic

1. See F. M. Powicke, *The Loss of Normandy* (Manchester, 1961), pp. 309 ff.
2. *Memoriale Walteri de Coventria*, ed. W. Stubbs (Rolls series, 1873), II, p. 196.
3. Matthew Paris, *Chronica Majora*, ed. H. R. Luard (Rolls series, 1874), II, p. 659.

annalists, but it also includes Gervase of Canterbury, Gerald of Wales and Adam of Eynsham, the biographer of St. Hugh of Lincoln.

3. Those who wrote after John's death, some after a lapse of a few years, some after a decade or so, some after a generation or more. This group of writers is less entitled than the first two to the description 'contemporary' and, within it, some were less 'contemporary' than others. One or two, although written in or after the middle of the thirteenth century, embody 'contemporary' material.

The importance of the first group of writers is considerable, for they provide clear evidence that John already enjoyed bad repute with some before he ascended the throne. The case presented by Richard of Devizes and William of Newburgh is that he had failed in Ireland in 1185 through vain and adolescent incompetence and an avaricious refusal to pay his soldiers, that he had treacherously deserted his father in 1189 and hence hastened his death, that, under Richard I, his lust for power led him into a perfidious attempt to seize the realm, into treasonable plots with King Philip of France and finally into an open but futile rebellion. This theme was developed dramatically by Richard of Devizes, who presented John, 22 years of age at his father's death, as a flighty youth, yet one capable of fearsome anger, who was seeking to displace Richard I and seize the realm, possibly as early as 1189, certainly by 1191. William of Newburgh's story is less highly coloured. He recognized the fact, later clearly established by Lionel Landon,[1] that Richard provoked John's treachery by recognizing Arthur of Brittany as his heir in the Treaty of Messina of 1190. Even so, John's treachery towards his brother provoked William into the famous comment which Kate Norgate used as a final judgment in *John Lackland*, 'John, nature's enemy'.

John's record in these years was bad. He betrayed his lord and brother, and, worse still, the lord and brother was a crusader. Even so, the case presented by Richard of Devizes in particular is decoratively stylized, at times almost hysterical. Howden and Diceto took a calmer view. Howden recorded John's unfortunate failure to pay his troops in Ireland in 1185 and preserved a mild account of his desertion of his father in 1189,

1. *The Itinerary of Richard I* (Pipe Roll Society, new series, XIII, 1935), pp. 196–208.

but his story lacks the vigorous hostility of Devizes or Newburgh. He plainly disapproved of John's behaviour in 1193 and attributed the cutting remark to Richard I that John was not the man to conquer a realm by force if he was opposed by force, but he also associated John with Richard's popularity in 1189 and gave a sympathetic account of his vigorous reaction to new suggestions of treason which King Philip apparently made in 1199. Furthermore, Howden did not let John's previous treachery affect his account of his early years as King. When he finished his work in 1201 he had presented no wayward tyrant, but a vigorous monarch, a ruler concerned to maintain his rights and realize his authority, a typical Angevin king, in short, whose accession had made little difference to the routine conduct of government. Howden had been a royal justice and knew what he was talking about. His narrative, rather than the more critical accounts of Devizes and Newburgh, was the main source for the next generation of writers. It was scarcely a sufficient herald of the outburst which was to come.

After 1201 the situation was soon changed by the accumulation of disaster. If a writer started to write of the events of John's reign after 1204, then he would write in the knowledge that Normandy had been lost. If he started to write after 1208, then he would write in the knowledge that an interdict lay on the land. If he started to write a year later, then he would know that the King was excommunicate. If he started to write in 1213, he would know that John had surrendered his kingdom to the Papacy to receive it back as a papal fief. A year later a writer would know of the defeat of the King's final attempt to recover his continental lands. By 1215 he would have seen the condemnation of John's methods of government in Magna Carta and a year later he would know of John's death in a country torn by civil war. Each successive incident might have a cumulative and often distorting effect on a writer's view of the whole reign.

This is obvious in the work of men who died before the accumulation of disaster was complete. Gervase of Canterbury, for example, stopped his *Gesta Regum* at the year 1210 and presumably died shortly afterwards. His account of John's reign is short, covering no more than 15 pages in the printed edition, and was written late in his life. Under the year 1200 he makes the following comment about John; he is referring to the Treaty of Le Goulet which brought a temporary halt to the Norman war in that year:

> The King would rather achieve peace by negotiation than fight for his own terms, and because of this his enemies and detractors call him John Softsword. But, as we shall see later, this softness was soon transformed into a cruelty unequalled in any of his predecessors.[1]

Now the second sentence was clearly written with John's expulsion of the Canterbury monks in 1207 and their consequent sufferings in mind, and it is probable too that the reference to John Softsword was made with the loss of Normandy in 1204 in mind. There are other examples. For instance the Margam annals treat the reign as a dramatic consequence of the denial of Arthur's rights in 1199. In describing John's coronation they state:

> Since William de Braose offended more than all the others in agreeing to his coronation, so he and all his house were punished more than the others by the judgment of God[2].

Here the account of 1199 is affected by the events of 1210. Similarly the Dunstable annalist finds truth in the prophecy of Peter of Wakefield in that John continued to reign only as a vassal of the Holy See for another four years.[3]

The results of the period up to John's death were mixed. There was splendid material for a condemnation of him in the disappearance of Arthur of Brittany, the loss of Normandy, the Interdict and all that followed from it, the attack on the Braose family, and the execution of Peter of Wakefield; and most or all of these points appear in the chronicles produced before the end of the reign. Some works were already markedly hostile: Gervase of Canterbury stated and typified the hostility of the monks; Adam of Eynsham levelled scandalous charges of irreligion, alleging that John never took the sacraments after he reached manhood; Gerald of Wales, who had already attacked John's early indiscretions, added fiery criticism at the end of his *De Principis Instructione*. However, this is not the whole story. There are several narratives which contain some or much of the material for a condemnation yet do not use it to reflect upon the

---

1. *The Historical Works of Gervase of Canterbury*, ed. W. Stubbs (Rolls series, 1880), II, pp. 92–93.
2. *Annales Monastici*, ed. H. R. Luard (Rolls series, 1886–9), I, pp. 24–5.
3. *Ibid.*, III, p. 34.

character and ability of the King. This is true, for example, of the continuation of the chronicle of Ralph Niger, which ends in 1212, of the annals of St. Albans which end in 1215, of one of the early texts in the Winchester–Waverley group of annals, of the annals of St. Edmund up to 1204, although not thereafter, and of the jejune annals of Battle which end in 1206 with a comment on John's gifts to the abbey.

When John died the legend of him was not yet complete and was not even unanimously agreed. Indeed it was only just beginning, for the narrative sources on which later generations have chiefly depended and from which the legend is chiefly derived were not yet written. Roger of Wendover was not writing about the end of John's reign until after 1225; abbot Ralph of Coggeshall, another important and hostile witness whose chronicle runs to 1225, probably did not begin his account of the period after 1207 until 1221 or thereabouts; the Barnwell chronicler most probably composed his work in the 1220s, and was adding to it as late as 1232; the biography of William Marshal was begun after 1219 and completed in 1225–6; the *Histoire des Ducs de Normandie* ends in 1220 and was probably composed after that date; the section in the annals of Waverley on the later years of John's reign was written after 1219, probably between 1221 and 1227; the Margam annals are probably even later; some annals, like those of Burton, are only known to us in late thirteenth-century versions.

Now there can be no doubt that time told against John's reputation; this is best illustrated in the succession of continental narratives written by Rigord, monk of St. Denis, and William the Breton, Philip Augustus' chaplain. Rigord's first version written *c.* 1196 is quite neutral to John and includes one story, concerning the recovery of a fragment of an image damaged by a mercenary soldier, which reflects credit on him. Moreover, Rigord's later continuation of the chronicle up to 1206 preserves this atmosphere and is perhaps more critical of Philip Augustus than of John. At this point William the Breton took over and produced three versions of a chronicle, based on and continuing the work of Rigord, all written between *c.* 1214 and 1227. In these the creditable story of the image is suppressed, and John is already presented as treacherous. The full blast of denunciation, however, was reserved for William's long account in verse, the *Philippide*, composed 1214–24, in which John's treachery is made a main cause of Henry II's death, in which he is accused of treachery again for his attack on Evreux in 1194, in which Arthur's claims are now given priority, and in which the King's marriage to Isabella of Angoulême is treated as rape in the classical style.[1] The legend still spread like a fog long after John had died. Matthew Paris, as is well known, improved on and added to the scandalous stories of Wendover;[2] Thomas Wykes, who wrote in the reign of Edward I, almost outdid the St. Albans chroniclers in presenting John as a king who had murdered the rightful heir to the throne and who equalled or exceeded the wantonness of Solomon in his carnal lusts.[3] Nor was the myth restricted to a monastic audience. The knights of Somerset who were charged in 1277 with the perambulation of the royal forests in their county were ready to assert that King John had afforested all England[4]; clearly almost anything could be said of John.

Hence there was a rapid and long-term decline in John's stock. But within this general trend the period of Henry III's minority was especially important. Those who wrote during Henry's minority were at work in a period in which the battles of John's reign were still being fought. These battles were largely won by the old opposition to the King. The old rebels were reinstated; some suffered territorial losses, it is true, but others went on to acquire both power and respect as loyal and efficient agents of the Crown. Magna Carta was reissued on three occasions and confirmed on several others. Many of John's old agents were excluded from influence; his alien administrators especially were driven from their control of offices and castles; Faulkes de Bréauté's power fell with Bedford castle in 1223 and Peter des Roches, the moving figure among the aliens, went abroad in 1227. In short the rebellion of 1215 was astonishingly successful viewed from a standpoint ten years later. It was in this atmosphere that the major narratives were written; they reflect John's posthumous defeat.

This had two obvious effects. First, the reissues and confirmations of the Charter made it far easier to assume that John's rule had been especially burdensome and contrary to custom. By

---

1. *Oeuvres de Rigord et de Guillaume le Breton*, ed. H. F. Delaborde (Société de l'histoire de France, 1882–5).
2. V. H. Galbraith, *Roger of Wendover and Matthew Paris* (Glasgow, 1944 p. 35).
3. *Annales Monastici*, IV, p. 53.
4. *Select Pleas of the Forest*, ed. C. J. Turner (Selden Society, 1899), p. cii.

1225 much of the ineffective settlement embodied in the Great Charter of 1215, which the Pope had quickly annulled, had become part of the law of the land. Hence men assumed that John had broken that law, and since law was closely identified with custom, they readily believed that John's rule had been uncustomary, arbitrary and tyrannical. Moreover, some writers paid little attention to their documents, for they confused the different versions of the Charter; many accepted the rebels' argument which traced a succession from the laws of Edward the Confessor and the Charter of Henry I to the demands of 1215; and few acknowledged the fact that many of the charges which they levied against John had also been levied by earlier writers against Henry II or against the government of Richard I. John's reputation had to carry the whole burden, his father's and brother's as well as his own.

Secondly, the political struggles of the Minority were concerned with disciplining and finally ejecting John's alien administrators; the established noble families were almost at one in this, no matter whether they had rebelled or remained loyal in 1215. This encouraged anti-alien feelings already enriched by the French invasion of 1216 and the behaviour of Prince Louis' entourage, and the resulting antagonism towards the foreigner is clearly reflected in the narrative sources written in the 1220s and later. It can be traced in Roger of Wendover, who refers to the King's wicked advisers; in the Coggeshall chronicle, in which the magnates are made to grumble about the promotion of Peter des Roches to the justiciarship; in the continuation of William of Newburgh, in which the cruelty of the aliens is made one of the main causes of the rebellion and in which John is portrayed as despising his native, free-born subjects; in the *Histoire des Ducs de Normandie*, which states that the King had many evil men; and, most emphatically of all, in the annals of Waverley, in which Peter des Roches is promoted to the justiciarship in order to subject the barons to the King's will, in which the King is presented as surrounding himself with aliens, and in which the barbarous foreigner ravishes the land. Even the most balanced of these writers, the Barnwell chronicler, took his final stand on this count:

> He was certainly a great prince, but he enjoyed no great success and, like Marius, met with both kinds of luck. He was generous and liberal to aliens but he plundered his own people. He ignored

those who were rightfully his men and placed his trust in strangers. Before his end his people deserted him, and at his end few mourned for him.[1]

The history of the aliens under John could not be divorced from their history during the Minority. Those writers who discussed one half of the story almost inevitably discussed the other and many of them were also critical of Prince Louis and his French followers. It was easy again to argue that John was responsible, for he was the one who had promoted the aliens and had used them to fight the civil war. The Waverley annalist, writing after 1219, commented on the promotion of Peter des Roches to the justiciarship in 1214 by saying that his conduct changed the anger of the barons into rage; 'nor', he added, 'has that rage subsided even now';[2] and when he described the downfall of Fawkes de Bréauté this same writer emphasized that Fawkes owed his position to John. Once again the legend grew in a period in which feeling against the alien rapidly increased. It is more obvious in Matthew Paris than in Roger of Wendover and it reappears in other later works.[3] Here John's reputation was made to carry the burden not only of the past but also of the future.

IV

The outcry against the aliens was not so much a national reaction against the foreigner as a politically inspired method of denigration. In Richard's reign John himself had apparently denounced William Longchamp for depriving free and lawful men of the land of their offices and giving them to unknown newcomers. Later Simon de Montfort was to be attacked as an alien and later still he and his supporters were to attack Henry III's relatives as aliens. The charge had some justification when levied against John. He had used aliens as officials and mercenaries – hence the demand for their ejection in Magna Carta.

1. *Memoriale Walteri de Coventria*, II, p. 232.
2. *Annales Monastici*, II, p. 281.
3. E.g. the annals of Worcester and the chronicle of Meaux.

Even so, the chronicles of the Minority present an exaggerated case. The aliens never formed more than a small group among the King's friends and agents. John's chief advisers were products of his own household, his chief political support came from men like William Marshal and Ranulf earl of Chester, and when he dined and gambled it was usually with some of his barons or with household knights of long standing like Brian de Lisle. The alien, in fact, was something of an Aunt Sally; in 1215 the drafters of the Articles and Magna Carta even muddled their names and relationships. The real complaint was against the King's distribution of office and the spoils of government. The aliens were simply the most vulnerable recipients. Those who attacked them were seeking, among other things, a cut for themselves. Yet this was reasonable, for medieval government depended for its stability on an acceptable distribution of office and influence among the great men of the land. This John had denied; he had sought administrative efficiency at the expense of political stability; worse still he had deliberately set one family against another: Leicester against Chester, Stuteville against Mowbray, de Say against de Mandeville.[1] That men were still vociferous in their denunciation of his agents long after he was dead is a measure of his failure. The circumstance of the minority of Henry III had not led men to invent this complaint: it simply allowed them to state it. Behind the smoke-screen raised by the chroniclers there was a real source of discontent which constitutes a significant criticism of King John. He had failed to manage the great noble houses of the land.

At this point the chroniclers bring us near to the truth, despite their omissions and exaggerations. Elsewhere their evidence is not so valuable. John was harsh and cruel, certainly, but a king was more likely to suffer disaster through kindness than through cruelty. John was not, like Stephen, 'a mild man, and soft and good'. Again, he was a profligate and enjoyed a good dinner, but it has yet to be shown that either a succession of mistresses or a healthy appetite are of necessity impediments to effective monarchical rule. These points, however, derive from the superficial decoration of the chroniclers' accounts. Underneath there are other more serious charges. John failed in the primitive

1. For discussions of these aspects of John's rule see S. Painter, *The Reign of King John*, c. 2, and J. C. Holt, *The Northerners*, c. 12.

tactical generalship of medieval warfare; he could conceive the strategy of a campaign, he could provide the necessary allies and resources, but he rarely fought one well. His failures may be explained by the superior resources of his opponents, but they were all of them inglorious. The nickname John Softsword may not recognize the circumstances against which John had to fight, but the sword was soft enough. This, like his failure to control and lead the aristocracy, was a crucial failure.

The chroniclers' opinions of John roughly follow the pattern of his career. They were hostile to his behaviour while Richard was on the Crusade; they reacted reasonably towards him by the time he was king and during his early years; they turned hostile again, this time excessively so, from the middle years of his reign and especially after his death. This ebb and flow of disapproval reflects two things: first, the critical circumstances in which John lived after Richard's recognition of Arthur and again after the loss of Normandy and during the quarrel with Rome; secondly, the manner in which John behaved in a crisis. Under Richard he engaged in treason; after 1204 he drove barons and knights into rebellion by the financial burdens, political discipline and monopoly of office which the search for the resources for effective war required. These two periods of crisis illustrate two qualities he enjoyed to the full: in the first case his genius for political negotiation, for intrigue and the manipulation of men; in the second his administrative ruthlessness, his interest and ability in governing. But they also illustrate his failings. Under pressure John owed most to the elaborations of his political genius and to his energy. He could deceive, cajole, bully or crush individuals; he could scheme, administer and muster resources. But he lacked what most helps a man in a crisis – a level head. Hence he betrayed Richard only to suffer a blot on his reputation, he abandoned Normandy only to attempt its reconquest, he challenged the Papacy only to find that diplomatic circumstances compelled him to surrender, he launched his last great campaign in France only to withdraw, and he sealed the Great Charter only to reject it and fight a civil war until his death.

The head of King John from his effigy in Worcester Cathedral
(*Photograph by Clive R. Haynes*)

5

KING JOHN'S DISASTER IN THE WASH

The loss of King John's baggage train in the Wash and the manner of this monarch's death have become part of that assorted collection of irrelevant incident which make up what every schoolboy and many adults know about the history of mediaeval England. The classical account of the King's disaster was published by Sir William St. John Hope in 1906.[1] His reconstruction of events has become orthodox; despite the fact that it was placed under a very damaging examination by Gordon Fowler in 1952,[2] it was still repeated in standard works, by Dr. Lane Poole, for example, in 1955,[3] and by Professor Frank Barlow in the same year.[4] The present paper is intended to reinforce, extend and deepen Fowler's criticism of St. John Hope and also to put forward a reconstruction of the disaster which differs from those they have advanced.

There are a number of fixed points which provide an unalterable framework for the story. Royal letters are attested at King's Lynn on 9, 10 and 11 October, and at Wisbech and Swineshead on the 12th. Thus between the morning of the 11th and the night of the 12th King John made a journey of some 50 miles from Lynn to Swineshead, via Wisbech, which he may have reached on the 11th but cannot have left before the 12th. It was on this journey that the disaster, such as it was, occurred.

On this framework St. John Hope erected a structure of detail held together by several interlocking assumptions. One was that John and his troops moved faster than their baggage, John travelling to Wisbech without the train which moved more slowly, and by a diverging route, to Cross Keys and then across the Wellstream towards Sutton. A second assumption was that the route which he allotted to John on the 12th, through Leverington, Tydd St. Giles and Tydd St. Mary, to Sutton, presented no special difficulties; this, St. John Hope felt, explains why the King and his army survived while the baggage train was lost. A third important assumption was that the baggage train was very large and its disaster complete; this led him to seek a point of crossing which was wide enough for the whole train to be engulfed at one and the same time. The last, which Fowler also shares, was that King John's visit to Wisbech was deliberate, a result of planning rather than unforeseen circumstances. There is no evidence to support any of these assumptions and a great deal to suggest that they are incorrect.

St. John Hope derived much of his story from the narrative of Roger of Wendover, written 1225–30. Roger, who specialized in the sensational,[5] made

---

[1] "The loss of King John's Baggage Train in the Wellstream in October, 1216," *Archaeologia*, lx, 93–110.
[2] "King John's Treasure," *Proceedings of the Cambridge Antiquarian Society*, xlvi, 4–20.
[3] *From Domesday Book to Magna Carta*, 2nd edn., p. 485, where Fowler's paper is noted.
[4] *The Feudal Kingdom of England 1042–1216*, p. 435.
[5] Cf., for example, his account of the loss of Hugh de Boves at sea. (Matthew Paris, *Chronica Majora*, ed. H. R. Luard (Rolls Series), ii, 623.)

the disaster total "He lost all his waggons, carts, and pack-horses, with his treasures and precious vessels, and everything which he loved with special care." "The ground opened in midst of the waves, and there were bottomless whirl-pools which engulfed everything, with men and horses, so that no man

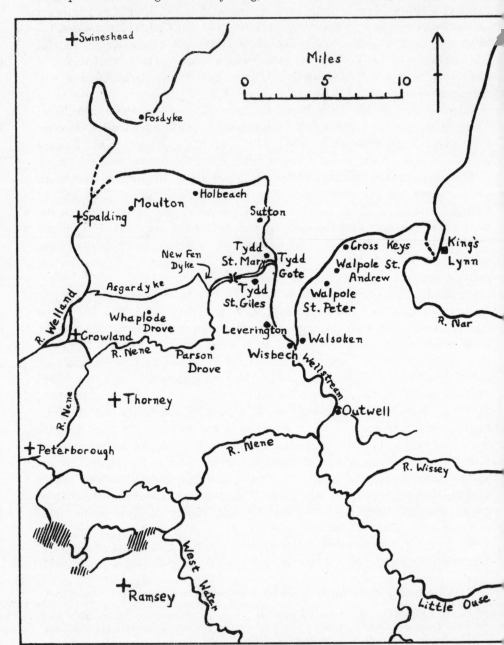

THE FENLAND IN THE TIME OF KING JOHN

escaped to tell the King of the disaster."[6] This St. Albans tradition was later embellished by Matthew Paris, who enumerated the King's losses further:— "his carts, his pack-horses, with loot and booty, and all his treasure and household goods," the quicksand "swallowing up men, arms, tents, victuals and all the King's valuable possessions except his life."[7]

As Fowler argued, these passages are undoubtedly exaggerated and unreliable.[8] Indeed, there is some possibility that they are little more than dramatic inflations of a source also used in the chronicle of the abbey of Coggeshall, which was composed some time before Wendover's work.[9] Both the Coggeshall text and Matthew Paris, for example, use the rare diminutive *supellectilis* for the King's household goods, and both have quicksand in their stories.[10] Moreover, Wendover's narrative contains contradictions which were possibly derived from a confused understanding of a sequence of events which Coggeshall gives correctly. Coggeshall states that John's final illness was accelerated by two things: first, by the arrival of messengers from Dover bearing the bad news that his garrison there was considering surrender, and secondly, by his grief at the losses he had sustained in crossing the Wash. Thus Coggeshall juxtaposes the arrival of messengers and the King's reaction to the disaster. So also, in a negative fashion, does Wendover, for he states, on the one hand, that the King scarcely escaped with his army, and, on the other, that no one survived to bear the tale to the King.[11] Why, if the King was so closely involved that he scarcely escaped, should there be any question of his learning of the disaster from survivors? Was not Wendover simply expressing some dim memory of a source in which messengers and the events in the Wash had been connected as causes of the King's decline? There is more than a hint in this that we have, not two independent stories of these events, but only one.

At all events, the Coggeshall chronicler presents a disaster on a much more modest scale. According to him, the King lost "his Chapel with its relics, and some of his pack-horses with divers household goods." "Many of his *familia* were drowned in the sea and sucked into the quicksand" because they had tried to cross "carelessly and too soon, before the tide had receded."[12] This is very different from the bottomless whirlpools of Wendover's fanciful imagination, and from the picture which St. John Hope accepted of the

---

[6] *Chron. Maj.*, ii, 667.

[7] *Historia Anglorum*, ed. F. Madden (Rolls Series), ii, 190.

[8] *Loc. cit.*, pp. 6–7. On the general value of these writers see V. H. Galbraith, *Roger Wendover and Matthew Paris* (Glasgow, 1944).

[9] *Chronicon Anglicanum R. de Coggeshall*, ed. J. Stevenson (Rolls Series), pp. 183–4. The evidence points to a common source rather than direct derivation because the St. Albans writers did not get the whole Coggeshall story. See below, pp. 121-2.

[10] "In vivo sabulone" (Coggeshall). Cf. "et sabulo qui vivus dicitur" (Paris).

[11] Cf. Wendover, "nec pes unus evasit qui casum regi nuntiaret" with Coggeshall, "Huc ergo cum venissent nuncii inclusorum castri Doverae et intimassent causam adventus sui" (*Coggeshall*, pp. 183–4).

[12] *Loc. cit.*, pp. 183–4.

engulfment of a baggage train two miles long.[13]   Moreover, even this modest
sketch may contain exaggeration and distortion. Like Wendover, the
Coggeshall writer wanted to make his disaster properly disastrous.

As Fowler has shown, St. John Hope's assumptions about the size of the
baggage train are unwarranted and unsound.[14]   King John travelled light,
with a household in which traditional offices were designed for a life of movement; the kitchen and buttery with its carters, the bearer of the King's Bed,
the tent-keeper, the napier, and the scullions, for example, each with his
pack-horse.[15]   In John's time the Wardrobe seems to have included a permanent
staff of five pack-horse men and several carters, two in 1209, four in 1212[16];
it was transported on "long" carts, a type of vehicle to which two men and
four or five horses seem normally to have been allotted.[17]   Other household
officers also had their carts; there was even a special one for the King's venison.[18]
At times the Wardrobe carters were reinforced.   Sometimes much of the work
was done by hiring small two-horse carts to meet special requirements; the
column which left King's Lynn may well have been increased in this way.
Hence it is impossible to estimate the number of vehicles and pack-horses
which were with the King on any one particular journey.   But modern authorities have concurred in assuming that the records convey an accurate impression
of the numbers involved, that where numbers are stated they cover all the
vehicles in use for a particular purpose at a particular time.   If this is so,
the "harness" and money of the Wardrobe might at times be carried in one
two-horse cart, or in one or two long carts.   In time of war more vehicles
must have been needed to carry arms and cash; sometimes four and even
seven carts operated together; but we must still imagine the resulting column
as a small one.[19]   Lady Stenton considers that the King's Chapel in John's
time was still carried on two pack-horses just as it had been carried two or
three generations earlier.[20]   In some respects government was still very personal
and still comparatively primitive.

The baggage train normally travelled with the King; this, indeed, was its
raison d'être. Sometimes part of the train might be immobilized and its
contents stored in some safe place, but this only points to the need to keep
the remainder moving efficiently.   Indeed, when the movements of the

[13] *Loc. cit.*, p. 104.
[14] *Loc. cit.*, pp. 8–9.
[15] Constitutio Domus Regis in *Dialogus de Scaccario*, ed. Charles Johnson, pp. 132, 133, 135.
[16] *Rot. Liberate*, pp. 118, 122, 128, 135, 159; *Documents Illustrative of English History in the thirteenth and fourteenth centuries*, ed. H. Cole (London, 1844), pp. 231, 233, 236, 259, 260.   These men also served the Chamber, from which, as yet the Wardrobe was but narrowly separated.   See T. F. Tout, *Chapters in Administrative History*, i, 167–9.
[17] See, for example, *Pipe Roll 13 John*, p. 44; *Documents Illustrative of English History*, pp. 242, 243, 248, 249.
[18] *Pipe Roll 11 John*, p. 27.
[19] See, in particular, T. F. Tout, *op. cit.*, i, 164–9 and J. E. A. Jolliffe, *Angevin Kingship*, p. 141.
[20] *English Society in the Early Middle Ages*, p. 22.

household baggage can be followed in detail, as, for example, when vehicles were hired, they usually tally exactly with the movements of the King. One such instance may be taken from June and July 1212, when, prior to a progress through the northern counties, the King left two of the Wardrobe carts at Kingshaugh on 10 June.[21] On the same day, one two-horse cart was hired to carry the tackle and money of the Wardrobe as the King journeyed north. The hire was paid at regular intervals, usually of two or three days, until the cart was finally discharged at Nottingham on 5 July. The cart's itinerary did not deviate at all from the itinerary of the King; it even accompanied him to the hunting lodges of Inglewood. Although the record does not make it absolutely clear that it always kept up with him, it certainly did so for most of the journey and there is no evidence that it fell behind at any point; it went from Bowes to Appleby in a day.[22]

All this was in time of peace. In time of war, in an area like the Fenland which was predominantly rebel in sympathy and where travel by road was difficult, there would be powerful reasons for keeping an undivided column. The army could not be separated from its supplies; government could not be separated from its impedimenta; the King, especially, was unlikely to let such of his regalia, money and precious movables as he had with him, far from his sight. In 1216 only some great urgency could have created the kind of separation which St. John Hope imagines between the King and his army, on the one hand, and the baggage train and treasure, on the other. There is no evidence for such an explanation of the King's visit to Wisbech on 12 October.

Indeed, there is some evidence that part of the usual baggage train must have accompanied the King, in that our knowledge of the visit to Wisbech is drawn entirely from attestations of royal letters. One enrolled letter close and two enrolled letters patent, one of which was made out in octuple form, were dated at Wisbech on 12 October.[23] Our knowledge of the detail of Chancery practice at this time is incomplete. Nevertheless, such a dating would normally imply that these letters were authorized at Wisbech on the 12th, and they may well also have been engrossed and sealed there. If this is so, then John must certainly have had some members of his writing office with him on this journey. Now these men would be drawn from the clerks of his Chapel, and, according to the Coggeshall writer, the Chapel was involved in the disaster. In this passage he was probably thinking of vestments, consecrated vessels and the like, for he goes on immediately to speak of relics, but, even so, those who manned the writing office and those who had charge of the King's Chapel were drawn from one and the same body. Thus there is evidence, albeit tenuous and fragile, which links part of the paraphernalia and personnel

---

[21] Rotulus misae 14 John, printed in *Documents Illustrative of English History*, p. 233. For the expenses of the carters and horses at Kingshaugh and later at Nottingham see *ibid.*, p. 248.

[22] *Ibid.*, pp. 233–5.

[23] *Rot. Litt. Claus.*, i, 291; *Rot. Litt. Pat.*, p. 199.

of government with John's journey to Wisbech. Moreover, the department concerned was identical, or closely related, to one stated to have been involved in the disaster. In view of this and the complete absence of any documentary or literary support for St. John Hope's hypothesis, we must assume that the royal army and its train were never divided, that they followed not two separate routes, but only one. On this basis, I shall first try to establish both the time and site of the disaster.

All indications are that the disaster had already occurred before Wisbech was reached. The strongest argument for this lies in the timing of the King's movements. On 11 and 12 October he only travelled 13 to 15 miles between Lynn and Wisbech. On the 12th itself he covered 40 miles or so between Wisbech and Swineshead.[24] Now it is reasonable to assume that some kind of disaster, with the resulting rearrangement of baggage and attempts at salvage, could have occurred during the first part of the journey, but, if it occurred after the King left Wisbech, it is very doubtful whether he could have reached Swineshead on the same day. The most likely hypothesis is that John left Lynn on the morning of the 11th, that he suffered the accident within an hour or so of low tide (11.15 a.m.),[25] that he stayed the night of the 11th at Wisbech, and that he set off again in the morning to take advantage of low tide (12 noon) on the 12th.

This receives some support from one of the letters patent dated at Wisbech. This consisted of a safe-conduct, covering the eight days beginning on 14 October, to one Ralf son of Walter and his ship which was taking the "goods and merchandise" of the King to Grimsby. Similar letters were authorized for seven other men and their vessels.[26] In brief, the King arranged at Wisbech to send a small fleet loaded with his possessions to Grimsby. Now there is no evidence that this fleet started from Wisbech; in fact, its point of departure is not mentioned; and there is nothing to establish the identity and provenance of any of the shipmen concerned.[27] Moreover, the two-day delay until the 14th May have been arranged so that the letters could be sent to the port in question. But it is not altogether easy to regard this business as routine, occurring as it did at a critical point and time in the King's journey. He had

[24] There are slight discrepancies between my milages and Fowler's. My calculations are based on a route from Wisbech to Swineshead via Spalding. Doubt as to the detailed route followed makes exact calculations impossible.

[25] I am following the tide tables given by St. John Hope (*loc. cit.*, p. 105).

[26] *Rot. Litt. Pat.*, p. 199. The phrase is "res et mercandise . . . nostre." The seven other recipients were Godfrey le Pohier, Osbert son of Walter, Benedict and Thomas de Beautr', William Alemannus, Reginald But and John son of Alan.

[27] Such indications as there are, however, point to Lincolnshire. In 1219 a Ralf son of Walter was a party to an action concerning property in Lincoln (*Rolls of the Justices in Eyre for Lincs. and Worcs.*, Selden Society, liii, case 816); a Reginald Buch' had property in Mablethorpe in the early thirteenth century (*Registrum Antiquissimum of the Cathedral Church of Lincoln*, vi, Lincoln Record Society, xli, 31–2); Alan son of Alan and John son of Alan had property in Boston in 1203 (*The Earliest Lincolnshire Assize Rolls*, Lincoln Record Society, vol. 22, cases 1252, 1290); a confirmation by King John of the possessions of the canons of Grimsby included a toft in Grimsby which had been given by a Hugh de Bautr' (*Rot. Chartarum*, p. 94).

just left Lynn, one of the greatest ports in the country, inferior only to London, Boston and Southampton.[28] Wisbech, by comparison, was little more than a fishing port, accessible only up a long and probably treacherous estuary. Lynn, not Wisbech, was the obvious place to arrange for the hire of ships and to buy and accumulate "goods and merchandise." Indeed, the purchase of winter supplies seems to have been one of the King's objectives in visiting Lynn, for while there he provided safe-conducts for victuals and wine which were dispatched to Philip Mark, sheriff of Nottingham, for the provisioning of Nottingham castle, and also arranged for the dispatch of "merchandise" of his own to Lincoln.[29] Thus much routine business of this kind had been completed before the King left Lynn.

There are grounds, therefore, for seeking some emergency behind the safe-conducts arranged at Wisbech on the 12th. They carry the scent of the disaster, for among the King's losses noted by Coggeshall were pack-horses. Baggage could be salvaged where pack-horses would drown, and, if the King was suddenly faced with a surplus of baggage over pack-horses, sea-transport was the obvious alternative. Thus the Wisbech writs can be viewed as a direct result of the disaster. They become part of a reconstruction into which the timing of the King's movements and the story of the Coggeshall writer also fit. This involves one new assumption, namely that the King himself intended to move north to Grimsby, or at least to its hinterland. This is not unreasonable. He had just travelled south from this area to Lynn and was certainly marching rapidly north into Lincolnshire once more when approaching death came to affect his movements.

The place of the disaster is a more complex and debatable issue. The chroniclers agree that it occurred in crossing the Wellstream.[30] This ran north through Wisbech to a broad estuary and, in 1216, carried the waters of all the major rivers of the Fenland, except the Welland and part of the Nene, the latter of which drained into the Wellstream estuary at Tydd Gote.[31] At Wisbech the sea banks confining the river were approximately a quarter of a mile apart, but the stream itself was normally only 40 yards wide[32]; at its mouth between Sutton and Cross Keys the estuary was nearly 5 miles wide. St. John Hope placed the accident at the widest point. Fowler, in contrast

---

[28] See *Pipe Roll 6 John*, pp. xliii–iv.
[29] *Rot. Litt. Pat.*, p. 199; *Rot. Litt. Claus.*, i, 291.
[30] *Coggeshall*, p. 184; *Chron. Maj.*, ii, 667; *Hist. Anglorum*, ii, 190. It was not until 1607 that Fosdyke, at the mouth of the Welland, was suggested as a site in the folio edition of Camden's *Britannia*. Sir Frederic Madden confused the Wellstream with the Welland (*Hist. Anglorum*, ii, 190); Miss Kate Norgate appears to have done the same (*John Lackland*, p. 282). This confusion existed earlier, for the 1607 edition of Camden centred the disaster at Fosdyle (*sic*) *and* the Wellstream (*Britannia*, London, 1607, p. 398).
[31] See the map, p. 76. This is largely based on Fowler's maps, the most useful of which is in *A Guide to Wicken Fen* (National Trust, 1947), p. 6. See also his map in *loc. cit.*, p. 11, and H. C. Darby, *The Medieval Fenland* (Cambridge, 1940), pp. 95–7. For a good impression of the estuary in the seventeenth century see Blaew's map of 1645 reproduced in W. H. Wheeler, *The Fens of South Lincolnshire*, p. 101.
[32] Gordon Fowler, *loc. cit.*, pp. 12–13.

placed it at the narrowest, between Walsoken and Wisbech itself.[33]   Although St. John Hope's case depended on unwarranted assumptions about the size of the column and the extent of the disaster, it is probable that he is nearer to the truth than is Fowler.

Fowler's case here was based on several points. First, he assumed that Wisbech lay on the usual route across the Fens. Secondly, he argued that the quicksands which figure in the chronicle stories could not be found in the lower reaches of the estuary. Finally he suggested that the disaster was caused by a tidal bore or eagre in the narrower part of the river.[34]   Much of this is unacceptable. Coggeshall clearly states that the disaster occurred, not because of an incoming tide, but because the tide had not yet receded. There is no sound reason for reversing his evidence at this point. The quicksands of contemporary narratives can also be confirmed. Drilling in the estuary, carried out under the direction of Professor W. D. Evans for objectives unconnected with King John, has revealed a thick layer of wet quicksand at mediaeval levels on or near the possible line of a natural causeway. Finally, there is no evidence to confirm that Wisbech lay on the normal route across the Fens in the early thirteenth century. King John had made the crossing in the opposite direction twice before, in 1205 and on 9 October, 1216. There is nothing to show that he passed through Wisbech on either occasion, or, indeed, that he had ever visited the place earlier in his reign. The Gough map of the fourteenth century makes no mention of Wisbech, but it names Fosdyke and Walpole, thus suggesting that these were then points of note on the route, perhaps even the sites of river crossings.[35]   The crossing cannot have been easy; if it had been, there would have been no accident; but it was probably better to tackle it where the waters spread out over sandy flats rather than at the point where they flowed deeper and faster within narrower confines. The estuary crossing would shorten the journey considerably; it was certainly used in the seventeenth century;[36] it had a parallel in the north-west of England in the similar passage over the Kent estuary.

The case for the estuary route is strengthened by the probable condition in 1216 of the west bank of the Wellstream from Wisbech to Sutton. Both St. John Hope and Fowler assumed that this provided an easy passage, but, in fact, the direct road between Wisbech and the villages of Holland must have been very difficult, for it involved the crossing of the western branch of the Nene, which flowed into the Wellstream at Tydd Gote.[37]   The Nene here was

---

[33] *Loc. cit.*, p. 13.   The suggestion was made earlier by F. J. Gardiner, *History of Wisbech* (Wisbech, 1898), pp. 5–6.   Cf. also N. Walker and T. Craddock, *The History of Wisbech and the Fens* (Wisbech, 1849), pp. 211–3.
[34] *Loc. cit.*, pp. 14–7.
[35] See Lady Stenton in *Medieval England*, ed. A. L. Poole (Oxford, 1958), i, 201–2.
[36] See the evidence presented by St. John Hope, *loc. cit.*, pp. 102–3.
[37] For the line of the Nene, or South Eau, see H. E. Hallam, *The New Lands of Elloe* (University College of Leicester, 1954), frontispiece, and the Ordnance Survey 1/25,000 maps of the area.

a navigable river which formed the boundary between Holland and Cambridge-shire; it was linked to the Welland at the famous triangular bridge at Crowland and to a second branch of the Nene near Peterborough,[38] which in turn connected it to the central rivers of the Fenland; it was one of the most important water-ways of the area.[39] In Dugdale's day it ended in a wide reach stretching from Tydd Gote upstream to the entry of the New Fen Dyke at Grange Hill Corner.[40] In mediaeval times it was bridged near Tydd St. Giles,[41] but it ran here through very low lying country. Leverington, Newton, and possibly also Tydd St. Giles, seem to have been established only in the course of the twelfth century.[42] The fen was being rapidly reclaimed on both sides of the river. Nevertheless, Asgardyke and New Fen Dyke were not made until John's time and may still have been under construction when war broke out in 1215.[43] The hamlets of Whaplode Drove, Holbeach Drove, Gedney Hill and Sutton St. Edmund, on the Lincolnshire side, and Parson Drove, on the Cambridgeshire side, were probably not yet in existence,[44] and the whole area, including Wisbech itself, lay under an ever-present threat of flooding.[45] Thus the Wisbech route presented not one, but two hazards, first the passage of the Wellstream at Wisbech itself, and secondly, the passage of the Nene and the   fenland which lay on both sides of it. It was in avoiding the latter that the chief advantage of the estuary route probably lay, for, in so far as there is any indication of its line, it ran from near Walpole, the point named on the Gough map, to somewhere north of Tydd Gote.[45a]

The most likely hypothesis on the present evidence is that on 11 October John's column met with an accident caused by an over-confident and hasty attempt to cross the Wellstream before low-tide; that this occurred on the route across the estuary from Walpole and that it necessitated a diversion to Wisbech, and perhaps subsequently to the alternative route through Wisbech, in order to rearrange the baggage and send some by sea.

What was lost? The only reasonably certain answer lies in the evidence of the Coggeshall writer and the implications of the Wisbech safe-conducts, that the King lost a number of his pack-horses. As it is unlikely that all their

---

[38] *Cartularium Monasterii de Rameseia*, ed. W. H. Hart and P. A. Lyons (Rolls Series), iii, 139–140, 143–144.
[39] See *ibid.*, iii, 144, for its use as a passage from Crowland to King's Lynn. The con-nections of these rivers are clearly represented on the Gough map, which, of course, refers to a later situation in which the outflow of the Wellstream had been diverted at Outwell to King's Lynn.
[40] *History of Imbanking and Draining* (2nd edn., London, 1772), map facing p. 218.
[41] H. C. Darby, *op. cit.*, p. 74, n. 2.
[42] H. C. Darby, *Domesday Geography of Eastern England*, pp. 269–72. Cf. *The Place-Names of Cambridgeshire* (EPNS, xix), pp. 271, 274, 283.
[43] H. E. Hallam, *op. cit.*, pp. 31–4. For similar activity on the Cambridgeshire side see Edward Miller, *The Abbey and Bishopric of Ely* (Cambridge, 1951), p. 289.
[44] Hallam, *op. cit.*, pp. 34–40; *The Place-Names of Cambridgeshire*, p. 277.
[45] *Cart. Rameseia*, iii, 139–40, 143–4; Dugdale, *op. cit.*, p. 299; N. Walker and T. Craddock, *op. cit.*, p. 214. See also in general, H. C. Darby, *op. cit.*, pp. 94–7, 55–60, 113–4, 151.
[45a] I am indebted to Professor W. D. Evans for this information.

loads would be salvaged, we may also accept the Coggeshall writer's inclusion of household goods, among which the Chapel and the relics would deserve special mention.   In such a disaster, members of the household staff may also have been lost, but, if so, they must have been insignificant, because no casualty was, or can now be, given a name.   Similarly, the loss of the Chapel did not involve the clerks who enrolled the King's letters.   A batch of letters patent covering 11 to 15 October was entered on the roll at Sleaford or Newark sometime after the 15th by the clerk who had been chiefly responsible throughout the year for keeping the roll up to date.[46]   Thus the evidence of the patent roll points to "business as usual."   The close roll is not quite so discouraging. Here a block of entries dated the 12th at Wisbech and Swineshead was entered on the roll by a clerk who had not apparently worked on it before.   But any possibility that the clerk usually in charge had been drowned is removed by the fact that later entries on the roll are the work of the scribe responsible for previous entries dated the 11th at Lynn and for many of the entries on the earlier part of the membrane.[47]   Thus the clerks responsible for the rolls survived and so did the rolls themselves.   These, indeed, are the only material we have which must have crossed the Wash on the King's last journey.   All four chancery enrolments, close, patent, charter, and fine, have come down to us in good order along with the duplicate copies.   There is some slight staining in the margin of Close Roll no. 14, but none of the other rolls show any sign of a wetting; the waters of the Wellstream never reached the panniers or chests in which they were carried.   Even individual letters survived, for at Newark, on or after the 18th, a letter dated the 11th at Lynn, which must have come through the journey as a draft, copy or minute, was entered on the roll.[48]   If the Chapel was lost in the disaster, as the Coggeshall writer states, it may well have been because the administrator in the royal clerk led him to think first of saving records rather than relics.

The Coggeshall chronicle mentions no precious goods apart from the Chapel and the relics.   Wendover also may have been thinking of consecrated vessels, but spoke more loosely of "treasures, precious vessels and everything which he loved with special care."[49]   Matthew Paris, not to be outdone, threw in *all* the treasure.[50]   Even in these narratives there is no specific mention of jewels or regalia, and, indeed, there is no direct evidence in any surviving source that the regalia or a collection of royal jewels were in any way involved. The absence of any mention of the regalia is especially significant in view of the Coggeshall reference to the Chapel and relics and Wendover's reference to precious vessels; so important a loss would probably also have been noted.

---

[46] Public Record Office, Patent Roll no. 15 (18 John), m.1.
[47] P.R.O., Close Roll no. 14 (18 John, part 1), m.1.
[48] Patent Roll no. 15, m.1.; *Rot. Litt. Pat.*, p. 199b.
[49] "cum thesauris, vasis pretiosis, et rebus omnibus, quas propensiori cura dilexit" *Chron. Maj.*, ii, 667).
[50] "omnem thesaurum" (*Hist. Anglorum*, ii, 190).

The only hint that the regalia may have been lost in the Wash lies in the fact that much of John's regalia never descended to his son.[51] But this permits no conclusive arguments, for it could well have suffered other fates. During the civil war John borrowed considerable sums from the Templars and from the citizens of Bordeaux and Ghent, and the regalia may well have been used as security. John had called in the Empress Matilda's regalia from its repository as early as May 1215, a great collection of plate in July 1215, and his own regalia last, in March and April 1216, at a critical point of the war.[52] It is as if he felt that his own regalia was the ultimate financial sacrifice. In June 1216 Hubert de Burgh was ordered to use the plate at Dover castle to pay the King's troops there,[53] and there is no reason to think that John acted differently with the plate in his own hands. By the summer of 1216 he was in dire financial need. In these circumstances, regalia, jewelry, plate, could leave the King's possession and vanish from record only too easily.

In the last resort the inclusion of treasure among the King's losses depends on the credibility of the St. Albans writers. Wendover clearly imagined that treasure, in the modern sense of the word, was lost. Matthew Paris creates a rather different picture, for he used the word in the singular and probably more usual contemporary sense to denote the contents of a treasury, namely, the financial resources, perhaps including plate, but consisting mainly of cash, which the King carried with him. These stories are best set beside an order which John made within a week of the accident. On 18 October he sent a force of 300 Welsh mercenaries to one of his commanders, Savaric de Mauleon, with instructions that their pay and arrears had been fully met up to and including 21 October and that Savaric was to see to their pay thereafter.[54] The pay of these men must have totalled at least £2 10s. per day.[55] It is possible that John had replenished his money chests since the 12th; if so, the source is not obvious for he had not visited any of the usual castle treasuries. In any case, this was scarcely the act of one who had just suffered financial ruin.

It is probable that the St. Albans references to treasure were simply decorations to a story the main elements of which these writers got at second hand. There is also another possibility. The accident probably occurred on 11 October. King John died at Newark during the night of the 18th. Once dead, he was robbed, like his father before him, by the members of his household, who looted his goods and left his body without decent covering.[56]

---

[51] See Lady Jenkinson's paper "The Jewels lost in the Wash" in *History*, viii (1923). 161, 168. A few items survived at Corfe; see *ibid.*, 167 and *Patent Rolls 1216–1225*, p. 321, [52] Lady Jenkinson, *loc. cit.*, pp. 163–5. See also *Rot. Litt. Pat.*, p. 174.
[53] *Rot. Litt. Claus.*, i, 274b.
[54] *Rot. Litt. Claus.*, i, 291b.
[55] They were normally paid 2d. a day; a few got double that sum (*Documents Illustrative of English History*, p. 260).
[56] For the robbery of Henry II see *Histoire de Guillaume le Maréchal*, ed. P. Meyer (Paris, 1891), ll, 9127–9143, and Gerald of Wales, De Principis Instructione, *Opera*, ed. G. F. Warner (Rolls Series), viii, 304.

All this was told to the Coggeshall writer by a clerk who met these men loaded with their booty as he entered Newark and who went to keep watch by the dead King's body and say mass for his soul.[57] For the men who did this deed the accident a week earlier must have been providentially convenient. If they now began to spread the story that the King had lost much more than in fact he had, they would not be the first or last to use the accidents of war to cover their own acquisitive misdeeds. Is it not axiomatic among soldiers that the transport destroyed by shell, mine or bomb, or indeed lost in some other way, is always the one which happened to be carrying the more desirable and valuable equipment? The story of John's treasure has roused human greed;[58] it could equally well have been a product of it. It is significant that the Coggeshall writer, who gives a restrained story of the accident, also knew of the robbery. The St. Albans writers, in contrast, who are the only ones to write of treasure, reveal no knowledge of the robbery. It is possible that, as unwitting accessories, they have foisted on later generations a tale of lost treasure first conceived by the jackals who surrounded John's bed as he lay dying in Newark castle.

[57] *Coggeshall*, p. 184.
[58] For some of the treasure hunts see Fowler, *loc. cit.*, pp. 4-5.

6

THE ORIGINS OF MAGNA CARTA

INTRODUCTION

Magna Carta was achieved by rebellion. The rebels
were not revolutionaries. Most of them were nobles;
they had no plan and made no attempt to subvert the
accepted social order. They were rather the recalcitrant, the dissatisfied, and the rejected—men who had
lost favour and fortune or who had struggled in vain to
achieve them, men with real or imagined personal
wrongs who now sought restitution from the King and
vengeance on his agents. Yet their work endured in the
Great Charter. That it did so is partly a story of other
men and later centuries. But it also sprang from the
nature of the rebellion, caused by the accumulation, as
much as the abuse, of royal power. It was directed not
only against a ruler, King John, but also against his
methods of government. Hence the rebels produced a
constitutional programme, a charter of governmental
reform. They had a strong case, one which gained
support from a wider social range than the baronial

ranks from which the rebel leaders came, one which was acknowledged by their opponents in the reissues of the Charter in 1216 and 1217. And they owed much to circumstances. This happened at a time when men were coming to think about law in a logical and sophisticated manner and when the English legal system was acquiring some of its characteristic fundamental features. This is why, in 1215, a rebellion of feudal magnates produced Magna Carta.

REBELLION IN FEUDAL ENGLAND

Rebellion in itself was an easy enough course. By twelfth-century standards England was a peaceful and orderly realm. Nevertheless, force lay only a little below the surface of everyday life and erupted frequently in the form of distraint and self-help in legal actions or of resistance to the sheriff and his bailiffs in the execution of their duties. The rebel received sufficient social adulation to provide heroes for thirteenth-century romances like *Eustace the Monk* and *Fulk fitz Warin*. Rebellion incurred little social stigma. King John himself had earlier rebelled against his brother Richard I, and both Richard and John had rebelled against their father, Henry II; if John's reputation had suffered through this, it was because his rebellion was considered treacherous. But rebellion did not necessarily seem so. Governments watched for and even expected it, especially during long absences of the king abroad or in the interval of diminished sovereignty between the death of one king and the coronation of another.[1] The feudal ties which bound the upper ranks

[1] For disturbances at the accession of Stephen, see *Gesta Stephani*, ed. K. R. Potter (London, 1955), pp. 1-4. For

of society made room for it through the formal process of defiance and renunciation of homage. It was by such a process that the barons declared war on King John in May 1215.

Whether the country suffered civil war or not depended on the political behaviour of the aristocracy, on the ambitions and reactions of a few dozen great families. Much of a king's concern and function was to cajole, bribe, bully, and discipline these powerful vassals. Much of their interest lay in the privileges, offices, and expectations which the royal favour brought, or in the evasion of the punishments, losses, and denials which followed inexorably on the enmity of the king. Few families managed to avoid this alternating state of enthusiasm and disenchantment; it made up one of the great themes of the epic minstrelsy which their households maintained.

No king could ignore his primary task of man management. Yet no king was able to perform it perfectly. Even the best could only distribute rough justice between the satisfaction of aristocratic interest and the need to preserve efficient government. The reign of Edward I was the first not seriously affected by civil war. Prior to that, neither the weak nor the strong, the capable nor the inept, avoided rebellion. It was an experience shared by Rufus and Henry III, by the Conqueror and Stephen, by

---

measures taken for the defence and preservation of the peace of the realm on the death of Richard I, see *Pipe Roll 1 John,* pp. xiii-xv; *Chronica Magistri Rogeri de Hovedene,* ed. W. Stubbs (Rolls series, 1868-71), IV, 88-92 (hereinafter cited as *Hoveden*).

It was not until the accession of Edward I, who was in Sicily when his father died in 1272, that the king's reign and authority antedated his coronation.

Henry I, "the Lion of Justice," and by John, who was soon reputed to be the cruellest and most tyrannical of English kings.

These aristocratic outbreaks make up much of what we know of the political history of England in the middle ages. Even so it is both inaccurate and unilluminating to interpret them as manifestations of a protracted, intermittent conflict of king *versus* barons. Kings and nobles ruled the realm in concert. They were mutually indispensable. No aristocratic rebels were republican; kings offended by adding to rather than by destroying the nobility. Rebellion was not a clash of constitutionally opposed forces, but a result of disturbed relationships within the ruling establishment, of feuds between families, even of squabbles within a single family, most likely of all within the royal family. Rebellions were organised and fought, not by a united baronage, but by factions, by small but troublesome minorities. Even in 1215, when revolt ran deeply through the feudal structure of the realm, the initial outbreak was the work of a few dozen men whose power was confined to the eastern and northern counties; some of the greatest nobles in the land, like the earls of Pembroke and Chester, remained loyal to John throughout.[2] Rebellion was not revolution. Rebel and loyalist might not be sharply divided by issues of principle. Their aims rarely went beyond those attainable through influence at court and the favour of

[2] Many more of the baronage were in rebellion when John died in 1216. By then the invasion of Prince Louis of France had increased the rebels' chances of success. For discussions of the rebel party and the proportion in rebellion, see F. M. Powicke, *Stephen Langton* (Oxford, 1928), pp. 207-12; Sidney Painter, *The Reign of King John* (Baltimore, 1949), pp. 286-99; J. C. Holt, *The Northerners* (Oxford, 1961), pp. 17-34.

the king. Civil war was often the continuation of political intrigue by other means.

Yet rebellion was a venture. The ties of a feudal society forced rebels into breaking the fealty which they owed to their lord. As time passed, the contrast between rebellion and civil peace was sharpened by the emergence of sophisticated doctrines of royal sovereignty and kingly majesty. Psychologically, rebellion became increasingly difficult. It also faced increasingly serious practical hazards as military techniques became more costly. Hence something more than personal ambition was necessary to drive men into rebellion, and something wider than the satisfaction of individual wrongs was essential if a programme of rebellion was to achieve success.

The more successful and dangerous rebellions occurred in contexts which supplied the rebels with broader motives and more general arguments than those which might arise from spontaneous discontents within the ruling establishment. Godwin's movement against Edward the Confessor in the eleventh century was concerned with French infiltration into English society; most of the rebellions against the Norman kings were concerned with the relationships between England and Normandy; the rebellion of Henry II's sons in 1173–74 was concerned with the control and descent of the various Angevin territories; and the growing hostility to Angevin government which culminated in the rebellion of 1215 was related to the manner in which the Angevin kings exploited England in order to maintain their possessions on the continent. In this last instance especially, a rebellion within the aristocratic establishment, which arose from a quarrel between the King and certain of his tenants, came to involve the relationships between

Crown and baronage, even between the Crown and all free subjects, and to affect the general capacities of the Crown within the political structure of the realm.

Although the rebellion of 1215 was not part of a general conflict of king *versus* barons or Crown *versus* subject, it nevertheless aimed at and achieved some of the heights which commanded such a field of conflict; although the rebels scarcely imagined any kind of inevitable and head-on opposition of royal and aristocratic interests, they were quite sure that the king as a feudal lord had certain rights and equally sure that his subjects as feudal tenants also had rights. About the definition of these respective rights there might well be argument and contention. This in fact was the nub of the quarrel.

The rebellion of 1215 presents two obvious aspects to the historian. First, it was an aristocratic disturbance of a type inseparable from the political and social structure of the Ancien Régime. It was a civil war caused by King John's failure to manage the great noble families, a failure which not only caused the war but also largely determined who would be loyal and who would rebel. Secondly, it was concerned with broader questions of royal rights, provoked by the continued demands of war abroad and by the development of law at home. It was from these contexts that the rebels derived their assumptions and drew their public arguments and policies, the means whereby they generalized their personal complaints and demands. These were two aspects of the same human actions, two facets of the same movement. Without the impetus provided by personal wrong there would have been no rebellion. Without the experience of the legal and political context of the government of the Angevin kings, that rebellion would not have produced Magna Carta.

THE GOVERNMENT OF KING JOHN

In both its aspects, the rebellion was intimately concerned with the character and actions of King John, for he was at once the personal lord whom the rebels now denied and the representative of the Crown whose policies and powers they set out to limit. Much of the fable of John's evil genius is derived from an anachronistic use of hostile narrative sources, chief among which were the two St. Albans chroniclers, Roger of Wendover and Matthew Paris.[3] Most of these sources suffer from being written in the early years of Henry III or even later, after John had met defeat and disgrace and ended his days in a land rent by civil war. On the other hand, the evidence of government records, which has done much to revive John's reputation, poses its own problems, since the extent of John's personal responsibility for the efficient development of his government is still far from clear.

Despite these contrasting difficulties, it is clear that certain features of John's rule were likely to provoke rebellion. He was extremely energetic. He patrolled his kingdom incessantly. From 1204 onwards, unlike his predecessors, he was almost continuously resident in England. He took an active interest in government, in the maintenance of royal rights, and in the operations of the Exchequer and the courts of law. Royal administration in his reign bore an increasingly personal stamp, in the increased use of the privy seal, of the Wardrobe and Chamber as major financial offices, and in the promotion

[3] For a criticism of these writers, see V. H. Galbraith, *Roger Wendover and Matthew Paris* (Glasgow, 1944).

of men who had learned their trade as administrators in John's own household. John was a real power in the land; among medieval kings his administrative capacity was exceptional, comparable to his father's (Henry II) or his grandson's (Edward I). Yet even at his best, his character was heated and strident, his methods too clever, his will ruthless. He obtained loyalty, but not through powers of leadership or a capacity to inspire it. He was mercurial and unreliable. He was an educated man by the standards of contemporary lay society. Some contemporary traditions suggest that he jested on the wrong occasions at the wrong targets.[4] He was a driving force, not a steadying influence.

In one important respect John failed to meet what men required of kings. He was not a successful warrior. He was effective and ruthless with the odds on his side, but he failed in his major campaigns in France. In 1204 he lost Normandy, the origin of Norman power in England, the homeland of the Norman aristocracy. "Shame upon a conquered king," Henry II had cried on his deathbed.[5] Henry II was spared defeat until his final years. John carried defeat with him throughout most of his reign. By 1204 he had acquired the name "Softsword."[6] This was to damn any medieval king.[7]

[4] See the stories of impolitic levity retailed in *Magna Vita Sancti Hugonis,* ed. Decima L. Douie and Hugh Farmer (London, 1962), II, 142-44.

[5] Thus according to Gerald of Wales, who was an eyewitness. See *Giraldi Cambrensis opera,* ed. G. R. Warner (Rolls Series, 1891), VIII, 297.

[6] *The Historical Works of Gervase of Canterbury,* ed. W. Stubbs (Rolls Series, 1880), II, 92-93.

[7] For the best short account of John's character, see A. L. Poole, *From Domesday Book to Magna Carta* (2d ed.; Oxford, 1955), pp. 425-58, and for a discussion of the evidence,

John had no personal mystique on which the loyalty of his tenants might be nurtured. However, he had a genius for politics, a keen insight into men's behaviour, an ultrasensitive suspicion of their motives, and a sure touch in manipulating royal patronage. Increasingly as his reign wore on, he sought to win loyalty by the distribution of rewards—by appropriate grants of land, office, privilege, wardships, marriages, and various financial benefits—or tried to enforce it by the imposition of heavy monetary penalties, by the denial of royal favour, by the exaction of pledges and guaranties, and by the threat or fact of dispossession, disinheritance, imprisonment, outlawry, or exile. These contrasting methods were traditional instruments of royal policy. John used them enthusiastically, and often with great cleverness. But he used them too frequently, too obviously, as if drawn to one pole or the other. As a result he divided the baronage against itself. Those in the royal favour and those out were more and more sharply distinguished one from another. By the same process he confused loyalty with subservience and converted the conventional ties of a feudal society into instruments of political discipline. Homage and fealty were diminished to the

---

see J. C. Holt, *King John* (Above, 85-109). Stubbs is the outstanding critic of John among the older school of writers. His most anachronistic and hostile assessment is to be found, curiously enough, in his introduction to the chronicle that comes closest to defending John's character and reputation. See *Memoriale fratris Walteri de Coventria,* ed. W. Stubbs (Rolls series, 1872-73), II, xi-xix. Kate Norgate's biography, *John Lackland* (London, 1902), is a scholarly work which still repays attention. W. L. Warren's *King John* (New York, 1961) presents a lively account, incorporating much recent work, but is unreliable.

level of a political bargain. John weakened social bonds
by distorting them. He drove both himself and his
opponents into civil war by revealing the reality of force
behind convention. This was to appeal to force and to
encourage others to do the same.

Such methods of government were often very successful. From the accession of John to the winter of
1204-5 Ranulf, Earl of Chester, was among John's most
dangerous and suspect vassals. A lord of tremendous
territorial power both in England and Normandy, he
was among those who tried to bargain for their loyalty
at John's accession; he was closely associated with some
of John's Norman rebels; he opposed the King's policies
in Wales and came close to open rebellion in December
1204, with the result that John ordered the seizure of his
estates. From 1205 onwards, in contrast, he was one of
the most loyal supporters of John's regime, and one of
those who ensured the succession of Henry III in 1216.
This *volte-face* is readily explicable, for in March 1205
John largely acknowledged Ranulf's claims to the possession of the great lordship of Richmond.[8] This marked
the accession of Ranulf into the King's favour. John's
thinking can only be guessed. He may have decided that
Ranulf was too dangerous an enemy. It is also significant that Robert de Beaumont, Earl of Leicester, had
died in 1204; this left a vacuum in the Midlands which
Ranulf could conveniently fill and removed the last direct

---

[8] Ranulf was the second husband of Constance, Duchess of
Brittany and Countess of Richmond. They were divorced in
1198 on grounds of consanguinity; the marriage was childless.
Constance subsequently married Guy de Thouars but died in
1201. Guy de Thouars held Richmond until he sided with
Philip of France in 1203. See *Early Yorkshire Charters,* ed.
C. T. Clay (Yorkshire Archaeological Society, 1935), IV, 79.

male heir of a family traditionally opposed to the
territorial ambitions of the earls of Chester. Robert
had held Richmondshire since September 1203.[9]

The methods which secured Ranulf's support were
also used to retain it. In the civil war of 1215-17 he
acquired the earldom of Lincoln and the shrievalties of
Lancashire, Staffordshire, and Shropshire; one of his
stewards, Walter of Coventry, became sheriff of Lincolnshire.[10] Ranulf's history is one of many similar
stories and is only remarkable for the suddenness and
completeness of the change in his relations with the
King. Other leading barons of the Welsh Marches
were managed in a like manner. William Marshal, Earl
of Pembroke, was in and out of favour throughout the
greater part of the reign. Suspect at times of a readiness to compromise with the King of France, at others of
being too close to John's enemies in the Welsh Marches
and in Ireland, he faced bitter accusations from the King
and subsequent demands for hostages. Then, in 1213-
14 he was restored to favour and granted the custody of
important Welsh castles. With Ranulf of Chester and
other lords whose support John sought at this time,

[9] *Rotuli de liberate ac de misis et praestitis,* ed. T. Duffus
Hardy (Record Commission, 1844), pp. 63-64.
[10] For Ranulf, see Painter, *The Reign of King John,*
pp. 25-29; Holt, *The Northerners,* pp. 205-7, 241. For the
earlier history of the family, its territorial ambitions, and its
relations with the earls of Leicester, see J. H. Round, "King
Stephen and the Earl of Chester," 10 *English Historical Review* 87-91 (1895); F. M. Stenton, *The First Century of
English Feudalism* (2d ed.; Oxford, 1961), pp. 249-56;
H. A. Cronne, "Ranulf de Gernons, Earl of Chester," *Transactions of the Royal Historical Society,* 4th series (1937), XX,
103-34; R. H. C. Davis, "King Stephen and the Earl of
Chester Revised," 75 *English Historical Review* 654-60 (1960).

William was largely responsible for ensuring the loyalty of the Welsh Marches and Ireland during the civil war.[11] These were the more successful of John's increasingly frantic attempts to secure loyalty throughout the realm by the grant of material reward.[12]

Such measures had a reverse side. Their effect was to canalize royal patronage to a favoured few. The rest, increasingly, were denied the reasonable expectancy of office and privilege which they might claim from status, family connections, or the laws of inheritance. They might be able to buy the possession or custody of land, or the wardship of a wealthy minor, or the right to arrange the marriage of a well-endowed widow or heiress—but at a price. Patronage was dispensed as if through a market, in which the bidding was often competitive and into which feudal lords were driven to plunge by family ties, by territorial and political ambitions, and by the social conventions of their time. They were encouraged all the more in this by the long-standing assumption that the Exchequer would not be excessively pressing in the collection of debts incurred by this kind of speculation.

John upset this delicately adjusted machinery. He sold privileges for a very high price. From the middle years of the reign onwards he required stricter accounting for debts, setting stiff and regular terms of repayment. At the same time he was ready to grant a relaxation of terms or even pardon the whole or part of a debt in return for political subservience. He kept the system of account under his own personal control and

[11] For William Marshal, see Sidney Painter, *William Marshal* (Baltimore, 1933); Painter, *The Reign of King John*, pp. 244-47, 277-78; J. C. Holt, *Magna Carta* (Cambridge, 1965), p. 119.

[12] For similar measures in northern England, see Holt, *The Northerners*, pp. 96-98, 105-6.

was able to adjust it to political requirements and his changing relationships with his subjects. Thus his likes and dislikes, his momentary whims, intruded into the ordinary operations of the Exchequer.

This method of government was all the more pernicious since debt to the Crown was difficult to avoid. The more cautious of John's subjects might refrain from excessive speculation in wardships and marriages. None could avoid the compulsory payments which were incidental to the feudal tenure of land. All had to pay reliefs or fines on the succession to their estates. All had to perform military service, or pay scutage or fines in lieu of service. All were liable to monetary penalties or amercements for breaches of the law, or for failing to perform the many duties required of feudal tenants in attendance at the local courts and the like. Many such pecuniary payments were almost formal and necessarily small and unimportant. Others, in particular the reliefs or fines for succession to estates, were not, and John used these as major financial resources and instruments of political discipline. He demanded enormous sums and allowed political considerations to affect the amount demanded, the terms set for repayment, and the manner in which those terms were enforced. From this kind of financial pressure there was no easy escape. If the indebted landowner turned to the Jews for aid, he was simply jumping out of the frying pan into the fire. Such loans carried extortionate rates of interest, and debts owed to a Jew reverted to the Crown on the Jew's death.

By contemporary standards the sums involved in these transactions imposed real burdens on the debtors. Offers for privileges varied with what was being bought. Exemption from jury service, for example, might involve relatively trifling sums. Wardships, on the other hand, often cost thousands of pounds. Widows might offer similar sums to avoid compulsory remarriage. It was just as expensive to purchase the marriage of an heiress. In 1213 Geoffrey de Mandeville, Earl of Essex, offered the unprecedented sum of £13,333 for the hand of John's divorced wife, Isabella, Countess of Gloucester. The costs of litigation in the royal courts could be equally burdensome. In 1200-1201 William de Mowbray offered the King £1,333 to ensure that he would be treated justly in an action in which William de Stuteville was laying claim to the Mowbray barony; de Mowbray was required to account for this sum despite the fact that the case ended in a compromise favourable to de Stuteville.[13]

These offers were made and accepted at a time when £500 per annum represented an exceptional baronial income. William de Mowbray never recovered from the debt in which his proffer of 1200-1201 involved him. Nicholas de Stuteville, who offered £6,666 for the succession to his brother William's estates in 1205, was never able to recover the manor and castle of Knaresborough, which he released to the King as a pledge of payment.[14] For some families indebtedness meant the depletion of their landed estates. The Buissels, barons of Penwortham, Lancashire, burdened by debt incurred in the course of family litigation, were compelled to surrender their barony to a neighbouring potentate and favoured agent of the King, Roger de Lacy, Constable of Chester, who was able and eager to absorb both their lands and their debts.[15]

Debt on such a scale was easily exploited as a means of enforcing political discipline. The relaxation or pardon

[13] See Holt, *The Northerners,* pp. 22, 172-73.
[14] *Ibid.,* pp. 27, 173, 239.   [15] *Ibid.,* p. 240.

of a debt, in whole or in part, was a privilege frequently granted to the King's friends and officials. Those out of favour, in contrast, were harried by demands for payment which were difficult if not impossible to meet. Even larger monetary penalties could be imposed for failure to pay, and men might be forced to place the whole of their land in pledge to guarantee these new amercements. The ultimate penalties were imprisonment and deprivation of estate. When John's suspicions concentrated on his old supporter, William de Braose, in 1208, he was able to take action by demanding that William should meet the agreed terms of the large proffer of £3,333 which he had made for Limerick in 1200-1. When these demands drove William into open resistance, John was ready to admit him and his wife to the peace on the payment of an enormous penalty of £33,333. This "settlement," which far exceeded William's capacity to pay, drove him into exile. His wife and eldest son died in prison. Yet John was able to argue that he had followed perfectly lawful procedure in collecting a debt according to "the law of the Exchequer" and in exiling a recalcitrant vassal "according to the custom of the realm." William's fate stood as a terrible warning of John's readiness and capacity to turn debt against real or suspected foes.[16]

By the last years of his reign, John had developed

---

[16] For accounts of John's quarrel with Braose, see Kate Norgate, *John Lackland* (London, 1902), pp. 287-88; Painter, *The Reign of King John,* pp. 242-50; Holt, *The Northerners,* pp. 184-86. See F. M. Powicke, *The Loss of Normandy* (2d ed.; Manchester, 1961), pp. 315-22, for the thesis that William knew too much about the fate of Arthur of Brittany, whom John was thought to have killed. For John's statement of his charges against de Braose, see *Foedera, conventiones, litterae et cujuscunque generis acta publica,* ed. T. Rymer; new edition ed. A. Clarke and F. Holbrooke (Record Commission, 1816), I, part 1, 107-8.

these techniques into an intricate system of control.[17]
Many of its features are well illustrated by the arrangements he made with John de Lacy, Constable of Chester
and lord of the honour of Pontefract, who succeeded to
his estates in 1213 after a minority of nearly two years.
The King demanded a fine of £4,666 for the succession
to his lands. He required de Lacy to pay this sum in
three years but agreed to remit £666 if he received the
faithful service he expected from him. The arrangement was guaranteed by twenty knights of de Lacy's fee,
who pledged his loyalty by charter and agreed that they
would transfer their fealty to the King if de Lacy proved
disloyal. De Lacy also had to surrender his castles of
Pontefract and Castle Donington as further pledges of
his good behaviour. He had to make a regular contribution for their upkeep, and his tenants had to give him aid
in paying his enormous fine.[18] The only element missing
from the arrangement was the surrender of hostages;
presumably, since John de Lacy was a young bachelor,
there were none suitable to be demanded.

The subsequent history of this transaction is as significant as its content. John de Lacy accompanied the
King's expedition to Poitou in 1214. In June he was
given delay in the terms of repayment, and in July the
King restored Castle Donington to him. On March 4,
1214, he was one of the few English barons to take the
Cross for the Crusades along with the King. A day

[17] See Holt, *The Northerners*, pp. 170-74. There is valuable
material and comment on this aspect of John's rule in the introductions to the edited Pipe Rolls of these years. See especially
Pipe Roll 10 John, pp. xvi-xix; *Pipe Roll 11 John*, pp. xix-xx,
xxiii-xxv; *Pipe Roll 12 John*, pp. xxii-xxvi; *Pipe Roll 13 John*,
pp. xxx-xxxiv.
[18] *Rotuli de oblatis et finibus in turri Londinensi asservati*,
ed. T. Duffus Hardy (Record Commission, 1835), pp. 494-95.

later his remaining debts to the Crown, which included £2,800 still outstanding under the arrangement of 1213, were pardoned. John de Lacy sold his support dearly. By the end of May 1215 he had joined the rebellion against the King and at Runnymede was made one of the committee of twenty-five barons chosen to secure the terms of the Charter.[19] In this agreement the King had reduced feudal loyalty to a matter of barter. This was a game which his subjects as well as he could play.

The King was entirely responsible for developing this technique of government. It is now quite uncertain how far it was an unnecessary and provocative expression of his own suspicious nature. No attempt to defend King John can afford to write off the contemporary attitude which his actions helped to create, for the hostility to him was not simply that of outraged monks and clergy, bent on destroying the reputation of a King who had challenged Innocent III and despoiled the Church; it was also expressed in works which betray the views of the lay aristocracy, in the biography of William Marshal in which John appears as hot-tempered, unpredictable, distrustful, and untrustworthy, or in the acid comment of Bertrand de Born:

> No man may ever trust him
> For his heart is soft and cowardly.[20]

Nevertheless, even in these aspects of his government, the King's personal behaviour was underlain by facts which go far to explain it. He lost Normandy in inglorious circumstances, but the French financial accounts of 1202-3 demonstrate that Philip Augustus

[19] Holt, *The Northerners,* p. 174.
[20] *The Political Songs of England,* ed. Thomas Wright (London, 1839), p. 6.

could deploy resources for war along the Norman border which were far greater than those which John could muster.[21] Common sense rather than laziness or a failure of nerve led to John's withdrawal without a serious fight.[22] And after the loss of Normandy he had cause to be suspicious, for one of the factors in his defeat had been his betrayal by the Norman baronage; the Norman interests of Ranulf of Chester and William Marshal go far to explain his distrust of them.

Yet damage to prestige and royal suspicion were not the only consequences of the events of 1204. The first clear symptoms of the monopoly of office and royal favour by a small group of the King's friends and officials came in the years 1204-7 when John made room in English administration for those who had served him well in Normandy, Maine, and the Touraine. Some of these were Poitevins or Normans by birth. The magnates later demanded in the Great Charter that officials should know the law of the land and that the King's Poitevin agents should be dismissed from office.[23] Yet after the disasters on the Continent John had to choose between abandoning these men or providing them with due reward in England. He probably saw profit for himself in choosing the latter, but it is difficult to argue that it was the wrong choice. It is even more difficult to maintain that John should have accepted the decision of 1204 as final. In fact he did not. In the years which

[21] Ferdinand Lot and Robert Fawtier, *Le Premier Budget de la monarchie française* (Bibliothèque de l'École des Hautes Études; Paris, 1932), pp. 135-39.

[22] "He preferred to withdraw in time, with some loss of reputation and goods, than deliver himself and his men to annihilation." *Memoriale fratris Walteri de Coventria,* ed. W. Stubbs (Rolls series, 1872-73), II, 197.

[23] Magna Carta, chapters 45, 50.

followed he was sidetracked into campaigns in Scotland, Ireland, and Wales, and Innocent III provoked him into an attempt to preserve the traditional position of the English Crown in the matter of ecclesiastical appointments. But there was never any real doubt either in his own mind or among his contemporaries that he would try to recover what he had lost; not even Henry III, who was of a much weaker frame of mind, was ready to accept the *fait accompli* until the Treaty of Paris of 1259.

Hence John was committed to the accumulation of resources for a campaign of reconquest, with all the military and diplomatic expenditure which that required. This urgent need lay behind the enormous reliefs, amercements, and charges for privilege which he placed on his vassals. In 1213, when he was preparing for the campaign in Poitou, he arranged for considerable numbers of his debtors to provide the service of knights and sergeants in lieu of payment.[24] Others at this time were required to accept agreements with early terms of payment in order to line the King's pocket before he sailed to Poitou in February 1214.[25] Such measures emphasised the close relationship between John's schemes on the Continent and his financial persecution of the English baronage. He was requiring them to carry the costs of war.

John's conduct of his relations with his vassals was the major reason for the outbreak of rebellion at the end of the reign. In 1212 a small group of dissident barons, headed by Robert fitz Walter and Eustace de Vesci, plotted to use the opportunity of a campaign against the

[24] Holt, *Magna Carta,* pp. 109-10.
[25] See Dr. Patricia M. Barnes's comments in *Pipe Roll 16 John,* pp. xxiii-xxiv.

Welsh to murder the King or desert him in the face of the enemy. That the rebels were ready for regicide is a measure of their discontent. The plot was discovered, the leaders were outlawed, and those suspected of complicity were loaded with penalties.

From this point onwards John's attempts to control his vassals became more blatant. The surrender of hostages and castles became an increasingly frequent incident of tenure.[26] The country was plunging towards a serious political crisis. But if this explains why there was a rebellion, it does not explain why that rebellion produced the Great Charter, or why men who hated John enough to attempt his murder should within three years lead the baronage to a very different kind of cure for their political ills. John's character, his relations with his baronage, and his methods of political control were in fact only part of the story and, in relation to the total content of the Charter, only a small part.

WAR AND FINANCE IN ANGEVIN ENGLAND

John inherited most of his problems. Most obviously, he inherited the Angevin empire and the task of defending it. His failure in 1204 was less a personal failure than a culmination of a long process which began in 1173 when the sons of Henry II, with French encouragement, rebelled against their father. Henry II died amidst defeat in 1189 after agreeing to pay a large indemnity to the French. Richard I increased this at his succession and abandoned the Angevin claims to Berri

[26] See Holt, *The Northerners,* p. 83; Holt, *Magna Carta,* pp. 105-24.

and the Auvergne. He surrendered most of the Norman Vexin in the Treaty of Louviers of 1196 and spent the rest of his life in recovering it at enormous cost in military effort. John confirmed the arrangements of Louviers and also surrendered the county of Evreux in the Treaty of Le Goulet of 1200. In 1204 Normandy fell through the chaos and wastage of continued war.[27]

But if the cost of war was more obvious in Normandy, its effects went far deeper in England. England became the milch cow of the Angevin empire. The taxation of the realm, the exploitation of the country's economic and the Crown's feudal resources, the management of the royal demesne, of wardships and escheats, of shires and hundreds, even the administration of justice—all became more and more tightly bound to providing the resources of war. The increasingly pressing need was for men, money, and the political stability at home essential to fight prolonged and recurring campaigns abroad. England bore all this for thirty years, and then for a further ten while John attempted the recovery of the lost possessions. Magna Carta was the direct result.

The first concern of the Angevin kings was for a properly organised and adequate army. For this they were in part dependent on the military service due from their vassals. Henry II first ensured, in investigations carried out in 1166, that the service due to the Crown was properly acknowledged. He and his sons required service more frequently; by John's time the campaigns had become almost annual. The increasingly critical nature of the Norman wars led Richard and John to demand that service should be performed in person; the same circumstance led many of their tenants who still

[27] Poole, *From Domesday Book to Magna Carta*, pp. 347-84; Powicke, *The Loss of Normandy*.

had interests in Normandy to provide it. The duration of the campaigns and the distances involved led to an alteration in the terms of service; the barons now sent fewer men, but for longer periods than the old limit of forty days, which was of little value for this type of expedition. The total result was to transform feudal military service in England.

Yet feudal service was only a proportion of the military resources of the Crown. Normans and Angevins, both kings and nobles, had frequently employed mercenaries; and mercenaries became more and more essential in long-drawn campaigns which turned on the capture and defence of castles. Hence Henry, Richard, and John all insisted that those vassals who did not serve should pay compensation sufficient to make a substantial contribution towards the pay of hired troops. Henry took this in the form of scutage, which was levied at a fixed and general rate, frequently at £1 per fee. Richard and John went further and often demanded that those who did not serve should compound for their absence by paying an arbitrary fine. Meanwhile even those who served as feudal vassals approached more and more closely to the position of mercenaries; by the end of John's reign they frequently received cash advances during their period of service in the army.[28]

It was quite impossible to maintain this type of military organisation or pay for the vast schemes of

---

[28] See Powicke, *The Loss of Normandy,* pp. 209-32, for these developments. For payments on account to the feudal host, see J. C. Holt, Introduction to Praestita Roll 14-18 John, in *Pipe Roll 17 John,* pp. 71-80. J. O. Prestwich, "War and Finance in the Anglo-Norman State," *Transactions of the Royal Historical Society,* 5th series (1954), IV, 19-43, and C. W. Hollister, *The Military Organization of Norman England* (Oxford, 1965), are important studies of an earlier period.

fortification[29] or subsidise allies on the continent simply from the sums due as scutage and fines from those feudal tenants who did not themselves serve. The Angevin kings sought to develop all potential sources of revenue. They and their servants tried to reassess taxation on land, especially in the carucage of 1198; from the old feudal aid they developed taxes on revenues and chattels, which, at the rate of a thirteenth, yielded £60,000 in 1207; in 1202-5 they imposed the first national customs system, which yielded £5,000 in the first two years of its operation; they taxed imported dyestuffs, attempted to impose a national system of weights and measures, and nationalized the Cornish tin-mining industry, which under John developed phenomenally high production.[30]

New forms of taxation were invented, and new weight was given to old methods of exploitation. Increments and profits were demanded from sheriffs over and above the ancient farms due from their shires; custodians of the royal demesne or of escheats and wardships were required to account for the total receipts of the estates in their charge; the forest law was maintained and extended not only in order to preserve the King's game but

[29] Château Gaillard, which was built in 1197-98, cost nearly £50,000. Powicke, *The Loss of Normandy,* pp. 194, 204-6. For other castle work in this period, see R. A. Brown, "Royal Castle Building in England, 1154-1216," 70 *English Historical Review* 353-98 (1955), and H. M. Colvin, *The History of the King's Works* (London, 1963), pp. 64-81.

[30] See S. K. Mitchell, *Studies in Taxation under John and Henry III* (New Haven, 1914); S. K. Mitchell, *Studies in Medieval Taxation,* ed. Sidney Painter (New Haven, 1951). See also the introductions to the Pipe Rolls of the relevant years, especially 1198 and 1207. For the customs system, see *Pipe Roll 6 John,* pp. xliii-xlv, and N. B. Gras, *The Early English Customs System* (Cambridge, Mass., 1918), pp. 48-53, 217-22. For Cornish tin, see G. R. Lewis, *The Stannaries* (Cambridge, Mass., 1924), pp. 35-37, 133-36.

also as a method of exploiting the agrarian development
of the country through annual charges assessed on newly
cultivated land within the forest; the Jews were taxed
with increasing severity, the administration of their
debts was overhauled, and these debts were collected
with new rigour when the death of a Jew brought them
into the hands of the Crown.[31] All this was in addition
to the stringent exploitation of the feudal incidents due
to the Crown and the increasingly demanding and
efficient collection of the debts which resulted both from
this and the sale of privileges.[32]

War was not the sole impetus to these developments.
They occurred amidst increasing population, rapid eco
nomic expansion in agriculture, trade, industry, and
credit facilities, and steeply rising prices. This situatior
both presented governments with opportunities and
subjected them to financial pressures. Inventive, active
efficient administration was both possible and necessary
It was provided by men, both clerk and lay, who took an
increasingly professional interest in it. By the end of the
twelfth century they had produced the first great com

[31] On the royal demesne, see R. S. Hoyt, *The Royal Demesn*
in English Constitutional History: 1066-1272 (Ithaca, N.Y.
1950), pp. 92 ff. For increments and profits, see Mabel H
Mills, "Experiments in Exchequer Procedure," *Transactions o*
the Royal Historical Society, 4th series (1925), VIII, 151-70
Painter, *The Reign of King John,* pp. 122-23; Holt, *Th*
Northerners, pp. 152-57; B. E. Harris, "King John and th
Sheriffs' Farms," 79 *English Historical Review* 532-42 (1964)
On the forests, see the introductions to the *Pipe Rolls* of 1198
1207, and 1212, and Holt, *The Northerners,* pp. 157-63. O
the Jews, see Cecil Roth, *History of the Jews in Englan*
(3d ed.; Oxford, 1964), pp. 18-37; Alice C. Cramer, "Th
Origins and Functions of the Jewish Exchequer," 16 *Speculur*
226-29 (1941); H. G. Richardson, *The English Jewry unde*
the Angevin Kings (London, 1960), pp. 135 ff.
[32] See pp. 134-9, *supra.*

mentary on the laws of England, which passes under the name of Glanville, Henry II's Justiciar, and the first administrative study by a civil servant, the *Dialogue of the Exchequer* of Richard fitz Neal, Henry's Treasurer. Men became schooled in government, both central and local. Families provided administrators in successive generations, and these administrators served successive kings. Some contributed as much to Angevin government as the kings did themselves. Hubert Walter, Richard's Justiciar and John's Chancellor, was one of the greatest administrators of medieval England; his predominance was unmatched until the time of Wolsey.

THE GROWTH OF DISCONTENT

As a result of these influences, the rule of the Angevin kings was one of continuous administrative and political development. Certain years were particularly critical; 1193-94 marked the return of Richard from captivity in Germany, the resulting financial burdens necessary for the payment of the enormous ransom (equivalent to £100,000), the renewal of the war in Normandy, and the beginning of the Justiciarship of Hubert Walter. Walter's appointment marked the beginning of a decade of remarkable administrative development which also saw the first hints of resentment and resistance. "England was reduced to penury from sea to sea by such exactions, both just and unjust. And before they were ended there came another kind of torment inflicted on the men of the realm by the Justices of the Forest . . . ." Thus wrote the level-headed chronicler, Roger of Howden, about the forest eyre of 1198.[33] Since he himself

[33] *Hoveden,* IV, 62-63.

had been a justice of the forest, his comment is all the more significant.

By this time there were varied undercurrents of unrest. In 1196 there had been riots against oppressive taxation and the dominance of the municipal oligarchy in London. Hubert Walter helped to suppress them brutally. Other objectors were less easy to coerce. In 1197 the bishops of Lincoln and Salisbury resisted demands for service overseas. They were unable to maintain their case, but it represented more general resentment, which was shared by the knightly tenants of the Abbey of Bury St. Edmunds.[34] In 1199 a group of important landowners refused to acknowledge John unless their rights were restored—some of these were granted their claims—and in 1201 some of the earls apparently advanced a similar demand as a condition of service overseas.[35]

John's succession in itself added little to this incipient discontent. Some of his continental vassals objected strongly to his supersession of his nephew, Arthur of Brittany, but there was no open resistance in England, where John was well known, nor yet was opinion particularly hostile to him. The decisive turn of events came with the loss of Normandy in 1204 and the death of Hubert Walter in 1205. The first multiplied John's difficulties abroad and his demands at home. The second removed a great royal minister at a time when John's activities were confined more and more to Eng-

[34] J. H. Round, *Feudal England* (London, 1895), pp 528-38; Helena M. Chew, *The English Ecclesiastical Tenants-in-Chief* (Oxford, 1932), pp. 39-45; *The Chronicle of Jocelin of Brakelond,* ed. H. E. Butler (London, 1949), pp. 85-86

[35] *Hoveden,* IV, 88, 161. See also Painter, *The Reign o. King John,* pp. 13-16.

land. From this point on his rule became more personal, and his officials more directly dependent on his will. His restless journeying throughout the land gave him a knowledge of his realm unequalled by his predecessors.

John brought his rule home to his subjects, and this had an important effect on the development and nature of the growing opposition. He spread government and discipline evenly. He required the same efficiency and obedience from the northern counties as he did from the South and West, the traditional sources of power and support for the Angevin monarchy. Henry II visited the North rarely; Richard not at all, north of Nottinghamshire; John, in contrast, almost annually.[36] Here his government bore down ruthlessly on men and families which had experienced little of it hitherto and on areas which enjoyed considerable feudal independence and long traditions of independent action. When the Earl of Chester came near rebellion in the winter of 1204-5, he was able to find support in the northern counties. The Exchequer was in the process of collecting a scutage; the King now found it expedient to pardon it in Northumberland and Lincolnshire, and the Exchequer apparently abandoned its collection in Yorkshire.[37] The North was already a matter for the King's special concern. In 1212 it was one of the main centres of the plot against his life; in 1213 and 1214 the Northerners led the resistance to his demand for service in Poitou; they were among the first to make war on John in 1215 and the last to make peace with his son in 1217. The North had not been a special centre of trouble hitherto, nor was it to be again until the fourteenth and fifteenth

[36] Holt, *King John*, pp. 13-14. See above pp. 95-6.
[37] Holt, *The Northerners*, pp. 89-90, 205-7.

centuries. The violent outburst of 1215 was a response to the burden of Angevin government and the personal supervision of King John.[38]

The crisis which began in 1194 and continued with heightened intensity after 1204 originated in the continental fortunes of the house of Anjou. So also did the events which precipitated the final collapse. From 1212 onwards England was near rebellion. John went to new lengths to propitiate and to new depths to browbeat. But he continued to prepare for the coming campaign on the Continent. He was able to sail in February 1214, leaving a small but determined body of recalcitrants in the North. The great majority of those who were to rebel a year later served with him or sent their service or contributed to the payment of the Poitevin army.[39] There was no rebellion in England behind his back.

What victory would have meant for John is now imponderable. In fact, his Flemish allies were defeated at Bouvines in July, and it is clear enough that he recognised that this defeat abroad entailed defeat at home. He prepared at once for civil war in England. Resistance to the scutage for the Poitevin campaign spread like an epidemic once the Exchequer tried to hold account for it in the autumn, and this increasingly general refusal of a recognised service made a major political crisis inevitable. Bouvines led directly to Runnymede.

The final crisis came suddenly. Even so, the King's opponents made demands which spread over the whole range of governmental methods developed by the Angevin kings. John himself recognised that this was likely to occur. In 1212 he reacted fiercely to the treasonable plot against his life by making dire threats against those

[38] *Ibid.*, pp. 194-216.   [39] *Ibid.*, pp. 98-100.

whom he suspected and by insisting on the surrender of hostages and castles. But he also started to promise or to make concessions—concessions which amounted to something more than bids for individual support. He promised to relax the collection of Jewish debts in the hands of the Crown. The sheriffs of Yorkshire and Lincolnshire were dismissed and enquiries ordered into their activities. Some attempt was also made to lighten the general burden of shire government by abandoning the collection of increments over and above the shire farms. He investigated the activity of some of the forest officials. A new forest eyre which had begun in 1212 was quietly abandoned. Nothing was done to follow up a great enquiry into feudal tenures which had been carried out in June and July of 1212.[40]

All this foreshadowed Magna Carta. It, too, provided for the regulation and amelioration of Jewish debts.[41] It, too, arranged for enquiries into the behaviour of the King's sheriffs, foresters, and bailiffs.[42] It, too, forbade increments[43] and insisted that feudal tenants should not be subjected to demands for excessive service.[44] But the Charter necessarily probed far deeper into the structure of government than had John's concessions of 1212-13. It attempted to regulate the assessment of scutage and aids, the collection of debts due to the Crown, the processes of amercement, and the operations of the law courts, to name but a few of the topics it covered. It was passing comment not only on John but on Angevin rule as a whole.

[40] Holt, *The Northerners*, pp. 85-88; Holt, *Magna Carta*, pp. 125-29; *Pipe Roll 16 John*, pp. xxi-xxiii; B. E. Harris, "King John and the Sheriffs' Farms," 79 *English Historical Review* 540-41 (1964).
[41] Chapters 10, 11.   [42] Chapter 48.   [43] Chapter 25.
[44] Chapter 16.

The argument was pursued with great sophistication on both sides. The King's opponents attacked his weakest spot—his need for service overseas. There had already been some attempt to barter service for concessions in 1201.[45] Now, in 1213-14, they met John with a blunt refusal to serve. Their arguments were varied. Some initially alleged that the King was excommunicate, which may have sufficed until his absolution on July 20, 1213; some pleaded the exhaustion of their resources; in the North some advanced the peculiarities of certain northern tenures as sufficient reason for their refusal.[46] Finally, they resolved to try to impose a geographic limit on overseas service by limiting it to Normandy and Brittany.[47] Their argument was that John's demands for service in Poitou in 1214 were unlawful and unfounded.[48]

This case was skilfully conceived. By appealing to the terms of tenure they were avoiding a blunt refusal of an acknowledged service and were driving John towards legal action or arbitration. But the final form of their argument had even wider implications. In trying to restrict service to Normandy and Brittany the barons seem to have been arguing that they were liable to

[45] See p. 148, *supra.*

[46] Holt, *The Northerners,* pp. 88-92.

[47] "Unknown" Charter, chapter 7.   For the text, see W. S. McKechnie, *Magna Carta* (2d ed.; Glasgow, 1914), p. 486; Holt, *Magna Carta,* p. 303.

[48] Little-known evidence on this is to be found in Faulkes de Bréauté's complaint to Pope Honorius III in 1225: "The men of England often debated whether they were bound to follow the King to Poitou, and after much argument, contrary to the will of the King, they denied that they were bound to do such service. And so this was one of the articles for which England, with the encouragement of the Archbishop, rebelled against the King's father." *Memoriale fratris Walteri de Coventria,* ed. W. Stubbs (Rolls series, 1872-73), II, 269.

overseas service only in those areas in which the Norman and Breton adventurers who had followed William the Conqueror had an interest at the time of the Conquest of England, that they were not liable to service in lands which had come to the English Crown after the establishment of their baronies. Hence they had no responsibilities in the Angevin and Aquitanian lands which Henry II and Eleanor, his wife, had allied to the old Anglo-Norman realm. The argument was not supported by precedent. The English baronage had assisted Henry II's campaign to Toulouse in 1159 with men or money; they had followed John in large numbers to Poitou in 1206; and they were to serve there again under Henry III. But it had a logic of its own which matched a practice, fairly general thoughout Europe, which restricted unpaid feudal service within the boundaries of the realm.[49]

THE CASE AGAINST THE CROWN: CUSTOM AND INNOVATION

The argument on overseas service was not isolated. It was part of a general pattern of thinking in which Angevin rule was regarded as unlawful innovation standing in sharp contrast to the good and ancient custom of the Anglo-Norman kingdom, itself partly derived from pre-Conquest England. This pattern was pieced together from myths and facts which had survived from the eleventh and early twelfth centuries; from the tradition of saintliness attached to the character of Edward the Confessor, canonized in 1161; from the confirmation by the Conqueror of the laws of Edward;

[49] Holt, *Magna Carta*, pp. 64-66.

from the traditional reputation of Henry I as a Lion of Justice and a Guardian of the Flocks; from the early twelfth-century legal collections known as the Laws of Edward the Confessor and the Laws of Henry I; and from the fact that Henry I had issued a Coronation Charter in which he promised a wide range of concessions on feudal incidents and other aspects of royal administration.

The material for the baronial arguments thus lay ready to hand. The Angevin kings provided the impetus which led men into assembling it into a philosophy of criticism and opposition. Henry I's Charter remained a dead letter in Henry's day and in the years which followed. The rebellious barons of the reign of Stephen never used it either as a programme or as a justification. Neither Henry II nor anyone else remarked on it when in his Coronation Charter he confirmed the concessions, liberties, and free customs granted by Henry I. Henry I's Charter was in fact defunct until it was turned against King John. The appeal to it was politically conceived. The same was true of the interest in the Laws of Edward Confessor and Henry I, into which late twelfth-century editors made interpolations which emphasised the king's responsibility to exercise justice and to consult the great men of the land both in this and in the demands he made on his subjects.

This appeal to tradition is of the greatest importance in understanding the crisis of 1215 and the influences which formed the Great Charter. The barons did not appeal to practice under Richard in order to condemn John. They did not appeal to practice under Henry II in order to condemn his sons. They appealed to pre-Angevin conditions in order to condemn or review the practices and methods of government of all three. They recognised the impossibility of distinguishing effectively between Henry II's administration and that of his sons. The latter was derived from and was based on the former. The former provided the justification and the legal basis for the latter. All had to stand or fall together. The point was clearly appreciated at the time. The barons' demands, Abbot Ralph of Coggeshall wrote, were for the abolition of the "evil customs which the father and brother of the king had introduced to the detriment of church and kingdom, along with those abuses which the king himself had added."[50]

The argument was not developed in a rigid or purely destructive manner. The barons did not pursue their argument about military service far enough to include any geographic restriction in the Charter; they may well have found that the precedents on the King's side were too strong. On certain issues an appeal to pre-Angevin conditions was unnecessary; no precedent was required for the demand that John should surrender the hostages and charters of fealty which he had taken as a guaranty of good behaviour. On other matters the barons wanted to regulate rather than destroy what the Angevins had done; they accepted the whole of the legal work of Henry II and his sons, simply confining themselves in the Charter to providing detailed improvements. They wanted more, not less, of the kind of justice which the English courts had come to provide.

Nevertheless the appeal to tradition served a useful purpose. It was based in part on fiction, for England in the early twelfth century was very far from the idyllic condition the appeal assumed; Henry I had been an active enough ruler, who had innovated like the Ange-

[50] *Radulphi de Coggeshall chronicon Anglicanum,* ed. J. Stevenson (Rolls series, 1875), p. 170.

vins. But in many spheres of government it did roughly
fit the facts: in the development of taxation or scutage,
for example, or in the administration of the debts of the
Jews. Its implications are perhaps seen at their clearest
in the case of the royal forests. The administration of
the forest law was the cause of some of the bitterest
complaints against the Angevin kings. In 1215 the
barons tried to reform the forest law and administration
and also restrict the area in which they were in force. It
followed logically that they had to attack Henry II as
well as, indeed even more than, his sons, for Henry had
been chiefly responsible for the extension of the royal
forests in the second half of the twelfth century. To
have accepted the afforestations of his reign as lawful
would have meant the acceptance of the existing situation, for neither Richard nor John had afforested to any
important extent; on the contrary, their reigns had seen
the beginning of extensive disafforestation. Hence the
demand for the restoration of the bounds to what they
had been in 1154. Here the appeal to pre-Angevin
conditions brought tangible gains; when this provision
was executed in 1218-19 barons and knights could and
did perambulate the bounds of the areas so released
from the royal forest law.[51]

The barons of 1215 did not appeal to the past in a
mood of blind instinctive reaction, reaching out to

[51] For the various provisions on the forest in 1215-17, see
"Unknown" Charter, chapter 9; Magna Carta, chapters 47, 52,
53; Charter of the Forest, chapters 1, 3. For discussion of the
history of the forest, see G. J. Turner, *Select Pleas of the
Forest* (Selden Society, 1899); C. Petit-Dutaillis, *Studies
Supplementary to Stubbs' Constitutional History* (Manchester,
1908-14), II, 147-251; Poole, *From Domesday Book to
Magna Carta,* pp. 29-35; Doris M. Stenton, *English Society in
the Early Middle Ages* (3d ed.; London, 1962), pp. 97-119;
Holt, *The Northerners,* pp. 157-63.

destroy all that the Angevin kings had done and seeking to revive the imagined glories of an anarchic past. They appealed to the past because this was part of the general attitude of mind in an age when law, custom, and tenure depended on precedent and long usage. They were not alone in this; popes, kings, and bishops did the same.

The argument also brought them real political gains. Some historians have used it to condemn the barons as reactionaries who set themselves against the tide of orderly administrative progress.[52] It should be used rather as evidence of their growing political awareness and their increasing political skill. Their achievement may not seem great. In a more sophisticated age long usage may seem a feeble basis for political criticism and no basis at all for constructive political theory. But the opponents of King John achieved one thing which has eluded many more sophisticated theorists and revolutionaries; they achieved relevance and the capacity to apply their arguments in practice. They produced, not a political theory, nor yet a blueprint for social reorganisation, but a justification for intervention in everyday administration and a method whereby the legality of that administration could be tested. What they set out to do was to bring government into line with ancient custom, partly by restricting it, partly by glossing custom so that it was made relevant to the circumstances of their own day. And this is what Magna Carta did.

This approach and this solution did not come easily or quickly. It appeared in 1213 as a simple demand that the King should confirm his subjects' ancient liberties. Men assumed that John was committed to some serious

[52] Compare Petit-Dutaillis, *op. cit. supra* note 51, I, 127-45; J. E. A. Jolliffe, *Angevin Kingship* (New York, 1955), pp. 301-50.

attempt at reform by the coronation oath which he had renewed when he was absolved from excommunication by Archbishop Stephen Langton on July 20.[53]   This became the starting point of the wrangling which followed.[54]   In the summer the growing opposition concentrated on the refusal of overseas service, and at the beginning of November the Northerners, who were the leaders in that resistance, met the King at Wallingford and obtained some kind of promise which again referred to the restoration of ancient liberties.[55]

The details of these interchanges were not very clearly remembered at the time and soon became distorted and exaggerated.   The more dramatic the story, the more vigorously it flourished.   Roger of Wendover, who compiled this section of his chronicle some fifteen years later at St. Albans, told of promises by the King's ministers that the laws of Henry I would be observed and of a theatrical incident at St. Paul's on August 25, in which Archbishop Stephen Langton secretly revealed the existence and contents of the Charter of Henry I to a group of astonished and delighted barons.[56]   Wendover's questionable reliability provides a frail and solitary warrant for these stories.   In fact the growing opposition to the King seems to have developed more slowly and more hesitantly than he suggests.   It

[53] Holt, *Magna Carta,* pp. 132-39.

[54] See the report of Walter Mauclerc, the King's agent at Rome in 1215.   *Foedera, conventiones, litterae et cujuscunque generis acta publica,* ed. T. Rymer; new edition ed. A. Clarke and F. Holbrooke, (Record Commission, 1816), I, part 1, 120.

[55] Holt, *The Northerners,* p. 95.

[56] *Matthaei Parisiensis, monachi sancti Albani, chronica majora,* ed. H. R. Luard (Rolls series, 1872-73), II, 551, 552-54.   For comment, see Holt, *Magna Carta,* pp. 129, 133, 137-39.

was not until after the defeat at Bouvines on July 27, 1214, that the opposition became powerful and organised enough to compel negotiation about precise demands. But after Bouvines this stage was quickly reached. The dissidents met the King at London on January 6, 1215. The discussions ended in deadlock, and further debate was postponed until April 26 at Northampton.

The dissidents now formed a coherent body bound together by some kind of covenant. They were capable of receiving and were given safe-conducts until the renewal of discussions in April. They immediately sent delegates to the papal Curia to plead their case against the King. And they now had a clear demand: namely, that John should solemnly confirm the Charter of Henry I. Indeed at this time, or shortly afterwards, they began to gloss the Charter of Henry I in an attempt to adjust it to current problems.

The first clear indication of their thinking is to be found in a document, known to English historians as the "Unknown" Charter, which has resided since the thirteenth century in the French royal archives. This consists of a text of the Charter of Henry I with additional clauses presented as concessions by King John. Some of these simply developed those sections of Henry's Charter which were concerned with feudal incidents. The rest were concerned with some of the characteristic features of Angevin rule: with overseas service, which was to be limited to Normandy and Brittany; with the extent of the forest, which was to revert to the bounds of 1154; with scutage, which was to be assessed at the low rate of 13s. 4d. per fee unless the barons agreed to pay more; with the administration of the forest law; and with the collection of the debts of the Jews.[57] The baronial programme was now launched, and implications of the appeal to ancient custom were clearly indicated.

This emerged from a period of confused negotiation which lasted from January to Easter 1215 and thereafter in a much more acrimonious manner to the meeting at Runnymede in June. Part of the discussion turned on where the line between ancient custom and unlawful innovation was to be drawn. John handled this theme skilfully. At or before the meetings arranged for April 26 at Northampton he offered to abolish the evil customs which had arisen during his own and his brother's reigns. He also said that he would submit any customs established by Henry II to the judgment of his court, if any were considered evil. John well knew how much his government relied on the precedent of his father's reign; it would have been impossible to draw the distinction he suggested.

Nevertheless, discussion of this point must have continued, for ultimately it left its imprint on the Charter itself. On the restoration of rights which had been seized unjustly by the Crown, on the settlement with the Welsh and the Scots, on disafforestation, and on other matters, the Charter drew a distinction between John and his predecessors: John was bound to make immediate reparation for his own acts, but he was given three years' respite as a Crusader for those of Richard and Henry.[58] Since his proposals of April he had gained the ten years of Richard's reign; 1199, not 1189, was now

[57] For the text and discussion, see McKechnie, *Magna Carta* pp. 171-75, 485-86; Holt, *Magna Carta*, pp. 296-303.

[58] Articles of the Barons, chapters 25, 44, 45, 46; Magna Carta, chapters 52, 53, 57, 59.

used to distinguish the more from the less heinous
offences of the Crown. There was good reason for this.
John was still alive to make reparation and could be
called to account for his own acts. It was less easy to
load him with the arbitrary actions of Henry and
Richard.

THE CASE AGAINST THE CROWN:
CHARTERED PRIVILEGES

By June 1215 the baronial appeal to ancient custom
had produced a detailed debate on the line of demarcation between the more and the less acceptable. There
must have been related discussions, too, of specific
proposals for administrative reform. Yet this only tells
part of the story of the crisis of 1215. Angevin methods
of government and the resulting response did much to
determine the content of the baronial programme. But
they did not, by themselves, determine its form. Hatred
of John could have been expressed, simply and directly,
in assassination or deposition, in the measures attempted
in 1212. Complaints against Angevin rule could have
been met by reforming ordinances, by a general eyre
investigating complaints, or by some kind of development of John's own concessions of 1213. A charter was
a very different matter. It was designed not simply to
ensure reform, but to declare law. It was intended to be
permanent. It included and was accompanied by measures to ensure its own enforcement. John might have
agreed to issue and even execute reforming ordinances in
the hope that he could shrug them off in time. But the
Charter went far beyond this. It attacked the sovereignty of the Crown. Such a challenge could be maintained and countered only by war.

This demand for a charter was apparently first expressed in January 1215, when the barons asked John to confirm the Charter of Henry I. By Easter it had developed further into the demand that John should affix his seal to a list of baronial complaints. Such a list was ultimately agreed and sealed as a preliminary to the final gathering at Runnymede in June, and this document, the Articles of the Barons, itself envisaged that the final settlement would be embodied in a charter.[59] In seeking such a grant the barons were true men of their time. They did not envisage the Charter as some kind of contract. They simply turned to the most solemn form of conveyance known to the law of their day as the most appropriate vehicle for the concessions they envisaged. This was no occasion to invent new forms. Routine procedure was the most likely to prove reliable and permanent.

They were led to this by all their past experience. The fabric of royal and aristocratic patronage depended on the grant of privileges. The Angevin kings had used the dispensation of privilege as a major financial resource. But the sale of privilege had two aspects, the buyer's as well as the seller's. If for the king it was an easy way of making money, for his subjects it was a method of evading the worst features of royal administration. It expressed their social and political aspirations. Hence for many years before 1215 they were able to buy many of the privileges which later appeared in the Charter. Widows frequently offered money that they should not be compelled to remarry. The custody and marriage of minors could be purchased by relatives or other interested parties. Men paid sums to avoid the burdens of jury service and attendance at the local

[59] Articles of the Barons, chapter 1, *forma securitatis*.

courts. They bought office, or paid to cultivate land within the forest, or paid fines for just treatment in the courts of law. Liberties had not been unobtainable. They had been available—at a price.

This traffic in privilege increased with the financial and political difficulties of the Crown. Richard sold offices wholesale in order to finance his Crusade. John sold privileges of all kinds in order to finance the closing stages of the Norman wars. At their worst they sold off the permanent resources of the monarchy in return for immediate financial gain. In so doing they whetted their subjects' appetite not only for the privileges they were ready to sell but also for privilege in general.

Such liberties were not restricted to individuals. At a very early stage in these developments, they were acquired by communities. The first in the field and the best organised were the towns. By the end of the twelfth century many towns had bought privileges roughly similar to some of those later incorporated in Magna Carta. Several had bought freedom from relief or heriot or a fixed limitation of these charges. Others had acquired regulations governing wardship, aids, and purveyance which foreshadowed the provisions of 1215. In many of the major towns the size of amercements was restricted.[60]

Such grants established examples not only of the kind of liberties which the barons came to seek in 1215 but also of the corporate tenure of such liberties by a group. The example was soon followed by other communities which were less close-knit and less clearly defined. In 1190 Richard I accepted £133 from the men of Surrey as a payment for the partial disafforestation of their county and £100 from the men of Ainsty wapentake,

[60] Holt, *Magna Carta,* pp. 48-51.

Yorkshire, for the total disafforestation of their wapen-take. At about the same time Count John, the future king, accepted £500 from the men of his honour of Lancaster in return for a concession of forest privileges. During the crisis of the Norman war in 1203-4 total or partial disafforestation was purchased by the men of Devon, Cornwall, Essex, Shropshire, and Staffordshire; Somerset and other areas soon followed.

Nor were forest concessions of this kind the only attainable attraction. In 1199 the men of Lancashire offered £66 and the same sum again in 1204 in order that Richard de Vernon might be their sheriff. The forest charter which the men of Devon purchased in 1204 included arrangements which aimed at restricting exploitation by the sheriff. By the end of the reign the men of Dorset, Somerset, and Cornwall had also bought privileges which gave them some control over the choice of sheriff.[61] Such forest and administrative privileges were extremely expensive; they might cost anything between £800 and £3,000 or more. The payments were negotiated by the men of the shire. In effect they must have been agreed upon, and the arrangements with the king concluded, by the shire court under the leadership of the more influential local landowners. The result was that shires, like towns, held liberties and privileges. From this there was but a short step to the concept of the liberties of the realm.

Magna Carta was thus a direct development from the growth of communal and corporate liberties. Municipal privilege was not isolated. Many towns derived their privileges from feudal lords. Thus John fitz Robert, one of the twenty-five guarantors of Magna Carta, was the author of the charter which gave the

[61] *Ibid.,* pp. 51-55.

burgesses of Corbridge freedom from arbitrary purveyance, and William Marshal, who sealed the Great
Charters of 1216 and 1217, was responsible for the
limitation of reliefs at Haverfordwest.

Communal ideas originating in the towns seem to have
infected the whole baronial movement. As early as
1199, the records mention the "commune of the shire"
of Buckinghamshire and Bedfordshire which negotiated
with the King to pay the carucage of 1198.[62] In 1215
the Charter talked of the "commune of the whole
land";[63] in effect the scheme whereby all pledged loyalty
to the terms of the Charter and support for the baronial
guarantors seems to have been derived from the communal movements of the Continent and more immediately from the commune established at London in 1191.
Such ideas spread all the easier as a result of the close
association between the barons and the Londoners, of
the fact that Robert Fitz Walter, one of the baronial
leaders, was banneret of the city, and of the inclusion of
the Mayor of London among the twenty-five guarantors
of Magna Carta.[64]

But the barons were not simply applying ideas inherited from others. When in 1207 Peter de Brus, Lord
of Danby and Skelton, purchased the wapentake of
Langbargh in Cleveland from the King, he proceeded
to grant a charter of liberties to the men of the wapentake which regulated the assessment of forfeitures in
the wapentake court, limited the number of officials
within the wapentake, arranged to ensure their good
behaviour, and required them to swear to observe the
terms of the Charter.[65] Peter de Brus was one of the
foremost northern rebels in 1215. Among the witnesses

[62] *Pipe Roll 1 John,* pp. 112, 113.   [63] Chapter 61.
[64] Holt, *Magna Carta,* pp. 48-49.   [65] *Ibid.,* pp. 58-59.

were two of the twenty-five guarantors of Magna Carta, Eustace de Vesci and Robert de Ros.

THE CASE AGAINST THE CROWN: THE DEMAND FOR LAW

The Charter of 1215 was a natural progression from these earlier grants; like them it was a privilege, a grant of liberties. But it was also a new departure. First, men were fighting for it, not buying it. John himself had encouraged this development through his attempts to win political support in 1214-15 by granting freedom of election to the Church and a new municipal charter to the City of London. The London Charter was in fact a reply to a petition from the Londoners which John failed to match; hence their support for the rebels.[66] John's grants to individuals had developed even more obviously into a business of political barter;[67] from political barter to open rebellion was but a short step.

Secondly, men were demanding for the community of the realm what they had sought hitherto only for local communities. In doing so they were moving beyond the concept of individual privilege to the idea of public right, for many of the privileges stated in the Charter could only be held by the community as a whole.[68] Here they

[66] The Charter of May 16 granted the coveted right of the election of a mayor. *Rotuli chartarum in turri Londinensi asservati,* ed. T. Duffus Hardy (Record Commission, 1837), I, 207. London fell, or rather went over, to the barons on the following day. For the Londoners' petition, part of which was met in Magna Carta, see Mary Bateson, "A London Municipal Collection of the Reign of John," 17 *English Historical Review* 726 (1902).

[67] See pp. 132-9, *supra.*

[68] J. C. Holt, "Rights and Liberties in Magna Carta," *Album Helen Maud Cam* (Louvain, 1960), I, 57-69, especially 64-65. Here, 203-15, *infra,* esp. 210-11.

matched the concept of the rights and majesty of the Crown, which, under the impetus of the revived study of Roman law, had been making rapid progress into political thought since the mid-twelfth century.[69] Both sides in the argument met on common ground; both equally could appeal to the "rights" or "utility" of the realm, either to justify or criticize the power of the Crown.[70] Magna Carta was granted "in emendation of our realm"; it was annulled as inimical to the King's right and dignity.[71] However, the Charter revealed little conscious inheritance from the studies of the canonists and civilians. It approached the concept of public law pragmatically, perhaps even unconsciously.

The progression from individual or local liberties to general liberties carried deep implications. Local or individual privileges could be viewed as exceptions which proved the rule, as acts of grace which did not infringe the general superiority of the Crown. Liberties granted to the community as a whole could not be so regarded. To promise just judgment to individual subjects did not diminish the King's power to direct the course of justice; on the contrary, it demonstrated and added to it. But to promise just judgment to all subjects was a very different matter. This involved a permanent and general definition of the power of the Crown. This was why the issue

[69] P. N. Riesenberg, *Inalienability of Sovereignty in Medieval Political Thought* (New York, 1956), pp. 81-112; H. G. Richardson, "The Coronation in Medieval England," 16 *Traditio* 111-202, esp. pp. 151-61 (1960); E. H. Kantorowicz, *The King's Two Bodies* (Princeton, 1957), pp. 347-58; Gaines Post, *Studies in Medieval Legal Thought* (Princeton, 1964), pp. 415-33.

[70] Holt, *op. cit. supra* note 68, pp. 62-63; Holt, *Magna Carta,* pp. 100-4. See here, 208-9, *infra.*

[71] *Selected Letters of Pope Innocent III,* ed. C. R. Cheney and W. H. Semple (London, 1953), pp. 215-16.

of the Great Charter could only be resolved by war.

This was no sudden leap into the dark. John's control of the administration tended to confine office to a small favoured group. But there were still men with administrative experience on the baronial side; Saer de Quenci, Earl of Winchester, who conducted the final negotiations prior to Runnymede, had been a Baron of the Exchequer; other rebels had acted as justices or sheriffs. Moreover, it would have been impossible, even if the King had wanted, to deny administrative experience to the members of the great aristocratic families. They necessarily gained it in war, on the Crusades, in the law courts, in the transaction of family business, and in the management of their estates; they mixed with great officials in both church and state. Increasingly they took a responsible attitude towards affairs of state, or at least stated their own policies in terms which reached beyond the mere assertion of self-interest. They were becoming politically educated. They had the experience derived from the lengthy and repeated absences of all three Angevin kings abroad. During the longest and most critical of these, Richard's Crusade and captivity in Germany 1189-94, they had remained loyal to his representatives and helped in the maintenance of law and order, despite the quarrels between the Chancellor, William de Longchamps, and Count John, and despite the latter's machinations with Philip Augustus of France.

Indeed this provided the occasion for the assertion of some of the principles which later appear in the Charter itself. In the agreement between Count John and William de Longchamps in 1191 it was laid down that:

Bishops, abbots, earls, barons, knights and free tenants shall not be disseised of lands and chattels by the will of the justices or ministers of the lord King, but shall be dealt with by the judgment of the court of the lord King according to the lawful customs and assizes of the realm or by the mandate of the lord King.[72]

This agreement was remarkable not only as an early and coherent assertion of lawful process; it also demonstrated a very practical turn of mind which, with Richard safely absent in the Holy Land, saw no conflict between the custom of the realm and the will of the king.

Of all the influences at work on the mentality of the baronage, infinitely the most important was law and legal procedure. This was part of the elemental structure of the feudal state. One of the king's prime duties, as defined in his coronation oath, was to give just judgment and maintain just laws. One of the vassal's prime duties was to attend his lord's court. One of the prime assumptions of feudal justice was that peer should judge and be judged by peer. These were principles accepted far beyond the shores of England and long before the accession of the Angevins. But in England, and especially under the Angevins, they assumed characteristics which had a determining effect on Magna Carta.

First, the development of English society in the twelfth century avoided hard and fast division within the landowning class. Tenants-in-chief were also undertenants; knightly and baronial families intermarried; some knights were wealthier and more powerful than many barons. Barons carried certain judicial privileges and liabilities, for as direct tenants of the king they were immediately justiciable in his courts; similarly, tenure by military service was recognised as the highest form of lay tenure; but these distinctions were not so deep as the great division between those who held their lands freely

[72] *Hoveden,* III, 136.

and those who did not. Henry II made his legal innovations not for the barons and his other immediate tenants, nor yet at the other extreme for all his subjects; he provided them for those who held freely. Similarly Magna Carta conveyed its privileges to the free tenant, the *liber homo;* few of its clauses were restricted to the barons at one end of the social scale or extended to the villeinage at the other.

Secondly, Henry II's legal measures provided ready access to legal process and established a national system of justice, which rapidly expanded into spheres of justice which the increasing complications of feudal tenures and the fragmentation of fees were forcing the feudal courts to abandon. Henry not only did this, he also established routine legal processes which greatly facilitated litigation, especially litigation about land, which was one of the prime concerns of the courts. Seisin and title, succession and inheritance, were defined and protected; tenant right was strengthened; division, sale, and mortgage were determined in increasingly complex forms. The landowning class was becoming accustomed to a logical, routine system of justice. Sometimes it might be slow, sometimes it might be rough, but it was incomparably better than what had gone before or was obtainable in most feudal courts. Landowners, from barons down to sokemen, resorted to it readily and frequently. Indeed it owed its success to their acceptance of it. In Magna Carta they tried to improve it, not destroy it.[73]

This development steeped the baronial class in law.

[73] See R. C. van Caenegem, *Royal Writs in England from the Conquest to Glanvill* (Selden Society, vol. LXXVII; London, 1959) ; Doris M. Stenton, *English Justice between the Norman Conquest and the Great Charter* (Philadelphia, 1964).

It was a much more complex, sophisticated law than that which they inherited from the feudal independence of the past. But it was not dissociated from it. The judicial superiority of the Crown had developed in part out of the feudal action of tolt.[74] The law was administered in the courts of shire and hundred, the old local courts of Anglo-Saxon England, dominated now as then by the county landowners. The Angevins had built on an established foundation. They had not destroyed ancient custom. They had developed it. Indeed long usage, established title, the fact of possession, underlay many of their new legal procedures.

Such a system both provided legal process and educated those who used it. It created assumptions and provided standards which placed other actions of the Crown in increasingly sharp contrast. What were men of such legalistic bent to make of the rapid advance of the royal administration? The law was not yet so clearly defined as to distinguish judicial from legislative and executive business, nor were these men very clear on how custom and law developed. Yet they were faced with an inventive administration which was producing new procedures which went far beyond any customary limitations conceivable at the beginning of the century. Necessarily, administrative development could not be customary; there could be no ancient custom to determine how Jewish debts should be collected or scutage assessed, or when assizes should be held, or whether men should serve in Poitou; these were all problems created by the rule of the Angevin kings. Custom was incompetent in the face of change. Yet administrative development created custom by the accumulation of prece-

[74] G. J. Turner, *Brevia Placitata* (Selden Society, vol. LXVI; London, 1947), p. lxiii.

dents as it moved logically from one step to the next.

Occasionally a king might acknowledge the problem this created. When in February 1204 John wrote to the clergy and laity of Ireland asking for an aid for the defence of Normandy, he made it clear that he was seeking it as a demonstration of friendship, not as a custom;[75] similarly in 1208, in asking the barons of Lancashire for assistance in repairing the moat of Lancaster Castle, he was ready enough to assert that he sought such aid not as a custom but as an act of grace and for this occasion only.[76] On certain issues it was recognised and accepted that there had to be some process of consultation between the king and some at least of the magnates of the realm. But this was no insuperable obstacle to change; there is no evidence that any such gathering opposed royal policies prior to the final years of the reign of John.[77]

Thus the barons were confronted with a system of administration which was moving beyond the confines of tradition and which created its own law through the development of its own precedents. In 1215 they sought to call a halt to this process, partly by opposing it directly, partly by incorporating some of its achievements in a statement which related custom to contemporary circumstances. They did this with varying confi-

[75] *Rotuli chartarum in turri Londinensi asservati,* ed. T. Duffus Hardy (Record Commission, 1837), I, 133b-34.

[76] *Rotuli litterarum patentium in turri Londinensi asservati,* ed. T. Duffus Hardy (Record Commission, 1835), I, 87.

[77] In 1205, however, the magnates, headed by Hubert Walter and William Marshal, opposed a campaign on the continent, advancing various reasons for thinking it impolitic. *Radulphi de Coggeshall chronicon Anglicanum,* ed. J. Stevenson (Rolls series, 1875), pp. 152-53.

dence. They had no hesitation in regulating feudal incidents; they showed more in dealing with the collection of the King's debts or with the appointment of his officials, in matters which lay more within the private purview of the Crown. Even here, however, they made some remarkable gains. The forest provisions of the Great Charter of 1215 and the Charter of the Forest of 1217 marked an assertion of custom and the establishment of law in a field recognised hitherto as totally dependent on the will of the King.[78]

This conflict was not limited to the problems created by administrative reform. It occurred in a much more dramatic and painful form in the administration of justice. The Angevins had provided justice as never before and trained their subjects in the law. Yet it was their justice to give, sell, or withhold as they wished and as political circumstance required and permitted. They respected the system they had built; they were all in favour of enforcing justice, John as much as his father; but they did not intend it to do anything but strengthen the authority of the Crown. They could direct it against their enemies and use it in support of their friends. They could place men in their mercy, enforce heavy penalties for readmission to their good will, and use the procedures of the Exchequer to harry their actual or suspected enemies. They disseised men by will, ordered the seizure of castles and hostages, even imprisoned and exiled.[79] From this stemmed one of the fundamental

[78] Compare the statement of Richard fitz Neal that the forest had its own laws based, not on the common law of the realm, but on the arbitrary regulations of the King. *Dialogus de Scaccario,* ed. C. Johnson (London, 1950), pp. 59-60. This is an authoritative statement of twelfth-century practice.

[79] Jolliffe, *Angevin Kingship,* pp. 50-109.

cries of 1215 : the demand for justice and the principle, laid down in chapter 39 of the Charter, that judgment should precede execution.

In some ways this was a simple aim. One of the common currencies of medieval thought was the distinction between kingship and tyranny, between rule according to the law and the exercise of arbitrary will. This appeared as part of the refined political theory of the *Policraticus* of John of Salisbury, as one of the assumptions of John's hostile monastic critics, and as an argument used by laymen in the courts of law against arbitrary action by the Crown.[80] King John himself accepted this distinction.[81] But if it was easy to quote as a political cliché, its implications were not so easily followed out in practice. Any king might flout the law occasionally and in anger; John had done this, as had many others. Few, however, had shown such skill as his in using the law for his own ends. He was interested in the administration of law. He was perhaps more likely to insist that established procedure should go forward despite any special instruction of his own than vice versa.[82] But established procedure in the Exchequer landed some of his men in prison, and established procedure in the shire court sent others into exile as

[80] Holt, *Magna Carta,* pp. 75-78, 117-19.

[81] "The King to Geoffrey fitz Peter. We order you in the fealty by which you are bound to us that you should make diligent enquiry whether Geoffrey de Lucy was disseised of the manor of Newton by our will or by the judgment of our court. And if you find that he was disseised by our will, then you shall reinstate him in seisin . . . ." *Rotuli litterarum clausarum in turri Londinensi asservati,* ed. T. Duffus Hardy (Record Commission, 1833-34), I, 136b.

[82] Doris M. Stenton, *op. cit. supra* note 73, pp. 89-93; Holt, *Magna Carta,* pp. 81-82.

outlaws. It was this skill in manipulating the law which made the demand for judgment and lawful process one of the main themes of the Great Charter.

The task of the King's opponents in 1215 was intricate and difficult. It was not simply a matter of stating custom; it was a matter of extending and defining custom and lawful procedure in the light of new administrative practice. They set out to do in three years what the Crown had been doing over two generations or more. But they were doing it with different interests and objectives in view. Hence there was a real conflict of principle. The barons were invading a field where the initiative had lain hitherto with the Crown. This was the essential struggle and achievement of 1215. They won a charter, but in effect they were originating what later generations would have called statute law; it was not without justification that the Great Charter became the first item in the manuscript and early printed collections of statutes. But they were doing this without any agreed procedure or accepted form, and without the conscious realisation that this was where their efforts would lead. Hence they embodied their statement of law in the form of a charter, and they tried to ensure the full execution of that charter by the performance of oaths and by arming the twenty-five guarantors with the primitive weapon of distraint.

Thus the Charter embodied a mixture of the ambitious and the antiquated. When the barons, at Brackley at the end of April, asked the King to seal a list of articles, they asked for something he was bound to refuse. The most John was prepared to concede in letters of May 9-10 was that the issues should be submitted to a committee representing both parties

sitting under the arbitration of Pope Innocent III[83]
The difference was irreconcilable; the barons had already renounced their allegiance and declared war on
May 5. The apparent reconciliation at Runnymede in
June came about only because London fell to the rebels
on May 17. Even then John had no intention of
accepting the Charter as a permanent solution. Within
a month of the meeting at Runnymede he wrote to Pope
Innocent asking for formal papal annulment. He had
found no means of reconciling the malcontents which he
was prepared to accept. The barons were placed in a
much more difficult quandary. They had asked that
their demands should be met by an act of royal self-
limitation embodied in a freely given grant. But John
obviously was submitting to compulsion. Thus the
circumstances in which the Charter was obtained
amounted to a grave imputation of its validity, and this
was all the more serious since both parties had appealed
to Rome. Indeed, the barons pressed their demands in
May in contravention of, or without waiting for, Innocent's decision on the appeal.[84] He was scarcely likely to
give his blessing now to an agreement so obviously
reached under duress.

Hence at Runnymede the barons were demanding an
unreliable guaranty of something which the King would
not in the long run surrender. They made the best of a
bad job by trying to exclude any further papal interven-

[83] *Rotuli litterarum patentium in turri Londinensi asservati,*
ed. T. Duffus Hardy (Record Commission, 1835), I, 141;
Rotuli chartarum in turri Londinensi asservati, ed. T. Duffus
Hardy (Record Commission, 1837), I, 209b.
[84] Cheney and Semple, eds., *op. cit. supra* note 71, pp. 194-97;
C. R. Cheney, "The Eve of Magna Carta," 38 *Bulletin of the
John Rylands Library* 311, at pp. 315-18 (1956); Holt, *Magna
Carta,* pp. 293-95.

tion[85] and by insisting on the retention of London.[86]   He
bided his time.

However, both sides negotiated terms vigorously.
No documents survive from the period between the royal
offer of May 10 and the Articles of the Barons, which
were agreed to as a preliminary to the full meeting of the
two parties which took place at Runnymede on June 15,[87]
but there are sufficient differences between the Articles
and the Charter to show that a great deal of hard thinking and hard-fought argument remained to be completed
between June 15 and June 19, when firm peace was
agreed.   It was not until this stage that John gained
respite on the disseisins and afforestations of Richard
and Henry, that amercement of barons by their peers
was included, or provision made on the methods of
summoning the Great Council.[88]   Furthermore, clause
after clause of the Articles was amended in detail in a
manner which suggests that the King's justices and clerks
had worked hard to provide legally watertight provisions.[89]

Hence the Charter finally appeared as a serious and
coherent set of provisions.   It went too far at many
points, but then so had John.   It was often vague where

[85] Articles of the Barons, *forma securitatis;* compare Magna
Carta, chapter 62.

[86] For the agreement on London, see *Foedera, conventiones,
litterae et cujuscunque generis acta publica,* ed. T. Rymer; new
edition ed. A. Clarke and F. Holbrooke (Record Commission,
1816), I, part 1, 133, and Holt, *Magna Carta,* pp. 171-74.

[87] For discussion of the negotiations of May and June and the
role and date of the Articles, see Cheney, *op. cit. supra* note 84;
J. C. Holt, "The Making of Magna Carta," 72 *English Historical Review* 402-22 (1957); and Holt, *Magna Carta,*
pp. 156-60, 304-6. See here, 217-38, *infra.*

[88] Articles of the Barons, chapter 25; Magna Carta, chapters
14, 21, 52, 53.

[89] Holt, *Magna Carta,* pp. 195-96.

greater precision would have been desirable, but precision was difficult to achieve in the face of the manoeuvrability of the king's government and the danger of political division. It was treated seriously. Some believed in and hoped for a permanent settlement. Certainly the Archbishop, Stephen Langton, had striven for a compromise since his return to England in 1213 and had acted as an intermediary through all the negotiations.[90] Even those who doubted whether a settlement could be permanent had good reason to negotiate seriously, for there was a large body of middle opinion to be won over or lost. Many only joined the movement against the King in the months or even weeks before Runnymede. Some abandoned it in the summer as war drew nearer. Others, more radical in temper, continued fighting despite the peace agreed at Runnymede.[91] In the short run John and these recalcitrants were more realistic: the agreement could not last. But in the long run Langton and the moderates were right—right by accident because the Charter achieved its permanence as a result of the minority of Henry III.

But they deserved their luck, for the Charter had stated something worth preserving. In attempting to resolve the political stresses within English society, it had assembled the experience of a generation well enough to provide a pattern and an example both for the immediate future and for generations yet to come.

[90] F. M. Powicke, *Stephen Langton* (Oxford, 1928), pp. 102-28; Holt, *Magna Carta,* pp. 130-44, 187-94, 255-67.
[91] For these movements, see Holt, *The Northerners,* pp. 105-10, 120-22.

7

THE BARONS AND THE GREAT CHARTER

THE rather broad title under which this paper appears covers an investigation into the attitude of the English layman towards problems of government and political theory in the generation or so prior to the sealing of Magna Carta at Runnymede in 1215. Briefly, I hope to show that men of the baronial and knightly class were slowly moving, in this period, towards a grasp of the ideas which were put into practice in 1215, and further, that occasionally, as individuals or groups, they were coming to demand and even apply some of the measures which were eventually laid down in the Charter. The reader may in the end feel, with the writer, that the outcome of this attempt is rather vague, both as regards conclusions and evidence. Despite this, the attempt is worth the effort and has at best two justifications. First, in its results, it may help to explain the attitude, perhaps sometimes the motives, of the men who met at Runnymede in 1215. Secondly, in its methods, it may illustrate some ways in which government records may be used to throw light on men's assumptions and ideas.

The topic has a controversial aspect in that it is relevant to the question—who designed Magna Carta? In answering this, historians have differed markedly. While Stubbs considered that the baronage were at least partly responsible,[1] and Tout wrote of Robert fitz Walter as 'the first champion of English liberty',[2] Miss Norgate firmly asserted that the barons were incapable of rising to the ' lofty conception embodied in the Charter ' and that Stephen Langton and the bishops were its chief authors.[3] Some later authorities have restated her views, in whole or in part,[4] while recently Dr. Lane Poole has looked to King John's friends and supporters, rather than the rebel leaders, for evidence of political experience and sagacity.[5] Sir Maurice Powicke, in contrast, has argued that, as important administrators, justices and associates of

[1] *Constitutional History of England*, 6th edn., i. 579 ff.
[2] *Dictionary of National Biography*, vii. 222.   [3] *John Lackland*, pp. 233-4.
[4] For views emphasizing the importance of Langton see W. S. McKechnie, *Magna Carta*, 1st edn., p. 62; and C. H. McIlwain, *Constitutionalism and the Changing World*, p. 103. Professor Painter's attitude to the role of Langton and the character of the baronage is similar to Miss Norgate's. See *The Reign of King John*, pp. 314-15, 347 and ' Magna Carta ', *Amer. Hist. Rev.* liii (1947), 47-8.
[5] *From Domesday Book to Magna Carta*, pp. 470-9.

lawyers and clerks, the barons were bound to absorb and hold views on the organization of the state.[1]

The present paper is not directly concerned with these different opinions. The problem of the origin of the Charter is a dual one. In one aspect it involves a detailed analysis of the politics of John's last years, in which the roles played by many individuals, both clerk and lay, must be evaluated. In its other aspect, the one treated here, it requires a study of the slow development of the ideas eventually embodied in the Charter, and indeed of the problems which gave rise to it. The two methods of approach are largely separate. Thus, to argue that the laity came to make assumptions and use ideas which eventually found form in the Charter does not conflict with the view that Stephen Langton, or other churchmen, or indeed the king's friends, had a powerful influence over the course events took at Runnymede. Whether they did so or not is a problem of political detail. It must also be agreed that, even if laymen did come to think in this way, their views may well have been affected, in the long run, by ecclesiastical and other modes of thought; ultimately, it becomes unrealistic to draw a harsh dividing line between clerical and secular ideas. But none of this invalidates the view that laymen could make an independent and intelligent approach to political problems. To argue that they could, increases their stature; it also increases the stature of those among the clergy, who, like Langton, may well have influenced them.

These arguments involve an obvious assumption which can only be discussed briefly. The Charter must be read as a criticism of a system of government, not of the behaviour of a single monarch, for we cannot argue that the ideas of 1215 developed gradually without also arguing that the problems the Charter was designed to meet were of long standing, John's government and his failures abroad simply precipitating events. As early as 1892 Charles Bémont pointed to the existence of some of these problems under Henry II [2] and J. H. Round emphasized them in his work on the pipe rolls of this reign.[3] Later authorities have reinforced these views [4] and the accumulation of printed material in recent years has demonstrated the strong element of continuity both in the aims and methods of the Angevin government throughout the period

---

[1] *Stephen Langton*, pp. 120–4; *Medieval England*, pp. 60–4, 238 ff.; ' Reflections on the Medieval State ', *Trans. Roy. Hist. Soc.*, 4th ser., xix (1936), 1 ff.

[2] *Chartes des Libertés Anglaises*, pp. xv, xxii.

[3] *Magna Carta Commemoration Essays*, p. 62. He paid particular attention to the heavy reliefs, amercements and *oblata* demanded in Henry's later years. See *Pipe Roll 22 Henry II*, pp. xxii ff., *Pipe Roll 23 Henry II*, pp. xxiii, xxv-vi, *Pipe Roll 28 Henry II*, pp. xxii ff.

[4] In reviewing the pipe rolls of the middle years of Richard's reign Lady Stenton commented that ' they give the impression of a country taxed to the limit '. (*Ibid. 9 Richard I*, p. xiii.)

1154–1215.[1] King John was nothing if not traditional. We can find examples of arbitrary disseisin or imprisonment in the reign of his father, as we can under him.[2] The taking of hostages, again, seems to have been a normal disciplinary method of government.[3] Even John's exactions of heavy financial payments as guarantees of good behaviour, the charters of fealty in which men promised loyal service on pain of distraint or disinheritance, both find a close parallel in the measures Philip Augustus used to tie the continental baronage to his cause.[4] In France, as in England, men had to

[1] This is clearly illustrated in the continuous treatment given in modern works to the administrative history of the period. See, for instance, Dr. Lane Poole, *op. cit.* chap. xii, R. S. Hoyt, *The Royal Demesne in English Constitutional History*, ch. iv and v, and S. K. Mitchell, *Taxation in Medieval England*.

[2] For arbitrary disseisin and imprisonment by Henry, see *infra*, p. 14 and the cases of Adam de Hales, quoted by Dr. Lane Poole, *op. cit.* p. 209, n, and of Thomas Bardolf (*Bracton's Note Book*, ed. F. W. Maitland, case no. 49). For alleged arbitrary disseisin by King Richard see the case of Geoffrey de Say (*Rot. Litt. Claus.* i. 168b). *Cf. The Complete Peerage*, v. 119–20.

[3] There are many references to hostages in the pipe rolls of Henry II's reign. Some of these were probably taken from the Irish or Welsh. For a hostage taken on the order of Hubert Walter in 1194, see *Three Rolls of the King's Court*, ed. F. W. Maitland (Pipe Roll Soc.), p. 9.

John certainly took hostages from many individual barons. See, for example, the cases of Roger de Lacy (*Chronica Rogeri de Hovedene*, ed. W. Stubbs (Rolls Series), iv. 91–2, *Rot. Chart.* p. 102b), William de Albini of Belvoir (*Hoveden*, iv. 161), John de Curcy (*Rot. Litt. Pat.* p. 45b), Robert de Ros (*ibid.* p. 59b, *Rot. Litt. Claus.* i. 99), Roger de Montbegon (*Rot. de Oblatis et Finibus*, p. 275), Robert de Vieuxpont (*Rot. Litt. Pat.* p. 89b), William de Braose (*Rot. Litt. Pat.* p. 80b) and William Marshal. (*Histoire de Guillaume le Maréchal*, ed. P. Meyer, ll. 13257–78, 13355–419, 14319–428, and *Rot. Litt. Pat.* p. 94b). How far the king exceeded contemporary practice, it is difficult to say. William Marshal seems to have been quite ready to surrender his sons on demand (*Histoire de Guillaume le Maréchal*, ll. 13403–6) and in most of the cases given above there were good reasons for taking hostages. Wendover's muddled account of a general demand for hostages following the Interdict finds little supporting evidence. (Matthew Paris, *Chronica Majora*, ed. H. R. Luard (Rolls Series), ii. 523–4).

It is an exaggeration to suggest, as Mr. Jolliffe has done, that the surrender of hostages had become ' almost a normal incident of tenure ' by 1212, either in the north or any other part of the country (*The Constitutional History of Medieval England*, p. 249 and n.). Of the cases he quotes seven families had provided hostages for the king of Scotland (*Rot. Litt. Claus.* i. 137b). In the six remaining cases, certainly two men, Earl David and Richard de Unfraville, had surrendered hostages because of their suspected participation in the fitz Walter conspiracy of August 1212 (*Rot. Litt. Pat.* p. 94b, *Rot. Litt. Claus.* i. 122b). This is also most probably true in the cases of Robert de Muschamp and Roger de Merlay (*Rot. Litt. Pat.* pp. 99, 106). Richard de Lucy's daughter, also mentioned by Mr. Jolliffe, was probably a royal ward, not a hostage (*Rot. Litt. Pat.* p. 96b, *The Complete Peerage*, viii. 248). Only in one case he quotes, that of Robert de Vaux, were hostages clearly taken for disciplinary reasons prior to the plot of 1212 (P.R.O., Pipe Roll 13 John, rot. 15, m. 2r, *Rot. Litt. Pat.* pp. 95, 96). Here they were taken to guarantee the payment of money.

John resorted to taking hostages frequently after the treasonable plot of 1212, but this was natural enough, and it is probably to the hostages taken after this time that the demands for restoration in the Great Charter largely referred.

[4] See *Layettes du Trésor des Chartes*, ed. A. Teulet (Paris, 1863), vol. i, nos. 478, 773, 805, 870–1, 881–7, 892–6, 932, 954–5, 988–94, 996–1001, 1026, 1040. There are many other examples both in this work, the *Catalogue des Actes de Philippe Auguste*, ed. L. Delisle (Paris, 1856), and in a register of Philip Augustus preserved in the Vatican Library (MS. Ottobon, 2796) and described in *Archives des missions scientifiques et littéraires*, 3rd ser. vol. vi (1880).

surrender castles to the king to atone for political errors or pledge their loyalty.[1] Indeed, in financial matters one baron could treat another just as stringently as John dealt with his vassals,[2] and nowhere in his dealings with individuals did the king lay down harsher penalties than those provided by the advice of the magnates lay and ecclesiastical in the writ of April 1205, organizing the defences of the country against invasion.[3] In these circumstances it is not surprising to find that William Marshal and his colleagues took from the *reversi* of 1217 charters of fealty which were closely similar to those exacted by the late king.[4]

All this makes it difficult to accept John's harshness as something particularly individual or unique, or to attribute the grievances of 1215 solely to his actions. His character and his failures certainly added something, as did the passage of time and the recurrence of heavy demands and harsh measures, but the causes of much of the discontent were already there when he came to the throne. After 1199, the mass of information in the chancery enrolments makes it easier to trace them, but this in itself constitutes a strong warning against assuming that John's accession marked a clear or decisive break in the policy of the Angevin government. Abbot Ralf of Coggeshall put the point concisely in stating that the baronial demands at the end of the reign were for the abolition of the ' evil customs which the father and the brother of the king had created to the detriment of church and kingdom, along with those abuses which the king himself had added '.[5]

---

[1] See the letters of Guy des Roches surrendering the castle of Montfort-le-Roger to Philip Augustus (*Layettes du Trésor des Chartes*, no. 799).

[2] The exaction of ransoms after the civil war was used by the victors to force their opponents to transfer estates. See, for instance, the losses suffered by William de Mowbray (*The Coucher Book of Furness Abbey*, vol. ii, pt. 2, ed. J. Brownbill, Chetham Society, new ser. lxxvi (1916), p. 291), Maurice de Gant (*Rolls of the Justices in Eyre for Yorkshire, 1218–19*, ed. Lady Stenton, Selden Soc., vol. lvi, no. 1133), and Henry Bec (*Rolls of the Justices in Eyre for the Counties of Lincolnshire 1218–19 and Worcestershire 1221*, ed. Lady Stenton, Selden Soc., vol. liii, no. 898).   [3] *Rot. Litt. Pat.* p. 55.

[4] The Chancery Miscellanea still include a set of some twenty charters of fealty made out by the *reversi* at the end of the civil war. All the grantors pledge their land as security for their faithful service and agree to accept the penalty of disinheritance should they withdraw from the service of the king or his heirs. These charters were probably drawn up to a form provided by the chancery. The witness lists usually include the names of William Marshal, Ranulf of Chester, the earls of Arundel and Warenne, and Hubert de Burgh. (P.R.O., Chancery Miscellanea, 34/8, nos. 1–23.)

[5] *Chronicon Anglicanum Radulphi de Coggeshall*, ed. J. Stephenson (Rolls Series), p. 170. The Waverley Annalist makes a similar statement. ' Hoc anno magna orta est discordia inter regem Angliae et barones: his exigentibus ab eo leges Sancti Edwardi, et aliorum subsequentium regum libertates, et liberas consuetudines. Nam tempore patris sui et maxime suo tempore corruptae nimis et aggravatae fuerant ' (*Annales Monastici*, ed. H. R. Luard (Rolls Series), ii. 282).

That the practices of all three Angevin kings were in question in 1215 is implied by the Papal bull annulling the charter (*Foedera*, i, pt. 1, 135–6) and the letters of Peter des Roches and his associates covering the bull ' Mirari cogimur ' (*ante*, xliv (1929), 90 ff.). The point is made quite clearly in John's letters to the pope of 29 May 1215 (*Foedera*, i, pt. 1, 129) and specific reference is made to the reigns of Henry II and Richard I in the

As kings, the Angevins were bound by oath to preserve and govern according to law and custom. Within these general limitations, they were further held to protect and defend the rights of their tenants-in-chief, to whom they stood as feudal lord. Both in practice and by definition, the king could not claim absolute power. To the medieval thinker, unbounded authority was not an attribute of kingship but of tyranny, for while the king governed according to the law, the tyrant ruled according to his will. This distinction between law and will receives full attention from John of Salisbury.[1] It is also used or mentioned almost incidentally by Gerald of Wales,[2] Roger of Howden,[3] Richard fitz Neal[4] and Glanville,[5] and was so ingrained in the medieval mind as to become a generally accepted premise for political discussion. In practice, however, law and will might be complementary rather than mutually exclusive. The government of a country raised many matters for which custom provided no rule or precedent and on these the king, suitably advised, might decide or arbitrate. As a result, the distinction between law and will was often of immediate concern both to the king and his subjects, and it became so generally current that it was reflected frequently, almost unconsciously, in many of the writs issued by John's chancery. The king, for instance, might order an assize to proceed ' unless reason or the custom of our realm ' ran counter to it;[6] he might lay down that cases should proceed according to custom despite any special instruction he had issued to the contrary,[7] or that the justiciar should do nothing contrary to custom on the authority of a royal mandate.[8] Sometimes he might order the restitution of land if it could be shown that the plaintiff had been disseized ' by our will ' rather than by the ' judgement of our court '.[9]

Perhaps the distinction between law and will was not the only premise from which political discussion might start. The tenets

' unknown ' charter cap. 9 and Magna Carta caps. 52 and 53. The Charter, of course, affected many administrative practices established before John's accession. Compare, for instance, cap. 44 with cap. 12 of Howden's record of the forest eyre of 1198 (*Hoveden*, iv. 64) and cap. 11 of the Forest Assize of 1184.

[1] For an analysis of John's treatment of the subject, see J. Dickinson, ' The Medieval Conception of Kingship and some of its limitations as developed in the Policraticus of John of Salisbury ', *Speculum*, vol. i (1926), 325 ff.

[2] ' Rex autem qui a regendo dicitur, primo se ipsum, deinde subditum sibi populum, regere tenetur; tyranno vero . . . proprium est violento dominatu populum opprimere ' (*Opera*, ed. J. S. Brewer and G. F. Warner (Rolls Series), viii. 54).

[3] See his description of the dispute between William de Stuteville and William de Mowbray in the king's court in 1201, when the parties were reconciled ' consilio regni, et voluntate regis ' (*Hoveden*, iv. 118).

[4] See his discussion of the royal forest where he distinguishes between common right and the will of the king (*Dialogus de Scaccario*, ed. Charles Johnson, pp. 59–60).

[5] See his well known passage on reliefs, *De Legibus et Consuetudinibus Regni Angliae* x, chap. 4, ed. G. E. Woodbine, pp. 126–8.

[6] *Curia Regis Rolls*, ii. 223.   [7] *Ibid.* iii. 57.   [8] *Ibid.* iii. 27–8.
[9] See letters dealing with Geoffrey de Lucy (*Rot. Litt. Claus.*, i. 136b).

of civil law could well provide alternative and more absolutist views on the nature of the ruler's authority. The *Corpus Juris Civilis* undoubtedly had a great effect on the development of English thought, particularly in the legal field. Under John, civil law was taught at Oxford and many important men, probably including Hubert Walter, had had some training at Bologna.[1] Occasionally, an authoritarian note sounded in the government records. In 1194, for instance, the royal justices roundly condemned the excommunication launched by Archbishop Geoffrey of York against William de Stuteville with the phrase—' consideratum est excommunicatio illa facta est contra regalem dignitatem et excellenciam '.[2] During the Interdict, too, Alexander the Mason apparently upheld royal authority in the strongest terms, the king being the ' rod of the wrath of the lord, ruling his people like a rod of iron and dashing them in pieces like a potter's vessel '.[3]

Certainly the king had extensive and ill-defined powers ; the legal records, in particular, demonstrate the wide variety of problems which were referred to his decision.[4] John, too, was the kind of man we might expect to seize every argument and occasion to bolster up and demonstrate his authority. He even pilloried the treason of a vassal by referring to it in the dating clauses of his charters.[5] On occasions, his writs, while contrasting custom with a royal order, insist that the latter should take precedence,[6] but nowhere do the records suggest that he considered his power absolute and free from traditional limitations. In asking the barons and knights of the honour of Lancaster for aid in repairing Lancaster castle in 1208, he stated that he was not seeking this aid as a customary one but as of grace and only for this particular occasion.[7] In defending his rights he was quick to base his argu-

---

[1] *The Liber Pauperum of Vacarius*, ed. F. de Zulueta, Selden Soc., xliv (1927), pp. xiii-xix; H. G. Richardson, ' The Oxford Law School under John ', *Law Quart. Rev.* lvii (1941), 319-38); A. Allaria, ' English Scholars at Bologna during the Middle Ages ', *Dublin Rev.* cxii (1893), 66-83. But see also below, p. 202.

[2] *Three Rolls of the King's Court*, ed. F. W. Maitland (Pipe Roll. Soc.), p. 50. See also a damaged entry on the roll of the pleas at Westminster in 1194, where a novel disseisin is apparently stated to have been made ' in lesionem coronae domini Regis Ricardi ' (*Rot. Curiae Regis*, i. 31).

[3] The quotation is used by Wendover (Matthew Paris, *Chronica Majora*, ed. H. R. Luard (Rolls Series), ii. 527). See also Sir Maurice Powicke, ' Alexander of St. Albans: a Literary Muddle ', *Essays in History presented to R. Lane Poole*, pp. 246 ff.

[4] C. T. Flower, *Introduction to the Curia Regis Rolls, 1199-1230*, Selden Soc., vol. lxii (1943), 15-16.

[5] *Cal. Docs. France*, ed. J. H. Round, no. 391 and a charter to Saer de Quency of March 1203 in the Bodleian Library (MSS. Wykeham-Musgrave, C37, parcel 1) which ends . . . ' Data per manum Hugonis de Wellis apud Pontem Aldomar ' i die martii anno regni nostri quarto quo R. comes Sagiensis proditionem fecit nobis apud Alenconem '.

[6] *Curia Regis Rolls*, iii. 215; *Pleas before the King or his Justices, 1198-1202*, ed. Lady Stenton, Selden Soc., vol. lxviii, no. 759.

[7] *Rot. Litt. Pat.* p. 87. A similar distinction is made in John's letters of February 1204 requesting aid from the clergy and laity of Ireland. (*Rot. Chart.*, pp. 133b-34.)

ments and claims on custom,[1] often referring to his father's reign,[2] and on one occasion apparently, seeking his precedents in the reign of Edward the Confessor.[3] In his famous *pièce justicative* dealing with William de Braose he paraded the custom of the realm to justify his actions,[4] and when war finally broke out, it was the rebels whom the papal agents, headed by Peter des Roches, accused of destroying the approved customs of the kingdom and introducing ' nova iura '.[5]

It is impossible, of course, to decide how far these and other letters reflect the personality of the king. Many may well represent the views of the chancery clerks. On the other hand, the cases quoted were not matters of routine administration, but important questions on which the king's own words might well be reflected in his writs. That this probably happened in other instances has already been shown by Professor Galbraith.[6] But whatever our conclusion on this point, it is clear that traditional ideas and arguments found their way into official correspondence. · They were sometimes too useful to be ignored, and too firmly rooted to be flouted. At an earlier date Ranulf Glanville had sustained the privileges of the monastery of Abingdon, stating, according to one version of the local chronicle, that the ' lord king neither

---

[1] See his letters to the Irish baronage of May 1207; ' Miramur plurimum super mandato quod nobis fecistis per litteras vestras patentes unde videtur nobis quod novam assisam creare paratis in terra nostra sine nobis, quod est inauditum tempore antecessorum nostrorum et nostro scilicet quod assisa nova statuatur in terra alicujus sine assensu principis terre illius '; (*Rot. Litt. Pat.* p. 72); also his letters of the same month to the clergy assembled at St. Albans forbidding them to institute anything new ' contra regni nostri consuetudinem ' (*ibid.*).

[2] See *infra*, p. 197, n. 2.

[3] The well-known record of the conversations between John and the papal legates in 1211, given in the Annals of Burton, represents the king as appealing to the tradition of Edward the Confessor and Wulfstan to justify his claim to control ecclesiastical appointments (*Annales Monastici*, i. 211). The late date of the Annals, the form of the dialogue and its inaccuracy both on detail and essential points throw considerable doubt on its value. (See Professor C. R. Cheney, ' The Alleged Deposition of King John ', *Studies in Medieval History presented to F. M. Powicke*, p. 107). It should be noted, however, that the letters patent sent by the Irish barons to the king in 1213 refer to the pre-Conquest rights of the kings of England in conferring bishoprics. These letters, themselves based on similar ones provided by the English baronage, in all probability follow a formula provided by the government. (H. G. Richardson and Professor G. O. Sayles, *The Irish Parliament in the Middle Ages*, pp. 285–7.) There is a second version of the dialogue, differing in detail, in a fourteenth century chronicle of John's reign in the Bodleian Library (Digby MS. 170, fos. 58–62ᵛ). These two versions may well have been based on some other original. The earlier part of the chronicle in the Digby MS. covers the period of 1199–1210 and has some similarities with the work of Gervase of Canterbury. For other versions see Professor C. R. Cheney, *loc. cit.* p. 103.

[4] *Foedera*, i. pt. 1, 107–8.

[5] Sir Maurice Powicke, ' The bull Miramur plurimum and a letter to Archbishop Stephen Langton ', *ante*, xliv (1929), 92. See also John's arguments as they are given by the Barnwell chronicler (*Memoriale fratris Walteri de Coventria*, ed. W. Stubbs (Rolls Series), ii. 223, 224).

[6] Professor V. H. Galbraith, *Studies in the Public Records*, pp. 124 ff.

wished nor dared to attack or alter such ancient and just customs ' ; [1] under John royal justices readily noted on their rolls that an inquest had been made ' on the order of the lord King, not by the considera- tion of the court or according to the custom of the realm '.[2]

This last passage is particularly suggestive. The justices felt that where there was a conflict between custom and a royal order, this fact should be stated. The strength of the doctrine of the limited nature of royal authority is clearly demonstrated ; so are its possibilities as a weapon of criticism in situations where royal authority exceeded good and ancient custom. As men experienced the increasing demands of the Angevin régime, as the speed of development led to a widening gap between customary practice and administrative innovation, they were more and more inclined to feel that the more burdensome practices of the government were the product of tyranny and stood in marked contrast to the custom of the realm. We have a strong suggestion that this had occurred by John's reign in the speciousness with which the king argued that custom was on his side in his dealings with de Braose, and in the subtle arguments of des Roches and his associates at the begin- ning of the civil war. The king and his agents had to place royal actions within the letter of the law. But the royal interpretation of the law was not acceptable to all. The doctrine of the limited powers of kingship and tyrannical nature of absolute authority was already being used by contemporaries to generalize their criticisms of the royal government. To William of Newburgh, for example, William Longchamp was an ' unbearable tyrant ' [3] and Richard of Devizes described the chancellor's activities in similar terms.[4] Tyranny again formed the burden of the charge against John and his officials. The ' Invectivum contra regem Johannem ' invari- ably describes him by some such phrase as ' John, not a king, but a cruel tyrant '; [5] the Waverley Annalist stated that ' his tyrannical

---

[1] *Chronicon Monasterii de Abingdon*, ed. J. Stevenson (Rolls Series), ii. 298.

[2] *Rot. Curiae Regis*, ii. 189. This case, significantly enough, dealt with a disputed succession similar to that affecting the throne in 1199, although here the dispute lay between uncle and grand nephews not between uncle and nephew. For a case be- tween uncle and nephew which was pending ' ex voluntate domini Regis ', see *Pleas before the King or his Justices 1198–1202*, ed. Lady Stenton, Selden Soc., lxviii (1949), no. 484.

[3] ' Denique ipsum illo tempore in Anglia et plusquam regem experti sunt laici, et plusquam summum pontificem clerici; utrique vero tyrannum importabilem ' (*Chron- icles of the reigns of Stephen, Henry II and Richard*, ed. R. Howlett (Rolls Series), i, 333).

[4] *Ibid.* iii. 389.

[5] Brit. Mus., Cottonian MSS., Vesp. E III, fos. 171–178[v]. This is a heretical tract coming from the period 1216–27 written by a member of a sect of which Peter of Wakefield had been a member. The author writes in the name of Christ and urges immediate reform on the clergy and laity of England. The following is typical of his attitude towards John: ' Ego dominus universe carnis creator, humani generis amator, vidi Johannem infidelem in operibus carnis humane maledictum quondam Anglie non regem sed tirannum crudelem ' (fo. 175[v]).

will was his law ',[1] and similar terms creep in in other chronicles.[2] More important than this general disapproval of the king, however, was the fact that men were beginning to explore the implications of the distinction between kingship and tyranny. If a king ruled according to the law, what was the law? How should his powers be limited? What, in fact, was the custom of the realm which the king should observe?

Perhaps in this form these problems were only perceived dimly; the twelfth century approach to political questions was usually much more empirical; but ideas were provoked which approximated closely to those put into practice in 1215. The additions made to the laws of Edward the Confessor and Henry I in the edition drawn up in the first few years of the thirteenth century provide an admirable instance of this development.[3] They contain the usual distinction between law and right on the one hand, and will and force on the other,[4] and the king is given his customary function of protecting the church and maintaining the laws of his ancestors.[5] After this the editor was particularly interested in two points. First, he was concerned with questions of taxation and the performance of services. Nothing, for instance, was to be taken or demanded unless by right and reason, according to justice and the judgement of a court.[6] Secondly, he emphasized the role played by the magnates of the realm. Justice was to be dispensed by their counsel[7] and they were to meet along with the knights and freemen in regular folkmoots.[8] These moots were to see to the election of sheriffs and constables every year[9] and were to deal with emergencies as they arose.[10] Here, on the question of the election of officials, we find regulations far more stringent than the related clauses in the Great Charter.

---

[1] *Annales Monastici*, ii. 282.

[2] The Barnwell chronicler describes the baronial embassy to the pope in the winter of 1214–15 in the following terms: ' Miserunt et ipsi pro sua parte de injustis exactionibus et quasi tyrannide conquerentes ' (*Walt. Cov.* ii. 218). Wendover adds to his list of the king's evil advisers the phrase, ' qui, regi in omnibus placere cupientes, consilium non pro ratione sed pro voluntate dederunt ' (*Chron. Maj.* ii. 533). See also the views of Gerald of Wales (*Opera*, ed. J. S. Brewer and G. F. Warner (Rolls Series), viii. 328).

[3] Liebermann dated the earliest surviving version of the ' London ' Leges as *c.* 1205 (*Gesetze der Angelsachsen*, iii. 340 and ' A contemporary Manuscript of the " Leges Anglorum Londoniis Collectae " ', *ante*, xxviii (1913), 732 ff.). H. G. Richardson has suggested that the original may date from Richard's reign (' The Commons and Medieval Politics ', *T.R.H.S.*, 4th ser., xxviii (1946), 24, n. 1; ' The English Coronation Oath ', *Speculum*, xxiv (1949), 60–1; ' Studies in Bracton ', *Traditio*, vi (1948), 75, n.).

[4] *Gesetze*, i. 635, Leges Edwardi, cap. 11 1A 6.

[5] *Ibid.* i. 635–6, Leges Edwardi, caps. 11 1A, 11 1A 7. For the first time the duty of preserving the rights of the crown is added, *ibid.* cap. 11 1A 2 (H. G. Richardson, *Speculum, loc. cit.* pp. 61–2).   [6] *Ibid.* i. 554, Leges Henrici, cap. 8 1b.

[7] *Ibid.* i. 635–6, Leges Edwardi, caps. 11 1A 6, 11 1A 8.

[8] *Ibid.* i. 655, Leges Edwardi, caps. 32 A5, 6.

[9] *Ibid.* i. 656–7, Leges Edwardi, caps. 32B, 32B 1, 32B 8.

[10] *Ibid.* i. 655, Leges Edwardi, caps. 32A 3, 32A 4.

A more entertaining but rather more dubious example of the same type of work appears in the ' De Principis Instructione ' of Gerald of Wales.[1] He tells of a Lincolnshire knight, one Roger of Asterby, who suffered from visions. In these he was instructed by St. Peter and the Archangel Gabriel to lay seven divine commands before Henry II. These commands were that the king should maintain his coronation oath and the just laws of the kingdom; that nobody, although guilty, was to be condemned to death without judgement; that inheritances were to be returned to their rightful owners and that right should be done; that justice was to be given freely and without charge; that the *servitia* of the king's ministers were to be restored, and finally, that the Jews should be expelled without their bonds and pledges which should be returned to their debtors, a point of some personal interest to Roger as he is stated to have been in debt to Aaron of Lincoln. Gerald goes on to say that Henry was impressed by the divine order and began to restore inheritances and rights which he had seized. This beneficent repentence, however, lasted for only a single night. On the next day the king procrastinated and nothing further was done. Here, in an embryonic form perhaps, we have some of the essentials of the programme of 1215, the demand for the expulsion of the Jews looking beyond 1215 to 1290.

Divine intervention apart, the story can be criticized severely. It has obviously been embellished and is simply one chapter in Gerald's account of Henry's moral decline. The most serious feature is the dating. It is placed shortly after the year 1175, but the ' De Principis Instructione ' was only written in the later part of John's reign and was not completed until about 1217.[2] It is in fact possible that Gerald placed something similar to the Great Charter in the middle years of the reign of Henry simply to add to the moral content of his narrative. If so, he may not have invented the story; more probably he was retailing a contemporary tradition which he appreciated. Whichever it was, it is of some significance that a man well acquainted with government circles should consider it fitted the political context of the reign of Henry II. This explanation, however, is not the only possible one for there was undoubtedly a Roger of Asterby living in Lincolnshire in the late twelfth century.[3] Further, Gerald himself spent some time at Lincoln about the year 1195.[4] The form of the story does not

[1] *Opera*, viii. 183–6.
[2] *Ibid.* viii. pp. xiv-xv, li-lii. See also Sir Maurice Powicke, ' Gerald of Wales ' *Bull. John Rylands Library*, xii (1928), 401, 408.
[3] *Pipe Roll 34 Henry II*, p. 74, *Pipe Roll 2 Richard*, p. 81, *Pipe Roll 3 & 4 Richard* pp. 5, 235, *Pipe Roll 3 John*, p. 10, *Documents Illustrative of the Social and Economic History of the Danelaw*, ed. Sir Frank Stenton, p. 391, *Transcripts of Charters relating to Gilbertin Houses*, ed. Sir Frank Stenton, Lincoln Rec. Soc. xviii, pp. xxiv, 106, 111, *Lincoln Records Abstracts of Final Concords*, ed. W. O. Massingberd, i. 49.
[4] Sir Maurice Powicke, ' Gerald of Wales ' *loc. cit.* p. 398.

suggest that Roger's name was dragged in just to provide corroborative detail. It is more likely that Gerald had met Roger or that he had heard local stories about him. At all events it seems possible that the ideas embodied in Roger's commands were current in Lincolnshire in the 1190's.

To argue that laymen were slowly moving towards the position occupied in 1215 is not immediately nonsensical. The Great Charter, after all, was in a form which they could readily grasp and its compulsive power depended on the weapon to which they were most thoroughly accustomed, distraint.[1] The medieval landowner, even down to the petty freeman, was before all else litigious, thoroughly versed, particularly since Henry II's time, in the practices of the law. He was employed in all grades of the administration, as a baron of the exchequer, sheriff, justice, or as a bailiff of the hundred, coroner or simple juror. Further, the practices of the administrative and legal system depended extensively on custom, not only on the custom of the kingdom but also on the custom of this or that shire, town and vill.[2] The legal records show men being summoned by the law of Norfolk,[3] judged by the law of Wiltshire,[4] even summoned according to the custom of Pickering.[5] The very existence of these phrases implies that the men meeting in the local courts knew what custom was and preserved and defended it. The same implication underlies the government's use of the inquest from Domesday onwards and the commonest assizes of Henry II.

Under John men defended local custom, privilege and traditional rights with particular tenacity. In 1214, for instance, the knights of four Devon hundreds entered on a running battle with the sheriff, Eudo de Beauchamp, in defence of a charter of privileges granted to the men of the shire ten years earlier. They carried the case from the hundred courts, through the shire court to the Curia Regis, claiming that it was a test case in defence of their charter, refusing to pass judgement on defaults in the hundreds, and arguing that the sheriff had tried to levy undue exactions on the hundreds as his predecessors had done before the charter had been granted.[6] An earlier case coming from Somerset illustrates the same pertinacity in more detail and demonstrates the feelings lying behind it. In Trinity 1204, as a result of a royal enquiry, twelve knights of the shire told the following story.[7] A certain William Dacus had

---

[1] See Professor T. F. T. Plucknett, *The Legislation of Edward I*, pp. 75–6.

[2] Glanville, *De Legibus*, book xii, cap. 23, ed. G. E. Woodbine, p. 156.

[3] *Pleas before the King or his Justices 1198–1202*, ed. Lady Stenton, Selden Soc., vol. lxviii (1949), no. 52. See also *ibid.* no. 9.

[4] *Three Rolls of the King's Court* (Pipe Roll. Soc.), p. 82.

[5] *Three Yorkshire Assize Rolls*, ed. C. T. Clay, Yorkshire Archaeological Soc. (Record Series), xliv. (1911), p. 2.

[6] *Curia Regis Rolls*, vii. 158–9. [7] *Ibid.* iii. 129–30.

produced in the shire court a writ ordering Alan the sheriff [1] to see that he received 60 m. damages which he had suffered as a result of disseisin by Richard Revel. Richard Revel the younger was in court and, on hearing this, he asked the sheriff to deal justly with his father, his brother and himself for they were native born and local gentry.[2] The sheriff replied that he was well aware of this but that he was bound to execute the writ. Richard repeated his statement and received the same reply. Richard again asserted that he and his family were native born and local gentry and added that the sheriff was a newcomer. The sheriff admitted that he came from other parts where perhaps, he added, he also might be considered as local gentry. Tempers must now have been roused for the rest of the story runs as follows. One of the sheriff's sergeants tried to execute a royal writ for the arrest of a clerk who was present in court. Richard prevented him, saying that the clerk ought not to be imprisoned without judgement,[3] and the sheriff himself had to arrest the clerk. William Revel here intervened to pacify his brother and to ask that the clerk should be released on pledges. The sheriff, for good measure, now tried to arrest both Richard and William. William retorted that he saw no royal order for his arrest and asked the court whether he ought to be imprisoned without such an order. He added that he had been in prison before for the king's sake and would go there again on his behalf whenever he desired. The interest of this case lies not only in its illustration of the deep-rooted prejudices of the local knight against the outsider, prejudices of special significance when related to the demands of 1215, but also in the skill with which Richard Revel and his brother played their hand, first whipping up the emotions of their audience, then stating that imprisonment should only follow a judgement and denying the sheriff's right to arrest without a royal writ, then appealing to the opinion of their fellows in the court and concluding with a little sarcasm at the expense of the king himself.

Just as local knights like Richard Revel were guardians of custom and traditional procedure in the shire court, so was the defence of the custom of the realm in the hands of the magnates. The barons were accepted repositories of tradition and sources of advice to whom frequent reference was made by the king.[4] To this must be added the experience they had gained in government

---

[1] Alan de Wihton', the under-sheriff to Hubert de Burgh in 1204 (*Pipe Roll 6 John*, p. 175).   [2] The phrase is ' naturales homines et gentiles de patria'.

[3] ' nisi per judicium '. The roll is defective here. One copy adds the words ' quod cor eorum desiderat ', which may refer to ' judicium ' (*Curia Regis Rolls*, iii. 130).

[4] For the postponement of important cases for consultation with the barons see C. T. Flower, *op. cit.* pp. 16–17. Many of the measures of John's reign are stated to have been made with the consent of the magnates. See the Winchester assize of bread (*Rot. Litt. Pat.* p. 41), the assize of money and the assize of arms of 1205 (*ibid.* pp. 54b,

during the absences of Henry II abroad and in particular during Richard's wars and captivity. If we may trust his biographer, William Marshal was confident enough in traditional forms of procedure to rely on his fellow barons to give him a favourable verdict against the king, and sufficiently self-assured in his judgement to argue with the greatest administrator of his day, Hubert Walter, on the succession to the throne.[1]

From this background emerged ideas and complaints identical with those put forward in 1215. By 1198, for example, it was already recognized that £100 represented a reasonable relief for a barony.[2] Some men asserted that they were not bound to grant any aid except for the ransoming of their lord's body, the knighting of his eldest son and the marriage of his eldest daughter.[3] Others claimed that the wasting of land during a wardship was contrary to the custom of the realm.[4] More significant than this, however, is the frequency with which men appealed to the custom of the kingdom. Robert de Courtnay and Alice his wife, for instance, offer money to be treated ' according to the custom and assize of the kingdom ' in their claims to the vill of Caldbeck.[5] William de Mowbray does the same to be treated ' justly according to the custom of England ' in the case arising from the claims of William de Stuteville to his barony.[6] Robert Bardolf asks the king to maintain and defend him ' according to the custom of England ' against his other lords.[7] Others ask for cases to proceed according to the custom of the realm,[8] or complain of actions contrary to the custom of the realm.[9] It might be thought that these were almost meaningless phrases, but, in fact, the men of the time knew what they meant. When they sought a special decision from the king, they asked him to do justice ' according to his will '.[10] When they were unwilling to accept normal and customary procedure they stated that the king ' can do his will '.[11] Indeed, baronial plaintiffs and their attorneys made exactly the same distinction between law and will which we find in contemporary writings. In a case involving the validity of several charters, the attorney of Gilbert de Gant claimed that one of them was invalid because it

---

55), and the writ for levying the thirteenth of 1207 (*ibid*. p. 72b). After the conquest of the Angevin possessions on the continent, Philip Augustus sought to establish his rights in his new dominions on information given by the baronage. See the letters of the leading Norman barons in which they discuss the relations between the duke, the baronage, and the church as they had existed under Henry II and Richard (*Layettes du Trésor des Chartes*, i, no. 785). William des Roches also reported from Anjou on the ruler's customary rights of marriage (*ibid*. i, no. 1062).

[1] *Histoire de Guillaume le Maréchal*, ed. P. Meyer, ll. 11861–908.
[2] *Pipe Roll 10 Richard*, p. 222.
[3] See the complaints of the tenants of Robert de Mortimer (*Curia Regis Rolls*, v. 39).
[4] *Ibid*. vii. 75–6.   [5] *Pipe Roll 8 John*, p. 45.   [6] *Ibid*. 3 John, p. 157.
[7] *Ibid*. 5 John, p. 103.   [8] *Curia Regis Rolls*, vi. 279.   [9] *Ibid*. i. 376.
[10] See the offer of Maurice de Gant, *Pipe Roll 10 John*, p. 89.
[11] *Curia Regis Rolls*, vi. 273–4.

had been made by Robert de Gant on his death-bed.   He concluded by saying that if Henry II had confirmed this charter ' he had done his will and not what he ought '.¹   In claiming land in Parham against the abbot of Westminster, Peter fitz Herbert stated that his father had held the land as of right and of fee in the time of Henry II and that he had been disseized by the will of that king.²   In answering a similar complaint of Ruald fitz Alan, constable of Richmond, the jurors stated that Henry II had disseized Ruald his grandfather ' of his own will and without judgement '.³   On one occasion similar terms were even used by a litigant who disapproved of his father's second marriage.⁴

While litigants paraphrased contemporary doctrine, the chroniclers seem to have turned to the phrases of the law courts in describing the politics of the period.   In describing promises made by royal agents in 1199 and demands of the barons in 1201, Roger of Howden uses the term ' ius ' in the legal sense it was given in the record of a proprietary action.⁵   Wendover does the same in recording promises made by John in July 1213,⁶ and he, Ralf of Coggeshall and the Barnwell chronicler, all use the word in dealing with events at Runnymede.⁷   In this last instance their words find a close parallel in the royal letters of 19 June 1215 announcing the restoration of estates.⁸   Gervase of Canterbury expands the word in his reference to John's oath of 1205 when the king apparently agreed to preserve the ' jura regni ' with the counsel of the magnates.⁹   Here he resorts to a phrase frequently used by Glanville to denote customary law.¹⁰   Wendover again gives us legal forms

¹ *Curia Regis Rolls*, iv. 43; ' libitum suum fecit et non quod debuit '.
² *Ibid.* vi. 176–7.   ³ *Ibid.* v. 148.
⁴ See the statement of Hamo Piron, a tenant of the honour of Wallingford, in *Three Rolls of the King's Court* (Pipe Roll. Soc.), p. 9; ' et dicit quod pater eius Henricus duxit Isabellam matrem Cecilie voluntate sua non ex dono Regis nec consilio Hamonis '.
⁵ ' praedictus Johannes Normannorum dux redderet unicuique illorum jus suum, si ipsi illi fidem servaverint et pacem ' (*Chronica Rogeri de Hovedene*, ed. W. Stubbs (Rolls Series), iv. 88), ' mandaverunt regi quod non transfretarent cum illo, nisi ille reddiderit eis jura sua ' (*ibid.* iv. 161).
⁶ ' . . . quodque singulis redderet jura sua ' (*Chron. Maj.*, ii. 550).
⁷ ' Ibi quoque jura sua baronibus, et aliis de quibus indubitanter constabat quod eis competebant, rex restituit ' (*Coggeshall*, p. 172).   ' Reddiditque in continenti rex unicuique jus suum ' (*Walt. Cov.* ii. 221).   ' . . . venerunt ad regem multi nobiles de regno, exigentes jura sua terrarum et possessionum. . . .' (*Chron. Maj.* ii. 606).
⁸ ' Sciatis quod pax hoc modo reformata est inter nos et Barones nostros quod nos statim reddemus omnes terras et castra et jura unde nos dissaisiri fecimus aliquem injuste et sine judicio ' (*Rot. Litt. Claus.* i. 215).
⁹ ' . . . jurare compulsus est quod jura regni Angliae de eorum consilio pro posse sua conservaret illaesa ' (*The Historical Works of Gervase of Canterbury*, ed. W. Stubbs (Rolls Series), ii. 97–8).
¹⁰ Glanville, admittedly, usually used the words in the singular.   For a use of the phrase ' judicium et ius regni ' by three members of the Twenty-Five, see the order for the surrender of Knaresborough Castle sent to Brian de Lisle by Geoffrey de Mandeville, Saer de Quency and Richard of Clare on 30 September 1215 (*Bull. John Rylands Library*, xxviii (1944), 443).

when he tells us that John promised to judge men according to the just judgements of his court.[1] This tendency to use legal words and phrases may cast doubt on the details of the incidents recorded by the chroniclers. On the other hand, there is circumstantial evidence to back part of their story and the evidence for this insistence on the restoration of rights is consistent throughout. There is no difference in principle, for example, between the incidents recorded by Howden in 1199 and 1201 and the individual actions fought by Ruald fitz Alan and Peter fitz Herbert, the terms of clause 52 of the Great Charter, or the wholesale restitution of property to which John was forced in the week following 19 June 1215. Further, legal terms are used in the chronicles with significant regularity, not only in one, but in all which deal with the nascent opposition to the king. The most likely explanation for this is that both the chroniclers and the barons were drawing on a common body of ideas.

Admittedly, this demand for the restoration of rights, by itself, scarcely represents a political opposition of much sophistication. Usually it referred to the restitution of property and it is not necessarily inconsistent with the picture of a baronage inspired by an 'all-consuming greed'.[2] With the demand for rights, however, were associated other ideas. The terms 'ius' and 'iura' were meaningless unless they implied just treatment according to lawful procedure and the maintenance of customary substantive law. The restoration of rights, just judgement and the maintenance of law were all closely associated in Roger of Asterby's 'commands'. Similarly, when men proffered money to acquire or defend property, they asked for just judgement and treatment according to custom. Ultimately, the questions were bound to arise . . . what was just judgement? what was custom? The questions were only answered slowly, empirically and often unsatisfactorily. Apart from the fact that opposition to a king such as John was a somewhat dangerous business, the questions themselves were extremely difficult.

The idea of a right to judgement was so ingrained in the medieval mind that judgement was almost equated with justice.[3] This right, even in the form of judgement by peers, was a traditional one,[4]

---

[1] '. . . et omnes homines suos secundum justa curiae suae judicia judicaret' (*Chron. Maj.* ii. 550). Cf. 'consideratum est quod prior replegiet eis terram suam et diem eis ponat in Curia sua de Reragiis redituum et serviciorum et deducat eos iuste iudicio Curie sue' (*Three Rolls of the King's Court* (Pipe Roll Soc.), p. 134).

[2] The words are Professor Painter's. See *The Reign of King John*, p. 347.

[3] The two words are inseparably associated in the writ of novel disseisin. See also Bracton, *Leges*, fo. 205 (ed. G. E. Woodbine, iii. 121) and *Bracton's Note Book*, ed. F. W. Maitland, case no. 530. In cases of disseisin the judgement of a private court was often entered as a plea of justification. See *Three Rolls of the King's Court* (Pipe Roll. Soc.), p. 134; *The Earliest Northamptonshire Assize Rolls*, A.D. 1202, 1203, ed. Lady Stenton (Northamptonshire Record Soc., vol. v, 1930), no. 782; *Rot. Curiae Regis*, ii. 117.

[4] See L. W. Vernon Harcourt, *His Grace the Steward and Trial of Peers*, pp. 205-14, and Sir Frank Stenton, *The First Century of English Feudalism*, pp. 58-60.

and the baronage readily expressed their views on the question long before 1215. In the treaty drawn up between John and Longchamp in 1191, for instance, it was laid down that free-tenants were not to be disseized by the will of the justices or the king's ministers, but only by the judgement of the king's court in accordance with the laws of the realm or by the order of the king himself.[1] This agreement is interesting not only in its early date but also in the way it illustrates the complexity of the situation. Here, judgement by a court is not contrasted with an arbitrary decision of the king, as we tend to assume it was in the Great Charter. On the contrary, the judgement of a court in accordance with the law and royal orders are treated as complementary and are both contrasted with arbitrary action by the king's ministers. Perhaps the reason for this lay in the political circumstances of the time, but even in John's reign there is no clear contrast between baronial demands for judgement on the one hand and arbitrary action by the king on the other, or between a baronial appeal to judgement by peers and a royal insistence on some other form of trial. Men were willing, even eager, to pay for a judgement in the king's court or for his decision or arbitration.[2] Further, John postponed important cases for consultation with the magnates, and even in political cases he was often able to achieve his ends without using methods which could be described as illegal or tyrannical. Much depended on the circumstances of each particular case. In 1201, for instance, he took action against Archbishop Geoffrey of York by the judgement of his court[3] and he used the same process against John de Curcy three years later.[4] In dealing with the Poitevin baronage, on the other hand, he tried to enforce trial by battle against expert champions, and was met with a demand for judgement by peers.[5] In his conflict with William Marshal in 1205 an offer of trial by battle was made by William, John countering with a demand for judgement 'by his barons' and later turning to his bachelors to find someone to stand against William.[6] In 1210, in contrast, William did not offer battle immediately, but put himself on the judgement of a court, again apparently consisting of the barons.[7] In three other famous cases, those of William de Braose, Robert fitz Walter, and Eustace de Vesci, the king relied on the customary procedure of outlawry for dealing with his opponents.[8]

[1] ' Sed et concessum est quod episocopi et abbates, comites et barones, vavassores et libere tenentes, non ad voluntatem justitiarum et ministrorum domini regis de terris vel catallis suis dissaisientur, sed judicio curiae domini regis secundum legitimas consuetudines et assisas regni tractabuntur, vel per mandatum domini regis ' (*Hoveden*, iii. 136).

[2] See *Pipe Roll 6 John*, pp. xxii ff. and the cases of Maurice de Gant and John Marshal (*Pipe Roll 10 John*, p. 89, *Curia Regis Rolls*, i. 374).

[3] *Rot. Chart.* p. 102.   [4] *Rot. Litt. Pat.* p. 45.   [5] *Hoveden*, iv. 176.
[6] *Histoire de Guillaume le Maréchal*, ll. 13149–256.   [7] *Ibid.* ll. 14311–18.
[8] *Foedera*, i, pt. 1, 107–8; *Rot. Litt. Claus*, i. 165b–166; *Coggeshall*, p. 165.

Some of this evidence may be unreliable, but in general it suggests that John usually resorted to lawful and traditional procedure. This argument is reinforced by the methods he used in dealing with heavily indebted barons. The *Dialogus de Scaccario* gives us a very detailed account of the regulations for the collection of debts and the use of distraint.[1] These regulations were amended in the king's favour in 1200–1,[2] but even then there were many apparent safeguards for the indebted subject. Distraint on land, for instance, was only mentioned as a method of recovering debts arising from reliefs. In contrast to this, John seems to have distrained on land without any hesitation[3] and he also imprisoned men for debt.[4] Here, at first sight, we have a complete disregard for the law. The *Dialogus*, however, does not give us the whole story. Fitz Neal states that in the last resort a defaulting baron was held in free custody after the end of the exchequer session until the court could discuss the case.[5] At this point, significantly enough, he ceases to guide us and it seems that there were no definite limitations to the court's powers in these circumstances. Thomas of Moulton almost certainly went through this procedure and finished up as a prisoner in Rochester castle.[6] Further, it was to the law and custom of the exchequer as well as to the custom of the realm that John turned to justify his actions against William de Braose.[7] This meant that the barons were faced with a long established court executing very heavy punishments. Perhaps when the Charter was drawn up, amercement by peers and even the phrase ' per legale judicium parium suorum vel per legem terrae ' were contrasted in their minds with the more sinister ' per legem scaccarii '. But they were faced with a king who had not blatantly disregarded the law. John's policy had been one of skilfully exploiting customary procedure in his own interests. It certainly aroused hostility; he had to produce an apologia for his treatment of de Braose and it was apparently necessary to ' pack ' the court

---

[1] *Dialogus*, ed. Charles Johnson, pp. 110–18.

[2] *Hoveden*, iv. 152.

[3] See the letters dealing with Peter de Scotigny and the orders for the distraint of Aaron's debtors (*Rot. Litt. Claus.* i. 72b, 98b).

[4] See the case of Thomas of Moulton discussed by Lady Stenton in *Pipe Roll 10 John*, p. xviii. Robert de Vaux, lord of Gilsland, suffered similar treatment. This case is summarized inaccurately by Professor Painter in *The Reign of King John*, p. 222. Robert's imprisonment occurred in 1211 and can have had no connexion with the fitz Walter conspiracy of 1212. See P.R.O., Pipe Roll 13 John, rot. 15, m. 2r.

[5] *Dialogus*, ed. Charles Johnson, pp. 117–18.

[6] The order for his imprisonment shows that he was in the hands of the barons of the exchequer (*Rot. Litt. Pat.* p. 85b).

[7] *Foedera*, i. 107–8. The regulations of 1200–1 also refer to the ' lex scaccarii '. See also *Memoranda Roll 1 John* (Pipe Roll Soc.), p. 32, where the subject is possibly treated as an exercise for sardonic humour by one of the exchequer clerks. ' Alter alterius honera portate et sic adimplebitis legem scaccarii.' The case is quoted by Sir Hilary Jenkinson in *Magna Carta Commemoration Essays*, p. 274.

which condemned fitz Walter; [1] but royal policy left little room for the barons to formulate their demands clearly. Clause 39 of the Great Charter was, and still is, vague and unsatisfactory.[2]

The vagueness with which the question of judgement was answered was matched by an apparently rigid precision in solving the problem of what was custom. Here men turned to demand the maintenance of the laws of Edward the Confessor and Henry I and the confirmation of the latter's charter.[3] It would be very easy to write this off as an immediate reaction of conservative minds. In fact, it was a very astute political move. To a certain extent, perhaps, this appeal to tradition was automatic. The history of the Normans in England formed a unity which could be clearly seen and understood. Baronial privileges, in particular their titles to land, could often be traced back to the Conquest, and in proprietary actions it is not unusual to find a statement of tenure ' de conquestu ' even though proof of tenure at the death of Henry I or the coronation of Henry II was all that was required in law.[4] Further, the charters of the various kings had traced custom and law back to the reigns of Henry I and the Conqueror, and so to pre-Conquest England. To this we must add the tradition of sanctity associated with Edward the Confessor, in particular since his canonization,[5] and the tradition of good government associated with the name of Henry I, ' the keeper of the beasts and the guardian of the flocks ' who ' did right and justice in the land '.[6]

In addition to all this, however, there is the strong possibility that an appeal to tradition was used deliberately as a political weapon.[7] To define custom in terms of the laws of Edward and Henry was

---

[1] *Rot. Litt. Claus.* i. 165b–66.

[2] The barons probably equated judgement by peers with a judgement of the Twenty-Five or some similar baronial gathering. See clauses 52 and 60 of the Charter. John, in contrast, on one occasion at least, equated it with a trial in his court. See *Rot. Litt. Pat.* p. 141 and Sir Paul Vinogradoff, ' Magna Carta, C. 39 ', *Magna Carta Commemoration Essays*, pp. 86 ff.

[3] *Walt. Cov.* ii. 217–18, *Coggeshall*, p. 170, *Chron. Maj.* ii. 550, 551, 552, 554.

[4] C. T. Flower, *op. cit.* pp. 143–4.

[5] Late twelfth-century writers sometimes illustrated Edward's sanctity in a very interesting way. Gerald of Wales, for instance, tells a story of Edward seeing the Devil sitting on the bags of money in the treasury which had been collected as Danegeld and remitting the tax as a result (*Opera*, viii. 130).

[6] The quotation is from the ' London ' Leges (*ante*, xxviii (1913), 739). Late twelfth-century opinions on Henry II were usually much less glowing. The author of the ' London ' Leges, for example, describes him in almost similar terms to those he uses for Henry I and then adds: ' Crimina vero sua fuerunt publica et valde notoria ' (*ibid.* p. 742). Henry II's comparative unpopularity must not be attributed solely to the harshness of his administration, although this certainly played a part (see Gerald of Wales, *Opera*, viii. 160); the murder of Becket rendered any balanced judgement impossible.

[7] The additions made to the laws of Edward and Henry in the ' London ' edition may provide an example of this. The ' Pseudo-Cnut de Foresta ' almost certainly does in that it attempts to make out that the royal forest rights were founded on pre-Conquest custom (F. Liebermann, *Gesetze der Angelsachsen*, iii. 335–7).

to level an implicit charge of unlawful innovation against the Angevin kings. It contrasted the 'evil customs' of Henry II, Richard and John with the 'good old times'. In part the 'good old times' were an invention, hardly consistent with what we know of the reign of Henry I from his one surviving pipe roll, but the baronial argument did in part fit the facts, for many of the administrative practices they were attacking were the product of the last half century. Thus 'custom' was to be founded in the earlier formative phases of the monarchy prior to the Angevin regime. The argument was of great and immediate significance [1] and the king saw the point of it; he had based his rights too often on the situation during his father's reign to miss it.[2] He fought the baronial views skilfully and in the end with some success. In the spring of 1215 he was prepared to go to great lengths in making detailed concessions to the barons, but when it came to the wider question of 'evil customs' he apparently tried to create confusion by making an impossible distinction between those of his own and his brother's reign, which he agreed to abolish, and those of his father's reign, which he said he would submit to the judgement of his faithful men.[3] His policy bore fruit for at Runnymede he was given a crusader's respite on several matters arising not only before 1189 but also before 1199.[4]

Necessarily, it is not until the final crisis of the reign that we hear of a clear demand for the laws of Edward and Henry I. Individuals and groups might demand the restoration of rights; men might argue with the king on forms of judgement; but they could not force their interpretation of custom on him and apply it to his administration without organizing rebellion. Until this point had been reached, however, they could and did alleviate some of the harsher aspects of the régime by buying privileges. For over twenty years before Runnymede men had been freeing themselves from the forest laws, starting with the men of Surrey who bought the deforestation of part of their shire in 1190.[5] Others were quick to seize an advantage from John's financial difficulties at the end of the Norman campaigns, and by the end of 1204 the men of

[1] On the question of the extent of the royal forests, for example, a demand to put the clock back to 1154 would have entailed wholesale deforestations. To demand a restoration of the bounds of 1189 or 1199 would have affected comparatively small areas. (Miss Margaret L. Bazeley, ' The Extent of the English Forest in the Thirteenth Century ', *T.R.H.S.*, 4th ser. iv (1921), 140 ff.)

[2] In November 1201, for example, he ordered the chief forester, Hugh de Neville, to keep the royal forest as it had been kept in the time of Henry II (*Rot. Litt. Pat.* p. 3b). Inquiries into royal rights, in particular into the royal demesne, often took the coronation of Henry II as a starting point (*Curia Regis Rolls*, i. 252, 419, 428, *Rot. Litt. Claus.* i. 55).

[3] *Foedera*, i, pt. 1, 129.

[4] Magna Carta, caps. 47, 52, 53. Cf. the ' unknown ' charter, cap. 9.

[5] *Pipe Roll 2 Richard*, p. 155.

Devon, Cornwall, Essex, Shropshire, Staffordshire, and certain wapentakes in Yorkshire and Lincolnshire had obtained charters of deforestation.[1] By 1214, the men of Somerset had also acquired forest liberties of some kind.[2] All this was in addition to a large number of similar grants obtained by individuals. A limited control of the shire government was also frequently sought. The forest charter granted to the men of Devon also laid down that the sheriff's turn should only be held once a year, that the shire court should have the power of giving bail for men the sheriff had arrested and that any sheriff who oppressed the men of the shire should be replaced by someone who would treat them better. In 1199 and 1204 the men of Lancashire made offers that Richard de Vernon might be their sheriff.[3] Thomas of Moulton's offer for the shrievalty of Lincolnshire in 1207 probably represented a bid to place him in the office by a group of gentry who acted as his guarantors.[4] A year later the king agreed to choose the sheriff of Cornwall from residents in the shire[5] and in 1210 the men of Dorset and Somerset obtained a similar agreement which specifically excluded William Briwerre and his men.[6]

The price of these privileges was high. The men of Devon offered 5,000 m. for their charter of 1204, while the administrative privileges of the men of Cornwall cost 1,300 m. and those of the men of Dorset and Somerset 1,200 m.[7] In none of the cases which have been cited, except that involving Thomas of Moulton, is there any indication that any single individual predominated in offering or paying these large sums.[8] Probably the decision to acquire grants of this kind was made initially by a small group. But even if this were so, the rest of the more important landowners of the shire had to be convinced. The purchases must have been preceded by extensive discussion. Agreement was necessary on the exact privileges to be obtained, and the amount to be offered to the king. We can easily imagine men airing their grievances and expressing their views on the administration and the king's financial needs.

---

[1] See *Foedera*, i, pt. 1, 89 for the Devon charter. The rest are in *Rot. Chart.* pp. 121, 122, 122b, 123, 128, 132b–3. The king's eagerness to profit from the forests at this time is illustrated by letters of July 1203, authorizing Hugh de Neville ' to make our profit by selling woods and demising assarts ' (*Rot. Litt. Pat.* p. 31b).

[2] In this year they were called to send twelve discreet knights of the shire to the king to discuss an offering they had made to Hugh de Neville during the last forest eyre for the preservation of their liberties. Similar letters were sent to Devon and Cornwall (*Rot. Litt. Claus.* i, 181).

[3] *Rot. de Oblatis et Finibus*, p. 38, *Pipe Roll 6 John*, p. 6.

[4] *Rot. de Oblatis et Finibus*, pp. 369–70.

[5] *Pipe Roll 10 John*, p. 183.   [6] *Ibid. 12 John*, p. 75.

[7] *Ibid. 6 John*, p. 85, *ibid. 10 John*, p. 183, *ibid. 12 John*, p. 75.

[8] In the case of Devon, both the bishop of Exeter and the earl were excluded from the agreement initially, and the fact that a special commission was used to collect the offering suggests that a very large number of men must have contributed (*Pipe Roll 6 John*, p. 85, *Rot. Litt. Claus.* i. 10b).

The buying of privileges must, in fact, have been prefaced by discussions and arguments similar in many ways to those which preceded the final revolt. In the one case perhaps, the advantages were weighed against money; in the other against risks to land, life, and limb. In the one case the knights of the shire were discussing business, and in the other politics and war. But the dividing line between business and politics was faint and the object was the same in both cases. The difference lay simply in intensity and method.

Occasionally these charters foreshadowed the arguments which were to be used by the barons at the end of the reign. The Devon forest charter, for example, re-established the bounds and customs of the forest as they had existed under Henry I. Further, they provided a legal defence for privileges and rights, to which an appeal might be made just as appeals were made to the Great Charter after 1215.[1] In one case, an apparently unimportant one, the close relationship between this purchase of privileges and the demands of 1215 is made startlingly clear by a private charter surviving in the chartulary of Guisborough abbey. In 1207 Peter de Brus, lord of Skelton, purchased the wapentake of Langbargh in Cleveland, Yorkshire, for 400 m., promising the annual render of the ancient farm and an increment of £20.[2] Sometime between then and Michaelmas 1209, he made the following grant to his knights and free-tenants of Cleveland:[3]

> Omnibus hanc cartam visuris vel audituris, Petrus de Brus salutem. Noveritis me concessisse, et hac præsenti carta mea confirmasse, militibus et libere tenentibus Clivelandæ et hominibus eorum, quod nullus eorum summoneatur, nec implacitetur ad Wapentagium de Langeberge, nisi per considerationem Wapentagii, vel per rationabilem sacrabord,[4] nec aliquis eorum causetur; et si aliquis (eorum) in forisfacturam ceciderit, amensurabitur secundum catella sua, et secundum delictum per quod ceciderit. Præterea concessi eis quod servientes (mei), qui in Wapentagio fuerint, jurent quod libertates secundum tenorem cartæ meæ fideliter servabunt et manutenebunt; et si aliquis eorum inde convictus fuerit, removebitur per me et hæredes meos, et alius per me et hæredes

---

[1] The quarrel between the Devonshire knights and the sheriff of the county in 1214 has already been mentioned [*supra* p. 189]. Here an appeal was made to the charter granted to the men of the shire in 1204. A similar case occurred in Lincolnshire in 1226, but on this occasion the sheriff's opponents relied on the terms of the Great Charter. (*Bracton's Note Book*, ed. F. W. Maitland, case no. 1730.)

[2] *Pipe Roll 9 John*, p. 70.

[3] *The Chartulary of Guisborough*, vol. i, ed. W. Brown, Surtees Soc. lxxxvi (1889), 92–4. Robert Walensis, who witnessed the charter as sheriff, ceased to hold office at Michaelmas 1209 (*Pipe Roll 11 John*, p. 126, *Pipe Roll 12 John*, p. 148).

[4] A 'sacrabar' or 'sacrabor' was an official peculiar to the Danelaw whose function seems to have been that of a public prosecutor. See Sir Frank Stenton, *The Danes in England*, pp. 35–6. But see also below, p. 202.

meos præsentabitur. Præterea concessi eis, quod summus serviens de Wapentagio non nisi tres equos habeat et tres servientes sub se in equis, scilicet duos in Clivelanda, et unum in Wytebistrand, et pro hiis libertatibus habendis idem milites et libere tenentes concesserunt, quod si serviens de Wapentagio de Langeberge per rationabilem compotum monstrare poterit, quod ad firmam Domini Regis, scilicet quadragenta marcas, et ad rationabiles expensas suas de exitu Wapentagii pervenire non poterit, ipsi milites et libere tenentes debitam firmam persolvent secundum quod defecerit de XL marcis, salvis rationabilibus expensis capitalis servientis secundum testimonium meum et senescaldorum meorum. Has prædictas liberates concessi militibus et libere tenentibus de Clivelanda et haeredibus suis, tenendas et habendas de me et heredibus meis in perpetuum. Hiis testibus. Rogero Contabulario Cestriæ, Roberto de Ros, Eustachio de Vescy, Roberto Walense, tunc Vicecomite Ebor., Waltero de Faucumberge, Roaldo Constabulario Richemund, Briano filio Alani, Johanne de Birking, Willelmo filio Radulfi, Waltero de Bovingtona, et multis aliis.

Peter de Brus later took part in the rebellion of 1215–17. Of the witnesses who were still alive, Robert de Ros, Ruald fitz Alan, Brian fitz Alan, and John of Birkin were also rebels; [1] Eustace de Vesci, of course, was one of the most important figures in the movement.

With this remarkable document our case can well rest. There is some suspicion, certainly, that Peter may have made this agreement at the demand of his tenants,[2] but this scarcely affects its significance. Some of the provisions of 1215 were being applied in the wilds of Cleveland at least six years earlier. Here, as at Runnymede, the agreement was drawn up as a charter. While the Great Charter used the term ' liber homo ', Peter's grant was made to the knights, free-tenants and their men. While the Great Charter forbad that men should be put to their law on the unsupported complaint of a bailiff, Peter promised that men should be impleaded ' per considerationem Wapentagii vel per rationabilem sacrabord '. Peter's officers, like John's in 1215, had to swear to observe the agreement, and both documents show the same desire to avoid burdensome government by local officials. In one clause the Cleveland charter is identical in intention and similar in wording not only to the Great Charter but also to the charter of Henry I. On the subject of monetary penalties the three documents run as follows:

---

[1] For Ruald fitz Alan, Brian fitz Alan and John of Birkin, see *Rot. Litt. Pat.* p. 163b, *Rot. Litt. Claus.* i. 338, 339b, 375b.
[2] He was heavily in debt to the king at the time (*Pipe Roll 10 John*, p. 143). This may have enabled his tenants to put pressure on him.

The charter of Henry I	*The Cleveland charter*	*Magna Carta*
Si quis baronum sive hominum meorum foris-fecerit, . . . secundum modum forisfacti ita emendabit sicut emendasset retro a tempore patris mei . . .	Si aliquis eorum in forisfacturam cecid-erit, amensurabitur secundum catella sua et secundum delictum per quod ceciderit.	Liber homo non amercietur pro parvo delicto, nisi secundum modum delicti; et pro magno delicto amercietur secundum magnitud-inem delicti, salvo contenemento suo;

Whether Peter or some other party to the agreement knew of Henry I's charter, it is impossible to say. Versions of it were sufficiently common for this to be possible.[1] But, whether they knew of it or not, it is clear that ideas similar to those in Henry's charter were familiar to this group of Yorkshiremen long before the end of the reign. If we accept Wendover's dramatic story of Langton's meeting with the barons at St. Paul's,[2] we must attribute the surprise and joy of the assembled company not to the fact that Henry's charter gave them a policy, but to the discovery that some of their ideas already had the authority of a royal charter bearing a king's seal. The archbishop gave them not their principles, but simply a debating point, albeit a strong one.

The views advanced in the preceding pages carry one important implication. It is unlikely that the attitude expressed in Peter de Brus' charter was unique; more probably it was common to most of the baronage. Hence it would be unwise to assume that the rebels of 1215 and the great lords who supported the king differed much in principle in their approach to the general problems discussed at Runnymede. There is little reason for doubting that William Marshal's re-issues of the Charter in 1216 and 1217 were made in perfectly good faith.[3] One of the great loyalists, Ranulf of Chester, followed up the Charter of 1215 by granting similar concessions to the men of his palatinate,[4] and fourteenth century

---

[1] F. Liebermann, ' The Text of Henry I's Coronation Charter ', *T.R.H.S.*, new ser. viii (1894), 22 ; Ludwig Riess, ' The Reissue of Henry I's Coronation Charter ', *ante*, xli (1926), 321–4.

[2] *Chron. Maj.* ii. 552–4.

[3] The marshal's biographer takes a very curious attitude to the civil war. The poem contains little information on the war up to John's death, but is very full for the period after. The author must have had ample sources available for the earlier period in addition to his own experiences. He seems to have regarded the war as a tragedy which should never have occurred (*Histoire de Guillaume le Maréchal*, ll. 14842–59, 15031–6). This may well represent the marshal's own views for the writer notes William's abhorrence of the excesses which were committed (*ibid.* ll. 15053–60).

[4] *The Chartulary or Register of the Abbey of St. Werburgh, Chester*, pt. i, ed. James Tait, Chetham Soc., new ser. lxxix (1920), 101–9. This charter was issued before John's death. Admittedly it was made in a difficult political situation and at the petition of Ranulf's men. Certain requests were refused.

tradition held that he had openly criticized John for his treatment of the wives and daughters of the barons and for his violation of the laws of St. Edward.[1]   Of all the lords who gave their advice in the granting of the Charter, only one, William Briwerre, can be shown to have opposed any of the later confirmations.[2]   The elimination of many articles from the re-issues of 1216 and 1217 suggests that there may have been differences in detail between the views of loyalists and rebels.   Immediately, however, the side men chose was probably determined by their personal relations with the king and it seems wisest to try to explain their choice and their frequent changes of side in terms of detailed politics.   Simply to label either rebel or loyalist as irresponsible, self-centred or greedy, obscures the need for this explanation.   Further, these terms are so general that they might be applied to almost all concerned in the crisis of 1215.   Even Stephen Langton did not escape criticism from his contemporaries.[3]   Many lawless, sometimes treasonable acts, can be attributed to men on both sides, but this is not necessarily incompatible with events at Runnymede.   Hard practical interests were simply translated into principles of law.   We may decry the men concerned, but their contemporaries and successors did not do so; the men of this period were prolific in providing subjects for *gestes*.[4]   We may judge them if we like, but first we must understand.

[1] *Eulogium Historiarum*, ed. F. S. Haydon (Rolls Series), iii. 108, *The Brut or the Chronicles of England*, pt. i, ed. F. W. D. Brie, Early English Text Soc. cxxxi (1906), 166–7.

[2] *Chron. Maj.* iii. 76.   William's objection was made in 1224, on the grounds that the original grant had been exacted by force.   Here he followed the argument put forward by Innocent III in his bull annulling the Charter of 1215 (*Foedera*, i, pt. 1, 136).

[3] The ' Invectivum contra regem Johannem ' accuses him of absenteeism.   ' Et tu qualiscunque pastor et rector Cantuariensis ecclesie ad animas cure et doctrine tue subditas carandas et salvandas frequenter absens et raro in ecclesia tua tibi ad regendum animas commissa residens . . . ' (Brit. Mus. Cotton MSS., Vespasian, E. III, fo. 171).

[4] Apart from the life of William Marshal which in its form at least belongs to this class of literature, *gestes* were written on Fulk fitz Warin, John de Curcy, and Ranulf of Chester.   Eustace the Monk was also used as a subject.   (J. H. Round, *Peerage and Pedigree*. ii. 258 ff.

NOTE

1   The suggestion that Hubert Walter studied at Bologna (above, p. 184) is no longer accepted as likely. See C.R. Cheney, *Hubert Walter* (London, 1967), p. 18.

2   Further evidence on the 'sacrabar' is provided in Doris M. Stenton, *English Justice between the Norman Conquest and the Great Charter 1066-1215* (Philadelphia, 1964), and Sir Frank Stenton's interpretation (above, p. 199, n. 4) is cogently challenged by J.M. Kaye, 'The Sacrabar', *E.H.R.*, lxxxiii (1968), 744-58.

8

RIGHTS AND LIBERTIES IN MAGNA CARTA

In 1236 John the Scot, Earl of Chester, was summoned before King Henry III to answer charges that he had deprived certain heirs of their rightful inheritance. In his objections to the charge the Earl finally alleged that as this was a common plea it should be held in a definite place and not before the King; the procedure was therefore contrary «to the liberties and charter granted by the Lord King» ([1]). He was referring of course, to Magna Carta ([2]). This kind of appeal to the terms of the Great Charter was frequently made both in important legal actions and in political crises in the course of the thirteenth century. The document had a practical value and, as Miss Faith Thompson has shown ([3]), this contributed in no small measure to its survival as a factor in English history.

This, however, is not the whole story. Lawyers, historians and politicians have for centuries seen the Charter not just as a collection of practical regulations but as a statement of principles. Individual liberty, trial by jury, freedom of trade, the supremacy of the law, the separation of justice from politics, all these ideas and others have been read in, and sometimes into, it. We may reasonably ask whether this is justified. The original charter was a very uncertain political compromise, unacceptable to many of the parties involved and legally valid for only a few months in the summer of 1215. How did this document come to dominate English history as it has done? Was it simply a result of the way in which re-issues and confirmations were piled one upon the other, buttressed by appeals, interpretations and misinterpretations? Or was there in addition, at the start, some kind of Promethean act? If so, wherein, for contemporaries, lay its creative quality?

The bull of August 24th 1215, whereby Pope Innocent annulled the first charter did not kill it stone dead. Despite the fact that the 1225 version was the only one binding in law, the 1215 charter

---

([1]) *Bracton's Note Book*, ed. F. W. MAITLAND, case n. 1213.

([2]) Cap. 11 of the 1225 version: cap. 17 of the 1215 version.

([3]) *The First Century of Magna Carta; Why it persisted as a document.* Minneapolis, 1925.

was still being transcribed faithfully into legal collections at the end
of the thirteenth century ([1]).The apparently clumsy errors made by
Roger of Wendover and Matthew Paris in entering the charter into
their chronicles show that some men failed to distinguish between
the various re-issues even to the extent of imagining that the Charter of the Forest of 1217 was first made at Runnymede two years
earlier ([2]). To contemporaries then, the *fons et origo* was the 1215
document: to it Wendover in the late 1220's and Paris thirty years
later traced an unbroken line of political ideas and administrative
practices. This continuity was not a fancy of the St. Albans writers
but was there in fact. Ten out of the twenty five *defensores* of 1215
were numbered among the witnesses to the charter of 1225.

This interest in the 1215 document could yield no practical value
in the courts of law. We may even doubt whether there would have
been such frequent appeal to the 1225 document if to contemporaries it had constituted a set of rules and regulations and nothing
more. One hundred and twenty five years earlier King Henry I had
issued a coronation charter which defined procedure on several
important issues in feudal practice and other matters. But while, as
we have seen, John, Earl of Chester, was quick to appeal to Magna
Carta in 1236, his great-grandfather Ranulf Gernons, Earl of Chester, that great tormentor of King Stephen, showed no interest, as far
as we know, in the charter of Henry I; nor did any of the other
turbulent figures of his period. Henry's charter indeed never enjoyed
such constitutional significance as Magna Carta achieved, until it
became a cardinal point in the baronial attack on John and was
hence involved in the genesis of the Great Charter itself. Clearly,
for the survival of such a document as a political force, practical
concessions, even several of them, were not enough. We may accept
that the political situation after 1215 was different from that after
1100 in many ways, and that English society and government had
changed in the century or so between the two documents. But behind all this there is the simple stark fact that Henry's charter, as
far as we know, aroused little feeling at the time. Magna Carta, in
contrast, set light to passions and ideas which burned immediately,
fiercely and permanently. It is with this in mind that I intend to

[1] See for example BM Harleian MS 746, where on f. 64 the names of the
Twenty Five are also listed.
[2] V. H. GALBRAITH, *Roger of Wendover and Matthew Paris*. Glasgow, 1944.

examine what Magna Carta and certain closely associated documents have to say about «rights» and «liberties».

The Great Charter in the first place uses these words in a quite common, traditional sense. Rights and liberties are those things to which we are entitled by law. Of the two, «rights» is perhaps the wider term, for «rights» may be enjoyed by custom whereas «liberties» are more usually privileges to which we are entitled by royal grant or prescription. But the terms were close enough to each other to be frequently associated, as, for example, when the corroboration clause of the Charter refers to the «liberties, rights and concessions» which it contains. Rights and liberties might be incorporeal but they were not abstract. Men could petition for them, sue for them and be sued for them. They had a value which could be assessed. In this sense, if not tangible in themselves, the profits they yielded were usually so. Cap. 52 of the 1215 Charter, which provided for the restitution of rights and liberties of which individuals had been unlawfully deprived, and the various writs in the Close Rolls executing this clause, make perfectly clear what might be comprehended under these terms. One man recovers a castle ([1]), another land ([2]), another the right to hold a market and fair ([3]), another the liberty whereby his dogs could run freely within the royal forest of Northumberland ([4]). Some recover «liberties» in the more specific sense of jurisdictional franchises ([5]). All this would have been readily comprehended two or three generations earlier. We are faced with a traditional use of words and with traditional ideas, part and parcel of the everyday assumptions men made about the feudal society in which they lived, part and parcel too of those concepts of hierarchy and status which stemmed back to the Investiture controversy and far beyond.

These simple usages which we find in the Charter were not the only ones in force in the early thirteenth century. The influence of

---

([1]) *Rot. Litt. Pat.*, pp. 143 b, 144, where the restoration of Richmond and Fotheringhay is ordered.

([2]) *Rot. Litt. Claus.*, i, 216 b, where William de Lanvallei recovers the manor of Kingston, Somerset.

([3]) See the concessions to Robert de Brus, *ibid.*, i, 217 b.

([4]) See the concession to Eustace de Vesci, *ibid.*, 216 b.

([5]) See the general confirmation of the liberties of the honour of Gloucester to Geoffrey de Mandeville, *ibid.*, i, 216 b.

canon and Roman law in the course of the twelfth century had had here a marked and important effect. Thus «ius» and «iura» came to be used not only in the sense of right or title but also in the sense of law. This is clearly marked in the work of Glanville where the word is used in both senses; he not only talks of the right of an heir or the right to an advowson ([1]) but also of the *ius et consuetudo regni* and the *iura regni* ([2]). To him the *ius* or *iura regni* constituted a body of substantive law, something which might be associated with the custom of the realm, but something which was stronger than custom, [3] something which might be compared with the canons of the Church and the Roman law of the *Corpus Iuris Civilis* ([4]).

The distinction between these two senses of the word *ius* or *iura* is easily grasped and was easily grasped in the twelfth century. The most cursory glance at Justinian's Institutes would make the difference in usage clear ([5]). But confusion might and did in fact occur. The most obvious example of this is the Great Charter itself. It is in fact a grant of rights and liberties ([6]), but it became a body of law, the first item in the Statute Book, and, as Maitland put it, «the nearest approach to an irrepealable fundamental statute that England has ever had» ([7]). Its unique character arose partly from this confusion. Unlike a normal grant of liberties the grantee was not a precisely named individual or institution, nor was there a clearly established procedure of suit or doctrine of seisin and ownership which might be used to reinforce and protect the original grant.

([1]) *Leges* ed. WOODBINE, New Haven, 1932, pp. 81, 95.

([2]) *Ibid.*, pp. 59, 24.

([3]) «Quicquid autem diversarum patriarum consuetudines super hoc teneant, secundum iura regni non tenetur quis in testamento suo alicui personae praecipue nisi pro voluntate sua aliquid relinquere». *Ibid.*, p. 105.

([4]) «Et quidem licet secundum canones et leges romanas talis filius sit legitimus heres, tamen secundum ius regni et consuetudinem nullo modo tamquam heres in hereditate sustinetur vel hereditatem de iure regni petere potest». *Ibid.*, pp. 111-2.

([5]) Thus the opening words, derived from Ulpian, run «Iustitia est constans et perpetua voluntas ius suum cuique tribuens». (*Inst.* I, i.i) Cf. «Constat autem ius nostrum aut ex scripto aut ex non scripto; «Scriptum ius est lex». (*Inst.* I, i. 3).

([6]) «Homines in regno nostro habeant et teneant omnes prefatas libertates, jura et concessiones» (cap. 63). Cf. the 1217 version which refers simply to «consuetudines predictas et libertates» (cap. 60).

([7]) POLLOCK and MAITLAND, *History of English Law*, i, 173.

Unlike the custom of the land, the Charter as law was an obvious artefact, worse still an artefact about which men had argued and fought. It therefore lacked in many of its sections the long usage then considered so essential to substantive law. It was something new in its principles even more than in its provisions. It was no accident that it required such frequent confirmation in the years which followed.

The reasons for this confusion and the way it had developed provide an important clue in understanding the Great Charter and the rôle it came to play in the thirteenth century. There were many different, sometimes conflicting, influences at work on English legal thinking and Englishmen's assumptions about government. There were the normal feudal notions of the king's responsibilities towards his vassals and of the exercise of government by their advice. There were older ideas of law as an expression of the will of a community. Roman influences were pointing, very hesitantly and uncertainly, towards a concept of kingship as a legally supreme public authority. While early twelfth century legal collections treat royal power as personal and speak simply of the rights of the King([1]), at the beginning of the next century men will talk of the rights of the Crown ([2]). But if these ideas were giving emphasis to royal authority, an equally powerful train of thought stemming from the Church was teaching that kingship was office and that a king carried heavy responsibilities. In 1215 itself, Archbishop Stephen Langton was a powerful influence behind such views with the emphasis he laid upon John's coronation oath ([3]).

The effects of these cross-currents are most clearly seen in the work of the well known anonymous writer, perhaps a Londoner, who

(1) «Hec sunt iura que rex Anglie solus et super omnes homines habet in terr; sua». *Leges Henrici Primi*, 10, 10, 1. F. LIEBERMANN, *Die Gesetze des Angelsach-sen*, i, 556.

(2) «De .iure et de appendiciis corone regni Britannie» *Leges Edwardi Confes-soris*, 11 1A, 32E. *Ibid.*, i, 635, 639. For further discussion of this trend see POLLOCK and MAITLAND, *History of English Law*, i, 512 ff.; Ludwik EHRLICH *Proceedings against the Crown* in *Oxford Studies in Social and Legal History*, ed Vinogradoff, vol. vi, 11 ff. For a recent treatment see P. N. RIESENBURG, *Inaliena-bility of Sovereignty in Medieval Political Thought*, Columbia, 1956, especially pp. 98 ff. See also J. C. HOLT, *The Barons and The Great Charter*, in *Englisi Historical Review*, LXIX (1955), 5-6. See above, pp. 183-4.

(3) F. M. POWICKE, *Stephen Langton*, pp. 102 ff.

produced a new edition of the Laws of Edward the Confessor at the
beginning of the thirteenth century. The additions which he made
to the traditional text clearly illustrate the dilemma of his period.
There is hint of it in the title he gives this section for he is concerned
on the one hand with the rights of the Crown, and on the other with
the office of the King. We then read «The King ought by right,
to preserve and defend completely, in their integrity and without
delapidation, all lands and honours, all dignities and rights and liberties of the crown of this kingdom, and restore with all his power to
their due and former state the *iura regni* which have been dispersed,
destroyed or lost» [1]. By the side of this he can state that the king
is *vicarius summi Regis* who has the duty to protect and defend the
people of God and Holy Church, and within a few lines he is busy
subjecting him very strictly to the advice of the magnates of the
realm and prescribing that he should rule according to the law [2].
Clearly we cannot look here for the logic of an expert in political
theory. Nor should we seek it either now or later. Bracton's difficulties on the relationship of the king to law are well known. King
John, when the situation required conciliatory language, would
express his personal concern at complaints directed against his
sheriffs [3]. Henry III, in similar circumstances, would emphasize
his regard for the «common interest of the whole kingdom» [4],
and that celebrated martinet in the matter of baronial franchises,
Edward I, would on other matters happily exploit the tag *quod
omnes tangit ab omnibus approbetur*.

Nevertheless political views need not be logical to be influential
or dangerous or even successful. At the heart of this idea of the *iura
coronae* there was an essential vagueness similar to that I have already

---

[1] «Debet vero de iure rex omnes terras et honores, omnes dignitates et iura
et libertates corone regni huius in integrum cum omni integritate et sine diminu-
tione observare et defendere, dispersa et dilapidata et omissa regni iura in pristinum
statum et debitum viribus omnibus revocare». Leges Edwardi, 11, 1A2; *Gesetze*,
i, 635. For the development of these views in the coronation oath see H. G.
RICHARDSON, *The English Coronation Oath*, in *Speculum*, XXIV (1949) 44 ff.
For a parallel development in Bracton's views on franchises see Helen M. CAM,
The Evolution of the Mediaeval English Franchise, in *Speculum*, XXXII (1957),
439 ff.

[2] Leges Edwardi, 11, 1A6; 11, 1A8; *Gesetze*, i, 635, 636.

[3] *Rot. Litt. Pat.*, p. 97.

[4] «Communi utilitati totius regni» *Close Rolls* 1231-4, p. 588; quoted by
F. M. POWICKE, *King Henry III and the Lord Edward*, i, 148.

noted in the Great Charter itself. Among these *iura coronae* was the exercise of justice. The concept of the rights of the crown quickly passes into Glanville's concept of the laws of the kingdom. The *iura Coronae* are not just rights, they are also responsibilities to which the King is bound not just in his own interest but by virtue of his office. The different possibilities here were laid bare in 1215 and 1216. Innocent III denounced the Charter as decreasing and impairing John's royal rights and dignity to the detriment of the *ius regalis* and the shame of the English nation ([1]). Prince Louis of France in contrast could condemn King John for failing to preserve the «rights and customs of the church and realm of England» ([2]). Once in this last position we are passing from the rights of the Crown, through the idea of the *iura regni* as the laws of the realm to the idea of *iura regni* as the rights of the kingdom. This last was the crucial step in the attack on the government of the Angevin monarchs.

This step was taken very early in the barons' campaign against the government. As early as 1205, according to Gervase of Canterbury, they compelled the King to swear that he would preserve the *iura regni* by their advice ([3]). By 1213 they were coming to identify their own liberties and rights with the liberties and rights of the kingdom for which warrant might be found in customary law and especially in the laws of St. Edward and Henry I. The Coggeshall chronicler thus sees the Northern barons in 1214 as working to force the king to reform the liberties of the church and the kingdom and to abolish evil customs ([4]). This transference from baronial liberties to the liberties of the realm, from ancient rights to ancient laws, was much facilitated by the baronial exploitation of the Charter of Henry I, a document which like the Great Charter itself, partook of the character both of a grant of privileges and of a legal enactment.

The Great Charter itself will have none of this. Here we see all the passions and prejudices and propaganda of the quarrel through

---

([1]) *Selected letters of Pope Innocent III*, ed. C. R. CHENEY and W. H. SEMPLE, pp. 215-6.

([2]) Chronicle of William Thorne, R. TWYSDEN, *Scriptores Decem.* London, 1652, ii, col. 1869.

([3]) *The Historical Works of Gervase of Canterbury*, ed. W. STUBBS (*Rolls Series*), ii, 97-8.

([4]) *Chronicon Anglicanum R. de Coggeshall*, ed. J. STEPHENSON, (*Rolls Series*), p. 170.

a glass skilfully darkened by chancery clerks who were concerned to produce a document in which there should be no avoidable diminution of the King's majesty and which should come as close as possible to the normal diplomatic forms. The equation of baronial liberties with the laws and liberties of the kingdom is something they cannot stomach. They will not accept the opposition claim to act for the *regnum*. Hence the liberties in the Charter are not granted to the *regnum* or to a community. Well established institutions they will accept. Thus the city of London is to have all its ancient liberties and customs under cap. 13 and cap. 1 states that the English church shall be free and shall hold its rights and liberties unharmed. Less fortunate mortals outside these corporate bodies, however, are only permitted to enjoy their newly won grant severally. The liberties of the Charter are granted not to the kingdom but to the freemen of the kingdom. This form is used consistently throughout the whole document. Only in cap. 61 where there is a reference to the commune of the whole land, is there the slightest hint that all free men might constitute a community or a *regnum*, and this perhaps represents ideas emanating from London rather than from the main line of the baronial argument.

At this point the Great Charter clearly plays into the hands of those later critics who have seen in it a grant of privileges or liberties and nothing more. But the interpretation which the chancery clerks placed on the document can and should be questioned. Many of its clauses, naturally enough, place no difficulty in the way of this interpretation. The regulations about baronial reliefs in cap. 2 represent concessions which every tenant-in-chief of the Crown can hold as an individual. Widows and minors likewise, can hold severally the concessions made in their interest. But who is to hold the concession in cap. 40 that right and justice shall not be sold, denied or delayed ? And, if the cynic insists on dismissing this clause as windy piety, who is to hold the concession of cap. 45 that only those who know the law of the land and are willing to observe it shall be employed as justices, constables, sheriffs and bailiffs? Who again is to hold the concession that shires, hundreds, wapentakes and tithings must be held at the ancient farms ([1]), or the concession of the charter of 1217 regulating the sheriff's tourns ([2]) ? Clearly in these instances,

[1] Cap. 25.
[2] Cap. 35.

whatever Magna Carta says about itself, we are faced with rights which, if they are to mean anything, must be held not severally but in common, by a community, whether that community be hundred, shire or kingdom.

If the men who drafted the Great Charter would not recognize this, others would. The Dunstable Annalist, an almost contemporary authority, refers to the *Chartae super libertatibus regni Angliae* ([1]). Documents closely associated with the Charter, some drawn up in greater haste, others originating outside the Chancery, also show fewer inhibitions in accepting the baronial arguments and assumptions. Thus cap. 48 of the *Articuli* bluntly states that the king has conceded customs and liberties to the kingdom. More strikingly still the treaty concerning the temporary custody of London was drawn up between the King on the one hand, and on the other, the baronial leaders, who were named, and «other earls barons and free men of the whole kingdom». It goes on to refer to the «Charter concerning the liberties and security granted to the kingdom» ([2]). The attitude represented in these words was perhaps best summed up three months after Runnymede, when three of the baronial leaders, in letters addressed to one of the king's agents, Brian de Lisle, referred to the *commune carta regni* ([3]).

In recent years there has been some trenchant and justified criticism of the way in which Stubbs used the concept of the nation ([4]). Whatever may be said of other instances, these phrases I have cited clearly give him some warrant for using this concept in the case of Magna Carta. Some contemporaries, if they did not believe that the Charter belonged to the nation with all the nineteenth century assumptions which Stubbs might attach to that word, at least believed that it belonged to the kingdom. They were not, of course, attempting to argue that there were two separate powers, *rex* and *regnum*, related to each other by covenant. The Charter is not, and was not imagined as, a social contract. But they were claiming that the good of the *regnum* was not simply a matter for the King and his immediate advisers, that if the Crown could claim

---

([1]) *Annales Monastici*, ed., H. R. LUARD, (*Rolls Series*), iii, 43.

([2]) *Foedera*, i, pt. i, 133.

([3]) H. G. RICHARDSON, *The morrow of the Great Charter*, in *Bulletin of the John Rylands Library*, XXVIII, 1944, 443.

([4]) See especially Helen M. CAM, STUBBS, *Seventy Years after*, in *Cambridge Historical Journal*, IX, 1947, 134 ff.

rights then the kingdom as a whole could claim rights and that, in this situation, baronial opinion was not just representative of the baronage or even of other groups as well, but was representative of the whole community, of the whole realm. Within a few years Roger of Wendover will put into the mouth of yet another notable recalcitrant baron, Earl Richard Marshal, these words «the King is not as powerful as God and God is justice itself. In Him I place my trust in seeking and preserving my own and the kingdom's right»([1]). Wendover's great successor, Matthew Paris, will later casually note on the death of Warin de Montchensy, a baron whose chief distinction lay apparently in his great wealth, that he was *zelator pacis et libertatis regni* ([2]).

The crux of the baronial argument lay in the construction they were placing on one single word, *regnum*. This, in their view denoted a social group, a community, which could be possessed of both rights and functions. The King was a part of this, certainly, but a part whose relationship to the whole could be prescribed and was now in fact being prescribed by a process of royal grant or kingly self-limitation. The royal interpretation of the word, as expressed by the chancery clerks in the early versions of the Charter, was quite different. Here the *regnum* is a royal possession, that area which the rule of their master, as king, pervades. The liberties of the charter are to be held «by all men of our realm within our realm of England» ([3]). To the king the realm is always *regnum nostrum*, an assumption against which the rebels of 1215 now set an increasingly damaging question mark.

In Magna Carta we are dealing with the origins of the concept of the community of the realm. It is the first great expression of the will of that community, and thereafter its rallying cry. But care is needed. The «community of the realm» has never been, and can never be. Interests conflict; some men govern others. The community of the realm exists not in fact but in the arguments and minds of men. What the barons claim in 1215 the knights and bachelors will claim in 1259 and the peasantry in 1381. Too much has perhaps been made of the fact that the Charter of 1215 was granted not to

[1] *Chronica Majora*, ed. H. R. Luard, *Rolls Series*, iii. 258.

[2] *Ibid.*, v. 504, quoted by F. M. Powicke, *King Henry III and the Lord Edward*, i, 142.

[3] See the preambles of the 1217 and 1225 versions.

the baronage but to the freemen of the kingdom, that it was concerned with legal procedures which were enjoyed by all freemen, and that it contained concessions to townsfolk and those concerned in trade. English law recognized few distinctions between the great tenants-in-chief of the King and the free tenants at large. Throughout the 12th century and particularly in the latter half, both groups had been associated more closely and often in interchangeable rôles in the work of government. There were barons who were comparatively poor and insignificant. There were men of simple knightly rank who were wealthy and held sway over the minds of kings and the lives of men. Most barons engaged in trade, sometimes directly, more usually through factors. Some barons were also burgesses. Some burgesses, in contrast, became knights and occasionally barons. Some burgesses were treated as barons. All this points to the rashness of thinking that any particular group of clauses in the Charter illustrates a high minded baronial concern for the interests of other sections of the population, for these interests and their own could not be separated. Such thinking acquires an additionally reckless air when we remember that the protagonists of the Charter were concerned with acquiring political support in a very critical situation. In 1215, as at many other times, knights and burgesses, and barons too, could be bought.

But if we are playing in some newly sprung and potent fount of self-deception, it derived from waters deep and plentiful. The close-knit society of the English shires, the *patria*, the county; the remarkable cohesion of the King's government; that England was «fortunate in littleness and insularity», as Maitland put it; that she had come under the hand of William the Conqueror by conquest and yet by a very peculiar conquest; these and many other influences combined to give a real background to the idea of the community of the realm. It was derived from social facts. If we reject the picture of the baronage as high minded idealists it must not be to paint another of them as logic-chopping and argumentative dons. We may see too many principles where in fact there were only the subtleties of political debate. In cap. 12 of the 1215 charter, for example, King John's opponents were not concerned with the principle of national consent to taxation, nor even with the practice of baronial consent to feudal aids, for neither John nor his predecessors had needed to attack this; they were simply trying to use the established procedure on aids to create a quite novel and revolutionary procedure in the matter of scutage. Here we are faced with muddled thinking, but muddled thinking to a very material and immediate purpose.

This concern for immediate mundane matters was never far distant. In a famous legal action in 1226 a group of Lincolnshire knights and gentry chose to attack the sheriff's administration of justice in the courts of Lincolnshire and Kesteven. Their case was a simple one, namely that he had exceeded his duties as laid down by custom and chapter 35 of the 1217 charter. Led by two knights, Theobald Hautein and Hugh of Humby, they argued that the sheriff had behaved «contrary to their liberty which they ought to hold by the charter of the Lord King». «As they held these liberties from the Lord King, it seemed to them that the position of the shire court could not and ought not to be changed except with the Lord King and the magnates of the realm» ([1]). Here an appeal to the Charter takes us straight from local privilege and practices to the concept of the king and magnates as the guardians of the law, into ideas typical of the political debates of the thirteenth century. This case was typical of its time, too, in that in 1234 the King and barons came to decide on some of the points which had been raised and drew up an ordinance which clarified cap. 35 of the 1217 charter ([2]). It was also later extracted by Bracton into his Note Book ([3]). Knights, barons, a famous king's justice and the King himself all had an interest in it. But what were Theobald Hautein and his fellows concerned with immediately? They had spent one day at the shire court hearing pleas, so they alleged, from dawn to dusk. They did not want to be troubled by a second day's hard work. The shire court must last for the customary single day and no more. When the sheriff attempted to transfer the outstanding cases to the next meeting of the wapentakes of Kesteven they were even unwilling to allow him this short cut. They saw themselves vexed with exactions and injuries. It was a simple as that. The Charter was thus a very material defence of custom and privilege of a very material kind. It was long to remain so. A volume dealing with Sherwood

---

([1]) *Curia Regis Rolls,* xii, 435, 461. The case is quoted in POLLOCK and MAITLAND, *History of English Law,* i, 549-50.

([2]) «De interpretatione clausule contente in libertatibus, qualiter debeat intelligi» *Close Rolls* 1231-34, pp. 588-9. See F. M. POWICKE, *op. cit.,* i, 148 f.

([3]) *Note Book,* ed. F. W. MAITLAND, case n° 1730.

forest in Nottinghamshire, written early in the fifteenth century, is prefaced with the following note: *Memorandum,* the charter of the forest is under patent in the hands and custody of Lord Ralph Cromwell Junior, and the charter of liberties is under patent in the hands and custody of Nicholas of Strelley, and the perambulation of the forest of Sherwood made in the time of Henry III is under patent in the hands of William Jorce of Burton (¹). Like good lawyers, the landowners of Nottinghamshire were still keeping the essential works of reference at their elbow.

(¹) P.R.O. Treasury of Receipt, Forest Proceedings, 76, f 4.

The Articles of the Barons sealed by King John at Runnymede, 1215
Actual size: 10½ x 21¾ in. *(British Library, Additional MS. 4838)*

9

THE MAKING OF MAGNA CARTA

MODERN studies of the negotiations at Runnymede in 1215 have been dominated by W. S. McKechnie's *Magna Carta*.[2] In this work McKechnie argued that on the first day of the conference, 15 June, John was forced to accept the demands of the barons and signified this acceptance in the document we know as the Articles of the Barons [3] which was drawn up and sealed on the spot. Magna Carta, however, despite its date of 15 June, was not in faet completed until 19 June, the day when firm peace was reached and when several originals were solemnly sealed and delivered to the barons.[4] These views were not new for they were derived essentially from Blackstone's *Commentary on the Great Charter* of 1759.[5] They have been criticized in detail and one modern authority, Professor Galbraith, has raised deeper issues by doubting the existence of an ' original ' Charter.[6] Nevertheless, they are still generally current and have been followed in essentials by such authorities as Dr. A. L. Poole,[7] Mr. A. J. Collins,[8] and Professor Painter.[9]

McKechnie's argument involved two important assumptions, first, that the *Articuli* were not written and sealed until 15 June, and

[1] In working on this paper I have been very much indebted to Professor V. H. Galbraith, in conversations with whom many of the ideas it contains were first developed. Professor J. S. Roskell also read an earlier version in typescript and has made a number of valuable suggestions. For the views advanced I alone am responsible.

[2] First edition, Glasgow, 1905. Second edition, from which all references below have been taken, Glasgow, 1914.

[3] This title seems to be derived from a combination of the heading of the document —' Ista sunt capitula quae Barones petunt . . .' and the later endorsement—' Articuli magne carte libertatum sub sigillo regis Johannis '. It is not used by Spelman who heads the document ' capitula super quibus facta est Magna Charta Regis Johannis'. Wilkins, *Leges Anglo-Saxonicae* (London, 1721), p. 356), or by Blackstone who refers to the ' articles or heads of agreement ' (Commentary on the Great Charter, *Law Tracts* (Oxford, 1762), ii. p. xxiv). Richard Thompson refers to the ' Articles of Magna Carta ' (*An Historical Essay on the Magna Charta of King John* (London, 1829), pp. 49 ff). The Articles of the Barons ' appears as a title in Stubbs, *Select Charters* (6th edn. 1888), p. 289. [4] *Op. cit.* pp. 38–41.

[5] See his *Law Tracts* (Oxford, 1762), ii. pp. xxiv–xxxviii, from which edition all references below have been taken.

[6] *Studies in the Public Records* (London, 1948), pp. 122–4, 135.

[7] *From Domesday Book to Magna Carta* (Oxford, 1951), pp. 473–4.

[8] ' The Documents of the Great Charter ', *Proc. Brit. Acad.* xxxiv (1948), 233–79.

[9] *The Reign of King John* (Baltimore, 1949), pp. 315–28.

secondly, that one of the main features of the firm peace of 19 June was the formal delivery of Magna Carta to the barons. For neither of these assumptions is there any direct evidence and, indeed, McKechnie admitted that what exactly happened on the two crucial days of the 15th and 19th is a matter of conjecture. The views advanced in the following pages are primarily concerned with an examination of these assumptions and, like McKechnie's, are conjectural. Briefly, I shall argue that although the *Articuli* were accepted verbally as a draft settlement on 15 June, this document was written and sealed before that date, and was in fact a record of an agreement reached between the king and baronial delegates in a meeting held at Runnymede on 10 June. I shall also suggest that, although the terms of Magna Carta had been settled by 19 June, there was no formal delivery of an original sealed Charter to the barons as part of the firm peace of that day. The actions underlying the documents, not the documents themselves, constituted the decisive steps in the negotiations.

Two hypotheses have usually been advanced in explanation of the *Articuli*: first, that they were presented by the barons on 15 June and conceded by the king forthwith,[1] and secondly, that they were not drawn up until the 15th itself in the first general discussions between the two parties at Runnymede.[2] Neither hypothesis is satisfactory. The first is inconsistent with the language of the document. In caps. 48 and 49, where the *Articuli* approach the official form of the Charter, the king's consent to the baronial requests is clearly stated.[3] More convincingly still, the document is headed *Ista sunt capitula quae barones petunt et dominus* Rex *concedit.* There is little possibility that this sentence was added after the rest of the document was compiled.[4] It can scarcely have been written

[1] This argument is followed by Charles Bémont, *Chartes des Libertés Anglaises* (Paris, 1892), p. xxi, by Stubbs in *Select Charters* (6th edn., 1888), p. 290, by H. W. C. Davis in *Select Charters* (9th edn., 1921), p. 285, and in *England under the Norman and Angevin Kings* (London, 1921), p. 376, by C. Petit Du Taillis in the *Feudal Monarchy in France and England* (London, 1936), p. 332, by C. H. McIlwain in *Constitutionalism and the Changing World* (Cambridge, 1939), p. 102, and by Professor Painter, *op. cit.* p. 315. It is also followed by the descriptive notes on the *Articuli* at present in the showcase at the British Museum.

[2] Blackstone, *op. cit.* ii. pp. xxiv, xxvii; W. S. McKechnie, *op. cit.* pp. 37 ff., where it is also suggested that the barons brought a list of demands to the Runnymede meeting; G. C. Crump, 'The Execution of the Great Charter', *History*, xiii (1928), 250–1, and A. J. Collins, *loc. cit.* p. 234, where the views of Blackstone and McKechnie are followed. Miss Norgate also seems to adopt this approach, but her account is rather confused (*John Lackland* (London, 1902), pp. 233–4).

[3] 'Omnes autem istas consuetudines et libertates quas rex concessit regno tenendas. . . .' '. . . libertates quas dominus rex eis concessit et carta sua confirmavit.'

[4] The title seems to be coeval with the rest of the document and there is no sign of an erasure. The argument that the title was added later would involve the assumptions that a document of such length and importance would be drawn up without a title but with a space where one could be inserted, and that such a title was later added by the same scribe who wrote the rest of the document with no noticeable difference in pen or ink. Collectively these assumptions are most improbable.

before the king's acceptance of the petitions. It is simply a statement of fact. The writer of the *Articuli* knew that the king had conceded the baronial petitions when he wrote the document. The sentence further implies that the *Articuli* were not produced in a purely baronial gathering but by both·sides in concert, and this finds strong support in two further points. First, the handwriting of the document is characteristic of the royal chancery. This fact, taken with the presence of the great seal, points to the drafting of the *Articuli* by a chancery clerk.[1] Secondly, the process of amendment which separated the *Articuli* from the Charter did not produce exclusive benefits for either party. Much of this amendment was limited to points of drafting. On some questions the barons gained advantages,[2] on others the king,[3] and certain amendments were not clearly to the exclusive benefit of either.[4] In contrast to this we might expect that a purely baronial petition would present the rebels' demands at their maximum and that subsequent amendment would be almost entirely in the king's interest. Similar arguments would apply, *mutatis mutandis*, if we treated the *Articuli* as a document of purely royalist origin, as some kind of acceptance of earlier baronial petitions.

[1] McKechnie suggested that the document was the work of a chancery clerk (*op. cit.* p. 39). I am unable to see, with Blackstone (*op. cit.* p. xxvii), any marked change in hand after caps. 45 and 46. The scribe varied the formation of some of his letters, in particular the d's, g's and small and capital s's. His hand simply became more current as he wrote the document.

The hands on the chancery rolls of 1215 are in general more florid than that of the *Articuli*. The horizontal abbreviation strokes are bolder, the loops of the g's and d's more prominent, the capitals more ornate. Usually, too, the writing is larger than that of the *Articuli*. But some of the hands on the patent rolls in particular, can only be distinguished from that of the *Articuli* after considerable study. Indeed, the difference between the hand of the *Articuli* and that of a patent roll entry is often no greater than that between one entry on the rolls and another. It should also be noted that where the scribe brackets the addition *nisi aliter* . . . to caps. 45 and 46, he does so in the manner of a chancery clerk; similarly, his paragraph marks at the opening of each clause are similar to those found on the chancery enrolments.

[2] The most important instances are the clarification of cap. 1 of the *Articuli* in cap. 2 of Magna Carta, the additions to cap. 3 of the *Articuli* in cap. 4 of Magna Carta, the addition of cap. 21 of Magna Carta, providing for the amercement of barons by their peers, and the passage in cap. 53 of Magna Carta dealing with afforestations by Henry II and Richard I. Neither of these last two points are raised in the *Articuli*. Compare also caps. 7, 14, 15, 19 and 45 of the *Articuli* with caps. 16, 24, 26, 29, and 58 of Magna Carta.

[3] The most important instances are the replacement of the last section of the *forma securitatis* of the *Articuli* by the passages in Magna Carta providing for the Letters Testimonial and the alteration of cap. 32 of the *Articuli* in cap. 12 of Magna Carta whereby all reference to tallage was omitted. Compare also caps. 3, 23, 27, 31 and 33 of the *Articuli* with caps. 6, 33, 37, 41 and 42 of Magna Carta. The important group of clauses dealing with the restoration of rights (*Articuli*, caps. 25, 44, 46; Magna Carta, caps. 52, 57) were also amended in such a way that the king was given a crusader's respite against pleas of disseisin by Henry II and Richard I. These clauses are discussed further, *infra*, p. 225 n. 1.

[4] Perhaps Magna Carta cap. 14 should be included here. See also *Articuli*, cap. 13 and Magna Carta, cap. 19; cap. 1 of Magna Carta which confirms the liberties ot the church ; and the curious insertion of cap. 54 of Magna Carta dealing with appeals by women.

The *Articuli*, then, were the product of discussions between the two parties. It does not follow, however, that the document was not drawn up until 15 June; this hypothesis, indeed, leads to grave difficulties. Most obviously, there is the simple question of time. On this matter there was some inconsistency in McKechnie's arguments, for while he maintained that the amendment of the *Articuli* into the form of the Charter and the engrossment of the latter formed the principal business of 16, 17, and 18 June, he also considered that the *Articuli* were produced in the course of one single day, 15 June. That the process of amendment took several days is highly probable,[1] but if this was so, it is unconvincing to argue that the preliminary agreement of the *Articuli* could have been produced on the first day of the discussions, for it was in the *Articuli* that most of the major problems were first settled. We cannot have it both ways.

An obvious apparent escape from this difficulty might be found in the argument that discussions between representatives of the two parties had settled so much before 15 June that the production of the *Articuli* was a largely formal matter. Behind the *Articuli*, it might be argued, there were earlier drafts of a settlement which have not survived and on which the *Articuli* themselves were based. This is a possible hypothesis, but one incapable of detailed proof.[2] Further, if so much had been agreed before 15 June, we might wonder why the two parties drew up a document of such peculiar form as the *Articuli* on the 15th itself, and why they did not proceed straight from these hypothetical earlier agreements to the Great Charter. The *Articuli*, in this view, if cast in their traditional rôle, soon seem redundant, and in the end these arguments, far from confirming 15 June as their date, suggest an earlier one. There is no need to predicate lost documents of the period prior to the 15th, if the *Articuli* themselves fit this rôle better than that which has usually been given to them.

The negotiations between the king and his opponents in 1215 were covered by a series of letters of safe-conduct. The first of these was issued under the date of 14 January and announced that the archbishop, several bishops and a number of earls and barons had guaranteed the safe-conduct up to 26 April of those who had come to the discussions in London at Epiphany.[3] This would have covered their attendance at and departure from a meeting to

---

[1] See cap. 25 of the *Articuli*.

[2] It might be argued that the 'unknown charter' filled this rôle. This document by itself, however, would have helped little in the rapid production of the *Articuli* on the first day of the assembly. It might equally have hindered it, for it was far more stringent in some of its provisions than the *Articuli*. (See *infra*, p. 229, n.3.) The Brackley schedule may well have coincided at many points with the *Articuli* but in the absence of a version of the former, this cannot be proved. Further, the schedule, like the king's offer on 10 May was rejected. On this see *infra*, p. 221 and p. 226, n. 3.

[3] *Rot. Litt. Pat.* p. 126b.

be held at Northampton in Easter week. This meeting, of course, never took place, nor is there any evidence that an intervening meeting at Oxford on 22 February, for which the king provided letters of safe-conduct to the ' Northerners ' under the date of 19 February, was ever held.[1] Despite this apparent breakdown in the discussions, however, general letters patent of 23 April provided for the safe-conduct of those who came with Stephen Langton to speak with the king or carried the archbishop's letters patent. This safe-conduct covered the period up to 28 May.[2]

During the period covered by these last letters events moved very rapidly. At least two proposals for a settlement were made, one by each party, and both were rejected. The first consisted of the schedule which the barons, according to Roger of Wendover, sent to the king from Brackley at the end of April.[3] This John rejected and in reply the barons renounced their homage on 5 May.[4] John's counter-offer was contained in letters patent of 10 May which in effect suggested that the issues at stake should be submitted to papal arbitration. These were accompanied by a charter of 9 May stating the conditions attached to the proposals.[5] Presumably after he had heard of the baronial rejection of this offer, John issued general letters under the date of 12 May ordering the disseisin of his opponents.[6] In the war which followed the actions of 5 and 12 May the decisive factor was the fall of London to the rebels on 17 May. By the end of the month the atmosphere of abortive negotiation had vanished. Letters of 25 May provided a safe-conduct up to the 31st for Saer de Quenci, earl of Winchester, to come and speak with the king.[7] Letters of the 27th provided for a similar safe-conduct for Stephen Langton and those who came with him to Staines.[8] In letters of the same day four royal agents were informed that a truce had been arranged.[9] Letters announcing the conditions and duration of this truce were not enrolled and have not survived, but it cannot have extended beyond 10 June, from which date it or a subsequent truce was extended to 15 June.[10]

The truce notified on 27 May was the beginning of a period of intensive negotiation which lasted for three weeks or more. We must presume that at the start there were some points of agreement between the two parties, for while safe-conducts simply implied a willingness to talk, a truce implied some confidence in the outcome of discussions because it involved a suspension of hostilities. The barons in particular must have had high hopes, for they were

---

[1] *Rot. Litt. Pat.* p. 129.   [2] *Ibid.* p. 134.
[3] *Matthaei Parisiensis, Chronica Majora*, ed. H. R. Luard (Rolls Series, 1874), ii. 586.
[4] *Annals of Southwark and Merton*, ed. M. Tyson (Surrey Archaeological Collections, xxxvi, 1936), p. 49.
[5] *Rot. Litt. Pat.* p. 141; *Rot. Chart.* p. 209b.   [6] *Rot. Litt. Claus.* i. 204.
[7] *Rot. Litt. Pat.* p. 138b.   [8] *Ibid.* p. 142.
[9] *Ibid.*   [10] *Ibid.* p. 143.

forgoing the advantages gained from the capture of London at a time when the king's troops were being rapidly reinforced by foreign mercenaries. These negotiations were apparently not continuous. They must have begun on or immediately after the 27th, for baronial agents were with the king on the 29th, when he was still repeating his offer of papal arbitration first made on 10 May.[1] How long discussions continued after this it is impossible to say, but in all likelihood they had finished by 5 June. On that day John, who had moved restlessly between Reading, Odiham, and Windsor since the end of May, began a short and rapid journey which took him as far as Winchester and led him through an area thick with royalist troops.[2] This may perhaps indicate that he momentarily considered breaking off negotiations, but if so, the numbers and condition of his troops can scarcely have been propitious for an immediate campaign, for the project was soon abandoned. New letters of safe-conduct to those who came *ex parte baronum* were dated at Merton on 8 June, covering the period from 9 June to midnight on the 11th.[3] On the 9th royal letters were dated at Odiham,[4] but by nightfall the king was probably back at Windsor,[5] where he stayed until the 26th.

At this point the story is illuminated by an account of the election of Abbot Hugh of Bury St. Edmunds, derived from a man who was probably an eyewitness of many of the incidents described. The writer tells us that Hugh set out to seek royal approval of his election on 5 June. He found both John and Stephen Langton at Windsor on 9 June and the king told him to appear in the ' meadow of Staines ' on the following day where he hoped to settle the matter. Hugh duly appeared there on the 10th. The chronicler tells us that he had to wait a long time, but after much discussion and exchange of views the abbot was given the royal kiss of peace and was asked to dine at Windsor.[6] The chronology of this narrative is fully confirmed, for letters patent announcing Hugh's election and granting him the temporalities of the abbey were issued from the chancery under the date of 11 June.[7] This story provides clear evidence that the king was at Runnymede on 10 June, for the words ' the meadow of Staines ' can scarcely mean anything else. He would not have gone there simply to settle the case of Abbot Hugh. The safe-conduct issued to the baronial

---

[1] *Foedera*, I. i. 129.

[2] See *Rot. Litt. Pat.* p. 138b. Savaric de Mauleon and his Poitevin followers were based on Winchester (*ibid.* pp. 136b, 137b). While at Winchester on 6 June John ordered Faulkes de Bréauté to send 400 Welsh troops to his half-brother at Salisbury (*Rot. Litt. Claus.* i. 214).

[3] *Rot. Litt. Pat.* pp. 142b–3.   [4] *Rot. Litt. Claus.* i. 214b.

[5] *Electio Hugonis Abbatis, Memorials of St. Edmunds Abbey*, ed. T. Arnold (Rolls Series, 1892), ii. 128.   [6] *Ibid.* pp. 127–8.

[7] *Rot. Litt. Pat.* p. 142b. Letters of 2 June had previously ordered the transference of the abbey to the custody of Thomas de Barewe (*ibid.*).

representatives on the 8th and the fact that Langton was with the king on the 9th make it almost certain that the main problem to be settled at Runnymede on the 10th was not Abbot Hugh's election, but the issues between the king and the rebel barons. The discussions which had probably ceased when the king went to Winchester, were by now reopened.

The phrases of the letters of safe-conduct issued between the 25 May and 8 June suggest that the negotiations were producing something concrete. The letters of the 25th and the 27th issued in favour of Saer de Quenci, Langton and his companions, state that these men were coming *ad tractandum de pace*.[1] The letters of the 8th, in contrast, state that the baronial agents were now coming *ad pacem faciendam et firmandam*.[2] Thus something definite seems to have been expected from the negotiations of the 9–11th. It seems probable, too, that something was achieved, for on the 10th the king's military agents throughout the southern and midland counties were informed that the truce had been extended to the early morning of the 15th.[3] Whereas earlier negotiations had been in the hands of envoys, now, apparently, arrangements were being made for a full assembly of the opposing parties. There is a strong inference that some agreement had been reached on 9-10 June which made this change possible.

The most adequate explanation of the characteristic features of the *Articuli* is that they constitute this agreement. The document thus records terms agreed between the king and baronial envoys. Although the evidence for this hypothesis can only be indirect, taken as a whole, it amounts to a strong inferential argument. It is in general improbable that a conference as large as that held at Runnymede would have met without an agreed draft, a draft which must in the circumstances have been written down. Apart from the difficulty of managing such a conference without this, it is unlikely that the barons would have agreed to meet the king without some kind of preliminary commitment on his part. Roger of Wendover, indeed, asserts that in April the barons had demanded that their schedule of petitions should be sealed as a preliminary condition of peace,[4] and we know that the whole trend of the baronial programme had been towards a new confirmation of the charters of the king's predecessors.[5] By June, too, much time had been lost in the vague promises and the postponement of discussions

---

[1] *Rot. Litt. Pat.* pp. 138b, 142.   [2] *Ibid.* p. 142b.

[3] *Ibid.* p. 143. The addressees were William of Salisbury, Savaric de Mauleon, Richard fitz Roi, William Briwerre, William de Cantilupe, Waleran the German, John of Bassingborn, William de Harcourt, Roger de Neville, Stephen Harengod, and Geoffrey de Martigny.   [4] *Chron. Maj.* ii. 586.

[5] *Memoriale Walteri de Coventria*, ed. W. Stubbs (Rolls Series, 1873), ii. 218; *Radulphi de Coggeshall Chronicon Anglicanum*, ed. J. Stevenson, (Rolls Series, 1875), p. 170; *Chron. Maj.* ii. 584. See also Walter Mauclerc's report to John on the activities of the baronial agents at Rome (*Foedera*, i. i. 120).

which John had skilfully forced upon his opponents. Now, he was to be tied to specific points and concessions before final negotiations began.

If the *Articuli* are accepted as this draft, then many of the difficulties created by earlier interpretations of the document vanish. The title now presents no problems. The chancery hand in which it is written is simply what we would expect. Also it is easier to imagine a document of such length and complexity as the work of a small committee slowly reaching common ground over the period of a fortnight, than as the product of the first day of the general assembly at Runnymede, when any dissentient tongue or ragged temper might lead discussion into irrelevance and recrimination. Thus, chronologically, the hypothesis presents no difficulties. Even the fact that the *Articuli* eventually came into Langton's possession [1] falls neatly into place, for he would be the obvious man among those present on 10 June to hold the record of the committee discussions and carry the document to the rebels at London as evidence that the negotiations had reached a satisfactory conclusion. [2]

One detailed piece of evidence goes far to confirm the date I have advanced for the *Articuli*. On 19 June the chancery began to produce letters of restitution in execution of cap. 52 of the charter. One of these ordered the surrender of York castle to William de Mowbray until his hereditary claim to it had been investigated. [3] Two days later the sheriff of Yorkshire was ordered to enquire into the authority and personnel of an inquest which, according to de Mowbray, had investigated his claim to the custody of the shire, castle and forest of Yorkshire along with the manor of Pocklington. [4] The sheriff was now told to repeat the enquiry. This case was a very remarkable one. First, the Mowbray claim went back to Stephen's reign and William had presumably argued that his ancestors had been disseised by Henry II. [5] Secondly, such a claim was valid under cap. 52 of the Charter only if proceedings had begun before the king took the Cross (4 March). In view of de Mowbray's strained relations with the Crown throughout the reign and his open hostility since 1214, this is most unlikely. Thus he had probably

[1] See A. J. Collins, *loc. cit.* pp. 234–43.

[2] The evidence that the *Articuli* came into Langton's hands and that the archbishop was present at the negotiations of 10 June corroborates Sir Maurice Powicke's view of him as the great mediator between the two parties (*Stephen Langton*, Oxford, 1928, pp. 102 ff.).

Langton seems to have made several journeys between the two parties in the last weeks before Runnymede. He received the Brackley schedule from the barons, took it to the king and brought back the king's reply (*Chron. Maj.* ii. 586). Apparently he was with the barons in London in the latter half of May (*Electio Hugonis*, p. 127) and he probably joined the king on or immediately after 27 May when a safe-conduct was issued to him. It is probable that he would take the *Articuli* to the barons at London, just as earlier the Brackley schedule had been given to him for transmission.

[3] *Rot. Litt. Pat.* p. 143b.   [4] *Rot. Litt. Claus.* i. 215.   [5] *The Complete Peerage*, ix. 370.

taken action on the authority of cap. 25 of the *Articuli* which still left disseisins by Henry II open to question. Finally, de Mowbray had informed the king by 21 June that an inquest into his claim had been held. This inquest had not been authorized by the king ; de Mowbray must have acted himself, perhaps through the offices of a baronial sheriff of Yorkshire ; but, whatever the machinery used, the whole process must have started before 15 June. Even the eleven-day interval between 10 June and 21 June, which is the maximum the date I have suggested for the *Articuli* would permit between the initiation of the action and de Mowbray's knowledge that it was complete, can only be considered adequate if it is assumed that he was acting in unseemly haste in exploiting the document in his family interests.

If this instance tends to confirm the date I have advanced for the *Articuli*, the general form of the document does something to confirm the function I have suggested. The *Articuli* are often surprisingly provisional and vague in character. Thus cap. 12 simply asks that something should be done about weights and measures. In cap. 1 the ancient relief is *exprimendum in carta* and in the *forma securitatis* the king or his justiciar are to repair wrongs *infra rationabile tempus determinandum in carta*. Most important of all, cap. 25 seems to refer the problem of the king's respite as a crusader against pleas of disseisin by his brother and father to the judgement of the archbishop and bishops.[1] This in turn affected the restitution of similar disseisins to both the Welsh and the king of Scotland,[2] and the

---

[1] The reading of the last section of cap. 25 is not easy, in particular the force of the word *inde*.

There would seem to be three obvious possibilities:

(i) That the king's rights as a crusader were to be considered in all cases of disseisin, whether committed by him or his predecessors. This is McKechnie's interpretation (*op. cit.* p. 449), but I am unable to accept it. Cap. 25 clearly specifies that John's disseisins and his predecessors' were to be treated differently. Where John had disseised there was to be immediate restitution; the earlier cases, on the other hand, were to be judged by peers in the king's court Cap. 44 provides a convenient gloss on cap. 25 in that it makes clear that John's disseisins were to be restored *sine placito*. These distinctions strongly suggest that his disseisins could not have been subject to the crusader's privilege. The effect of caps. 25 and 44 in these cases is to by-pass the whole judicial process, the restitutions appearing as acts of grace. The stay against legal action to which a crusader was entitled would therefore not arise.

(ii) That if the king was to have the privilege of a crusader, the judgement of the archbishop and bishops was to replace the judgement of peers in cases of disseisin by Henry II and Richard I. This seems to be the obvious construction of the Latin. For a similar use of the word *inde* see the *Articuli* cap. 37 and Magna Carta cap. 55.

(iii) That the archbishop and bishops were to decide whether the king was to have the crusader's privilege where cases of disseisin by Henry II and Richard were raised. If the passage means this, it is phrased in a rather odd manner. This, however, seems to have been the sense accepted for it was precisely this problem which the archbishop and his colleagues settled in the period intervening between cap. 25 of the *Articuli* and cap. 52 of Magna Carta.

[2] *Articuli*, caps. 44, 46.

restoration of Welsh hostages and those of the king of Scotland was also submitted to ecclesiastical judgement.[1] In the *Articuli*, in fact, a large sector of the issues between the king and the rebels and their allies was deliberately and intentionally referred to a committee of churchmen. To this we may add the informal language of the *Articuli*. Only in cap. 48 and the *forma securitatis* does it approach the solemn formulae of a grant. Elsewhere its sections are cast as requests or promises. The chapters of the *Articuli* are *conventiones ;* the Charter, in contrast, contains *concessiones*.[2]

It is arguable on general grounds that this tentativeness and informality is more likely to have been produced in the committee discussions of 10 June than in the general meeting of 15 June. Indeed, it is not easy to see why the barons should have insisted on producing a written preliminary agreement on 15 June, when that agreement envisaged and provided for its own amendment and elucidation. If this argument seems at first sight weak, it is immeasurably strengthened by a consideration of the most striking and difficult feature of the *Articuli*—the fact that they bore the king's great seal. For such a document to be sealed was quite abnormal, if not unique. It had little of the characteristic form of a charter or letter patent. Legally, it did not convey or grant anything. There was nothing in it to be strengthened or made valid by the appending of the king's great seal. Given the normal practices of the Angevin chancery, that the seal should be placed on the *Articuli* in the circumstances of 15 June seems completely meaningless.

The sealing of the *Articuli* is more comprehensible if we imagine that they were to be sent to someone. If, as I have argued, the points they contained were agreed by 10 June, then it is easy to imagine that the sealed draft was sent to the rest of the barons at London as a warrant that their envoys had reached a preparatory agreement with the king on a large number of problems. This despatch of a sealed document may, indeed, have been essential, for according to Wendover the barons had already asked that the Brackley schedule should be sealed and had defied the king on his refusal.[3] Whatever the relationship of the schedule to the *Articuli*, in the sealing of the latter we seem to have a reply to this demand. But the demand, it should be noted, was made in circumstances identical with those of 10 June, for in both instances the negotiations were in the hands of envoys. In the first instance the sealing of an informal document was demanded and in the second it occurred,

---

[1] *Articuli* caps. 45, 46.   [2] Compare the two versions of the *forma securitatis*.

[3] Some confirmation of Wendover's evidence at this point is found in the king's charter of 9 May where reference is made to the fact that the barons had already sent *articuli* to the king (*Rot. Chart.* p. 209b). This word seems to fit Wendover's description of the Brackley schedule well enough. This reference, of course, cannot refer to the *Articuli* proper. These must have followed the royal offers of 10 May which were still being repeated on 29 May. See *supra*, p. 222.

when the opposing parties had not yet met in a plenary conference.

If the *Articuli* were accepted on 10 June, then the whole problem of the date of Magna Carta is thrown open, for one of McKechnie's main arguments for allocating the latter to 19 June was that there was insufficient time for the production of both documents in one day. This now loses weight, for although the *Articuli* were probably sent to London, the committee which produced them must still have had the minutes on which they were based; the baronial envoys and the king, therefore, could have continued discussions after the 10th and had the Charter ready by the 15th. This date was the one given to Magna Carta by Stubbs, Miss Norgate, and Charles Bémont,[1] and although their views that a sealed Charter was delivered and executed on that day may not be acceptable, it is still possible that the Charter was drafted by or on that day. The dating of the Charter to the 15th could be taken to indicate a baronial acceptance of a draft Charter.

At this point the documents themselves are of little use for they are legal instruments not historical records. They refer to events in the past tense on the assumption or in the knowledge that these events would occur as part of the settlement, not in the knowledge that they had taken place at the time of drafting. Thus the *forma securitatis* of the *Articuli* refers to the peace and liberties which 'the lord king has conceded and confirmed by his charter' at a time when the Charter could not even have been drafted, still less sealed and delivered. Similarly, the *inspeximus* of the Charter provided in the Letters Testimonial cannot have existed when cap. 62 of the Charter was drafted with the words *fecimus eis fieri litteras testimoniales*. Equally significant is the fact that the writ in which the king informed Stephen Harengod that firm peace had been reached on the 19th, is dated 18 June and was presumably authorized and perhaps drafted on that day.[2] Thus, although the Charter refers to events which we may attribute to 19 June, it may well have been drafted earlier.

Despite this, however, the evidence on the whole suggests that the Charter had not been drafted as early as 15 June. First, the

---

[1] C. Bémont, *Chartes des Libertés Anglaises*, p. xxi; Kate Norgate, *John Lackland*, p. 234. Stubbs states that the *Articuli* were sealed on 15 June and the Charter 'issued' or 'executed' on the same day (*Constitutional History of England*, (6th edn., 1897), i. 569; *Select Charters* (6th edn., 1888), p. 290).

[2] *Rot. Litt. Pat.* p. 143b. Miss Norgate has argued that the 'die Veneris' (19 June) of this and other writs is an error for 'die Lunae' (15 June) (*op. cit.* p. 234, n. 2). McKechnie, in contrast, followed Blackstone in arguing that the enrolling clerk erred in transcribing *xxiii* as *xviii* (*Magna Carta.* p. 41; *Law Tracts*, ii. p. xxxvii). There is no sound reason for assuming that either mistake occurred. The writ is preceded on the rolls by writs of the 18th and followed by writs of the 19th. The situation is easily comprehensible if we imagine that John knew on the 18th that homage would be renewed on the following day and that he immediately authorized writs forbidding acts of war after the 19th with the intention of issuing them as soon as homage had been renewed.

reference of the problems involved in cap. 25 and related sections of the *Articuli* must have taken time and perhaps necessitated the summoning of the bishops to Runnymede to discuss them. Secondly, the fact that firm peace was delayed until the 19th suggests that the terms of the settlement were still being discussed after the 15th. There were, it is true, other matters besides the terms of the Charter to settle : the custody of London,[1] the choice of the Twenty-Five barons of the *forma securitatis*, and perhaps also the methods of putting the Charter into effect locally. It is also possible that the attendance at Runnymede was insufficiently complete in the first few days of the conference for a formal peace to be concluded. Nevertheless all parties must have felt some urgency. Apart from the simple desire for a settlement, Staines and Windsor must have been crowded with the households of the barons and the supporters of the king, and the problem of finding provisions for such a large concourse must have been a difficult one. There is therefore some reason for thinking that a formal peace would be concluded as soon as possible. The four-day delay after the 15th thus implies that the Charter was not yet drafted and that its terms were still being discussed. This view finds strong support in the chronicle evidence, for according to the Barnwell Chronicler the agreement at Runnymede was only reached after much discussion,[2] and the impression conveyed by this statement is confirmed by Roger of Wendover.[3] Lastly, the final extension of the truce was quite precise in specifying that it ran until the early morning of the 15th.[4] This implies that some definite and immediate action was expected when the two parties first met which would either make peace certain or render

[1] Although there is no conclusive evidence, I am inclined to believe that the agreement between the king and the barons on the custody of London should be dated 15–19 June. It is scarcely likely that the king would agree to terms of peace without some arrangement being made on the fate of the capital. The treaty's reference to the letters patent of the 19th providing for the taking of oaths, and its similarity to the writs of the 19th both in this matter and its provision for the restoration of estates, would suggest that it was produced at the same time as these writs (*Foedera*, I. i. 133). The treaty was in fact an essential supplement to the writs in that it imposed a time limit for their execution (15 August). *Cf.* the treaty with the writs to William of Salisbury (*Rot. Litt. Claus.* i. 215) and the general letters ordering the oath to the Twenty-Five and the inquiry into evil customs (*Rot. Litt. Pat.* p. 180b). The treaty does not, as McKechnie states (*op. cit.* p. 43, n. 4), refer to the letters to sheriffs and the juries of the counties of 27 June (*Rot. Litt. Pat.* p. 145b).

Mr. H. G. Richardson has argued that the treaty belongs to a meeting held at Oxford in the third week in July basing this argument on the fact that it was entered on the dorse of the membrane of the close roll covering 18–19 July (' The Morrow of the Great Charter ', *Bulletin of the John Rylands Library*, xxviii (1944), 424). This may prove nothing more than that the treaty was entered on the roll at this time. Even if it proves this, which is problematical, the date of the composition of the treaty is quite another matter. [2] *Walt. Cov.* ii. 221.

[3] ' Tandem igitur cum hinc inde varia sorte tractassent, rex Johannes, vires suas baronum viribus impares intelligens, sine difficultate leges subscriptas et libertates concessit ' (*Chron. Maj.* ii. 589).

[4] *Rot. Litt. Pat.* p. 143. *Cf.* the safe-conduct of 8 June which ran to the 11th ' ad diem completam ' (*ibid.*).

any continuation of the truce pointless. Whatever was to occur, it was not expected to require extended discussion. Now a baronial acceptance of a draft Charter at this stage would probably have entailed lengthy debate and this would be true of any document which departed from the terms of the *Articuli*, on the basis of which the general conference was being held. It seems therefore that the action which was expected early on the 15th was simply a solemn verbal acceptance by all parties of the *Articuli* as a draft settlement. Such an act would have great significance. It would make it certain that a formal peace would now be concluded ; it would provide a point of authorization for the final terms of the Charter, a document clearly foreseen in the *Articuli ;* finally, it would raise the *Articuli* from the status of a draft produced in committee to that of a preliminary settlement to which all who agreed at Runnymede were committed.

There are strong reasons for thinking that such an acceptance of the *Articuli* would be the first important act at Runnymede. In 1215 the concept of delegates exercising full authority on behalf of a community still lay in the future. Despite the fact that the *Articuli* enjoyed the prestige of the great seal, neither the king nor the baronial envoys of 10 June can have been certain that they had any validity as a draft agreement until they had been publicly accepted by a very large majority of the rebels. Whatever the bonds imposed by a *conjuratio*, the envoys of 10 June were simply representative of an *ad hoc* association loosely held together by a common hostility to the king. In recounting events at Runnymede on and after the 15th, the Barnwell Chronicler states that some of the ' Northerners ' left the meeting and on the excuse that they had not been present, proceeded to make war.[1] This statement cannot be tested adequately. But whether it is true or false, if a contemporary could imagine a rejection of the Charter in these terms, then the king and the baronial envoys could far more easily imagine that the *Articuli* might be rejected in similar terms. The danger of this would seem all the greater if the *Articuli* did not meet all the proposals which were in the air. That they did not indeed do so is demonstrated by the fact that one highly important section of the Charter, dealing with the amercement of barons by their peers,[2] found no place in the *Articuli*. Further, neither the Charter nor the *Articuli* contained such stringent regulations on overseas service or the forests as appear in the ' unknown ' charter.[3] Thus, while the *Articuli*

---

[1] *Walt. Cov.* ii. 222.　　　　　　　[2] Magna Carta, cap. 21.

[3] ' Unknown charter ', caps. 7, 9, 10 and 12. The text is readily accessible in McKechnie, *op. cit.* pp. 485–6 and in C. Petit Du Taillis, *Studies Supplementary to Stubbs' Constitutional History* (Manchester, 1908), i. 117–18.

This document has normally been allocated to the period November 1213–June 1215. See McKechnie, *op. cit.* pp. 171 ff., where the older views on the document are summarized, and Sir Maurice Powicke, *Stephen Langton*, pp. 117 ff., Professor S.

represented a surrender by the king, they also represented a withdrawal by the envoys from previous baronial plans.

If the authorization of the Charter is to be found in a general acceptance of the *Articuli* on 15 June, then the Charter cannot have been drafted until some time later. That it had been drafted by the 19th is almost certain, for letters of that date provided for the execution of caps. 48, 49, 52, and 61.[1] Indeed, the king knew on the 18th that the barons were to renew their homage on the following day,[2] and so it is probable that final terms had already been agreed by then and that the Charter already existed in some kind of draft. It is not, however, until the day after the conference broke

---

Painter, *op. cit.* pp. 314 ff., Dr. A. L. Poole, *op. cit.* pp. 471 ff., and Professor V. H. Galbraith, *op. cit.* pp. 133-4. The reference made by the barons in January 1215 to the oath sworn by the king at Winchester in July 1213 and not to any intervening commitment, suggests that the document followed the Epiphany negotiations at London (*Coggeshall*, p. 170; *Chron. Maj.* ii. 584; *Foedera*, i. i. 120). Indeed, the phrasing of cap. 1 may mean that it followed the royal offer of 10 May.

The problem of dating is obscured by the form and archaisms of the document. These difficulties, however, and the fact that we have the document in a rather careless transcript, do not render it valueless. The fact that it gives us a text of the re-issue of Henry I's charter independent of but similar to those of the Quadripartitus and the Red Book of the Exchequer suggests that the originator of the document had access to a Treasury copy of Henry's grant (J. H. Round, ' An Unknown Charter of Liberties ', *EHR*, viii (1893), 288). Further, whatever the peculiarities of the concessions it attributed to John, these peculiarities were relevant to the situation in 1215. It is possible that some of its points were discussed at Runnymede. Unlike the *Articuli* or Magna Carta, it contained detailed regulations on the administration of the forest law. These have a parallel in the Charter of the Forest of 1217 (' unknown charter ' caps. 10 & 12, Charter of the Forest, caps. 4, 9 & 10). Wendover's allocation of the Charter of the Forest to 1215 seems less surprising if we assume that these sections of the ' unknown ' charter were still a matter of debate at Runnymede. It is also worth noting that the author of the ' Histoire des Ducs de Normandie et des Rois d'Angleterre ' (ed. F. Michel, Paris, 1840, p. 150) states that John promised in 1215 that a man should not lose life or limb for any wild beast that he took. This promise is identical with cap. 12 of the ' unknown charter '.

[1] *Rot. Litt. Pat.* pp. 180b, 143b; *Rot. Litt. Claus.* i. 215. It is a possible but not very likely hypothesis that these letters were in execution of the interim agreement of the *Articuli* and that the terms of the Charter had not been settled by the time of the ' firm ' peace of the 19th. This would assume that the rebels would be prepared to go through the formalities of peace before the final terms were settled, an assumption which is improbable in view of the importance of many of the problems which the *Articuli* left open for discussion. It should also be noted that cap. 25 of the *Articuli*, dealing with royal disseisins, was one of the chief debatable clauses. All the cases of restitution from the 19th onwards which I have examined, with the exception of the peculiar Mowbray case dealt with above (pp. 408-9), covered disseisins by John only. This suggests that the position of disseisins by his predecessors, left open in cap. 25, had been settled by the 19th. Further, the letters of restitution sometimes dealt with castles, a point not mentioned in cap. 25 of the *Articuli*, but inserted in cap. 52 of the Charter. The writ of the 19th to William of Salisbury is especially significant in this respect for while it makes a temporary exception in the case of Trowbridge castle it clearly states that the terms of peace provided for the restoration of castles. ' Sciatis quod pax hoc modo reformata est inter nos et Barones nostros quod nos statim reddemus omnes terras et castra et iura unde nos dissaisiri fecimus aliquem injuste et sine judicio ' (*Rot. Litt. Claus.* i. 215).

[2] *Rot. Litt. Pat.* p. 143b.

up,[1] 24 June, when two, and probably a further five, copies of the Charter were delivered for distribution,[2] that we can be certain that a sealed engrossment of it was in existence.

McKechnie's argument at this point was that the formal delivery of a sealed engrossment of the Charter formed part of the business of 19 June. These views have been reinforced by Mr. A. J. Collin's who has suggested that the Letters Testimonial and the Charter were exchanged on this day, the two fulfilling a rôle ' analogous to the counterparts of an indenture '.[3] But there is no direct evidence that a sealed engrossment of the Charter was completed by 19 June. It is true that the general writs to the sheriffs of this date refer to the Charter *quam inde fieri fecimus,* but evidence of this type, as we have seen, is inconclusive.[4] Further, the writ to Stephen Harengod makes it perfectly clear that the essential feature of the firm peace of the 19th was not, as we might expect, the delivery of the Charter, but the renewal of homage,[5] for by this and this alone was the state of war consequent on the baronial *diffidatio* technically brought to an end. One section of the Charter, in fact, makes it certain that the execution and delivery of the document must have followed, not preceded, the renewal of homage. The object of the writ to Stephen Harengod was to restrain the king's agents from further acts of war after the dead-line of the 19th. It found a complement in the Charter in a royal pardon of transgressions arising from the quarrel between the two parties covering the period from Easter 1215 *usque ad pacem reformatam.*[6] These words clearly refer to the firm peace of 19 June, and they are similar to those used in the writ of that date announcing the peace to William, earl of Salisbury.[7] This section of the Charter may have been drafted before 19 June, but it could not have been executed until the state of war had been brought to an end by the renewal of homage. That this also applied to other sections is demonstrated by the following writ of 21 June addressed to Saer de Quenci : ' Mandamus vobis quod ex quo Comes David nobis homagium suum fecerit, ei castrum suum de Foderingeya quod vobis commisimus custodiendum reddi faciatis, et si forte obierit antequam nobis homagium suum fecerit, tunc castrum illud nobis reddatis.'[8] Earl David was not to enjoy the benefits of cap. 52 until he was once more the king's man.

This evidence is reinforced by more general considerations. A royal charter was not a treaty but a freely given grant, made in the

[1] Royal writs were dated at Runnymede on the 21st, 22nd and 23rd (*Rot. Litt. Pat.* pp. 143b–4). Several of the baronial leaders attested a charter dated 20 June at Runnymede (*Rot. Chart.* p. 210b) and Saer de Quenci, Eustace de Vesci and Philip fitz John all received copies of the writ ordering the enquiry into evil customs sometime between the 19th and the 24th (*Rot. Litt. Pat.* p. 180b).

[2] *Rot. Litt. Pat.* p. 180b.   [3] *Loc. cit.* pp. 245, 249.

[4] *Rot. Litt. Pat.* p. 180b. See *supra*, p. 227.   [5] *Rot. Litt. Pat.* p. 143b.

[6] Cap. 62.   [7] *Rot. Litt. Claus.* i. 215.   [8] *Rot. Litt. Pat.* p. 144.

case of John's Magna Carta *intuitu Dei et pro salute anime nostre et omnium antecessorum et heredum nostrorum ad honorem Dei et exaltationem sancte Ecclesie.* Such an act, whether royal or private, was invalid if issued under duress. Now John, certainly, was acting under strong compulsion when he issued the Charter. Pope Innocent annulled it partly on the grounds that it had been granted under duress,[1] and one of the king's friends, William Briwerre, later used the same argument to oppose the confirmation of 1224.[2] But our concern here is not so much with the fact of force as with its appearance. The king would not have executed a solemn grant in perpetuity in favour of men who were not yet in his peace.[3] To his opponents also it must have seemed essential that the Charter should appear to have been granted freely and without duress, for anything less would deprive it of validity and ease the way for papal annulment, the possibility of which they clearly recognized.[4] For different reasons both parties must have wanted to eliminate the impression that the Charter had been traded for a baronial renewal of homage, however much this impression represented the underlying situation.

From this point of view, the terms used in the Charter and related documents are interesting. The writs issued in execution of the Charter make it quite clear that a war had occurred. The letter patent to Stephen Harengod refers to the prisoners and hostages taken *occasione hujus guerre* [5] and several letters order the restitution of property *sicut ante guerram* [6] or mention the seizure of land and chattels *occasione guerre.*[7] More significantly still, in the agreement on London, Robert fitz Walter still styled himself ' marshal of the army of God and Holy Church ', and the threat which the baronial retention of London levelled at the king was but thinly veiled by the legal fiction that fitz Walter and his friends were holding the capital of the king's bail and along with the freemen of the whole kingdom.[8] In these documents the writers showed no inhibitions. In the Charter, however, the atmosphere is quite different. Although it describes itself as a peace,[9] it

---

[1] *Selected Letters of Pope Innocent III*, ed. Professor C. R. Cheney and Professor W. H. Semple (London, 1953), p. 215.   [2] *Chron. Maj.* iii. 76.

[3] It seems arguable at first sight that the king had already granted a charter to men technically his enemies, namely the charter of 9 May (*Rot. Chart.* p. 209b). To a large extent, however, this charter duplicated the letters patent of 10 May, and if any document was sent to the rebels at this stage it was the letters patent, accompanied by similar ones making individual concessions to Geoffrey de Mandeville and the bishop of Hereford. The charter of the 9th, in contrast, seems to have been a public announcement of the conditions John was attaching to his offer. Finally, none of these documents were grants in perpetuity. They simply announced temporary concesionss pending the arbitration of the committee of eight and the Pope. John's attitude to his offer is clearly indicated in his letter to the Pope of 29 May . . . ' in tantum nos humiliavimus quod haec praedicta eis optulimus ' (*Foedera*, I. i. 129).

[4] See the *forma securitatis* of the *Articuli.*   [5] *Rot. Litt. Pat.* p. 143b.   [6] *Ibid.* p. 143b.
[7] *Rot. Litt. Claus.* i. 215b–16b.   [8] *Foedera*, I. i. 133.   [9] Caps. 51, 55, 61.

mentions no war. The trouble has simply been a *discordia*,[1] a dispute, and the baronial acts of war simply *transgressiones*,[2] or breaches of the peace. The whole atmosphere of the Charter is one of legality. Thus, under cap. 61 a plaintiff was to *seek* redress of the king and, in the case of default, compulsion was to be achieved not by war but by *distringendo et gravando nos*. The difference in tone between the Charter and associated documents may be partly explained by John's unwillingness hitherto to admit publicly that the situation had been one of war.[3] But the main factor must have been that while the writs were simply administrative instruments, and while the agreement on London was not a grant but a *conventio* covering a limited period, the Charter was a solemn concession in perpetuity ' concerning the liberties and security of the kingdom '.[4] It must therefore contain no hint that force had gone into its making.

Three obvious questions remain to be answered. At what point and how did the terms of the Charter acquire legal validity? When was the first sealed engrossment of the Charter finished? When was such an engrossment first delivered? The first question is distinct from the other two because the English charter at this period was not a dispositive but an evidentiary document, which simply provided a record of a transaction agreed verbally by the parties concerned and executed by some kind of formal and public act. A charter was not even essential to a grant, nor did a grant presume a charter.[5] Magna Carta, therefore, would come into effect, not when the first engrossment was sealed or when such an engrossment was delivered, but when its terms were publicly and formally accepted. Such a formal acceptance did take place at Runnymede, for the Charter emphasized that both parties had sworn to observe its terms in good faith.[6] This oath must have followed the drafting

---

[1] Caps. 1, 61, 62. The term *discordia* was often used to mean a wider period than that of the war. See, for instance, Magna Carta, cap. 1. This distinction, however, was not always clearly made. See Magna Carta, cap. 62 and the writ to Stephen Harengod (*Rot. Litt. Pat.* p. 143b).   [2] Cap. 62.

[3] There is no reference to the baronial *diffidatio* or the capture of London in the letters John sent to the Pope on 29 May (*Foedera*, i. i. 129). In the letters patent of 10 May and those of the 27th dealing with the truce and safe-conduct the barons appear as ' our ' barons (*Rot. Litt. Pat.* pp. 141, 142) and in the public documents as a whole the seriousness of the situation is obscured. They refer to the ' barons who are against us ' (*ibid.* p. 141) or to the ' barons opposing us ' (*Rot. Chart.* p. 209b), but never to the ' barons making war on us '. It is in the more private correspondence between the king and his sheriffs, largely contained in letters close, that his opponents are bluntly and accurately described as ' our enemies ' (*Rot. Litt. Claus.* i. 204).

[4] The phrase is taken from the treaty on London (*Foedera*, i. i. 133).

[5] For a discussion of these problems see Professor T. F. T. Plucknett, *A Concise History of the Common Law* (London, 1948), pp. 577–9; Sir Frank Stenton, *Transcripts of Charters relating to Gilbertine Houses*, xviii (Lincoln Record Society, 1922), pp. xvi ff.; Professor V. H. Galbraith, ' Monastic Foundation Charters of the 11th and 12th centuries ', *Cambridge Historical Journal*, iv (1934), 205–22.

[6] Cap. 63 where the reference to the oath is inserted between the *Quare volumus* and witnessing clauses. For another and similar instance see the letters of the baronial guarantors of John's peace with Langton and the other exiled bishops in 1213, (*Foedera*, i. i. 112).

of the Charter and must have preceded the authorization of writs putting it into effect. Most probably, therefore, it was a counterpart to the baronial renewal of homage on the 19th. By it, John was tied by far stronger bonds than those of parchment, for if he broke them he would stand publicly condemned as a perjurer.

This oath provided the immediate guarantee of the execution of the Charter. A sealed engrossment could have been produced at any time after the document had been drafted and such an engrossment could have been delivered at any time after the renewal of homage, but there is no evidence that such a sealed engrossment was ready by 19 June or that the delivery of the document followed immediately on the renewal of homage on that day, nor is there any compelling reason for assuming that this occurred. While the oath provided the immediate guarantee, the sealed Charters provided a permanent one. They were, in effect, a record for those not present at Runnymede and for generations yet to come of what had been agreed. This record derived further authenticity from the Letters Testimonial which were drawn up ' lest anything should be added to or taken away from ' the terms of the Charter. But there is no reason for thinking that special significance was attached to the actual transfer of these letters to the barons.[1] Similarly, when copies of the Charter were delivered into the hands of some of the barons and the agents of the king, the aim was simply to ensure their distribution throughout the country.[2] Only in fact in the case of the indenture on the custody of London can we be certain that there was a formal exchange of documents between the two parties. At what exact point the first Charter was engrossed, sealed and delivered

---

[1] The Letters Testimonial were not guarantees of the settlement but guarantees that the record of the settlement would not be altered at some future date. They cannot have been drawn up until the first sealed engrossment of the Charter had been produced.

There may well have been a second motive in associating letters of this kind with the settlement. This section of the Charter replaced the much more stringent demand of the *Articuli* whereby the leading churchmen with the papal legate were to guarantee that the king would not appeal to the pope against the terms of the agreement. This must have proved unacceptable to the churchmen, for they could scarcely be expected to deny the right of appeal to the Curia, especially since John had surrendered his kingdom to the pope. It is probable therefore that the Letters Testimonial were intended as a weaker but acceptable method of committing the churchmen, and the papal legate in particular, to the terms of the Charter. It should be noted that the language of the clause of corroboration at the end of the Letters Testimonial comes fairly near to the closing words of the *Articuli*. ' Et ne huic forme predicte aliquid possit addi vel ab eadem aliquid possit subtrahi vel minui, huic scripto sigilla nostra apposuimus.' *Cf.* ' Preterea rex faciet eos securos per cartas archiepiscopi et episcoporum et magistri Pandulfi, quod nichil impetrabit a domino papa per quod aliqua istarum conventionum revocetur vel minuatur, et, si aliquid tale impetraverit, reputetur irritum et inane et numquam eo utatur.'

In the light of this and the wording of cap. 62 of the Charter, I find it difficult to accept Mr. A. J. Collins's argument that the Letters Testimonial were made out not for the barons, but for the king (*loc. cit.* pp. 244 ff.). It is possible, of course, that both parties received copies. [2] *Rot. Litt. Pat.* p. 180b.

it is impossible to say, but it may well have been some time after 19 June, for once the agreement had been executed *viva voce* by oath, the engrossment of the necessary documents could well be left to the chancery clerks.[1] The final word on the matter may be given to two contemporaries. Abbot Ralf of Coggeshall describes events at Runnymede in the following manner :

> Intervenientibus itaque archiepiscopo Cantuariensi cum pluribus coepiscopis et baronibus nonnullis, quasi pax inter regem et barones formata est, et tactis sacrosanctis ab omnibus inviolabiliter tenenda juratur, etiam a rege. Mox igitur forma pacis in charta est comprehensa, ita quod singuli comitatus totius Angliae singulas unius tenoris haberent chartas regio sigillo communitas. Ibi quoque jura sua baronibus, et aliis de quibus indubitanter constabat quod eis competebant, rex restituit.[2]

The Dunstable Annalist gives us roughly the same sequence of events :

> Tandem apud Runymede convenerunt, et die Gervasii et Protasii (19 June) facta est ibidem pax inter regem et barones; quae parvo tempore obtinuit. Et recepit ibi rex homagia, quae barones ei in principio guerrae reddiderant, in diffidatione facta apud Walingefort per quendam canonicum de Derham oriundum. Et tunc restituit rex plerisque castra et alia jura sua, et confectae sunt ibidem chartae super libertatibus regni Angliae, et per singulas episcopatus in locis tutis depositae.[3]

These two writers provide mutually independent and very valuable accounts of the reign of King John.[4] For them the peace agreement was reached *viva voce*, in the one case with the renewal of homage, and in the other with the oath accepting the peace. The engrossments of the Charter followed later and were designed immediately for distribution throughout the country. Neither writer mentions the formal transfer of an original as part of the peace settlement. Both, in contrast, associate the engrossment and

---

[1] It is perhaps relevant to note here that the baronial renewal of homage on the 19th was followed by a royal request for letters of fealty (*Rot. Litt. Pat.* p. 181). This was refused, but if they had been produced, there would have been a lapse of time between the act of homage and the letters recording it. The fact that the barons refused to issue them, it should be noted, did not render the homage invalid.

[2] *Coggeshall*, p. 172.

[3] *Annales Monastici*, ed. H. R. Luard (Rolls Series), iii. 43.

[4] Compare their narrative with the following from the Barnwell Chronicler: ' Assignato itaque loco, ubi partes commode convenirent, tandem post multas deliberationes amici facti sunt, rege illis omnia annuente quae volebant, et per cartam suam confirmante. Recepti sunt igitur in osculum pacis qui aderant, hominium et fidelitatem de novo facientes . . .' (*Walt. Cov.* ii. 221). Although this passage seems to point to a different order of events, the writer distinguishes between the king's agreement to the terms and his confirmation of them by charter. It is possible too, that the sentence ' Recepti sunt igitur . . .' is simply an explanation of the phrase amici facti sunt '.

delivery of the Charter with the king's restitution of baronial rights. As most of the writs of restitution were dated between 19 and 26 June, their evidence dovetails exactly with the note on the patent roll that seven charters were delivered for distribution on 24 June. In all likelihood these were the first engrossments to be completed.

NOTE

Since this paper was written, Professor C. R. Cheney has published his lecture entitled ' The Eve of Magna Carta '.[1] Our arguments are based on extensive common ground, particularly in questioning the accepted explanation of events in the summer of 1215. But at two important points they differ : in the dating of the *Articuli* and in the time at which the terms of Magna Carta were agreed.

1. The *Articuli*. Professor Cheney argues that the meeting of the 15th was arranged on the understanding that the king would agree to the Articles ' as we know them '. On the 15th itself, in his view, the actual document which has survived was copied by a royal clerk from a baronial draft, a few last additions were made, and the seal was affixed ' as a promise by the king that a charter would be made on the basis of the Articles' demands and suggestions '.[2]

This argument assumes the existence of a baronial list of articles identical, or almost identical, with the extant *Articuli*, an assumption considered above.[3] It also leads to one central difficulty, the striking contrast between the informality of the *Articuli* in both form and language and the fact that they carried the great seal. If Professor Cheney's hypothesis is correct, it has to be proved that the application of the great seal was a form of guarantee of John's good intentions which the assembled barons would insist upon or accept on 15 June. Yet, as Professor Cheney himself states, the barons ' understood better a system of oaths, hostages, and sureties '[4] and were, in his view, prepared to renew homage and accept a firm peace on the 19th, not only with the Charter unwritten, but with its final terms not yet settled.[5] Further, even if the seal was applied in these circumstancse, why was it applied to a document which contained none of the conventional formulae of a grant, especially when we are imagining that the extant document was written by a royal clerk on the 15th itself? If the document was to receive the normal validation by seal then we might expect that the clerk would insert part or all of the associated formulae. He did not do so, and he did not do so on a piece of parchment which still had room for the insertion of such formulae when the writing had been finished.

It is possible, of course, to circumvent these difficulties. It might be argued that the assembled company did not think of applying the seal to the *Articuli* until after they had been written, or that the clerk did not know that the seal was to be applied when he was writing. But there is no

[1] *Bulletin of the John Rylands Library*, xxxviii, no. 2 (March 1956), 311–41.
[2] *Ibid.* pp. 330, 325. [3] *Supra*, p. 220. [4] *Loc. cit.* p. 325. [5] *Ibid.* pp. 332–4.

prima facie case for suggesting such hypothetical detail. The basis for doing so is simply that 15 June saw the first general meeting at Runnymede and that something happened on this day which was regarded by the Chancery as " dating " Magna Carta. There is nothing to suggest that this " something " was the drafting or sealing of the *Articuli*.

On the whole the hypothesis that the *Articuli* were drafted and sealed on 10 June is stronger. Apart from the general reasons for this which I have advanced already, it is a hypothesis which explains why the seal was applied to such a peculiar document. The seal constituted not so much a royal promise as evidence to the baronial army at London of what the king and their envoys had agreed. Perhaps also, in circumstances in which more radical demands were in the air, the application of the seal to the *Articuli* gave the draft an official status which no other draft or set of proposals could enjoy and, by implication, gave the negotiators of 10 June a recognized position which no other group among the barons could claim.

2. Magna Carta. Professor Cheney and I are in agreement in believing that the engrossment of the Charter followed the ' firm ' peace of 19 June and he adduces evidence not considered above in support of this view. He suggests further, however, that the terms of the Charter were probably not settled until 23 June, both the document and its terms being ' disengaged from the recorded ceremonial of 19 June '.[1] My reasons for thinking that the terms of the Charter were settled by 19 June have been given above. Professor Cheney's hypothesis, which I admit is a possible one, is based on the following evidence:

(*a*) The interrelated annals of Merton, Southwark, and Waverley date the peace or the making of the Charter to 23 June, others giving various dates, the 15th (Wendover), the 18th (Melrose), and the 19th (Dunstable).[2]

(*b*) The probability, based on the narrative of the *Histoire des Ducs de Normandie* that Earl William of Salisbury, one of the counsellors named in the preamble of the Charter, could not have been present at Runnymede between 15 and 19 June.[3]

(*c*) The absence of reference to existing versions of the Charter prior to 24 June and the lack of record evidence apart from the dating clause of Magna Carta that the king was at Runnymede before 19 June.[4]

Of this evidence points (*a*) and (*c*) are the least convincing. It is difficult to make anything of the variety of dates provided by the chroniclers; there are no internal reasons, for example, for preferring the 23rd of the Waverley Annals to the 19th of the Annals of Dunstable. The fact that a Charter cannot be shown to have been in existence before the 24th does not imply necessarily that its terms had not been settled earlier. Nor does the absence of attestations at Runnymede prior to the 19th mean that the king was not there. In fact, if the date on the letter to Stephen Harengod is taken at its face value, this provides an attestation at Runnymede for the 18th.[5] As Professor Cheney points out, few

---

[1] *Ibid.* p. 333. [2] *Ibid.* pp. 327–8. [3] *Ibid.* pp. 328–9.
[4] *Ibid.* p. 326. [5] *Rot. Litt. Pat.* p. 143b.

letters were issued between the 15th and the 19th. After the 19th letters were attested both at Runnymede and Windsor up to the 23rd. Clearly John was 'commuting' at this stage. The few letters of the 15–19th could quite easily fail to reveal that he was also doing so earlier. Two further points should be considered. First, the more important letters putting the settlement into effect were attested at Runnymede, not at Windsor, as also were many of the letters of restitution to individuals. The first of these was attested on the 18th and they were authorized in large numbers from the 19th. In contrast, there were no letters executing the settlement prior to that which was addressed to Stephen Harengod on the 18th. Secondly, the paucity of letters of any kind for the period 15–19th and the flood of letters which accompanied and followed the 'firm' peace suggests that up to the 19th the settlement was being discussed, but that afterwards it was simply being administered.[1] It is difficult in any case to imagine that the discussion of the *Articuli* was still being continued on and after the 19th when so many individual claims were being pressed.

Professor Cheney's point (b) on the whereabouts of William of Salisbury is important, but not by itself sufficient to prove his hypothesis. First, as he agrees, the earl may have discussed proposed terms with John prior to the meeting at Runnymede, for John was at Winchester between 5 and 8 June and probably met the earl.[2] It is perhaps significant for my own hypothesis that this meeting took place just before John decided to meet baronial envoys at Runnymede on the 10th.[3] Secondly, the statement in the *Histoire des Ducs de Normandie* that the peace was made without William's knowledge may simply represent what the earl said to the Flemish mercenaries in his army. As he had already lost face with them during his campaign to Exeter, it may not have been the truth. Thirdly, even if we accept the sequence of events for the Exeter campaign provided by the *Histoire* and assume that William set out on 6 or 7 June and stayed four days at Exeter, it is still not impossible that he was back at Runnymede by the 19th. Finally, the fact that a letter close of the 19th was addressed to William implies little as to his whereabouts.[4] This letter ordered the surrender of the honour of Trowbridge, except the castle, to the earl of Hereford or ' his messenger the bearer of the present letter '.[5] It simply constituted a written authorization which would probably be sought by the earl of Hereford, or given to him, wherever William of Salisbury might be. If Professor Cheney's argument at this point were valid, we would have to assume not only that William of Salisbury was not present on the 19th but also that Hugh de Neville, another of the counsellors of the preamble, was not at Runnymede on either the 21st or the 23rd,[6] absent in fact on the very day Professor Cheney suggests for the final settlement of terms.

---

[1] This possibility is admitted by Professor Cheney, *loc. cit.* 330, n. 2.
[2] *Loc. cit.* p. 330, n. 1, *Histoire des Ducs de Normandie*, p. 148.
[3] *Supra*, p. 222.   [4] *Cf.* C. R. Cheney, *loc cit.* p. 329.
[5] *Rot. Litt. Claus.* i. 215.   [6] *Ibid.* pp. 215, 216.

A VERNACULAR-FRENCH TEXT OF MAGNA CARTA, 1215[1]

STUDENTS of Magna Carta have long been aware of a problem inherent in the events of 1215. How was the content of the Charter made known to the political community of England? An answer is easy enough in administrative terms: copies of the Charter were despatched to the sheriffs, who were to proclaim them throughout their bailiwicks.[2] This was the usual practice.[3] Apparently it was assumed that the men assembled in the shire courts would readily comprehend a long and complex document written in Latin. If so, the standard of literacy must have been high, certainly higher than most historians have been ready to allow.[4] If not, then the provision for the publication of the Charter and other documents published in a similar manner, must have been to a varying degree meaningless, even farcical, for of what value was an oath to observe an agreement which was not fully understood?

Historians have offered several solutions to this problem,[5] but neither the Charter nor the accompanying writs suggest that there was a quandary for contemporaries. One perceptive and reliable analyst, the 'Barnwell' chronicler, apparently saw nothing unrealistic in recounting that a copy of the Charter was carried round through towns and villages and that all swore to observe its terms.[6] It may be that in shire and hundred and other assemblies men relied on the clerks of the court to provide immediate *viva voce* translations of such proclamations. That the Charter was published in this way in 1300 seems to be implied by Rishanger who recounts that Edward I ordered that it should be read before an assembly in Westminster Hall, *prius litteraliter, deinde patria lingua*,[7] but there is no evidence

1. I am grateful to Professor M. Dominica Legge for commenting on a draft of the texts printed below and to Miss Claire Isoz and Dr. P. S. Noble who have kindly read them in proof. Any errors which remain are mine.
2. See the writ to sheriffs of 19 June (*Rot. Litt. Pat.*, p. 180b; J. C. Holt, *Magna Carta* (Cambridge, 1965), p. 345). The subject is discussed by R. L. Poole, 'The Publication of Great Charters by the English Kings', *ante*, xxviii (1913), 444–53, and by Faith Thompson, *The first century of Magna Carta*, (Minnesota, 1925), pp. 93–97.
3. H. G. Richardson and G. O. Sayles, 'The Early Statutes', *Law Quarterly Review*, i (1934), 544–8.
4. H. G. Richardson and G. O. Sayles have rightly questioned the assumption of widespread and deep-seated lay illiteracy (*The Governance of Medieval England*, Edinburgh, 1963, pp. 269–84).
5. R. L. Poole had 'difficulty in believing that so long and technical a document . . . could have been actually read aloud in Latin in the county courts' and suggested that only the writ of 19 June enjoining obedience to the Charter and the Twenty Five was proclaimed; though he 'would not venture to express an opinion as to the language in which the proclamation was made' (*op. cit.* pp. 449–51). Faith Thompson considered that the complete Charter was proclaimed as well as the writ but accepted that 'reading in Latin would have meant something to any clergy present, and must have been impressive, if not instructive, to the lay element' (*op. cit.* p. 95).
6. *Memoriale fratris Walteri de Coventria*, ed. W. Stubbs (Rolls Series, 1873), ii. 222.
7. W. Rishanger, *Chronica et Annales*, ed. H. T. Riley (Rolls Series, 1865), p. 405.

that something similar was done in 1215, probable though it may seem. Moreover this method was but a crude and inefficient means of communication, inadequate for reference and discussion. Hence the problem remains, and it is one of substance, for it involves the seriousness of baronial intentions in 1215 and the reality of the political community, brought together in local courts throughout the land, which was to enjoy the newly granted liberties.

Some fresh light is thrown on the difficulty from an apparently unlikely source, the cartulary of the lepers' hospital of S. Giles at Pont-Audemer in Normandy. This contains a vernacular-French text of Magna Carta, 1215. The text, which is printed below, has long been available to scholars. It was first published in the *Spicilegium* of Luc d'Achéry in 1675 and reprinted in the second edition of that work in 1723.[1] J.-A. Déville included it in the compilation of transcripts from the records of Upper Normandy which he submitted to the Record Commissioners in 1835. This MS. volume, which still survives in the Public Record Office,[2] was used intensively by J. H. Round for the *Calendar of Documents preserved in France*.

The text printed in the *Spicilegium* was noted by Blackstone, Richard Thomson and McKechnie[3] but has not attracted the attention of subsequent students of Magna Carta. The title which d'Achéry provided for the text does not properly identify it as a vernacular version of the Charter – 'Ordinationes Iohannis Regis Angliae queis statuit quid nobiles, quid plebeii observare debeant ad pacem et tranquillitatem Regni stabiliendam.'[4] Nor does his version indicate the source or date of the translation[5]; only close inspection by a linguistic scholar, inevitably hampered by d'Achéry's frequent inaccuracies, would be likely to reveal that it might be contemporary with the original Latin. But if the general failure to pursue d'Achéry's text remains surprising, Round's failure to call attention to Déville's is truly astonishing, for he retained a life-long interest in Magna Carta. To be sure, he restricted his selection of documents for the *Calendar*, with one exception, to the years up to 1206,[6] but, unless he strictly ignored anything of later date, he can scarcely have failed to note the familiar lengthy text occupying fifteen pages of Déville's volume. Moreover,

1. Luc d'Achéry, *Spicilegium*, (Paris, 1675), xii. 573–5; 2nd ed. (Paris, 1723), iii. 579–83.
2. P.R.O. Transcripts, 8/140A.
3. Blackstone (1759), p. xvii; R. Thomson (1829), p. 430; McKechnie (1914), p. 168.
4. *Spicilegium* (1675), xii. 573. The index contains a similar description. The abbreviated title in the table of contents is 'Ordinationes Johannis Regis Angliae'. The title is repeated in the second edition.
5. The first edition simply carried the note 'Eruit D. D'Herouval'. The transcript was evidently provided by Vyon d'Hérouval (d. 1689), who was a member of the learned circle centred on the congregation at Saint-Germain des Prés. On d'Hérouval, 'serviable et obligeant à l'infini, aimant avec passion l'érudition et l'histoire des temps passes . . . chercheur infatigable toujours à la piste des anciens documents', see E. de Broglie, *Mabillon et la société de l'abbaye de Saint-Germain des Prés* (Paris, 1888), i. 61–63.
6. *Cal. Docs. France*, p. vii.

Déville provided the clearest indication of its nature and importance in his title – 'Magna Carta Johannis (in gallico sermone translata seu forsan primum edita)'.[1] He repeated this title, with the addition – 'ad annum 1216' – which was taken from the margin of his text, in a list of contents at the beginning of his volume. This list was printed in Appendix C to the Report on *Foedera*.[2]

Both d'Achéry's version and Déville's were derived from the cartulary of S. Giles of Pont-Audemer. The translation must have been available at that house within a few years of 1215 for it is entered in an early thirteenth-century hand. There is no ground for thinking that it was made at Pont-Audemer or anywhere else in France. That it is written in French and that it survives in France have no bearing one upon the other. Latin was the language of record throughout western Christendom. French was the vernacular of the ruling class on both sides of the English Channel. Written translation was an arduous task not to be undertaken without a purpose. Much the most likely hypothesis is that Pont-Audemer acquired a vernacular text first produced in England. Indeed, all the evidence suggests that the translation was done to facilitate the publication of the Charter in Hampshire in the summer of 1215.

The main reason for this conclusion is that the Charter is followed immediately and in the same hand in the cartulary by a vernacular text of the writ of 27 June addressed to all the sheriffs of England and twelve elected knights of each shire, instructing them to seize the land and chattels of all those who refused to take the oath to obey the twenty five barons of the Charter. This version of the writ is addressed to the sheriff and elected knights of Hampshire, and the translation must have been made from the original letters issued to that county. The version entered on the Patent Roll cannot have been the source for it is addressed to Warwickshire. Moreover, this ends with the customary abbreviation used where appropriate in the enrolment – 'Teste ut supra, anno eodem',[3] – which indicates that the letters were issued on 27 June at Winchester. The translation in contrast ends with the complete formulae of a letter patent – 'Et en tesmoig d'iceste chose nos enveons cestes noz lettres overtes' – and is attested 27 June at Odiham. This establishes that Odiham not Winchester was the place of issue and that the 'Teste ut supra' of the enrolled version is a clerical error.[4]

---

1. P.R.O. Transcripts, 8/140A, no. 194.

2. *Report on Foedera*, Appendix C (n.d.), p. 147. The Report was not published. The *Appendices* were stored when the Record Commission was wound up in 1837; they were distributed in 1869. Appendix C was in proof in March 1836.

3. *Rot. Litt. Pat.* p. 145b; J. C. Holt, *op. cit.* p. 347.

4. The enrolled writ is the last of five items entered at the foot of m. 22 of the roll by a clerk whose hand intrudes at this point (P.R.O., Patent Roll, no. 14). The group begins with an entry dated 26 June at Odiham, continues with two dated 27 June at Winchester and ends with two 'teste ut supra'. It seems likely that the clerk failed to

These translations antedate by forty years anything similar known hitherto. Magna Carta 1215 now becomes the first document of political importance known to have been issued in the vernacular. The re-issues of the Charter of 1216, 1217 and 1225, the Provisions of Merton of 1236 and the *parva carta* of 1237 were all proclaimed in the shire courts, but no mention was made of the vernacular in the instructions for publication.[1] The next example comes from 1255, when in letters directed to the diocese of Coventry and Lichfield, Richard dean of Lincoln, one of the executors of the Innocent IV's confirmation of the *sententia lata* of 1253 against infringers of the Charter, ordered that the sentence was to be 'published clearly and lucidly both in the English and French tongue whenever and wherever it may seem expedient'.[2] No vernacular version of the *sententia* has so far come to light. Three years later the well-known royal letters of 18 and 20 October 1258, respectively confirming the Provisions of Oxford and promulgating ordinances for the reform of local government, were issued to every county both in French and English 'so that they might be read by the sheriffs and understood and observed intact by all men in the future'.[3] Vernacular texts of these have survived.[4] By this time French was becoming an official language in which much of the baronial programme of 1258

note that the last item in his batch of drafts was dated 27 June at Odiham. He was both careless and fussy about dates: he first dated his third entry at Windsor only to delete it and replace it correctly with Winchester; he also added 'Data eadem' to the penultimate entry of the previous scribe. The material which he recorded suggests that he intruded for a particular purpose. The first three of his entries record letters acknowledging the receipt of royal treasure from monastic repositories, the first dated 26 June at Odiham and the next two 27 June at Winchester. The fourth entry, ordering the issue of money from the treasure at Bristol is 'Teste ut supra. Data eadem'. If his chief interest was to record financial transactions, especially the receipt of treasure, he could well have grouped these items together, thus adding to the likelihood of error in his use of the 'ut supra' abbreviation in his fifth and final entry, the letters to the sheriffs and elected knights. The possibility of error in the use of the 'Teste ut supra' formula has been noted by C. Johnson in *Calendar of Liberate Rolls 1226–1240*, p. ix and further discussed by F. Cazel, 'The last years of Stephen Langton', *ante*, lxxix (1964), 689–91. They have indicated that the enrolling clerk might slip into the erroneous use of 'Teste ut supra' through recording successive items on different chancery rolls. This was not the source of error in this case; the clerk's hand does not appear on any other but the Patent Roll.

    1. R. L. Poole, *op. cit.* pp. 450–2; Faith Thompson, *op. cit.* p. 94; H. G. Richardson and G. O. Sayles, *op. cit.* (1934), pp. 545–6.

    2. Annals of Burton; *Annales Monastici*, ed. H. R. Luard (Rolls Series, 1864–9), i. 322.

    3. This is the comment of the Burton annalist, not part of an official text (*ibid.* i. 453).

    4. R. L. Poole, *op. cit.* p. 450; R. F. Treharne, *The Baronial Plan of Reform 1258–1263* (Manchester, 1932), pp. 119–20. The French text of the letters of 18 October is in *Foedera*, i, pt. i, 377–8; the English in W. Stubbs, *Select Charters* (9th edn., 1921), pp. 387–8. The French text of the letters of 20 October is in *Royal Letters illustrative of the reign of Henry III* ed. W. W. Shirley (Rolls Series, 1866), ii. 130–2 and the Annals of Burton (*Annales Monastici*, i. 453–5). I have found no English text of the latter and no Latin text of either.

and 1259 was recorded both as memoranda and final drafts,[1] but the use of the vernacular in 1215 can scarcely be explained in this way. The association of the Charter and the writ indicates that the translations were made for publication. In 1215 as in October 1258 the vernacular was a means of ensuring more effective communication with the men of the shires. Hence 1215, not 1255 or 1258, marks the first known attempt to reach out to a wider political community. The later dates mark, not the first use of the vernacular, but the first use of English as well as French.

This view of the translations is strongly supported by the texts. The writ is rendered exactly and in full. The Charter also is remarkably accurate and complete. *Mere* appears for *terre* in cap. 13. The opening phrase of cap. 14 is attached to the end of cap. 13, thus producing nonsense. A negative is lost in cap. 61 either through simple omission or through misreading *noluerint* as *voluerint* in the original Latin. Apart from a few literal slips, that is the sum total of error. The omissions are slight: the king is simply entitled *roi d'Engleterre* without any subsidiary honour, and Jocelin bishop of Bath appears without his second title of Glastonbury. Otherwise the Charter appears with all its trappings in a surprisingly accurate vernacular version of the finished text. It is written in French of good standard with some, but not many, Anglo-Norman forms.

In some ways this is unfortunate. Selection, compression or error might well have been more revealing than the almost mechanical accuracy which the translator achieved. Two points of detail are noteworthy. First in cap. 61 he developed the phrase *cum communa totius terrae* into *a la commune de tote Engleterre*. Secondly the linguistic constraints imposed by his task allowed him no ambivalence when faced with the famous *vel* of cap. 39, and he translated it disjunctively as *o* (*i.e. ou*). He thus adds a final clinching proof that it means 'or', not 'and'.[2]

The translations throw only a little additional light on the events of 1215. The well-known memorandum on the Patent Roll recording the issue of copies of the Charter and the accompanying writ of 19 June providing for the oath to the Twenty Five and the election of twelve knights in each county indicates that copies of the writ and the Charter were issued over a period, some as late as 22 July.[3] The

1. R. F. Treharne, *op. cit.* pp. 82–83; E. F. Jacob, *Studies in period of the Baronial reform and rebellion, 1258–1267* (Oxford, 1925), pp. 71–101; H. G. Richardson and G. O. Sayles, 'The Provisions of Oxford: a forgotten document and some comments', *Bulletin of the John Rylands Library*, xvii (1933), 291–321; F. M. Powicke, *King Henry III and the Lord Edward*, (Oxford, 1947), i. 400.

2. For a Latin text of Magna Carta, 1225, stemming from the confirmation of 1253, which reads *aut* not *vel* see J. C. Holt 'The St. Albans chroniclers and Magna Carta', *Transactions of the Royal Historical Society*, 5th ser., xiv. 81. There is also a French text of Magna Carta, 1225, in a fourteenth-century Anglo-Norman collection of statutes, National Library of Wales, MS. Peniarth 329a, pp. 5–13. This also reads *ou* for the *vel* of the Latin text. For the St. Albans version see below, p. 280.

3. *Rot. Litt. Pat.* p. 180b; J. C. Holt, *op. cit.* p. 345.

association of the Charter with the writ of 27 June in the present texts may indicate that the two were issued together to Hampshire. Elias of Dereham, the archbishop's steward, received the writ of 19 June for Hampshire along with four charters and eleven similar writs for other shires sometime after 24 June. Whether one of these charters or any of the six charters which Elias later received at Oxford on 22 July were intended for Hampshire is unspecified. Elias could well have been responsible for the translation, but there is nothing to connect him with the distribution of the writ of 27 June, of which nothing is known, and the hypothesis would seem stronger were the accompanying writ the earlier one of 19 June. Nevertheless he is the only person known to have had a hand in the distribution to Hampshire; he was firmly committed to the baronial cause, and the memorandum on the Patent Roll makes it clear that he was a key figure in the distribution of the Charter. This is the second hint, however vague, that he was not just a postman.[1]

Whatever the strength of Elias's claim, and it is admittedly fragile, there is no other obvious possibility. In 1258 Robert of Fulham, a clerk of the Exchequer, received 50s. for translating and drafting the French and English versions of the letters of 18 and 20 October.[2] It is improbable that the work was done centrally in 1215. Nor is the office of the sheriff of Hampshire a very likely source for he was William Briwerre, one of the staunchest supporters of King John who later acquired notoriety through resisting a confirmation of the Charter in 1224 on the ground that the original had been extorted by force.[3] He can have been no more enthusiastic than his master in ensuring effective promulgation of the settlement of Runnymede. Nor can he have been under great pressure, for Hampshire was not one of the centres of rebellion; indeed the king was progressing through the county at the end of June 1215 at the very time at which the writs of 27 June were authorized.

The texts themselves give little guidance on how this version of the Charter got from Hampshire to Pont-Audemer. There are hints in the personal and place-names of both English and French influence in the translation. William appears as *Willaume*, not *Guillaume*, in the preamble and cap. 59; Wales always as *Wales*, not *Galles*[4]; and Stephen as *Estievene* or *Stefne*, not *Etienne*.[5] There are a number of infelicities which may derive from ignorance of England and English organization: *wapulzac* and *treingues* in cap. 25, *Medoine* for the Medway in cap. 33 and *Roueninkmede* for Runnymede in the dating clause.[6] On the other hand the variant in the preamble

1. J. C. Holt, 'The St. Albans chroniclers and Magna Carta', pp. 86–87. See below, pp. 285-6.
2. R. F. Treharne, *op. cit.* p. 120 n.
3. Matthew Paris, *Chronica Majora*, ed. H. R. Luard (Rolls Series, 1872–84), iii. 76.
4. Caps. 56, 57.   5. Preamble, caps. 55, 62.
6. There is no confusion in the MS. between 'n' and 'u' in either *wapulzac* or *Roueninkmede*.

of William, bishop of Chester, for William, bishop of Coventry, can only have been the work of someone familiar with English episcopal titles.[1] All this is consistent with the hypothesis that the document was translated first in England and was subsequently copied at least once before its incorporation in the cartulary of S. Giles. This is also confirmed by the appearance of the text, which is neatly drafted with initial letters omitted for later rubrication. It is the earliest known version of Magna Carta to be arranged in paragraphs. It is clearly a formal copy rather than a working text.

However, it is by no means certain that this work was done at Pont-Audemer. The text of the Charter is an insertion in the cartulary, and the balance of probability is that it reached the house sometime between 1219 and 1226, almost certainly no later than 1234. This cartulary is composite. It is a compact MS., measuring 7 × 10 inches, of 106 folios, along with title folios and two unnumbered folios at the end; the numbering is modern. The first part of the volume, comprising fos. 6–53, was largely written by a single scribe who rounded off his work on fos. 50 and 51 by recording grants made by the priors and brethren of S. Giles. The latest dated entry for which he was responsible is of June 1219. Shortly after completion the book was rubricated by a single hand up to fo. 50[v]. The compiler of this part, who may be called the first scribe, had an eye for documents of hitsorical importance. He faithfully transcribed the letters of the Norman barons assembled at the council of Lillebonne, 1205[2], the treaty of Lambeth, 1217,[3] and the agreement between King John and Stephen Langton of May 1213.[4] He did not transcribe Magna Carta. It is unlikely therefore that it was available at Pont-Audemer by 1219.

The first scribe's work was soon extended. Other scribes filled the remaining folios of the last quire he had used with additional entries belonging to 1219–21.[5] This work was then continued on fo. 91 with charters arranged roughly chronologically beginning in 1221 and ending on fo. 105[v] with items belonging to 1250 and 1251. Folio 91 is the third of a new quire. Originally this was a direct continuation, for fos. 50[v]–53[v] and 91 are rubricated in the same hand. This does not appear on any intervening folio, even though there would have been work there for it to do. The latest

---

1. In John's time both Geoffrey de Muschamp and William of Cornhill were entitled bishops of Coventry when attesting royal charters. The alternative title of Chester was still in frequent official use in less formal circumstances. See *Rot. Chartarum, Rot. Litt. Pat.*, indices, *sub. nom.*, and *Handbook of British Chronology*, ed. Sir Maurice Powicke and E. B. Fryde (Royal Historical Society, 1961), p. 232 n. The titles were easily interchanged. King John's charter to the nuns of Farewell of 3 April 1200 refers to the land of the bishop of Chester, but was attested by Geoffrey de Muschamp as bishop of Coventry (*Rot. Chartarum*, p. 43).

2. Fos. 43[v]–44[v].   3. Fos. 46–47.   4. Fos. 47–48.

5. There is one entry in this section of a grant by Thomas, prior of S. Giles, dated February 1217, which is probably a stray.

dated document rubricated in this hand is of June 1221.[1] It is improbable that the intervening folios formed part of the book at that date.

These intervening folios contain three insertions: an incomplete copy of the *Compendium in Job* of Peter of Blois,[2] a copy of the decrees of the Fourth Lateran Council,[3] and the vernacular version of Magna Carta and the writ of 27 June. These insertions are the work of three distinct hands. The copy of the *Compendium* is considerably earlier than the rest of the MS. and there is no indication of when it was included. The decrees of the Fourth Lateran very probably formed part of the volume by 1234. They occupy a quire and the first folio of a half quire. The miscellaneous material added on the remaining folios includes a privilege of Pope Gregory IX for Pont-Audemer of 1228, followed by a chronological table written in 1234.[4] Hence there can be little doubt that this was already lodged at the house by that date. The version of Magna Carta and the writ occupy fos. 81–87^v, comprising seven folios of a single quire. It was certainly written in Normandy for it is followed in the same hand by a memorandum on the assessment and collection of *fouage* in the duchy.[5] Moreover, fo. 88^v, the last of the quire, contains a list of rents and services due to the Hospital which is continued on fo. 89, the first of the next quire in which, on fo. 91, the regular entry of the documents of 1221 and later years begins. This material which overlaps the two quires is the work of a single early thirteenth-century hand. Hence fos. 81–88, which contain the copy of the Charter, must have formed part of the cartulary at a very early date in its history. There is little real doubt that both the Charter and the Lateran decrees, and perhaps also the *Compendium*, were part of the MS. when the chronological table was written in 1234. Indeed it is probable that they were bound in with the first quire added for the material of 1221 and later. The latest dated entry on this is 1226.

However, none of these insertions seems to have been written at Pont-Audemer. The hands responsible appear nowhere else in the cartulary. The version of the Charter approximates sufficiently closely to the format of the cartulary to suggest that it may have been written for Pont-Audemer by a scribe who knew what was required.[6] But there is nothing to prove this, nor is there any obvious local slant in anything this scribe contributed. His memo-

---

1. Fos. 53^v.
2. Fos. 54–68. The text breaks off at the foot of fo. 68^v at 'Nichil moleste potest sustineri in hac morte vitali, quod ...' (*Petri Blesensis opera omnia*, ed. J. A. Giles, Oxford, 1846–7, iii. 61).
3. Fos. 69–77^v.   4. Fo. 78.   5. Fos. 87^v–88.
6. The margins and general pattern of ruling of the text of the Charter are generally similar to the first part of the cartulary, but there are 26 lines to the page instead of 24. The *Compendium* and the Fourth Lateran decrees are quite distinct since they are in double-column format; the main body of the cartulary and the text of the Charter are in single-column.

randum on *fouage* lists exemptions as far afield as Breteuil, Almenes-ches and Alençon.

Nevertheless Pont-Audemer was a natural resting place for such documents. Lying at the head of the tidal reach of the Risle, it provided the best route from England into central Normandy, indeed the only regular port of entry of any importance between the Seine and the harbours of the Cotentin. Originally one of the chief members of the Beaumont fee, it was seized by Richard I and soon became the centre of a bailiwick and a seat for assizes. There was a prison and a castle, hastily munitioned in the crisis of 1203. The town housed a Jewish community from which King John borrowed money. King Philip granted a commune in June 1204.[1] The priory of S. Giles, which lay outside the town, was founded by Waleran, count of Meulan, in the reign of Henry I. In the last years of Angevin rule it still enjoyed the patronage both of the royal house and of Robert, the last Beaumont count of Meulan. Such a community, enjoying links with the highest ranks of the Norman aristocracy, sited near a centre of ducal government and lying on a frequented route across the Channel was admirably placed to attract the documents which came to be lodged in the cartulary. The feared disease which it was founded to tend was not apparently an overriding deterrent. A deed of 1217-19 recorded in the cartulary, a confirmation to the brethren by Richard, bishop of Salisbury, of the tithes of Sturminster, refers to their generous hospitality to wayfarers.[2]

The links with England were not completely broken in 1204. The count of Meulan, dispossessed of all his Norman lands, survived as a pensioner of King John until 1210.[3] The pension was continued for his widow, a daughter of Reginald, earl of Cornwall, who survived in possession of two Cornish manors until 1221.[4] Their daughter was the wife of William, earl of Devon, who died in 1217.[5] Men of the count of Meulan were arrested at Shoreham in December 1205 and at Portsmouth in April 1206 and released on the king's instructions; these must in all probability have come from Pont-Audemer.[6] Margaret, sister and co-heiress of Robert, earl of Leices-ter, the last male descendant of the English branch of the Beaumont family, married Saer de Quency, earl of Winchester in 1207, and in in 1215 one of the leaders of the baronial movement. According to Roger Wendover, Saer accompanied Robert fitz Walter on an

---

1. F. M. Powicke, *The Loss of Normandy*, Manchester (2nd edn., 1961), pp. 71, 208 n, 261, 272; *Rot. Norm.*, pp. 72, 97, 113, 116; *Rot. Litt. Pat.* p. 25; *Recueil des actes de Philippe Auguste*, ed. H.-Fr. Delaborde and C. Petit-Dutaillis (Chartes et Diplômes relatifs à l'histoire de France, Paris, 1943), ii. no. 809.

2. 'Attendentes domus sancti Egidii de Ponteaudom' tenues et modicas esse facultates et nichilominus effusam in omnes transeuntes etiam supra vires eiusdem domus carita-tem' (fos. 34, 48 d).

3. *Rot. de Liberate ac de Misis et Prestitis*, pp. 192, 210, 226.

4. *Rot. Litt. Claus.* i. 345 b, 429 b, 449 b.

5. *Complete Peerage*, iv. 315-6.   6. *Rot. Litt. Claus.* i. 59 b, 69.

embassy to King Philip and Prince Louis of France in the winter of 1215–6.[1] In 1218 he must have crossed France again on his way to Damietta and his death at Acre.[2] Meanwhile Sturminster, where the church still belonged to the brethren of Pont-Audemer, passed to William Marshal in 1204 and descended to his heirs.[3] William retained his Norman barony of Longueville until his death in 1219. There were other possible points of contact. Elias of Dereham was in exile in France in the service of Prince Louis in 1217 and 1218.[4] By 1222 he was a canon of Salisbury[5] whose bishops had repeatedly confirmed the rights of the brethren of Pont-Audemer in Sturminster.[6] Stephen Langton himself spent part of his exile in northern France in 1216–18, travelled to Rome in 1220 and visited France yet again in 1222.[7] Peter des Roches, bishop of Winchester, must have passed through France in the spring of 1221 on his way to Rome or Compostella, again in 1227 on his way to the Crusade and yet again in 1233 en route to Rome once more.[8] He was scarcely a devotee of Magna Carta but, as bishop of Winchester and, from 1217 to 1224, sheriff of Hampshire and custodian of Winchester castle, he had direct access to the vernacular charter if it still lay either in the cathedral or shrieval archives. Any one of these great and influential men could have been the agent, direct or indirect, through whom the brethren of Pont-Audemer acquired the Charter. The matter is guess-work and the possibilities are embarrassingly rich.

The appearance of Magna Carta in the cartulary of Pont-Audemer is not then an accident. That it happens to be in the vernacular is a happy chance which throws new light on the condition of England

1. *Chron. Maj.* ii. 648.

2. *Complete Peerage*, xii. 750–1. At first sight the facts that Saer was earl of Winchester, where the translation must have been read in 1215, and that he married a Beaumont heiress whose family had founded S. Giles, seem more than coincidental. However, the cartulary does not contain any evidence that the English branch of the family had any interest in the house. Moreover, Saer seems to have played no part in the affairs of Hampshire, although as earl of Winchester he received the third penny. His chief territorial interests lay in the Midlands, and his activities during the civil war were divided between there and London.

3. *Rot. Litt. Pat.* p. 45 b; *Rot. Litt. Claus.*, i. 7 b; J. Hutchins, *History of Dorset* (London, 1861–70), iii. 336–7.

4. F. M. Powicke, *Stephen Langton* (Oxford, 1928), p. 136.

5. A. Hamilton Thompson, 'Master Elias of Dereham and the King's Works', *Archaeological Journal*, xcviii (1941), 7.

6. In addition to the charter of Bishop Richard mentioned above, 247, the cartulary also contains confirmations of Jocelin, bishop 1142–84, and Herbert, bishop 1194–1217. It is noteworthy that Elias is the only person who could have had access to all the relevant documents copied into the cartulary of Pont-Audemer: as Langton's steward, to the settlement between the archbishop and King John; as one of the chief agents of distribution, to Magna Carta; and as one excluded from, and therefore personally involved in its terms, to the Treaty of Lambeth. However, it is unlikely that the Charter was obtained at the same time as the other two. See above pp. 245-6.

7. *Acta Stephani Langton*, ed. Kathleen Major (The Canterbury and York Society, l, 1950), pp. 165–7.

8. For the confusion over Peter's journey in 1221 see *Walt. Cov.* ii. 260 and *Annales Monastici*, ii. 84; iii. 68. For the later journeys see *Annales Monastici*, ii. 85–7.

in 1215. But that it survives there at all is of equal interest. The scribes of a leper-house, with many more pressing and immediate concerns than great events as they are now seen by historians, nevertheless had the interest and made the time to record or acquire copies of some of the crucial documents of the years 1213–17. With the exception of the Fourth Lateran decrees those documents derived from England. More than a decade after the collapse of 1204 the Anglo-Norman world was still of interest, perhaps still a reality, to these men.

TEXTS

(Rouen, Bibliothèque Municipale, MS. Y 200, fos. 81–87ᵛ)

The texts printed below preserve the paragraphs of the MS. The conventional numbering of the chapters of Magna Carta is inserted. The MS. omits the initials of paragraphs throughout; these have been included in brackets.

The texts are printed by the kind permission of the Librarian, Bibliothèque Municipale, Rouen.

(i) MAGNA CARTA 1215

[J]ohan par la grace de Deu roi d'Engleterre, as arceveskes, as eveskes, as abbez, as contes, as barons, as justises, as forestiers, as viscontes, as prevoz, as ministres, e a toz ses bailliz e ses feels, saluz. Sachiez que nos,[1] par la grace de Deu e pur le sauvement de nostre alme, e de toz nos ancestres, e de noz eirs, e de l'enor de Deu, e le sauvement de seinte iglise, e l'amendement de nostre regne, par le consel de noz enorez peres l'arceveske Estievene de Cantorbire primat de tote Engleterre e cardenal de Rome, e l'arceveske Henri de Diveline, e l'eveske Will. de Londres, l'eveske Pieres de Wincestre, l'eveske Jocelin de Ba, l'eveske Hue de Nichole, l'eveske Gautier de Wirecestre, l'eveske Will. de Cestre, e l'eveske Beneit de Rovecestre, e maistre Pandol sodiacre nostre seignor l'apostoire, e nostre ami frere Aimer maistre de la chevalerie del Temple de Engleterre, e de noz barons Will. le Marescal conte de Penbroc, Will. conte de Salesbires, Will. conte de Warenne, Will. conte Arondel, Alain de Galwehe conestable d'Escoce, Warin le fiz Gerod, Peres le fiz Herebert, Hubert de Borc seneschau de Peitou, Huge de Nuevile, Matheu le fiz Herebert, Thomas Basset, Alain Basset, Philippe d'Aubeigni, Robert de Ropelee, Johan Marescal, e Johan le fiz Hue, e de nos autres feels:

1. MS. 'vos'.

(1) [P]remierement que nos avons otrié a Deu e le confermons par ceste nostre presente chartre, por nos e por noz eirs a toz jorz, que les yglises d'Engleterre seront franches, e aient lor dreitures franches e enterines e plenieres; e volon que eisi seit gardé; la que chose apert par ço que nos otriames par nostre pure volenté e de gré les franchises des ellections que l'en tienent por plus grant e por plus necessaire as yglises de Engleterre, devant que de la descorde fust comencié entre nos e noz barons, e la confermames par nostre chartre, e porchaçames que ele fu confermee par nostre seignor l'apostoire Innocent le tierz; laquele nos garderons e volons que nostre eir la gardent toz jorz en bone fei.

[N]os avon oncore otrié a toz les frans homes de nostre regne, pur nos e pur noz eirs a toz jorz, totes les franchises qui desoz sunt escrites, qu'il les aient e les tiegnent il e lor eir de nos e de noz eirs.

(2) [S]e acuns de nos contes, vo de noz barons, vo des altres qui tienent de nos en chief par servise de chevalier, mora, e quant il sera morz, e ses eirs sera de plein aage e devra relief, ait son heritage par l'ancien relief, ço est a saveir li eirs[1] ou li eir del conte, de baronie contal entiere por C. livres; li eirs ou li eir del baron, de la baronie por C. livres; li eirs ou li eir de chevalier, de fie de chevalier entier por C. sol. au plus, e qui meins devra meins doinst solon l'anciene costume del fie.

(3) [S]e li eirs d'aucun d'itels sera dedenz aage, e sera en garde, quant il sera parvenu a aage, ait son heritage sanz relief e sanz fin.

(4) [L]es gardeors de la terre de tel heir qui sera dedenz aage, ne pregne de la terre de l'eir fors reignables eissues e reignables costumes e reignables servises, e ce senz destruiement e senz vast des homes e des choses.

[E]t se nos avons livrié la garde de la terre d'aucuni[2] itel a visconte o a acune altre qui nos dei respondre des eissues de la terre, e cil de la garde fera destruiment o gast, nos prendrons de celui amende, e la terre sera livree a deus leals prodes homes de cel fei qui respoignent des eissues a nos, o celui que nos comanderons.

[E]t se nos avons doné o vendu a acunui la garde de la terre de aucun itel, e cil en fra destruiement o wast, perde cele garde, e seit livré a deus leials sages prodes homes e d'icele, qui[2] nos respoignent, si come nos avons devant dit.

(5) [E]t li gardeor tant dis com il avra la garde de cele terre, sostinge[3] les meisons, les viviers, les pars, les estans, les molins, e les altres choses qui apartient a cele terre, de eissues e[4] de cele meimes terre; e rendra a l'heir quant sera parvenuz en plein aage sa terre tote estoree de charues, de granges, solon ço que li tens de la gaignerie requera e les eissues de la terre poront musurablement soffrir reisnablement.

(6) [L]i heir seient marié sanz desparagement eissi ne purquant que ainz que li mariages seit fait, seit mostré al prochains del lignage de cel heir.

(7) [L]a veve enpres la mort de son mari maintenant[5] e sanz grevance ait son mariage e son heritage, ne riens ne doinst por son mariage ne por son doaire, ne por son heritage que ele e ses mariz tindrent al jor de la mort del mari, e seit en la maison de son mari puis qu'il sera morz xl. jorz, dedenz les quels jorz li seit ses doaires livrez.

---

1. MS. 'eir'.   2. MS. corrects 'que'.   3. MS. 'sostinges'.
4. 'e' has been inserted incorrectly.   5. MS. 'naintenant'.

(8) [N]ule veve ne seit destreite de sei marier tant dis come ele voldra vivre sanz mari, essi ne purquant que ele face seurté que ele ne se marira sanz nostre otrei, se ele tient de nos, o senz l'otrei de son seignor de qui ele tient, se ele tient d'autrui.

(9) [N]e nos ne nostre bailli ne seiseron terre ne rente del dettor por aucune dette, tandis com sis chatels soffisent a paier la dette, ne si plege ne seront destroit, tant dis come le chevetaigne dettor soffira a la dette paier. Et se le chevetaigne detor n'a de quei paier sa dette, respoigne li plege de la dette; e s'il volent, aient les terres e les rentes del dettor jusqu'il aient restorement de la dette qu'il ont devant paiee por lui, se le chevetaigne detor ne monstre qu'il en est quite vers cels pleges.

(10) [S]e acuns a emprunté as Jeus plus o meins, e muert devant qu'il lor ait paié lor avoir, ne croise mie la dette tant dis com li heirs sera dedenz aage; e se cele dette vient en noz mains, nos n'en prendron que le chatel que nos troveron en la chartre.

(11) [E] se aucun muret, e deit dette as Jeus, sa feme ait son doaire, e ne paiet nient de cele dette, e se li enfant qui remaindront del mort sont dedenz aage, pourveu lor seit lor estoveir raisnablement solonc le tenement qui fu del mort, e del remanant seit paiee la dette, sauf le servise des seignors; e en tel maniere seit feit de dettes que l'on deit a altres que a Jues.

(12) [L']en ne mettra nul escuage ne aie en nostre regne, fors par commun conseil de nostre regne, fors a nostre reimbre, e a nostre ainzné fiz faire chevalier, e a nostre ainznee fille marier une feiz; e a cestes choses ne face l'en aie se raisnable non.

[E]n cele maniere seit feit d'aies de la cité de Londres, [13]e estre ço la cité de Londres ait totes ses anciennes costumes, e ses franchises e par mer[1] e par aigue.

[N]os volons estre ço e otrions que totes les altres citez e li borc, e les viles, e li port aient en totes lor franchises, e lor franches costumes, (14) e aient[2] le commun conseil del regne, de l'aie a asseeir altrement que as treis cas, qui sont devant dit.

[D]e l'escuage aseer, ferons somondre les arceveskes, les eveskes, les abbez, les contes, les greignors barons, chascun par sei par nos lettres; e estre ço ferons somondre en commun par noz viscontes e par noz bailliz toz ceus qui de nos tienent en chief, a certain jor, ço est al terme de xl jorz al mains e a certain lieu; e nomerons la cause en totes lettres de ceste somonse. Et quant la somonse[3] sera issi feite voist li afaires avant au jor assigné solon le conseil d'icels qui seront present, ja seit ço que ne seient pas venu tuit cil qui furent somons.

(15) [N]os n'otrions a nul des ore en avant qu'il pregne aie de ses frans homes fors a son cors raimbre, e a son ainzné fiz faire chevalier, e a sa fille ainznee marier une feiz, e a ço ne seit fait aie se raisnable non.

(16) [N]uls ne seit destreinz a faire grenor servise de fieu de chevalier o d'altre franc tenement que tant come il tient e deit.

(17) [L]i commun plait ne suient mie nostre cort, mais saient tenu en alcun certain lieu.

1. 'Mer' is presumably in error for 'terre'.
2. At this point the opening phrases of cap. 14 has been attached to the close of cap. 13, thus producing nonsense.
3. MS. 'somose'.

(18) [L]es reconussances de novele dessaisine, de mort d'ancestre[1] e de darrain presentement ne seient prises fors en lor contez e ceste maniere: nos o nostre chevetains justisieres se nos sumes fors del regne, enveierons deus justises par chascun conté par iiii feiz en l'an, qui o quatre des chevaliers de chascun conté esleuz par le conté pregnent el conté, e el jor del conté e en certain lieu les devant dites assises, (19) e se les devant dites assises ne puent estre prises el jor del conté, tant chevaliers e franchement tenanz remaignent de cels qui furent present al conté en icel jor, par quei puisent li jugement estre feit sofisaument, solon ço qui li afaire sera plus grant o plus petit.

(20) [F]rans hom ne set amerciez por petit forfait fors solon la maniere del forfait, e por le grant forfait seit amerciez solonc la grandesce del forfait sauf son contenement; e li marcheant ensement sauve sa marchandise; li vilains[2] ensement seit amerciez salz son gaagnage, s'il chiet en nostre merci; e nule des devant dites merciz ne sera mise fors par le serement de prodomes e des leaus des visnez.

(21) [L]i conte e li baron ne seient amerciez fors par lor pers, e solonc la maniere del forfait.

(22) [N]us clers ne seit amerciez de son lai tenement fors solonc la maniere des altres qui devant sunt dit, e nun pas solonc la quantité de sa rente de s'iglise.

(23) [N]e vile ne home ne seit destreiz a faire ponz a rivieres, fors cil qui ancienement e par dreit les devent faire.

(24) [N]uls visquens, ne conestables, ne nostre coroneor, ne nostre altre bailli ne tiegnent les plaiz de nostre corone.

(25) [C]hascuns contez, hundrez, wapulzac, e treingues soient as ancienes fermes senz nul croisement, fors noz demeines maniers.

(26) [S]e aucuns qui tient lai fie de nos muert, e nostre visquens o altres nostre bailliz monstre nos lettres overtes de nostre semonse de la dette que li mort nos deveit, leissie a nostre visconte o a nostre bailli atachier e enbrever les chatels del mort qui seront trové el lai fie, a la vaillance d'icele dette que li morz nos deveit par veue de leaus homes, eissi ne purquant que riens ne seit osté jusque nos seit paiee la dette qui sera coneue; e li remanant seit laissié as executors a faire le testament del mort. E s'il ne nos deivent rien, tot li chatel seient otrié al mort, sauves les reignables parties de sa feme e de ses enfanz.

(27) [S]e aucuns frans huem muert senz testament, li chatel seient departi par les mains des prochains parenz e de ses amis par la veue de seinte iglise, sauves les dettes a chascun que le mort lor devoit.

(28) [N]us de noz conestables ne de noz altres bailliz ne pregne les blez ne les altres chatels d'aucun, se maintenant n'en paie les deniers, o il n'en puet aver respit par volenté del vendeor.

(29) [N]us conestables ne destreigne nul chevalier a doner deniers por la garde del chastel, s'il la voit faire en sa propre persone u par altre prodome, s'il ne la puet faire por auscune reignable achaisun; e se nos le menons o enveions en ost, il sera quites d'icele garde tant dis cum il sera par nos en l'ost.

(30) [N]us viscontes ne nostre bailliz ne altre ne pregne les chevals ne

---

1. The copyist has left the rest of this line blank.   2. MS. 'vilaint'.

les charettes d'aucun franc home por faire cariage, fors par la volenté de cel franc home.

(31) [N]e nos ne nostre baillie ne prendrons altrui bois a nos chastels o a nos altres ovres faire, fors par volenté de celui cui sera li bois.

(32) [N]os ne tendrons les terres de cels qui seront convencu de felonie, fors un an e un jor, e adons les rendrons as seignors des fiez.

(33) [T]ot li kidel seient d'ici en avant osté del tot en tot de Tamise e de Medoine, e par tote Engleterre, fors par la costiere de la mer.

(34) [L]i bries qui est apelez 'precipet' des ci en avant ne seit faiz a nul d'aucun tenement, dont frans hoem peust perdre sa cort.

(35) [U]ne mesure de vin seit par tot nostre regne, e une mesure de cerveise, e une mesure de ble, ço est li quartiers de Londres, e une leise de dras teinz e de rosez e de habergiez, ço est deus aunes dedenz listes; e des peis seit ensemel come des musures.

(36) [R]iens ne seit doné ne pris des ci en avant por le brief del enqueste de vie o de membres, de aucun, mais seit otree en pardon e ne seit escondit.

(37) [S]e aucuns tient de nos par feuferme o par sokage, e tient terre d'altrui par servise de chevalier, nos n'avrons mie la garde de l'heir, ne de sa terre qui est d'altrui fie par achaison de cele feuferme, o del sokage, o del burgage; ne n'avrons la garde de cele feuferme, o del socage, o del borgage, se cele feuferme ne deit servise de chevalier.

[N]os n'avrons la garde de l'heir ne de la terre d'alcun, que il tient d'altrui par servise de chevalier, par achaison d'aucune petite serjanterie, qu'il tient de nos par servise de rendre saettes, o cotelz, o tels choses.

(38) [N]uls bailliz ne mette des ci en avant alcun a lei par sa simple parole, fors par bons tesmoinz amenez a ice.

(39) [N]uls frans hom ne sera pris, ne emprisonez, ne dessaisiz, ne ullagiez, ne eissilliez, ne destruiz en aucune maniere, ne sor lui n'irons ne n'enveierons, fors par leal jugement de ses pers, o par la le· ⸏le la terre.

(40) [A] nulli ne vendrons, a nullui n'escondirons, ne ne p ⸍rloignerons droit ne justise.

(41) [T]uit li marchant aient sauf e seur eissir d'Engleterre, e venir en Engleterre e demorer, e aler par Engleterre par terre e par eve a vendre e a achater, sanz totes males totes par les ancienes dreites costumes, fors el tens de guerre, cil ki sunt de la terre qui nos guerroie; e se tel sunt trové en nostre terre el comencement de la guerre, soient atachié sanz domage de lor cors e de lor choses jusqu'il seit seu de nos o de nostre chevetein justisier coment li marcheant de la nostre terre seront traitié, qui donc seront trové en la terre qui contre nos guerroie; e se li nostre sunt ilueke sauf, seient li lor sauf en la nostre terre.

(42) [L]eise chascun des ci en avant eissir de nostre regne e repairier sauf e seur par terre e par eve sauve nostre fei, fors el tens de guerre par alcun petit tens por preu del regne; mais d'iço sunt jetté fors li emprisoné, e li utlagié solon la lei del regne, e la gent ki contre nos guerroie. Des marcheanz seit feit si come nos avon devant dit.

(43) [S]e aucuns tient d'aucune eschaette si come de l'honor de Walinge-ford, Notingeham, Boloigne, Lancastre, u d'autres echaetes qui sunt en nostre main, e sunt de baronie, e il muert, ses heirs ne doinst altre relief, ne face a nos altre servise qu'il feist al baron, se cele baronie fust en main del baron; e nos la tendrons en tele maniere que le baron la tint.

(44) Li home qui maignent fors de la forest ne viegnent de ci en avant devant noz justises de la forest par communes somonses, s'il ne sont en plait u plege de aucun ou d'aucuns qui seient atachié por la forest.

(45) [N]os ne frons viscontes, justises, ne bailliz, fors de tels qui sachent la lei de la terre e la voillent bien garder.

(46) [T]uit cil qui fonderent abbeies dont il ont chartres des reis d'Engleterre, o anciene tenue, aient en la garde quant eles seront voides, si com il avoir devent.

(47) [T]otes les forez qui sunt aforestees en nostre tens, seient maintenant desaforestees, e ensement seit feit des riveres qui en nostre tens sunt par nos mises en defens.

(48) [T]otes les males costumes des forez e des warennes, e des forestiers e des warenniers, des viscontes e de lor ministres, des rivieres e de lor gardes, seient maintenant enquises en chascun conté par xii chevaliers jurez de meimes le conté, qui devent estre esleu par prodeshomes de meismes le conté; e dedenz xl jorz apres ço qu'il avront feite l'enqueste, seient del tot en tot ostees par cels meismes, si que james ne saient rapelees; eissi ne purquant que nos le sachons avant, o nostre justise, se nos ne sumes en Engleterre.

(49) [N]os rendrons maintenant toz les hostages e totes les chartres, qui nos furent livrees des Engleis en seurté de pais o de feel servise.

(50) [N]ous osteron de tot en tot des baillies les parenz Girard d'Aties, si que des ci en avant n'avront nule baillie en Engleterre, e Engelart de Cigoigni, Peron, Guion, Andreu de Chanceas, Gion de Cigoigni, Gifrai de Martigni e ses freres, Phelippe Marc e ses freres, Gefrai son nevo, e tote lor siute; (51) e maintenant empres le reformement de la pais osterons de nostre regne toz les estranges chevaliers, aubelastiers, serjanz, soldeiers, qu'o chevals e o armes vindrent al nuisement del regne.

(52) [S]e alcuns est dessaisiz o esloigniez par nos senz leal[1] jugement de ses pers, de terres, de chastels, de franchises, o de sa dreiture, maintenant li rendrons; e se plaiz en comencera d'iço, a donc en seit fait par jugement des xxv barons, dont l'en parole desoz en la seurté de la pais.

[D]e totes iceles choses dont alcuns fu dessaisiz o elloigniez senz leal jugement de ses pers par le rei Henri nostre pere, o par le rei Richart nostre frere, que avons en nostre main, o altre tienent cui il nos covient garantir, avrons respit jusqu'al commun terme des croisiez, fors que celes choses dont plaiz fu comenciez o enqueste faite par nostre comandement devant que nos preissons la croiz; et se nos repairons de nostre pelerinage, o par aventure remanons del pelerinage, maintenaunt en frons pleine dreiture. (53) Cest meimes respit avrons e en ceste maniere de dreiture faire des forez desaforester, o que remaignent forez, que li reis Henri nostre peres, o li reis Richart nostre freres aforesterent, e des gardes des terres qui sunt d'altrui fie, que nos avons eues jusque ci par achaison de fie que alcuns teneit de nos par servise de chevalier, e des abbeies que furent fondees en altrui fie que el nostre, es quels li sires del fie di qu'il a droiture; e quant nos seron repairié de nostre pelerinage, o se nos remanons, nos en frons maintenant pleine dreiture a cels qui s'en plaindront.

(54) [N]uls ne seit pris ne enprisonez por apel de feme de la mort d'altrui que de sun marri.

1. MS. 'real'.

(55) [T]otes les fins e toz le amerciemenz qui sont feit vers nos a tort e contre la lei de la terre, soient tot pardoné, o l'en enface par jugement des xxv barons dont l'en parole desoz, o par le jugement de la greignor[1] partie de cels ensemble, o le devant dit arcevesque Stefne de Cantorbere s'il i puet estre e cels qu'il vodra apeler od sei. E s'il n'i pora estre, neient-meint ne voist li afaires avant senz lui, en tel maniere que se alcuns o alcun des devant diz xxv barons seront en tel querele, seient osté de cest jugement, e altre esleu e juré seient mis a ço faire en lieu de cels par le remanant des devant diz xxv barons.

(56) [S]e nos avons dessaisiz e esloigniez les Walais de terres o de franchises o d'altres choses senz leal jugement de lor pers en Engleterre o en Wales, maintenant lor seient rendues; e se plaiz en sera comenciez, se lor en seit fait en la Marche par jugement de lor peres, des tenemenz d'Engleterre solonc la lei d'Engleterre, des tenemenz de Wales solonc la lei de Wales, des tenemenz de la Marche solonc la lei de la Marche, e ço meismes facent li Walais a nos e as noz.

(57) [D]e totes celes choses dont alcuns des Walais fu dessaisiz o esloignié senz leal jugement de ses pers par le rei Henri nostre pere, o par le rei Richart nostre frere, que nos avons en nostre main, o altre tienent cui il nos covient garantir, avrons respit jusqu'al commun terme des croisiez, fors de celes choses dont plait fu comenciez o enqueste faite par nostre comandement devant que nous preissions la croiz; e quant nos serons repairiez o se par aventure remanons de nostre pelerinage, maintenant lor en frons pleine dreiture solonc les lez de Wales e les devant dites parties.

(58) [N]ous rendrons le fil Lewelin maintenant, e toz les hostages de Wales, e les chartres que l'en nos livra en seurté de pais.

(59) [N]os ferons a Alisandre le rei d'Ecoce de ses serors e de ses hostages rendre, e de ses franchises, e de sa dreiture solonc la forme que nos frons a nos altres barons d'Engleterre, se altrement ne deit estre par les chartres que nos avons de son pere Willaume, qui fu jadis reis d'Escoce; e ço sera fait par jugement de ses pers en nostre cort.

(60) [T]otes ces costumes devant dites e les franchises que nos avons otriees a tenir en nostre regne quant a nos apartient envers les noz, tuit cil de nostre regne, e clerc e lai, devent garder quant a eus apartient envers les lor.

(61) [E]t car nos avons otriees totes les choses devant dites por Deu, e por amendement de nostre regne, e por mielz apaisier[2] la descorde qui est comencié entre nos e nos barons, nos, voelliant que ces choses seent fermes[3] e estables a toz jorzs, faisons e otrions a nos barons la seurté desoz escrite; ço est que li baron eslisent xxv barons del regne tels qu'il vodront, qui dient de tot lor poer garder, e tenir, e faire garder, la pais e les franchises que nos avons otriees e confermees par ceste nostre presente chartre; eissi ço est a saver que se nos, o nostre justise, o notre bailli, o aucuns de noz ministres mesfaisons en alcune chose vers alcun, o tres-passons en alcun point de la pais o de la seurté, e nostre mesfaiz sera mostrez a quatre barons des devant dit xxv, cil quatre baron viegnent a nos, o a nostre justise, se nos sumes fors del regne, e nos mostrent nostre trespassement, e requierent que nos faceins amender cel trespassement

1. MS. 'greigor'.   2. MS. '[a^i]p[ı^c]aisi[e^i]r'.   3. MS. 'ferm[e^c]es'.

senz porloignement; e se nos n'amendrons le trespassement, o se nos sumes fors del regne, nostre justise ne l'amendera, devant xl jorz empres ço que il sera mostré a nos, o a nostre justice se nous sumes fors de la terre; adonc li devant dit quatre reportent cele cause as altres de cels xxv barons,e adonc cil xxv baron a la commune de tote Engleterre nos destreindront e greveront en totes le manieres que il poront, ço est par prendre chastels e terres e possessions, e en queles altres manieres qu'il poront, jusqu'il seit amendé solonc lor jugement, sauve nostre persone e de nostre reine, e de noz enfanz; e quant il sera amendé il atendront a nos eissi come devant. Et qui vodra de la terre jurt que a totes les devant dites choses parsivir, il obeira al comandement des devant diz xxv barons, e qu'il nos grevera ensemble o els a son poer; e nos donons comunement e franchement congié de jurer a chascun qui jurer vodra, e ja ne le defendrons a neis un; e toz cels de la terre qui de lor bon gré voldront[1] jurer as xxv barons de destreindre e de grever nos, nos les frons jurer o els par nostre comandement, si com devant est dit.

[E]t se alcuns des xxv barons morra, o partira de la terre, o serra destorbez en aucune maniere qu'il ne puist les choses qui sunt devant dites parsivir, cil qui seront remés des devant dit xxv barons eslisent un altre en lieu de celui solonc lor esgart, que jurera en tel manere com li altre ont fait.

[E]t en totes les choses que li xxv baron devent parsivir, se par aventure cil xxv seront present, e descorderont entre els d'aucune chose, o aucun de cels qui seront somons ne vodront o ne porront estre present, seit ferm e certain ço que la greignor partie de cels qui seront present porverra o recevra ensement com se tuit i aveient consenti.

[E]t li devant dit xxv baron jurent que totes les choses qui sunt devant dites, qu'il garderont feelement e feront garder de tot lor poer.

[E]t nos ne porchacerons d'alcun, par nos ne par altrui, rien par quei alcuns de ces otreiemenz o de cestes franchises seit rapelez o amenusiez, e se alcune tel chose sera porchacie, seit cassee e veine, e ja n'en userons par nos ne par altrui.

(62) [E]t totes males volentéz, desdeigz, rancors, qui sont nees entre nos e noz homes clers e lais, deske la descorde comença, avom plainement relaissiees e pardonees a toz, e estre ço toz les trespassemenz qui sunt fait par achaison d'iceste descorde des la Pasche en la sezain de nostre regne jusqu'al reformement de la pais, avom plainement relaissié a toz clers e a lais, e quant a nos aportient lor avom plainement pardoné e otrié; d'iço lor avom fait faire lettres de tesmoig overtes de seignor Stefne l'arceveske de Cantorbire, de seignor Henri l'archeveske de Diveline, e des devant diz evesques e de maistre Pandolf, sor ceste seurté e cez otreiemenz. (63) Por la que chose nos volons e comandons fermement que l'eglise d'Engleterre seit franche, e que li home en nostre regne aient e tiegnent totes les devant dites franchises, e les dreitures, e les otriemenz bien e en pais franchement e quitement, plainement e entierement, a els e lor heirs, en totes choses e en toz leus, a toz jorz si com devant est dit. Et si fu juré de nostre part, e de la part des barons que totes ces choses qui desus sunt escrites seront gardees a bone fei sanz ma engin. Tesmoig en sont cil qui sunt devant dit, e mult altre. Ceste chartre

---

1. MS. omits 'ne'. The translator perhaps misread 'noluerint' as 'voluerint'.

fu donee el pre qui est apelez Roueninkmede entre Windesores e Stanes, le quinzain jor de Juig l'an de nostre regne dis e septain.

(ii) LETTERS PATENT FROM THE KING TO THE SHERIFF OF HAMPSHIRE, 27 JUNE, 1215

[J]ohan par la grace de Deu reis d'Engleterre al visconte de Suthantesire, e as dosce esleuz en cel conté a enquerre e oster les malveises costumes des viscontes e de lor ministres, des forés e des forestiers, e des warennes e des warenniers, e des rivieres e de lor gardes, saluz. Nos vos mandons que senz delai saisisiez en nostre main les terres e les tenemenz e les chatels de toz celz del conté de Suthantesire qui ne vodront jurer as xxv barons solonc la forme qui est escrite en nostre chartre des franchises, o a cels qu'il avront a ço atornez; e s'il ne volent jurer, maintenant empris quince jorz compliz puis que lor terres e lor tenement e lor chatel seront seisi en nostre main, faites vendre toz lor chatels, e les deniers qui en seront pris gardez sauvement a metre en l'aie de la sainte terre de Jerusalem; e lor terres e lor tenemenz tenez en nostre main jusqu'il aient juré. E ço fu porveiu par le jugement l'Arceveske Stefne de Cantorbire e des barons de nostre regne. Et en tesmoig d'iceste chose nos enveons cestes noz lettres overtes. Tesmoig mei meisme a Odiham[1] le vint e septain jor de Juig, l'an de nostre regne dis e septain.

1. MS. 'Odi[h^i][a^c]am'.

11

THE SALISBURY MAGNA CARTA

The copy of Magna Carta 1215 (S) which is preserved in the Cathedral Library at Salisbury is the least known of the four surviving exemplars. In 1700 it was collated by James Tyrell with one of the versions (Cii) in the Cottonian library, but thereafter it was missing and was not rediscovered in the Salisbury muniments until 1814. Blackstone tried to trace it, without success, for his edition, *The Great Charter,* of 1759. The Record Commissioners also failed in 1806 and hence it was not collated in the text published in *Statutes of the Realm,* 1810, which gave prominence for the first time to the Lincoln version (L). Hence S played no part either in the first scholarly attempt to examine the originals or in the establishment of an officially authorised printed text. It missed the bus and it has never fully recovered despite the fact that scholars who have discussed the texts in the present century have accepted it as an authentic original.[1]

S, unlike the other three exemplars, has provoked some mild reservations. These have centred on two features. First, it contains more clerical errors than the other three, and secondly it is not written in a script characteristic of the royal chancery. Even so the weight of opinion has come down in S's favour. Despite the clerical errors, it is a good version which falls well within the limits acceptable for a medieval scribe dealing with such a lengthy document. Moreover the writing is not such a simple problem as it may seem at first sight. The various scribes who compiled the enrolled records of the chancery of King John used what may fairly be described as a chancery hand which also appears as the characteristic writing in many royal letters and writs. Charters were written in more formal and more decorative hands which show greater variety. Nevertheless they share characteristic features which also appear in Ci, Cii and L. S is a different matter. W.S. McKechnie accepted it too easily in saying that 'it resembles the Lincoln copy . . . in its fine leisurely penmanship'.[2] A.J. Collins was perhaps excessively critical when he wrote that the script suggests 'a decade or so later than 1215 and smacks of an ecclesiastical scriptorium', for that is to claim an unattainable precision both as

---

1. Fox, Sir John, 'The Originals of the Great Charter of 1215', *English Historical Review,* xxxix (1924), pp. 321-336; Collins, A.J., 'The Documents of the Great Charter 1215', *Proceedings of the British Academy,* xxxiv (1948), pp. 233-79.
2. McKechnie, W.S., *Magna Carta,* (2nd edn, Glasgow, 1914), p. 168.

regards dating and origin.[3] Mrs. Stroud draws too sharp a contrast in describing the script as 'book hand' and implying that there was a single 'business hand' used for chancery documents.[4] The truth is that there is ground for serious doubt. No-one familiar with the official royal documents of John's reign would readily accept the script of S as the work of the royal chancery. On the other hand no-one has been prepared to deny S authenticity on the purely paleographical evidence. The matter has to be put in such negative, hedging, fashion because the hands at work in the official documents have not yet been categorised systematically. Even if such an examination in the future were to show, as is likely, that the scribe of S is an odd man out, and S therefore suspect, there would still be room for argument, for no-one can be absolutely certain of what special measures might have been taken to produce copies of the Charter and the related writs in a hard pressed chancery working at a time of political crisis in the summer of 1215. All this explains why S has received the benefit of the doubt.

S also has one feature which counts in its favour. Although it has never been known to carry a seal, it does bear an M-shaped tear, now repaired, at the bottom centre from which a seal might have been appended. It is most unlikely that this was manufactured deliberately as Mrs. Stroud suggests, as a pretence to authenticity. When, in King John's time, the great seal was affixed on cords, it was usually done through holes arranged triangularly through the folded parchment so as to produce a handsome diamond pattern in the cords at the foot of the document. The remaining holes in L reveal that it was sealed in this way. There were also other methods, one of which relied on holes arranged as an inverted triangle or the angles of a capital M. It is just such a method which the tear in S indicates. It was used rarely. No-one deliberately seeking to create a false impression of authenticity would have been at all likely to have reproduced such an arrangement. For what it is worth, therefore, the evidence of the tear is that S bore a seal attached in an unusual but authentic fashion. That is unlikely to have been the case with an unauthentic document.

One nagging doubt remains, namely that the version written in the least convincing script is *also* the one with the most clerical errors. In addition it is well known that Wiltshire was one of the

3.   Collins, p.270, n.3.
4.   Stroud, Daphne, 'Salisbury's Magna Carta: was it issued by the Chancery?' *The Hatcher Review*, vol. 2. no. 12 (1981), pp. 51-58, especially p.51.

six counties omitted from the list entered on the dorse of the patent roll recording the despatch of charters and the accompanying letters patent. If it could be shown that this was other than coincidental, if it could be established that the peculiar features of S may have arisen from the fact that no charter was sent to Wiltshire in 1215, then S would stand condemned as an unofficial copy and a pretended original. This is the essence of Mrs. Stroud's argument.

In this the despatch list is critical. It is entered on the dorse of membrane 23 of the patent roll. The scribe who entered the writs of 19-23 June dated at Runnymede left a gap of four lines at the end of the entries for the 19th, presumably to leave room for the draft letters enforcing the Charter. If that was the purpose of the gap it proved insufficient and the letters were entered by the same scribe on the dorse of the roll. Some hint of the pressures under which the clerks were working is given by the indication that neither the draft nor a copy was available for insertion in its proper place on the face of the roll before the next documents, dated 21 June, were entered. The memorandum of despatch was also entered on the dorse immediately following the letters. But this was done by a different scribe and it is not a despatch list in the sense of a day-to-day record of issues. It is a fair copy of a despatch list or of notes of despatch. Except for the last sentence the whole memorandum was apparently written in one go and must have been entered after 24 June, for it records the issue of two writs to the bishop of Lincoln on that day. The last sentence was added in late July for it refers to the issue of six charters on the 22nd.[5] To all appearances therefore the memorandum is retrospective and that perhaps leaves greater room for omission. But, much more important, it is also unique. There is nothing like it anywhere else on the rolls. Letters destined to all counties were usually entered with a note — 'In like manner it is written to all sheriffs' or 'The same is ordered to all sheriffs'; the Chancery then saw to the distribution of such writs through the services of the king's messengers without further record of despatch. The memorandum, in contrast, records the issue of the letters of 19 June to members of the baronial party, to bishops and above all to Elyas of Dereham, steward of Stephen Langton, archbishop of Canterbury. Only one recipient, Henry de Vere, a prominent member of the royal household, who received writs for twelve

5. The memorandum is illustrated in Collins, plate 14.

counties, approximates at all to the normal method of distribution.

Now the entry of the memorandum on the patent roll is surely related to this unusual method of distribution. Despite the exceptional circumstances the recording clerk was quite meticulous in naming the counties to which the writs were addressed. This was omitted only in the case of Engelard de Cigogné, but since he was sheriff of Gloucestershire the destination in his case would have seemed obvious. For Worcestershire, the clerk neatly superscribed the county address, thus making plain that that was where the writ delivered to Walter, bishop of Worcester, was to go. He must have noted the addresses for a purpose: to avoid duplication, perhaps, or to ensure that copies reached all counties. It may also have guided him in despatching the writs to the counties not on the list which could well have been served by the normal service of the royal messengers. True, two of the missing counties, Durham and Chester, were palatinates and may not have received writs, but there can be no guarantee that the remaining three, Herefordshire, Hertfordshire and Wiltshire, did not receive them by the ordinary messenger service, which, precisely because it was ordinary, would go unrecorded.

The writs were addressed to the sheriff and officials of each county. The exemplars of the Charter had a general address and were treated differently in the memorandum. The clerk who was so pernickety in recording the addresses of the writs, was plainly not concerned at all to note the destinations of the charters. We may surmise that the charter received by the bishop of Worcester went to Worcestershire and we may guess that the two exemplars received by the bishop of Lincoln partnered the two writs he took for Oxfordshire and Bedfordshire. But thereafter all we know is that Elyas of Dereham received four charters on or after 24 June and six more on 22 July. Where they went we do not know. They could have gone to counties listed in the memorandum. Some could have gone to counties not so listed. Elyas could have retained one or more. Only one thing is certain: the charters, unlike the writs, were delivered only to the bishops and, most important of all, to Elyas of Dereham, steward of the archbishop. This fact, first pointed out by Professor Cheney,[6] deserves more emphasis than it has received hitherto as evidence of the Church's role in supervising the settlement of 1215.

6.   Cheney, C.R., 'The Eve of Magna Carta', *Bulletin of the John Rylands Library*, xxxviii (1956), p.340.

It is now apparent that the memorandum is irrelevant to the status of S. Wiltshire does not figure among the destinations of the writ but that does not necessarily mean that it did not receive one. Wiltshire does not appear as a destination for the charter, but nor does any other county. To the copies which we may surmise went to Worcestershire, Oxfordshire and Bedfordshire, we can add L, which bears the contemporary endorsement *Lincolnia* and Ci, which probably went to the Cinque Ports. Neither of these it should be noted, can be identified with the charters mentioned in the memorandum unless L was one of those received by the bishop of Lincoln. So in this, certainly one and probably two undoubtedly authentic exemplars are no different from S. We know nothing of the rest.

Does the political situation in Wiltshire shed any light on the problem? It probably does, but not necessarily from the angle adopted by Mrs. Stroud. While it is true that the beneficiaries of the grant of 1215 may have been left to obtain their own copies of the Charter, as Professor Cheney has suggested,[7] it does not follow that there was no exercise of central responsibility for the imposition of the settlement. Plainly there was, as is abundantly demonstrated by the careful note in the memorandum of the writs which prescribed the reading of the Charter, the exaction of oaths to the Twenty Five barons and the initiation of enquiries into local government. Henry de Vere was sent out with writs, just like Elyas of Dereham, and Engelard de Cigogné received a writ enforcing a settlement which required his own dismissal from office. So although in Wiltshire William earl of Salisbury was doubtless a powerful influence in the local balance of power, it may be doubted whether he was able to resist the tide. Moreover, as Mrs. Stroud and others have shown, the evidence on his attitude, even his whereabouts, is confused. But one fact seems reasonably certain. William was very immediately involved because the settlement required him to surrender the honour of Trowbridge to Henry de Bohun, earl of Hereford. This was announced to him by letters close of 19 June which were sent to him through de Bohun or his messenger.[8] In short the restoration of Trowbridge, the one immediate consequence of the settlement to which William of Salisbury would certainly object, was imposed on him directly by the hand of one of the Twenty Five barons of the Charter or his agent. So Wiltshire was not sealed off, as it were,

---

7. Cheney, p. 341.

8. *Rotuli Litteraram Clausarum*, ed. Hardy, T.D., (Record Commission, 1833-4), i. p. 215; also in Holt, J.C., *Magna Carta* (Cambridge 1965), which contains copies of all the documents discussed above.

from events at Runnymede. On the contrary it must have been among the first counties to receive news of what had happened there, and that from or on behalf of one whom the Charter had placed in a position of authority as one of the Twenty Five and who had a most immediate interest in applying its terms. Hence Wiltshire could well have received its charter early, rather than late or not at all.

In view of this there is no need to turn to later events to explain the location of S. That Elyas of Dereham, who was to contribute so much to the church of Salisbury, retained an interest in Magna Carta is possible. That he copied the terms of the Charter of 1215, as proposed by Mrs. Stroud, in order to preserve them from destruction by the royal party and in the face of the re-issues of 1216 and 1217 is entirely conjectural. It would imply a continuing commitment to the terms of 1215 as against those confirmed in 1217 and 1225 which would be very remarkable in so experienced and respected a man of affairs. True, the royal party sought the return of the 'charters of Runnymede' along with other documents in the negotiations which led to the Treaty of Kingston /Lambeth in 1217, but this was not part of the final terms of settlement.[9] Moreover there is no evidence at all that the intention was to destroy them. On the contrary, the letters testimonial in which the archbishop and bishops validated the Charter, which may well have been among the documents restored in the negotiation of 1217, were still preserved in the Exchequer in the early fourteenth century when they were copied into the Red Book.[10]

So in the end we are driven back to S, the document: to its errors, its script and to the method of sealing which the tear implies. One of its features it would be unfair to lay at Elyas's door. The scribe frequently preferred the future indicative to the more correct present subjunctive.[11] We might expect Master Elyas, university graduate, to have done better than that.

9.   Smith, J. Beverley, 'The Treaty of Lambeth, 1217', *English Historical Review,* xciv (1979), pp. 562-79.

10. Collins, pp. 249-50.

11. Fox, p.330.

12

THE ST ALBANS CHRONICLERS AND MAGNA CARTA[1]

THE St Albans chroniclers, Roger of Wendover and Matthew Paris, present a unique version of the documents of 1215. This, as it appears in Wendover's chronicle, consists, first, of a text of Magna Carta drawn from the 1215 version for its introduction and first clause, and thereafter from the re-issues of 1217 and 1225; secondly, of a text of the Charter of the Forest based on the versions of 1217 and 1225, and in the St Albans version falsely attributed to King John; finally, of a version of the *forma securitatis* of 1215 which includes sections found nowhere else, either in record or in chronicle. It is, in short, a complete muddle, and it was not improved by Matthew Paris, for he copied it into his *Chronica Majora* and then later proceeded to patch it with sections drawn from the 1215 text.

This version of Magna Carta misled generations of scholars. Matthew Parker's edition of the *Chronica Majora* of 1571 made it generally available nearly sixty years before two of the four surviving authentic originals of the 1215 charter came into the hands of Sir Robert Cotton.[2] Spelman copied it; later Wilkins printed Spelman's copy;[3] and it was not until Blackstone's *Commentary* of 1759 that the errors of the St Albans chroniclers were

---

[1] I have been greatly assisted in preparing this paper by Dr Richard Vaughan, Fellow and Librarian of Corpus Christi College, Cambridge. I have depended heavily on his published work on Matthew Paris. He has allowed me to inspect the manuscripts of the *Chronica Majora* and advised me on a number of points of detail concerning Matthew's handwriting.

[2] For Cotton's acquisition of the originals in 1629–30, see A. J. Collins, 'The Documents of the Great Charter of 1215', *Proceedings of the British Academy*, xxxiv (1948), pp. 260–61.

[3] *Leges Anglo-Saxonicae*, ed. D. Wilkins (London, 1721), pp. 367–73. Spelman also copied the Letters Testimonial from the Red Book of the Exchequer and made some attempt to collate this text of the 1215 charter with the St Albans version (*ibid.*, pp. 373–76).

first clearly indicated.[1] This long and influential reign of error may explain why some critics have been particularly severe on Roger and Matthew at this point. In his introduction to the *Chronica Majora*, Luard concluded that 'the charter as given here is such a piece of patchwork between the two [versions of John and Henry III] that it is clear the St Alban's historians thought they might pull about and piece together the two as they liked'.[2] Mr A. J. Collins has repeated Luard's opinion and added: 'Even Matthew Paris . . ., the ablest, the best-informed and the most careful writer of his age, was at no pains whatsoever to transmit to posterity an authentic version of Magna Carta . . . what Paris and Roger of Wendover, whom he followed, offered as the Great Charter of John to those for whose instruction they wrote was a patchwork of the various issues, still further embellished by insertions of their own'.[3] But criticism has not been unanimous. Dr Vaughan contented himself with a reference to Luard,[4] while Professor Galbraith has commented that Roger's 'virtues are those of the indefatigable narrator who sets down all he can find, and of every kind. He attempted, for example, and not without success, to incorporate the text of official documents—like Magna Carta and the bulls of Innocent III'.[5] This is a timely reminder that Roger of Wendover did at least try. It suggests, if not a conscious clash of modern expert opinion, at least the existence of a problem. Why and how did Roger of Wendover and Matthew Paris go wrong? Did they not know? Or did they not care? How 'document-conscious' were they?

The impression given by Luard is that the two chroniclers cared little about what they were doing, and that they constructed a patchwork from authentic texts which they had before them. A truer estimate would place more weight on ignorance than

---

[1] W. Blackstone, *Law Tracts* (Oxford, 1762), pp. xxxv, lxix. Many earlier commentators referred solely to the re-issue of 1225 or later versions of this re-issue. See H. Butterfield, *The Englishman and his History* (Cambridge, 1944), pp. 25–30, 54–56.

[2] [*Matthei Parisiensis*] *Chron*[*ica*] *Maj*[*ora*], ed. H. R. Luard (R[olls] S[eries], 1874), ii, p. xxxiv.

[3] *Ibid.*, pp. 259–60. *Cf.* W. S. McKechnie, *Magna Carta* (Glasgow, 1914), p. 176.

[4] R. Vaughan, *Matthew Paris* (Cambridge, 1958), p. 134*n.*

[5] V. H. Galbraith, *Roger Wendover and Matthew Paris* (Glasgow, 1944), p. 19.

insouciance; it would also distinguish sharply between Wendover and Paris. There is no evidence that Wendover ever saw an accurate text of any version of the charter;[1] Paris, in contrast, had accurate texts of both the 1215 and 1225 versions, but by his time the damage had been done; Wendover's text had got the authenticity of age, and Paris repeated his errors. However, the faults were not all Wendover's. Paris had more strident prejudices than his predecessor as well as wider knowledge, and it was largely these which prevented him from using his increased documentary resources properly. Roger went astray because he had not got the facts, Matthew because he was blinded to their proper use.

Wendover's work survives in three manuscripts:

1. A copy of his *Flores Historiarum* written *c.* 1300, now in the Bodleian Library, Douce MS. 207 (*W*).
2. A copy of his *Flores Historiarum* written *c.* 1350, now in the British Museum, Cotton MS. Otho B.v (*O*).[2]
3. The *Chronica Majora* of Matthew Paris, the relevant section of which is Corpus Christi College, Cambridge, MS. 16 (*B*).[3]

The relationship of these three manuscripts is securely established: *O* and *W* are both derived from an intermediate recension of Wendover's chronicle (*OW*) and thence on the original text (*b*); *B*, which is Matthew's working copy of the *Chronica Majora*, is based on *b* and is therefore the earliest and most immediate surviving copy of Wendover's work.[4] A fourth manuscript, British Museum, Cotton MS. Vitellius A.xx (*V*), is also relevant to the present topic. This is a chronicle extending from 1066 to

---

[1] There is no record that an original was sent to Hertfordshire in 1215 (*Rot. Litt. Pat.*, p. 180[b]), nor does the St Albans evidence support the view that a copy was deposited at the abbey at that time. *Cf.* Collins, *op. cit.*, pp. 259–60, 277–78.

[2] Wendover's chronicle has been edited twice: by H. O. Coxe, for the English Historical Society, 4 vols (1841–44), and by H. G. Hewlett, for the Rolls Series, 3 vols (1886–89). For comments on the editions, see Hewlett's introduction, *op. cit.*, i, pp. viii–x, and V. H. Galbraith, *op. cit.*, pp. 20–21.

[3] Ed. H. R. Luard, 7 vols (R.S., 1872–83). All references below to the work of Wendover and Paris are to this edition.

[4] Vaughan, *op. cit.*, p. 29.

1246; Matthew Paris wrote a short section of the text at the beginning and annotated other sections; the rest is the work of a single scribe. It is headed 'Cronica excerpta a magnis cronicis S. Albani a conquestu Anglie usque deinceps', and, as its title implies, it is largely an abridgment of the *Chronica Majora*; it also drew directly on Roger of Wendover.[1] V contains two texts of Magna Carta: the first, like b, a composite version of the charters of John and Henry III ($V1$);[2] the second a much more accurate version of the charter of Henry III ($V2$).[3] It also contains the Charter of the Forest, here correctly attributed to Henry III.[4]

There are, therefore, five surviving St Albans versions of Magna Carta: $V1$, $V2$, and the three derived from b in O, W and B. All five are derived from a single basic St Albans text[5] which had two identifying characteristics. First, in Chapter 2, it set the relief due from a baron at 100 marks, not £100. Secondly, it was a composite version of the charters of 1217 and 1225. Where there are minor textual differences between the 1217 and 1225 texts, all St Albans versions follow the 1217 text in the same eight instances,[6] and the 1225 text in the same four.[7] There is a similar pattern in the St Albans version of the Charter of the Forest, of which there are four surviving copies: one in V and three derived from b. This follows most of the minor variants of the 1217 text,[8]

---

[1] Vaughan, *op. cit.*, pp. 115 ff.   [2] Fos 93^v–97^r.   [3] Fos 99^r–101^v.
[4] Fos 98^r–99^r.

[5] It is obvious at a glance that the b and $V1$ texts are closely associated. $V2$ contains fewer errors, but still shares nearly half its minor textual variants with b and $V1$.

[6] Cap. 4, l.8, *committatur; committetur,* 1225; cap. 7, l.6, om. *ipsius;* cap. 8, l.3, *sufficiunt; sufficiant,* 1225; cap. 8, l.10, *solverint; solverunt,* 1225; cap. 27, l.8, *vel; nec,* 1225; cap. 31, l.5, *illa; ipsa,* 1225; cap. 36, l.4, *eam illi; illam ei,* 1225; cap. 37, l.1, *consuevit; solebat,* 1225. All references to Magna Carta are to the texts in C. Bémont, *Chartes des libertés anglaises* (Paris, 1892), unless otherwise noted.

[7] Cap. 7, l.5, *tenuerunt; tenuerint,* 1217; cap. 14, l.7, *sacramentum (sacrament', V2); sacramenta,* 1217; cap. 18, l.11, *et pueris suis;* om. 1217; cap. 36, l.4, *recepit; receperit,* 1217.

[8] Cap. 2, l.1, om. *vero;* cap. 3, l.1, *fuerunt; fuerint,* 1225; cap. 4, l.4, *predicti;* om. 1225, (cropped in V); cap. 4, l.7, *vastum, purpresturam vel assartum; vastum vel purpresturam,* 1225; cap. 8, l.3, om. *nostri;* cap. 9, l.1, om. *quem habet;* cap. 9, l.8, *ita quod; unde,* 1225; cap. 16, l.1, *vel alius;* om. 1225; cap. 16, l.6, om. *nostro;* cap. 17, l.9, *tam clerici quam laici;* om. 1225. In contrast there is:— cap. 4, l.9, *de vastis purpresturis et assartis,* as in 1225, (*de vastis et essartis et purpresturis, V*); *de vastis et assartis,* 1217.

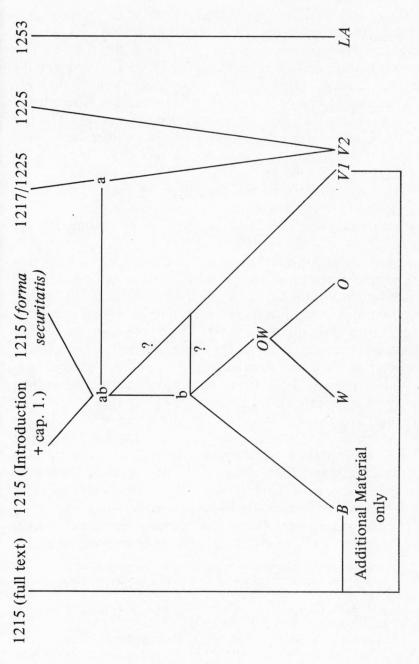

1215 (full text)　　1215 (Introduction　1215 (*forma*　　1217/1225　　1225　　1253
　　　　　　　　　　+ cap. 1.)　　　　*securitatis*)

THE ST ALBANS MSS AND MAGNA CARTA

but it also drew on the 1225 text for its introduction and for the material additions made in 1225 to Chapter 11.[1]

This basic St Albans text of Magna Carta is not represented in its entirety in any one of the five surviving versions. V1 contains only the first seventeen chapters of it, and the b texts differ markedly from V2 at certain points. The b versions end with the saving clause of 1217; V2, in contrast, here follows the 1225 charter exactly and ends with the reference to the Fifteenth and with an abbreviated, but still lengthy, list of witnesses. The text of the Charter of the Forest shows similar differences. The b versions have no proper conclusion and include the last sentence of Chapter 14 of the 1217 charter which was omitted in 1225. V ends by referring to the conclusion of the Great Charter of 1225[2] and excludes the 1217 material in Chapter 14. Thus, in both cases, b approximates to 1217, V—excluding V1—to 1225.

There are two obvious possibilities: either b was a version of the original text amended in the direction of 1217, or V2 and the associated text of the Charter of the Forest represent the original text amended in the direction of 1225. The latter kind of amendment seems generally more likely. The b texts show the greater dependence on the earlier of the two charters, b was composed long before V2 was written, and the order of the two final clauses of the b version of Magna Carta is more likely to have arisen from an initial dependence on the 1217 than on the 1225 text.[3] Hence the most likely explanation of the special features of V2 and of the V version of the Charter of the Forest is that somebody at St Albans between the compilation or acquisition of the basic text in or after 1225 and the writing of V after 1246 had access to accurate versions of the 1225 documents, from which he made additions and corrections to the basic text.

The b version also shows characteristic divergencies from the basic text. It is much the least accurate in detail of all the

[1] . . . *veniens ad nos ad mandatum nostrum . . . Idem liceat eis in redeundo facere sicut predictum est.* V and OW follow this exactly; B reads *liceat in redeundo eis facere.*

[2] It ends with *Hiis testibus ut infra*, the reference being to the V2 version of Magna Carta which follows immediately.

[3] At this point the saving clause and the confirmation of liberties appear in a different order in the 1217 and 1225 versions. The B texts follow 1217, V2 1225.

St Albans versions. Even by medieval standards it is a bad text. *W* contains less than half a dozen errors or variants peculiar to itself; *O* is an equally accurate copy; *O* and *W* share exclusively nearly twenty variants or errors, all of which were presumably in *OW*. Matthew Paris was not quite so accurate: he produced just over twenty variants or errors in *B*, some of which were serious. But even this is little compared with the seventy variants or errors common to *O*, *W* and *B*, all of which were presumably contained in *b*. These include two major omissions: the last section of Chapter 16,[1] and four lines of the printed text of Chapter 4,[2] the latter almost certainly a result of homoeoteleuton in the exemplar. There is one major variant in Chapter 29, which reads 'nec super eum ibimus nec eum in carcere mittemus'. There are also three obvious errors which vitiate the sense of the passages in which they occur. In Chapter 7 *O*, *W*, and *B* in its original version, all provide that a widow shall give nothing for her dower and homage, instead of—correctly—for her dower and marriage portion;[3] in Chapter 35 *O*, *W* and *B* all have the sheriff doing his term, instead of—correctly—making his tourn.[4] *O* and *W* also confuse the sense of Chapter 14 by altering *comites* to *comitatus*, thus providing that amercements should be imposed by the oaths of men, not of the neighbourhood, but of the neighbourhood of the shire. *B* inserts *comites* correctly, but also preserves the incorrect reading by retaining *comitatus*.[5]

All these major errors are avoided in *V*2. If they were present in the basic text, then the author of *V*2 must have corrected them by collation with the 1225 charter. But in view of *b*'s general inaccuracy, the fact that *V*2 was not so thoroughly corrected to remove all traces of the basic text, and indeed shares minor

[1] *O*, *W* and *B* om. *per eadem loca et eosdem terminos sicut esse consueverunt tempore suo.*

[2] *O*, *W* and *B* om. *qui de exitibus . . . duobus legalibus et discretis hominibus de feodo illo.*

[3] *O* and *W*, *nec aliquid det pro dote sua vel pro homagio suo.* Cf. *maritagio suo*, 1217, 1225. Matthew Paris gives the correct reading over an erasure in *B*.

[4] *O*, *W* and *B*, *Nec vicecomes aliquis vel ballivus suus faciat terminum suum.* Cf. *faciat turnum suum*, 1217, 1225.

[5] *O* and *W*, *sacramentum proborum et legalium hominum de visneto comitatus. Et barones . . . Cf. B, comitatus, comites et barones . . . Cf. visneto. Comites et barones*, 1217, 1225.

variants with *b* in two of the chapters in which the majoi errors occur,[1] it is more likely that *V*2 and *b* were derived from a common exemplar, which is preserved accurately in *V*2, where used, but carelessly in *b*. This is confirmed by a comparison of the *b* versions with Chapters 1–17 of *V*1, which, like *b*, is a composite version of the 1215 and 1217 charters. This shares many of the minor variants and several of the major features of the *b* text.[2] But *V*1 is on the whole a better version than *b*;[3] it avoids one of *b*'s major errors in that in Chapter 7 it has the correct reading *maritagio* instead of *b*'s *homagio*. *V*1, in short, seems to be derived, not from *b*, but from an exemplar shared with *b*, and it is quite possible that *b*, far from coinciding with the basic text, was in fact separated from it by an intervening recension from which both *V*1 and *b* were derived.

Hence, to sum up, there was a basic St Albans text (*a*), which was a reasonably accurate but composite version of the 1217 and 1225 charters. In one line of its development, it was amended in the direction of the 1225 version to appear as *V*2; in another, it went, either directly or, more likely, through an intermediate recension, into the *V*1 and the *b* texts, by which time it had acquired characteristic errors and omissions. *V*1 and *b* are also distinctive and different from *V*2 in that they are attributed to King John and are provided with introductions drawn from the 1215 charter and other suitable alterations. The final versions in *O*, *W* and *B* display cumulative error and distortion.

It is not easy to distinguish who was responsible. It is probable, however, that the basic conflation of the 1217 and 1225 texts in *a* was not done at St Albans, but came to the house ready made. The chronicle of Walter of Guisborough contains a text of the charters with features strikingly similar to the St Albans version.[4] Like *a* it puts the baronial relief at 100 marks; it follows the

---

[1] Cap. 4, l.8, *b* and *V*2, *committatur*, as in 1217 but not 1225; cap. 7, l.4, *b* and *V*2 om. *pro*; cap. 7, l.8, *b* and *V*2, *fuerit castrum*.

[2] It makes the same omissions as *b*, in cc. 4 and 16. Matthew Paris amended the *V*1 text of cap. 14 to conform to the reading in *B*.

[3] In cap. 1, *V*1 reads correctly *ante discordiam inter nos et barones nostros motam*, a phrase into which *b* inserts the word *manifeste*. In cap. 15, *V*1 reads correctly *debet* for *b*'s reading *debent*.

[4] *The Chronicle of Walter of Guisborough*, ed. Harry Rothwell (Camden, 3rd Series, lxxxix, 1957), pp. 162–72.

1217 variants of Magna Carta in seven of the same eight instances as *a*, and the 1225 variants in the same four;[1] it incorporates the same 1225 material as *a* in Chapter 11 of the Charter of the Forest, and the same 1217 material as *b* in Chapter 14. Yet it contains introductory and concluding sections to both charters which could not have been derived from any known St Albans text; similarly, the St Albans versions, in these sections, contain material not in the Guisborough text.[2] Neither Dr Vaughan nor Professor Rothwell have discovered any channel of communication between the two houses. They must have derived their versions of the charters from a common source which itself embodied elements of the 1217 and 1225 texts, and, as we shall see, it was a source also used in the Red Book of the Exchequer.

In the case of the much more corrupt text in *b*, there is a greater certainty, for, if *b* and *V*2 were derived from a common exemplar, *b*—like *V*2—must in all probability have been produced at St Albans. St Albans, therefore, must carry responsibility for the errors in *b* and for the textual reconstruction which accompanied the attribution to King John. This comprised the insertion of the introduction and Chapter 1 of the 1215 charter, and some readjustment of awkward references to previous kings. In Chapter 16 of the 1217 charter Henry III refers to Henry II as *avus noster*. *O* and *V*1 hopefully leave this as it stands, despite its inaccuracy in a charter supposedly granted by John. *B*, equally hopefully and less excusably, reads *Henricus primus, avus noster*. All *b* versions amend the reference to 'Richard our uncle' in Chapter 3 of the Charter of the Forest to 'Richard our brother', and they all omit the reference to King John which immediately follows. All this was done ineffectively and incompletely. In Chapters 35 and 37 of Magna Carta and Chapters 1, 4 and 5 of the Charter of the

---

[1] In cap. 31, l.5, this version has *baronia* for the *illa* of the *a* text. See p. 70, n. 6, above.

[2] The Guisborough version incorporates a full introduction which is abbreviated in *V*2 and replaced by the 1215 text in *b* and *V*1. It also has *Datum per manum venerabilis patris nostri domini R. Dunelmensis episcopi, cancellarii nostri*, which does not figure in any of the St Albans versions. The *b*, *V*2 and Guisborough versions of the conclusion of the Great Charter, and the introduction and conclusion of the Charter of the Forest each embody the 1217 and 1225 texts in different proportions, although even in these sections there are common variants.

Forest references to *Henricus avus noster* are left untouched in all versions.[1]

Wendover himself had a hand in this. It is clear that he not only wrote *b*, but also, at one point, had access to *b*'s source. The 1215 introduction in *b* and *V*1 omits the long list of names of those who counselled King John in granting the charter. However, Wendover had access to this list because he used it in the immediately preceding section of his chronicle to concoct a list of those who were *quasi ex parte regis* at Runnymede. Furthermore, if the narrative and the *b* version of the charter are compared, it is difficult to avoid the conclusion that Wendover tailored the *b* version to meet the needs of his narrative; having used the list in the narrative, he excluded it from the charter.[2]

To this extent Wendover can be shown to have tampered with his sources, and because of this he must remain the likeliest candidate, indeed the only candidate we have, for the dubious distinction of originating the *b* text. But this is the only piece of direct evidence; the rest of the case against him depends on collateral evidence. Professor Cheney, for example, has remarked that Roger's texts of papal letters are 'corrupt', 'much corrupted' or 'careless and incomplete'.[3] Occasionally Roger misread a document completely, as for example in the case of the famous summons of the reeve and four men of the vill to St Albans in 1213;[4] and where his transcripts avoid serious error, they usually contain minor variants: transpositions of words, alterations of tenses and moods, the insertion or omission of adjectives and suffixes, and the like. The numerous minor variants in *b* are similar, and if Wendover was responsible for these, then it is reasonable to assume that he was also responsible for *b*'s major errors and omissions, the inclusion of sections from the 1215

---

[1] *V*2 has none of these amendments. It has no introduction except for the king's name and title—*Henricus dei gratia rex Anglie etc. In primis concessimus* . . . , and it uses the 1217 version of cap. 1 (distinguishable from 1225 only by the omission of *omnia* in l.3).

[2] *Chron. Maj.*, ii, pp. 589, 590.

[3] *Selected Letters of Pope Innocent III*, ed. C. R. Cheney and W. H. Semple (Nelson's Med. Texts, 1953), pp. 211*n.*, 188*n.*, 207*n.*

[4] *Chron. Maj.*, ii, p. 550. See H. W. C. Davis, 'The St Albans Council of 1213', *Eng[lish] Hist[orical] Rev[iew]*, xx (1905), pp. 289 ff.; G. J. Turner, 'The St Albans Council of 1213', *Eng. Hist. Rev.*, xxi (1906), pp. 297 ff.

charter, and the attribution of both the Great Charter and the Charter of the Forest to King John.

Against this, there is the evidence of Wendover himself. When he came to the re-issue of the charters in 1225, he wrote: 'The content of these charters is given more fully above, where this history is concerned with King John, for there are no differences to be found between the charters of the two kings'.[1] Taken at its face value, this implies either that Wendover was not responsible for the corrupt text he produced in *b* or, more likely in view of the textual evidence, that he concocted the text himself under a genuine misapprehension of what King John had conceded in 1215. His documentary materials for 1215 seem to have been quite inadequate. There is no evidence that he ever saw anything of the charter of 1215 except the introduction, Chapter 1 and the St Albans version of the *forma securitatis*. It is probable, too, that they were only available to him as fragments. He presented the *forma securitatis* as something quite separate from the Great Charter, with the Charter of the Forest intervening between the two. This arrangement was repeated by Matthew Paris; in his time, Wendover's sources were still available at St Albans, for he reintroduced the names of the king's advisers into the margin of *B*, and at the end of the *forma securitatis* he noted that there was another exemplar which was dated in John's sixteenth regnal year.[2]

Wendover's own words, then, leave some room for doubt about his rôle. At the very least, they suggest that his errors arose in extenuating circumstances. Moreover, the maltreatment of documentary sources which produced *b* was not atypical of the age. Matthew Paris, for example, deliberately altered the date, the address and the content of documents in order to point the moral of his story.[3] Such intentional falsification was relatively rare. More important was a tendency to conflate, which at St Albans was almost an epidemic infection. The *a* text is a conflated version of the 1217 and 1225 charters. The scribe of *V* never completely eliminated the 1217 variants in *V*2; he simply adjusted it appropriately where it obviously diverged from the 1225 text.

---

[1] *Chron. Maj.*, iii, p. 92: . . . *cartae utrorumque regum in nullo inveniuntur dissimiles.*

[2] These additions were made in Matthew Paris' current hand, probably some time before his main additions of 1215 material in the margins of *B*.

[3] Vaughan, *op. cit.*, pp. 132–33; Cheney and Semple, *op. cit.*, pp. 1–2.

The same scribe reproduced in V1 the first seventeen chapters of the b versions which embodied pieces of the 1215, 1217 and 1225 texts, and used the 1215 text alone for the remainder. Matthew Paris first used b in B, and then added chapters from the 1215 charter both in B and V1. These writers were not lawyers; they did not see in the versions of the charters any need to distinguish between different, sometimes conflicting, legal enactments; they were churchmen and monks, who treated the different versions which came their way as if they were variants on a single thread of truth. Hence they conflated where they should have distinguished. They may have been encouraged in this by ignorance of authentic originals, but in the end conflation had become such a habit that Matthew Paris could not even recognize an authentic exemplification of the 1225 charter for what it was.[1]

These awkward facts are of some importance to constitutional historians. The differences between the 1215 and 1217 texts of the charter were important. In 1216 William Marshal and his advisers regarded the chapters which were ultimately excluded as *gravia et dubitabilia*; the exclusion of these chapters and the inclusion of new provisions in 1217 must have been a product of serious discussion and delicately poised political considerations. Historians now, and statesmen then, assumed that all this mattered, that the body politic was sensitive to these changes in the prescription for its ills. In fact it was easier to provide remedies than to arrange for their distribution and absorption. At St Albans they clearly had no predictable effect, and St Albans, according to Professor Galbraith, was one of the nerve centres of thirteenth-century constitutionalism, its chronicles *apologia pro baronibus*, which presented a Whig interpretation of history before its time.[2] The St Albans writers were not the only ones to make mistakes. The conflated version of the charters used at Guisborough has already been noted.[3] There is another version, apparently embodying the 1217 and 1225 texts in proportions different again, in the *Liber Niger* of Christ Church, Dublin.[4] Moreover, there

[1] See below, p. 280.
[2] Galbraith, *Roger Wendover and Matthew Paris*, p. 20.
[3] See above, pp. 73–74. See above, pp. 179-202.
[4] H. J. Lawlor, 'An Unnoticed Charter of Henry III, 1217', *Eng. Hist. Rev.*, xxii (1907), pp. 514–18. See also Professor Rothwell's comments, *The Chronicle of Walter of Guisborough*, p. 162n.

is a version of the charter, dated 11 February 1252, printed in the *Statutes of the Realm* and displayed in the British Museum, which includes part of the introduction of the 1217 charter in a text otherwise based on the 1225 document, and which substitutes marks for pounds in the baronial relief in Chapter 2.[1] These and other variants are so striking that Bémont dismissed this version as 'une grossière fabrication'.[2] Authentic or not, it represents yet another conflated text.

Error was encouraged by the historical circumstances of the 1220's. The re-issues of the charter seem to have convinced many that its principles were more important than its variants; hence they gave it a continuous history going back to Runnymede. Wendover stated that the treaty of Lambeth provided for the restoration of *all* the liberties which had been sought earlier in the quarrel between King John and his barons.[3] Again, according to him, Stephen Langton's request for a confirmation of the charters in January 1224 sought the liberties and free customs for which war had been fought against King Henry's father.[4] For Wendover the struggle for the charters was continuous from 1215 through the re-issues of 1217, the confirmation of 1224, the re-issue of 1225, and the temporary repudiation of forest liberties in 1227.[5]

Matthew Paris's treatment of these passages typifies the relationship between the two St Albans writers. He repeated them all, but instilled them with passionate moral comment all his own, asserting, for example, that the repudiation of forest liberties in 1227 created great discontent and bitter grief that the advice of wicked men had destroyed the work for which so much effort, blood and money had been expended.[6] Furthermore he distorted and fabricated history in an attempt to attribute his own attitude towards papal dominion, towards royal and papal taxation and towards the spread of 'foreign' influences in both church and state,

[1] *Statutes of the Realm*, i, pp. 28–31.
[2] *Chartes des libertés anglaises*, p. xxxin. R. L. Poole, in contrast, did not question its authenticity (*Eng. Hist. Rev.*, xxviii (1913), p. 452).
[3] *Chron. Maj.*, iii, p. 31. *Cf.* the annals of Waverley, *Annales Monastici*, ii, pp. 290, 291.
[4] *Chron. Maj.*, iii, p. 76; incorrectly dated 1223. See Kate Norgate, *The Minority of Henry III* (London, 1912), pp. 215–16.
[5] *Chron. Maj.*, iii, pp. 31, 76, 92, 122, 125.
[6] *Flores Historiarum*, ed. Hewlett, ii, p. 188. *Cf.* his comments on the re-issue of 1225, *ibid.*, ii, p. 182, and *Chron. Maj.*, iii, p. 92.

to men long since dead on whom Matthew's prejudices sit uncertainly, artificially and anachronistically. He makes the barons of 1215 fight his battles for him. They become vehicles for anti-papal invective; he even has them quote Juvenal and the prophet Isaiah.[1] Likewise he presents King John's surrender of the realm to the papacy as an outstanding blot upon his character. In the *Historia Anglorum* Savaric de Mauléon exclaims against the king: 'When have you seen or heard from anyone of a free king, whether Saracen or Christian, who subjected himself willingly to servitude? But you, who were the freest of monarchs, have consigned you and your realm to perpetual slavery that you may confound your native subjects the more vehemently'.[2] Matthew's final word was: 'Thus died John, king and first tributary of England'. 'Woe to the tottering crown of England'. To emphasize the point, he drew a falling crown to accompany his comment.[3]

Matthew did all this quite deliberately. At every stage he protected himself against possible reprisals. The barons of 1215 who inveighed against the pope are described as blasphemous and refractory; their views are lamentable; those who cursed the pope sinned beyond redemption, for 'it is written that "Thou shall not curse the ruler"; those transgress both truth and reverence who say that John the illustrious king of England was a slave; for to serve God is to rule'.[4] He could be remarkably sly in seeking to have it both ways.

Matthew's approach had a serious effect on his account of Magna Carta. First, he amalgamated the characters and policies of Henry III and John. They are presented as attacking, and their opponents as defending, identical lay and ecclesiastical liberties. Hence Matthew places John's ghost at Henry's elbow. In 1252 he has the bishops complaining that Henry had taken the cross for the same reason as John, namely to oppress his subjects;[5] a year later the bishops express the polite but ominous hope that Henry is learning from the example of his father's ultimate fate;[6] others

---

[1] *Chron. Maj.*, ii, pp. 620, 637, 645, 646–47.
[2] *Historia Anglorum*, ed. F. Madden (R.S., 1866–69), ii, p. 152. *Cf. Chron. Maj.*, ii, p. 647.
[3] *Chron. Maj.*, ii, p. 669n.
[4] *Chron. Maj.*, ii, pp. 637, 645, 647.
[5] *Ibid.*, v, p. 327.
[6] *Ibid.*, v, p. 360.

suggest that John would rather have died than be crushed under the heel of his subjects, as they imply Henry will be, following the confirmation of the charters in 1253;[1] thus John is made to reinforce a curialist doctrine—'Henry, be a king'. Non-curialists, in contrast, are made to hint that Henry took after his father in the favour shown to Poitevins.[2] Matthew even puts John to work on his deathbed, issuing suitable instructions for his son. He is made to renounce ill will towards his barons as a condition of his salvation, and then says: 'Tell my son Henry to do likewise lest my soul be burdened with his sin, and henceforth let him be warned and edified by my example so that he loves, cherishes and co-operates with his native-born subjects.'[3] Despite his hostility to King John, Matthew could portray him sympathetically if it served a greater purpose, the admonishment of Henry III.

The purpose and effect of these comparisons is to imply that John and Henry III were equal and alike in duplicity. Wendover had a small enough opinion of John's good faith; even so, Matthew found several points in the *Chronica Majora* to add notes on the king's readiness to go back on his word.[4] All his prejudice and despair is concentrated into the passage he included in the annal of 1215 in which he contrasts the high hopes which men had in the king's concessions with the insidious and provocative advice of his foreign advisers and his secret preparations for war: 'it was believed that fate had provided nectar for enjoyment while all the time she had prepared a bitter and poisoned cup'.[5] Matthew saw no improvement under Henry III, but only a wearisome reiteration of promises and confirmations, followed by backsliding and breach of faith. In describing the confirmation of the charters of 1237, he referred to the sentence against offenders of 1225, which he believed the king had infringed;[6] he referred to the confirmation of 1237 in describing the complaints against infringements of the charters in 1242 and 1244;[7] he treated the confirmation of 1253 as the lineal successor to Henry's earlier confirmations and John's original grant;[8] by this time he was complaining that Henry had given his promise on many occasions

---

[1] *Chron. Maj.*, v, p. 378.   [2] *Ibid.*, v. p. 443.
[3] *Historia Anglorum*, ii, p. 193.
[4] *Chron. Maj.*, ii, pp. 588, 613, 614. Cf. *Historia Anglorum*, ii, pp. 157, 158.
[5] *Chron. Maj.*, ii, pp. 610–12.   [6] *Ibid.*, iii, p. 382.
[7] *Ibid.*, iv, pp. 186, 187, 362–63.   [8] *Ibid.*, v, p. 375.

and this became the final note to which he returned in his annals of 1254, 1255 and 1257.[1]

Matthew presented royal government as an almost unrelieved denial of the charter, beginning with King John in 1215 and continuing with King Henry III up to 1257, a record only broken by the minority of Henry and occasional, isolated and unconvincing instances of royal repentance. Hence, for Matthew, the charter is never simply the charter of King Henry;[2] it is always the charter of King John, or the charter of King John which King Henry has confirmed.[3] Matthew described it thus despite the Crown's insistence that the charter which was being repeatedly confirmed was Henry's. He did so even though he could compare his own references to the charters as John's with letters in which Henry III referred to the charters as his.[4] He did it even when he acquired an authentic chancery exemplification of the 1225 charter used in the confirmation of 1253. This is a fine copy of the 1225 text. It contains only one major variant: it ends with the phrase 'Hiis testibus Stephano Cantuar' archiepiscopo et aliis', instead of the complete list of witnesses. It has a number of minor variants, mostly transpositions; one variant reading in Chapter 29 is of considerable interest, for it reads 'nisi per legale judicium parium suorum *aut* per legem terre'. This scribe, at least, was in no doubt about the disjunctive sense of the famous *vel*. Needless to say, the charter opens with the full titles of Henry III. Nevertheless Matthew Paris gave it the following heading, when he included it in the *Liber Additamentorum*:

'Magna carta regis Johannis quam rex Henricus III juravit iterum tenere in aula Westmonasterii et lata est sententia in infractores'.

This title, which was printed by Luard without the text,[5] seems

---

[1] *Ibid.*, v, pp. 451, 500–1, 623.

[2] The apparently exceptional references under the year 1242 are to Henry's 'parva carta' of 1237 (*ibid.*, iv, pp. 186, 187).

[3] For 1244, *Chron. Maj.*, v, pp. 362–63, 373; *Historia Anglorum*, ii, p. 491. For 1252, *Historia Anglorum*, iii, pp. 125–26. For 1253, *Chron. Maj.*, v, pp. 377, 449. For 1255, *ibid.*, v, pp. 500–1. For 1256, *ibid.*, v, pp. 540–41. For 1258, *ibid.*, v, p. 696.

[4] Compare *Chron. Maj.*, v, pp. 377, 449, with Henry's letters included in the *Liber Additamentorum* (*ibid.*, vi, pp. 249–50).

[5] *Chron. Maj.*, vi, p. 523.

to have had a mesmeric effect on historians, for it leads one to expect the usual St Albans pastiche. Certainly neither Luard nor anyone else has so far recognized that the *Liber Additamentorum* contains the sole known original of the confirmation of 1253. Here Matthew's errors have long survived him.

Matthew's description of this document shows that he was in no fit mental state to distinguish between the different versions of the charter. Yet he obtained not only the original of 1253, but also a good text of the version of 1215. This apparently only became available at St Albans after the composition of the *Chronica Majora*; it was not used by Wendover or by Paris when he first wrote *B*. The scribe of *V* had access to it, and Paris used it to make additions both to *B* and *V*. In all, he had the whole of the 1215 text, yet he never brought himself to question Wendover's statement, which he repeated *verbatim*, that the 1225 and 1215 texts were alike. Instead he seems to have assumed that he was adding sections which Wendover for some reason had omitted, or that he was supplying variant readings to Wendover's text. Where there was a conflict, he was uncertain which of the two texts, Wendover's or the newly accessible 1215 version, was the more authentic. Both he and the scribe of *V* copied into their texts Chapter 12 of the 1225 charter providing for annual circuits of justices to hear possessory assizes. The margin of *V* also contains the parallel Chapter 18 of the 1215 charter, which provided for three-monthly circuits. Matthew headed this *vel sic*.[1] Such uncertainty was an important ingredient of the St Albans conflation.

Matthew had no excuse. Where he added material from the 1215 charter, he did so at the right place; it is therefore evident that he was comparing the *b* version with the full text of the 1215 charter when he amended *B*. Yet all he did was to patch the *b* text. He had already introduced the list of royal advisers into Chapter 1, deriving it presumably from the source used by Wendover. Now he washed out the foot of the first column and the whole of the second column of Folio 38ᵛ, which contained Chapter 8 to the fifth word of Chapter 19 of Henry's charter.[2]

---

[1] Cotton MS. Vitellius A.xx, fo. 94ᵛ. In *B*, in contrast, he added the reference to the assize of darrein presentment from the 1215 text, but did nothing about the more important issue of the interval between circuits.

[2] The relevant points are noted by Luard as a change of hand (*Chron. Maj.*, ii, pp. 592*n.*, 595*n.*).

He then squeezed in the appropriate sections of the 1215 charter, thus introducing Chapters 10, 11, 12, 14, 15, 25 and 27.[1] He also added Chapter 42 at the foot of the first column on Folio 39, and made small amendments throughout the whole text, some of which were derived from the 1215 charter.[2] His new text thus included the 1215 provisions on debts to the Jews, on aids, on municipal privileges, on the summoning of the great council, on increments, intestacy and free entry into, and exit from, the kingdom. He selected his additions deliberately. Of the chapters he excluded some were in the St Albans *forma securitatis*,[3] some were of temporary significance only,[4] and some dealt with the forest which was covered in the St Albans version by the Charter of the Forest.[5] Only one chapter is missing which we might reasonably expect to be included: Chapter 45, which provides that justices etc. should be chosen from those who know the law of the land.

The scribe of V tried to solve the problem differently. V_2 shows that he realized that Henry's and John's charters were different; in this he had an advantage over Matthew Paris. But he was no more certain than Matthew about the relative authority of the different versions. In V_1 he followed the *b* versions, or a closely similar exemplar, up to Chapter 17 without including any of the newly available 1215 material; thereafter he turned to the 1215 text and followed that almost exclusively, to end correctly with the authentic *forma securitatis*, corroboration and dating

[1] He also amended the text of cap. 13 which incorporates both the *tam per terras quam per aquas* of 1215 and the *barones de Quinque Portubus et omnes* of 1217 and 1225.

[2] Cap. 6, Paris adds in the margin *ita tamen . . . ipsius heredis*; cap. 7, Paris corrects *homagio* to *maritagio* partly over an erasure, partly in the margin; cap. 20, Paris cancels *per* and puts *propter* in the margin; cap. 27, Paris writes *Nos non tenebimus* over erasure; cap. 29, Paris adds *aut exulet* in the margin; cap. 30, Paris inserts *et morari et ire tam* in the margin; cap. 31, l.5, Paris interlines *baronia*; cap. 33, Paris adds *antiquam* in the margin; cap. 35, lines 12–13, Paris adds *et quod . . . consuevit* in the margin.

[3] Cc. 50, 51.

[4] Cc. 49, 52, 55, 56, 57, 58, 59.

[5] Cc. 44, 47, 48, 53. Opposite the appropriate point in the text where Paris could have followed cap. 31 of the 1217 and 1225 charters (cap. 43 of the 1215 charter) with cap. 44 of the 1215 charter, he added in the margin *Homines qui manent extra forestam verte hoc folium*, this reference being to his text of the Charter of the Forest.

clause of 1215. Hence, unlike Matthew, he included all the chapters of temporary significance, the chapters concerning the forest, and he had the chapter concerning foreigners in the correct form and the right place. It is an example Matthew might have followed, but by now Matthew was in a rut. He, too, took a hand in $V1$, where he added in the margins the 1215 version of the end of Chapters 5 and 6,[1] and the whole of Chapters 10, 11, 12, 14, 15 and 18 of the 1215 charter. He worked a little more accurately here than in his amendments to B, but neither he nor the scribe of V obliterated the evidence of the initial dependence on a. This version is a patchwork with a lot of patches.

Most of the blame for what happened at St Albans must be carried by Matthew Paris. Wendover, it is true, had left incorrect texts and made the misleading assertion that John's and Henry's charters were the same; but, unlike Wendover, Matthew had the authentic text of 1215, and in V he had reasonable versions of the charters of Henry III. Wendover made do with a little; Matthew was confused by abundance and by his own prejudices and preconceptions. On this topic, Wendover emerges as the sounder writer, perhaps through no quality of his own, perhaps simply because he was closer to the events he was describing, and had not accumulated the prejudiced anachronisms expressed in Matthew's approach to the reign of John. Conversely it follows that Matthew had the better sources. Even though he was writing thirty years after the event, he was able to add to the St Albans chronicle a considerable body of fact which Wendover had not used and which was presumably not available at St Albans in his day. Matthew's surrender to prejudice should not obscure this important contribution.

In what form and how did the St Albans writers obtain their material? Their mistakes suggest that they had access to very few authentic originals. It is certain that they had one: the confirmation of 1253. It is possible that they also had the re-issue of 1225, for St Albans was the obvious deposit for the Hertfordshire copy, and an accurate text was used in $V2$. It is improbable that they had an authentic original of 1215 at the time of issue; Hertfordshire is not listed among the counties to which copies were sent,

---

[1] There are also additions to cap. 4, *et si dederimus . . . de feodo illo*, which is omitted in all the *b* versions, and to cap. 5, *et waynagiis . . . poterunt sustinere*. These are less certainly the work of Matthew Paris.

and it was not until after the composition of the relevant sections
of *B* that the full text was first used. At certain points they may
have had access to drafts of the official documents. Many of the
characteristics which the *a* version shares with Guisborough
could very easily have been produced in a draft of the 1225
charter. This possibility, first suggested by Professor Rothwell,[1]
is strengthened by the fact that almost all the minor 1217 variants
in *a* and Guisborough are also found in the version of the 1225
charter in the Red Book of the Exchequer.[2] Similarly, the St
Albans version of the *forma securitatis*, with its provisions for the
custody of castles, looks like a rejected draft of the authentic
forma of 1215.[3] However, the deepest impression of the evidence
is that there was a great deal of circulating and copying of texts
and fragments, particularly of the 1217 and 1225 charters, which
resulted in a number of unofficial, conflated versions—hence the
existence of the St Albans, Guisborough and Dublin texts, all of
which preserve the two charters of Henry in slightly different
proportions. Most of the larger houses must have had a rag-bag
of assorted documents, only some of which were copied into
registers, even if few can have competed with the materials which
Matthew Paris accumulated.

   In this light, it is only too easy to imagine possible sources
which Roger and Matthew could have tapped, and it becomes
hazardous to raise any one possibility above the rest. In Wendover's case we know too little; in Paris's case we know too much,
for his sources included Hubert de Burgh, Peter des Roches and
Alexander of Swereford, through whom he obtained copies of
Treasury documents;[4] any one of these might have been able to
provide him with the material he acquired on the events of 1215.
However, this material included not only the charter, but also

---

[1] *The Chronicle of Walter of Guisborough*, p. 168n.

[2] The Red Book version shares all the variants noted above, p. 70, nn. 6–7,
except *solverint* in cap. 8. It also shares other minor features with *V*2 and
Guisborough, *e.g.* cap. 1, l.5, *etiam et dedimus*; cap. 12, l.4, *mittet*; cap. 15,
l.2, *ab antiquo*; cap. 29, l.2, om. *aliquo*. However, it has the correct reading
centum libras in cap. 2, and contains characteristic errors of its own not
shared by any of the *b*, *V* or Guisborough versions. This text is collated in
Statutes of the Realm, i, pp. 22–25.

[3] See J. C. Holt, *The Northerners* (Oxford, 1961), pp. 116–18. *Cf.* H. R.
Luard in *Chron. Maj.*, ii, pp. xxxiv–vi.

[4] Vaughan, *op. cit.*, pp. 11–18.

the list of the twenty-five barons and a list of those who swore at Runnymede to obey the orders of the Twenty-Five.[1] This points to a source very closely involved in the settlement of 1215 and its enforcement, and there is one possible informant who has not so far been considered as one of Matthew's sources, namely, Elias of Dereham, canon of Salisbury, who died in 1245 and who had been steward successively of Hubert Walter, Stephen Langton and Edmund of Abingdon.[2]

Elias was very thoroughly involved in the events of 1215. After Runnymede he distributed copies of the charter and the accompanying writ to various shires;[3] he had presumably been present with his master at Runnymede. He continued to serve Stephen Langton until the latter's death, and then reappeared in the service of Edmund of Abingdon.[4] Thus, in addition to his own memories and resources, he could also tap the archives of the archbishopric. There are scattered, tantalizing indications of a link between Elias and Matthew. Elias must, at times, have been a reasonably close neighbour, for he was rector of Harrow. Matthew knew something about him; he noted his death,[5] and in the *Historia Anglorum* mentioned him with Walter of Colchester, sacrist of St Albans, as one of the designers of the new shrine of St Thomas at Canterbury;[6] thus Elias' building interests brought him into touch with a St Albans monk. Matthew used Elias at least once, for he included a diagram of the four winds 'secundum magistrum Elyam de Dereham' in the *Liber Additamentorum*.[7] Elias may explain why Matthew had texts which Wendover failed to use, and why he had such exact and detailed information on events at Runnymede. He may also explain other features of

[1] *Chron. Maj.*, ii, pp. 604–6. These lists are in Matthew's current hand and were probably written before his amendments to the body of the text in *B*.

[2] For Elias's career, see F. M. Powicke, *Stephen Langton* (Oxford, 1928); Kathleen Major, 'The Familia of Archbishop Stephen Langton', *Eng. Hist. Rev.*, xlviii (1933), pp. 529–53, and her *Acta Stephani Langton* (Oxford, 1949); A. Hamilton Thompson, 'Master Elias of Dereham and the King's Works', *The Archaeol. Journal*, xcviii (1941), pp. 1–35; C. H. Lawrence, *St Edmund of Abingdon* (Oxford, 1960), pp. 141–42; J. C. Russell, 'The Many-sided Career of Master Elias of Dereham', *Speculum*, v (1930), pp. 378–87.

[3] *Rot. Litt. Pat.*, p. 180^b.   [4] Lawrence, *op. cit.*, pp. 141–42.

[5] *Chron. Maj.*, iv, p. 418.   [6] *Historia Anglorum*, ii, p. 242.

[7] *Chron. Maj.*, vi, p. 465.

Matthew's story, such as the account of Hubert Walter's speech on John's accession, which, like the new information on 1215, was inserted by Matthew in the margins of *B*.[1]

Elias is an interesting possibility, but no more. He died in 1245. The handwriting of Matthew's insertions in the margins of *B* suggests, on Dr Vaughan's analysis,[2] that the new material was incorporated several years after this, probably *c.* 1250 or later. Furthermore there is no evidence of a direct link between the St Albans chronicles and the archiepiscopal records. The only hint of such lies in the fact that *V* and the thirteenth-century archiepiscopal register, Lambeth MS. 1212, both contain versions of the charter of Henry I of the type which Liebermann classed as a London forgery.[3] Here St Albans and the archiepiscopal archives were dependent, directly or indirectly, on a common source.

Matthew Paris collected his material with the instinct of a magpie. It is easy to erect theories explaining why he knew more about the crisis of 1215 than Wendover had known, but the answer may simply be that he was a little more energetic than his predecessor in examining the contents of the sacks, chests and presses at St Albans. Matthew was almost indefatigable; if Dr Vaughan is right, he died in harness.[4] Such a seeker of sources deserves admiration, but it is important not to distort his activity, or give him a 'record-consciousness' which he did not share. As I have shown, he preserved an original used in the confirmation of 1253. On its dorse someone other than Matthew entered a copy of letters of Innocent IV empowering Hugh of Northwold, bishop of Ely, to enforce reforming statutes on the Benedictine monks.[5]

---

[1] *Ibid.*, ii, pp. 454–55.

[2] The handwriting of the *B* text of Magna Carta and of the later amendments is illustrated in R. Vaughan, 'The Handwriting of Matthew Paris', *Trans. Cambridge Bibl. Soc.*, v (1953), plate xvi(*c*).

[3] F. Liebermann, 'The Text of Henry I's Coronation Charter', *Trans. Roy. Hist. Soc.*, New Series, viii (1894), pp. 21–48. Lambeth MS. 1212 contains two copies, the earlier at pp. 187–88 and the later at pp. 17–18. Both are derived from the same text. The main difference between these and the *V* text is in cap. 11, where *V* follows the Red Book and London versions: *ut sicut benignitas mea propensior est in eis, ita mihi fideliores sint.* This passage is omitted in Lambeth 1212. It should be noted that the *V* text of this charter is different from that copied by Wendover and Paris in their chronicles.

[4] Vaughan, *op. cit.*, pp. 7–11.

[5] *Chron. Maj.*, vi, pp. 234–35, 523. It is worth noting that Hugh of

Matthew himself entered two notes on the dorse, one concerning the death of Emperor Frederick II and the other about the battle of Walcheren of 1253.[1] A blank piece of parchment was still a useful space for memoranda, even if it had Magna Carta on the other side. The thirteenth century saw Magna Carta deeply engraved on English political life; but it was in this casual manner that some of the vital documents were transmitted to later generations.

Northwold was among the bishops present at Westminster on 13 May 1253, when sentence of excommunication was pronounced against transgressors of the charters (Rymer, *Foedera*, I.i.289). Matthew may well have derived this copy of the charter from him. Hugh died in Aug. 1254.

[1] *Chron. Maj.*, vi, pp. 252–55, 523n.

13

MAGNA CARTA AND THE ORIGINS OF STATUTE LAW

Magna Carta was the first English statute. It was the oldest and most venerable item in the manuscript collections of statutes of the thirteenth and fourteenth centuries. It was the first item in the printed collection of statutes of the sixteenth century. It was treated with special veneration by antiquarians, lawyers and statesmen in the seventeenth century. It has never lost its primacy. " Magna Charta, the Petition of Right, and the Bill of Rights, form that code which I call the Bible of the English Constitution ", declaimed Lord Chatham (1). It remained as the foundation stone of that code until eroded by utilitarian law reform in the nineteenth century (2).

The Charter owes its fame to this long history. It comprised two processes: one political and constitutional, the other legal. Each has received its fair share of attention. Dr. Faith Thompson and others have traced the political importance of the Charter from the thirteenth to the seventeenth century (3). Maitland, McIlwain, Plucknett, Professor Thorne and Mr. Gough have discussed the Charter as law: its relationship to later statute, to parliamentary sovereignty and judicial review; and the extent to which it came to be regarded as a fundamental statute or written statement of fundamental common law (4). The two processes

---

(1) Speech on the state of the Nation, House of Lords, 22 January 1770; *Parliamentary History*, XVI, p. 748. I owe the reference to the kindness of Mr. E.A. Smith.

(2) The Statute Law Revision Act of 1863 is of special importance.

(3) FAITH THOMPSON, *The First Century of Magna Carta*, Minnesota, 1925, *Magna Carta*, Minnesota 1948; DORIS M. STENTON, *After Runnymede, Magna Carta in the Middle Ages*, University Press of Virginia 1965; MAURICE ASHLEY, *Magna Carta in the Seventeenth Century*, University Press of Virginia 1965; W.H. DUNHAM, *Magna Carta and British Constitutionalism* in *The Great Charter*, intr. E.N. Griswold, New York 1965; Sir HERBERT BUTTERFIELD, *Magna Carta in the historiography of the sixteenth and seventeenth centuries*, University of Reading 1969.

(4) F. POLLOCK and F.W. MAITLAND, *History of English Law*, Cambridge, 1911, i. pp. 78ff; C.H. MCILWAIN, *Magna Carta and the Common Law* in *Magna Carta Commemoration Essays*, ed. H.E. MALDEN, London 1917, 122-79; T.F.T. PLUCKNETT, *Statutes and their interpretation in the first half of the fourteenth century*, Cambridge 1922, 26-31, *Concise History of*

were complementary; but for the interaction between the two, the Charter could scarcely have survived for as long as it did. It is unlikely that it would have become part of the law of the land in the thirteenth century, enforceable and enforced in the courts, but for the re-issues and confirmations which the recurrent political crises of the period brought about. Conversely it is unlikely that it would have retained much political force in the fourteenth century had it not been for the special regard which it enjoyed as an expression of law. It had nothing to say about the great issues of the time, about the control of the royal council or household, about the exercise of patronage or the management of finance as they had now developed (5). Yet it had become so deeply rooted in the law that it was able to sustain much of the legal and political thinking of this period (6). It was already a political cliché. Acts could now be condemned as contrary to " law, reason and the Great Charter " (7).

These and later phases of the Charter's history are well known. It nevertheless remains extraordinary that a document which was in origin a grant of feudal or communal liberties, an ineffective peace agreement which " had first an obscure birth from usurpation and was secondly fostered and shewed to the world by rebellion " (8), should have come to play such a role. That

---

the Common Law, London 1948, 318-20; S. THORNE, *Dr. Bonham's Case* in *Law Quarterly Review*, LIV 1938, 543-52; J.W. GOUGH, *Fundamental Law in English Constitutional History*, Oxford 1961, 12-29.

(5) The Charter was not mentioned at all in the articles of deposition of Edward II (*Foedera*, ii. 650). *Nullus liber homo* was advanced in cap. 44 of the articles of deposition of Richard II to counter his use of the Marshalsea (*Rotuli Parilamentorum*, iii. 420).

(6) Hence trial by peers and due process of law both sprang from of were grafted onto the original principles of *nullus liber homo* expressed in cap. 39 (1215). See FAITH THOMPSON, *Magna Carta*, 68-97.

(7) See the charge against Hugh Despenser the Younger in 1326 that the condemnation of Thomas, earl of Lancaster, had been secured " par un faux record contre ley et reson et la grante chartre ", G.A. HOLMES, *The Judgement on the Younger Despenser 1326* in *English Historical Review*, LXX 1955, 264. Cf. FAITH THOMPSON, *op. cit.*, 72-8.

(8) *The Prerogative of Parliaments*, first printed 1628, attributed to Sir Walter Ralegh, *Harleian Miscellany*, London 1810, v. 196. The reference to usurpation is to that of Henry I as well as that of John, the argument being that the consequent weakness of their position forced them to make concessions, which as a result were *de facto* and not *de iure*. This pamphlet is unusual in that it emphasises the derivation of Magna Carta from the Charter of Henry I; hence it states that Henry I first granted Magna Carta and the Charter of the Forest, *ibid.* 195.

the Charter was politically important in the thirteenth century is readily explicable. It is less easy to understand why men continued to flog Magna Carta into action time and again rather than change to a less antiquated vehicle for political and constitutional protest. There were alternatives: the Provisions of 1258-9 and their subsequent statutory expression in the Statute of Marlborough, the Ordinances of 1311, and later the Petition of Right and the Bill of Rights. Some of these were evanescent; none replaced Magna Carta as the torch of English liberties. The explanation seems to lie in the peculiar respect which the Charter enjoyed as law. But how was it that this particular document rather than any other came to enjoy such respect? It is with this question that the following pages are concerned and with a particular part of the answer which has not perhaps been given the importance it deserves.

At first sight there would seem to be a ready and easy explanation. The force of precedent, it might run, depended on antiquity; hence the older and more venerable the document the better, and hence the continuing prestige and influence of the Charter. This carries some weight. The Charter was the *fons et origo* on which " the whole of the constitutional history of England " was a " commentary " (9). But there is an important objection. Magna Carta was not the first of such documents. Throughout the twelfth century the charter of liberties of Henry I lay readily accessible in cathedral and monastic repositaries (10). There is no indication that it had the slightest political or legal importance at this time. It even remained infertile in the rich soil of the anarchy of Stephen. It was confirmed by Henry II, perhaps to indicate that royal concessions, like royal rights, were to be derived from his grandfather's reign and not from Stephen's, but it was not until the onset of the movement which culminated at Runnymede that men turned to it as a precedent for the new charter which they were seeking from King John. Only then, and only for a few years at the

----

(9) *Stubbs' Select Charters*, 9th edn., ed. H.W.C. DAVIS, Oxford 1921, 291. The phrase was Stubbs's own; cf. 8th edn., Oxford 1900, 296.

(10) F. LIEBERMANN, *The Text of Henry I's Coronation Charter* in *Transactions of the Royal Historical Society*, new ser., VIII 1894, 21-48; J.C. HOLT, *Magna Carta*, Cambridge 1965, 300.

most, did it play a role similar to that of its greater successor.

Hence Magna Carta was not the oldest possible precedent for the embodiment of law in an act of self-limitation by the Crown.● Essentially it derived its importance not from its antiquity but from its coincidence as a grant of liberties with the formative period of English legal development. It was concerned specifically with the operation of the legal machinery devised under Henry II and his sons; with the sessions of the central and local courts, with the relationship between royal and seignorial justice, with the legal powers of bailiffs and the legal qualifications of the King's justices and officials (11). In wider terms it sought to establish general principles of judicial procedure and financial administration which in effect created or affirmed substantive law (12). But this is not the whole story. The Charter was soon seen to enjoy a very special relationship to statute law. It was included as an essential item in the collections of statutes; the charter of Henry I was not, nor for that matter were the Assizes of Henry II (13); Henry I's charter was too early for such success, Henry II's assizes too concerned with procedural matters. This was not simply accidental. To understand it, it is essential to examine how the documents of 1215-7 were drafted.

The programme of these years can be traced in remarkable detail from the so-called " unknown " charter, which embodies the charter of Henry I, through the Articles of the Barons, to the four successive versions of the Charter of 1215, 1216, 1217 and 1225. The first important comparisons for the present purpose lie between the Articles and the Charter of Runnymede. Many of the differences between the two may be described as political. They involve some of the major issues about which the King and the barons were quarrelling (14). It may be assumed that they represent the work of the King, his advisers

---

(11) Caps. 17, 18, 19, 34, 38, 45 (1215).

(12) Eg. cap. 2 on reliefs, caps. 20-22 on amercements, cap. 39 *nullus liber homo* (1215).

(13) The Assize of the Forest, however, survived in collections of forest documents. See *The Sherwood Forest Books*, ed. HELEN E. BOULTON, Thoroton Society, Record Series, XXIII 1964, 59-62.

(14) J.C. HOLT, *The Making of Magna Carta* in *English Historical Review*, LXXII 1957, 403, *Magna Carta*, 161-2, 195-6. See above, p. 219.

and those negotiating for the barons; some certainly were determined by Stephen Langton and the bishops, for the Articles specifically referred some issues to them for resolution (15). However, there are many differences which cannot reasonably be
placed in this " political " category. In chapter after chapter
the Charter contains changes which simply amount to improvements in drafting. There are some forty amendments of this
kind all told (16). For example, cap. 2 makes clear that the
provisions about reliefs apply to tenants holding by military
service; cap. 5 indicates that the stock and crops on an heir's
land will vary with the season of the year; cap. 9 provides that
guarantors of a debt shall be responsible for payment if the debtor
should default; cap. 24 excludes constables, coroners and bailiffs,
as well as sheriffs, from holding pleas of the Crown; cap. 26 makes
it clear that sheriffs or other officers of the Crown must present
royal letters patent when summoning for payment of the debts
of a dead tenant-in-chief; cap. 33 excludes the sea-coast from
the prohibition of fish-weirs. Such amendments clarified points
already made in the Articles, or followed up their logical implications, or closed up escape-routes which the Articles had

---

(15) Articles of the Barons, caps. 25, 37, 45, 46.

(16) In the following list the precise amendment is only indicated where it is not immediately apparent from a comparison of the appropriate chapters. It does not include alterations of political importance or purely formal changes arising from the conversion of a petition into a charter.

Caps.	
2 (*Si quis... fuerit*)	39
5 (*secundum quod tempus...*)	40
9 *bis*	41 (*de Anglia... aquam*)
11 *quater*	42 (*salvo... aquam*)
16 *bis*	43
23	44
24	46
25	49 *ter*
26 *bis*	50 (correction of names)
27	51
29	52 *ter* (*legali, parium suorum; de... pacis; vel... suorum*)
33	55 *quater*
36	56 *bis*
37 *ter*	61 (*qui presentes fuerint*)
38	

left open, or made necessary exceptions which the Articles had
omitted. The total effect was to convert a petition into a watertight legal enactment. The work was well done. The Charter
was considerably amended in the re-issues of 1216 and 1217,
but all but a very few of these later changes were concerned with
more than drafting and clarification (17). There are also some
more extensive additions in the 1215 Charter which yet may
have been matters of drafting. Cap. 19 provides that knights
and free tenants shall remain in the shire court to determine
possessory assizes which cannot be completed on a single day.
Cap. 41 restricts the free movement of merchants in time of war,
and cap. 42 excepts prisoners, outlaws and enemy aliens from
the general guarantee of unimpeded entry to or exit from the
realm.

A comparison of the arrangement of the Articles and the
Charter tells the same story. The logical order of the Articles
is frequently weak or obscure; some items seem to have occurred
as afterthoughts; an amendment was made in the text to caps. 45
and 46, and space was left between the list of petitions and the
forma securitatis in which further addenda could have been inserted. The Charter makes a much better job of it. Chapter 5
of the Articles is concerned with baronial debts, chapter 6 with
the lord's right to levy an aid; the logical connection, if any,
lies in the fact that tenants-in-chief sometimes obtained permission to levy an aid from their tenants in order to pay their
debts. The Charter, in contrast, moves from cap. 9, which is
equivalent to cap. 5 of the Articles, to the consideration of debts
owed to the Jews in caps. 10 and 11. It then turns in caps. 12
and 14 to consider other financial matters, namely the levying
of aids, and the subject of cap. 6 of the Articles is only approached
in cap. 15 after the larger issue of royal aids has been settled.
Hence material arranged as cap. 5, 34, 35, 32, 6 in the Articles
was brought into a more logical order as caps. 9, 10, 11, 12, 13,
14, 15, in the Charter. There are other similar adjustments of
order. Cap. 17 of the Articles, concerned with the remarriage
of widows, was rearranged alongside cap. 4, concerned with widows'

---

(17) The 1216 version contains minor improvements in drafting in cap. 9. The 1217
version, cap. 28, replaces the simple *ad legem* of the 1215 version with the more precise *ad
legem manifestam vel ad juramentum*. It also gives clearer definition to disseisin in cap. 29.

dower, in caps. 7 and 8 of the Charter. The final clause of cap. 35 of the Articles was correctly associated with the provisions on custody in cap. 3, in caps. 4, 5 and 6 of the Charter. Cap. 13, concerned with the possessory assizes, was also correctly associated with cap. 8, in caps. 17, 18 and 19 of the Charter.

Not all the changes in order seem logical; that indeed could scarcely be expected from the circumstances of discussion and argument at Runnymede where much of the work was done. Here and there the Articles present a better order. Caps. 37 and 38, for example, associate the pardoning of unjust fines and amercements with the restoration of hostages and charters of fealty. The connection is obvious, for King John had demanded hostages and charters to guarantee the payment of fines and amercements. In the Charter, in contrast, the logic is broken, or rather replaced by another. Cap. 37 of the Articles was now associated with cap. 25, concerned with unjust disseisins, and with caps. 44, 45 and 46, which dealt with lands liberties, charters and hostages taken from the Welsh and Scots. They were now reorganised in a comprehensive and expanded set of provisions in caps. 52, 53 and 55-9 of the Charter. These chapters had one thing in common in addition to their concern with restitution in one form or another: all involved judgement by the Archbishop and his advisers. Cap. 38 of the Articles did not; hence it came to be separated from its proper context. In this instance the processes of political argument produced a new pattern. These chapters from part of a larger group, caps. 48-53 and 55-59, all of which appear at the end of the document because they only reached final form after discussions which took place between the preliminary and final agreement. When drafting began the earlier chapters were probably agreed, but these were still under debate (18).

---

(18) The forty-day limit inserted in cap. 48 is related to the similar limit in cap. 61, which in the Articles had been stated loosely as *infra rationabile tempus determinandum in rta*. It is worth recalling that the final section of cap. 48 appears as an addition at the foot of the parchment in two originals of the Charter, Ci and Cii, J.C. HOLT, *Magna Carta*, 313, 328n.

The provisions on foreigners (caps. 50,51) do not as they stand reflect extended argument intervening between the Articles and the Charter. However, much more radical demands on this point were in the air; see the St. Albans' version of the Charter, J.C. HOLT, *The Northerners*, Oxford 1961, 116-8.

Such political pressures are only rarely discernible in the documents. In their arrangement as in their content, they also reflect a workaday sensible improvement, which cannot very easily have resulted from the confusion and heat of negotiation. For immediate political purposes many of these changes were irrelevant. They are administrative in conception and objective; they indicate a determination that there should be no shabby or slipshod drafting, whatever the political origin and impact of the documents; they are the product of experienced and skilful secretarial effort. Painter, who discussed many of these changes, considered that " they may well have been made by the drafters on their own authority " (19), and indeed such a conclusion is inescapable. The Chancery clerks sought to produce in Magna Carta a document as well drafted and as watertight as any other issuing from their office. Their finished work was not perfect the extent and miscellaneous nature of the settlement scarcely permitted this. Moreover, the difficulty of securing agreement between the negotiating parties sometimes produced vague solutions as essential parts of the settlement (20). But on the whole the result was a document which made legal sense and was enforceable at law.

However, the argument cannot be left at that. It would be quite inadequate simply to maintain that the major change in the documents were political in content and were the work of the baronial leaders or the King and his advisers, and that the minor changes were the work of the Chancery clerks. The attitudes revealed by the amendments are more important than their origin. No doubt one or other of the barons, even perhaps the King, may have pointed to the need for an improvement in drafting. It is also possible that a question arising in the minuting or drafting of the documents provoked or contributed to an argument about content. Moreover, between the improvements in drafting on the one hand and the politically significant amendments on the other, there were changes which scarcely fit either category. For example, the amendments which dealt with the stock on a ward's lands in cap. 5, or laid down in cap. 26 that royal officers must present letters patent in summoning debtors

---

(19) *The Reign of King John*, Baltimore 1949, 316-7.

(20) J.C. HOLT, *Magna Carta*, 206ff.

of the Crown, or excluded the sea-coast from the provisions concerning weirs in cap. 33, or made the exceptions to freedom of travel in caps. 41 and 42, cannot have raised much political dust. Nor were they simply matters of drafting. They would appear rather to spring from minds familiar with the operations of government, minds which were carefully considering how the Charter would be enforced in practice. If the major changes can be attributed to the negotiating parties, and the minor changes to the clerks of the Chancery, these would seem to be the work of men who shared experience as barons of the Exchequer, as justices or as lesser officials of the king's court.

An attitude reasonably attributable to such men is represented more and more emphatically in the successive versions of the Charter. It is reflected not only in the amendments noted above, but also much more strikingly in the addition of entirely new provisions not directly related to the political crisis of 1215. Cap. 54 of the 1215 Charter — " No one shall be taken or imprisoned upon the appeal of a woman for the death of anyone except her husband " — provides the first obvious example. It had no apparent political relevance (21); it merely confirmed existing law (22); the reason for its inclusion is not apparent, and it still puzzles commentators (23). It remains puzzling,

---

(21) There is no evidence that appeals of this kind were a serious baronial grievance. Note, however, that Robert de Vaux, a baron of limited consequence but a classic illustration of John's victimisation of his vassals, offered five palfreys in 1210 for the King to " keep quiet about the wife of Henry Pinel ", *Pipe Roll 12 John,* 139.

(22) F. POLLOCK and F.W. MAITLAND, *History of English Law,* i. 485.

(23) MAITLAND was characteristically cautious, *loc. cit.* McKECHNIE's analysis of the chapter is vitiated by his assumption that the barons were responsible for its insertion, *Magna Carta,* Glasgow 1914, 451-3. However, he did note that " it restricts explicitly not appeals, but arrest and imprisonment following on appeal ", *op. cit.,* 453, n. 5. PAINTER's comment was that it " would seem to be intended to make rape less hazardous, but that can hardly have been its chief purpose ", *op. cit.,* 318. The reference to rape is quite irrelevant; indeed, on a literal interpretation the chapter limits legal process in cases of homicide but leaves it less restricted in cases of rape. Dr. WARREN suggests that the object was to limit a woman's right to appoint a proxy in an appeal of felony, *King John,* 2nd edn., Penguin Books, 1966, 296, n. 1. The chapter does not say this. Moreover, Dr. WARREN does not substantiate his claim that before the limitation imposed by this chapter " the possibilities of abuse were great ". McKechnie noted several cases in which before 1215 the courts ruled against attempts to extend a woman's right of appeal in cases of homicide, *op. cit.* 453, n. 4. Cap. 54 simply restated the grounds of appeal described by Glanville, book. xiv, c. 3, ed. G.D.G. HALL, London 1965, 174-5. It does not therefore impose new limitations.

for it is impossible to say who inserted it and why. But its difficulties are much reduced if it is accepted that it was inspired
by administrative and legal attitudes of which this was the first
obvious expression. Similar insertions were made in later versions of the Charter. In 1216 cap. 3 was thoroughly revised:
a lord was to take the heir's homage before he could enjoy custody
of an estate; the age of majority was now defined as twenty-one;
and the lord's custody was to extend until this term even if the
heir became a knight. These were points all in need of clarification. It is not surprising that the new provision was made
during a royal minority. Similarly the circumstances of civil
war are likely to have contributed to the extension of cap. 7
to provide an alternative house for a widow whose husband had
died seized of a castle, and to the more precise regulation of rights
of prise in caps. 19 and 21. Nevertheless these were treated as
routine amendments distinct from the *capitula... gravia et dubitabilia* which were set apart for later discussion.

This trickle of new material acquired much greater momen-
tum in 1217. The provisions on prises were further amended
to extend the period of payment (24). The widow's dower was
given its customary definition as a third of her husband's property (25). Cap. 31 laid down that the Crown's tenure of escheats
did not establish a right of prerogative wardship, thus settling
a possible difficulty which caps. 37 and 43 of the original Charter
had left undefined. The provisions of 1215 dealing with possessory assizes were also thoroughly revised (26). Cap. 35 introduced
regulations which had not appeared in the Charters hitherto
for the session of shire and hundred courts. Cap. 32 introduced
the problem of the sale of land which resulted in the loss of services to the vendor's lord, and cap. 36 forbade collusive alienation
in free alms. Both these provisions were new; both were starting

---

(24) Cap. 19.

(25) Cap. 7. Cf. Glanville, book vi, c. i, ed. G.D.G. HALL, 58-9; F. POLLOCK and F.W
MAITLAND, *op. cit.*, ii. 420-22.

(26) Cap. 12 reduced judicial visits to the shire from four to once per year. Cf. cap. 1
of the 1215 version. In place of the cumbersome arrangements of the 1215 charter, cap. 1º
for the continued session of the county court, it arranged for excess cases to be postpone
to a later point in the eyre. Cap. 13 removed cases of darrein presentment from the justice
in eyre to the Bench. Cf. cap. 18 of the 1215 Charter.

points for much subsequent legislation. The most striking development of all concerned the royal forest. The Charter of the Forest, now issued for the first time, settled matters already raised in 1215 concerning the extent of the forest and summonses to the forest courts (27). It also laid down points of forest law which were not mentioned at all in the earlier versions of the Charter (28), and it included detailed regulations for the forest courts and forest officials. These, which form the bulk of the document, were only foreshadowed in 1215 by the enquiry into local government, including forests, which was ordered under the terms of cap. 48.

Hence, to sum up, the documents taken as a series reveal a changing administrative concern. It was manifested first in improvements in drafting and arrangement, and in the definition and clarification of the original baronial petitions. It received its final and strongest expression in 1217 with the injection of measures which had not appeared at all in the earlier versions of the Charter. A grant of liberties was used as a vehicle for legislation.

This dual function was implicit in the Charter of 1215 (29). But this was a controversial document. Formally it settled a war; in fact it started a new one. Administrative concern was not the exclusive property of one political or professional group. The rebel barons may have been able to call on the advice of one of the most experienced judges of the time, Simon of Pattishall, when drafting the first Charter (30). During the civil war a number of royal administrators, Reginald of Cornhill, Hugh de Neville, Peter fitz Herbert, John fitz Hugh, and even some of the great earls in the King's party, Salisbury, Arundel and Warenne, moved over for a time to the rebel cause. Among the rebels, Saer de Quenci, earl of Winchester, had been a baron of the Exchequer. Others, Robert de Ros, William de Albini,

---

(27) Charter of the Forest, caps. 1,2,3. Cf. *Magna Carta* (1215), caps. 44,47,53.

(28) Some however, appear in the "unknown" charter, caps. 10 and 12, J.C. Holt, *Magna Carta*, 303.

(29) See above pp. 292-297.

(30) Simon of Pattishall seems to have been suspect and may possibly have sided with the rebels between May and December 1215. He was acting as a royal justice at the end of March 1216, *Rotuli Litterarum Patentium*, 138, *Rotuli Litterarum Clausarum*, i. 200, 244, 270.

Thomas of Moulton, Robert de Percy, Simon of Kyme, had judicial or administrative experience at a lower level of government. However, the experience of the rebels was never directly expressed after 1215. The Charter of 1216 was drawn up in the midst of civil war; that of 1217 within a few weeks of its end (31). Whatever direct or indirect influence the rebel leaders may have had over the political content of these versions, they can scarcely have been responsible for the new and detailed regulations affecting law and legal procedures. The same may be said of the loyalist magnates. William Marshal, Ranulf of Chester, Hubert de Burgh, Peter des Roches and the papal legate, readily appreciated that the reissues of the Charter were means of bringing peace to the land (32). They must have been responsible for the ultimate exclusion of the more debatable chapters of the original charter which were listed as *gravia et dubitabilia* in 1216. But they cannot have paid much attention in 1216 to the definition of wardship, for example, or in 1217 to the detailed organization of hundred courts or possessory assizes. They had their hands full of matters more urgent than the improvement of the local administration of the law. The impetus is much more likely to have come from the justices, from Simon of Pattishall, Roger Huscarl or Henry de Pont-Audemer, from the Chancellor, Richard Marsh, or from rising young clerks of the *curia regis* like Martin of Pattishall (33).

The influence exercised was not that of the canon law. The *volte face* in the papal attitude to the Charter was of great importance to its survival (34). Innocent III annulled the first

---

(31) The Treaty of Kingston with Prince Louis of France was agreed on 12 September 1217. The Charter of 1217 belongs to this date, or much more likely to the Council of Merton of 23 September, or to 6 November, which is the date of the Charter of the Forest, J.C. HOLT, *Magna Carta*, 273, n. 1. The final submission of many of the rebels only came in the last week of October and the first week of November.

(32) See the announcement of the coronation of Henry III and of the reissue of the Charter in letters sent to Ireland, *Foedera*, I, pt. i, 145, *Stubbs' Charters*, 333-5.

(33) For the early career of Martin of Pattishall and his association with Simon of Pattishall see *Rolls of the Justices in Eyre for Lincolnshire 1218-9 and Worcestershire 1221*, ed. DORIS M. STENTON, Selden Society, LIII 1934, xvi-xviii and *Rolls of the Justices in Eyre for Yorkshire 1218-19*, Selden Society, LVI 1937, xxi-xxiii. Like Simon of Pattishall he seems to have been suspect in June 1215, *Rotuli Litterarum Patentium*, 142b.

(34) This has rightly been re-emphasised by Professor V.H. GALBRAITH, *Runnymede*

Charter; the papal legate, Guala, along with William Marshal sealed the re-issues of 1216 and 1217, and Guala himself may well have drafted the letters announcing King Henry's coronation and the first re-issue (35). This change in papal policy was permanent. In 1254 Pope Innocent IV confirmed the *sententia lata* of 1253 (36), and in its interventions in the quarrel between Henry III and his barons the Curia accepted the Charters as lawful concessions now beyond recall (37). But this change of heart had little effect in the documents. Ecclesiastical pressure probably lay behind some of the changes in the new versions. In 1216 the provisions against " wasting " were extended to ecclesiastical lands in custody (38). In 1216 and 1217 the provision governing the amercement of clerks was improved to emphasise that lay fee alone, not ecclesiastical benefice, was to be assessed (39). The Charter of 1217 also protected carts of ecclesiastics, along with those of knights, from seizure by royal bailiffs (40). But all this lay within the framework of common law. Moreover, the new provision against collusive alienation in free alms, reveals that the tide was not running entirely in the Church's favour. The documents as a whole fail to reveal an increasing influx of concepts derived from canon law. Indeed the opposite is true. In the Articles of the Barons the Archbishop and his colleagues were required to arbitrate on unjust disseisins and fines, on the rights of the Welsh and Scots, and on the King's claim to crusading privileges (41). They completed their work in a few days.

Revisited in *Proceedings of the American Philosophical Society*, CX 1966, 307-17, and *A Draft of Magna Carta* (1215) in *Proceedings of the British Academy*, LIII 1967, 345-60, especially 359-60. See also C.R. CHENEY, *The Church and Magna Carta* in *Theology*, LXVIII 1965, 266-72.

(35) This was suggested by G.J. TURNER, *The minority of Henry III* in *Transactions of the Royal Historical Society*, new series, XVIII 1904, 255.

(36) *Councils and Synods*, ed. F.M. POWICKE and C.R. CHENEY, Oxford 1964, ii, pt. i. 474 n. 1.

(37) See the letters of Pope Urban IV confirming King Louis IX's award at Amiens, *Foedera*, I pt. 1. 436-7, F.M. POWICKE, *King Henry III and the Lord Edward*, Oxford 1947, 450-3, *Dictum de Kenilworth*, c. 3, *Stubb's Charters*, 408.

(38) Cap. 5.

(39) *Magna Carta*, cap. 22 (1215), cap. 17 (1216), cap. 14 (1217).

(40) Cap. 21.

(41) Caps. 25,37,45,46.

They determined the King's crusading privilege, but the other matters were referred in the Charter to the secular jurisdiction of the Twenty Five barons or of the royal court (42). Archiepiscopal arbitration was only retained in the matter of unjust fines (43), presumably because they might involve pledge of faith. The Articles likewise required written assurances from the Archbishop, the bishops and Pandulf that the King would make no appeal to Rome against the settlement (44). This they could not do; all that remained of the scheme in the Charter were the Letters Testimonial in which they provided an *inspeximus* of the King's grant (45). Their concern to maintain the distinction between canon and secular law and their commitment to the right of appeal to the papal Curia forced them to withdraw from, rather than intrude into, a largely secular agreement. After Langton's ineffective intervention in the summer of 1215, the Church blessed in general rather than interfered in detail (46). It came to owe as much to Magna Carta as the Charter did to the Church. From 1225 it reinforced the Charters with sentences of excommunication, but from Boniface to Pecham it did so increasingly in the hope of procuring a detailed and favourable exposition of the concession of cap. 1 that the Church should be free and hold its rights undiminished (47). In so far as churchmen influenced the changing content of the Charter it was not as canonists but as secular administrators experienced in royal government.

However, the men responsible for the additions to the Charter cannot have been entirely free from external influence. How can they have known what to add? The Charter of the Forest,

---

(42) Caps. 52,53,57,58,59.

(43) Cap. 55.

(44) Articles of the Barons, *forma securitatis*.

(45) Cap. 62.

(46) In 1218 Honorius III intervened on the question of the treaties agreed between John and William the Lion of Scotland, which were in question in cap. 46 of the Articles and cap. 59 of the 1215 Charter. This, however, was at the request of King Alexander II of Scotland, *Royal and other historical Letters illustrative of the reign of Henry III*, ed. W.W. SHIRLEY, Rolls Series 1862, i. 16-7.

(47) See the important paper by J.W. GRAY, *The Church and Magna Carta in the Century after Runnymede* in *Historical Studies*, VI 1968, 23-38. Cf. W. BLACKSTONE, *The Great Charter and The Charter of the Forest*, Oxford 1759, liii-lviii.

the regulations concerned with the hundred courts or with alienation were not conjured out of a hat, especially at a time when the country had scarcely emerged from civil war. The new material subsumes a basis of written information and only one source seems likely: the records of the inquests into local government arranged under cap. 48 of the Charter of 1215. No such records have yet come to light. But it is certain that the enquiries took place (48). An important addition in the final text of the Charter of 1215 laid down that the King or his Justiciar was to be informed before any evil customs were annulled (49). The King must therefore have received reports in the summer of 1215; enough was known of the work of these local inquests for the Archbishop and bishops to seal letters implying that the investigations were threatening the King's lawful rights within his forests (50). Much of the new material in the Charter of 1217, the regulations about assizes, the arrangement of the session of local courts, perhaps also the rules on alienation, and most of the provisions of the Charter of the Forest, are entirely consistent with such a source. The rebels did not direct the revision of the Charter. Nevertheless the complaints made during the inquest of the summer of 1215 in all likelihood provided the information on which those responsible for the revisions acted. There was nothing revolutionary in this, for the inquest of 1215 was a typical operation of Angevin government, attuned on this occasion to novel ends. Civil war had not destroyed the mutual dependence of central government and local community.

Such seems to have been the process of amendment. It presupposed an adequate basis. This the barons had provided in 1215 for they then sought and obtained what was in effect a statement of law. Hence baronial demands and administrative amendment are parts of the same story. But each was essential to the final emergence of the Charter as the great archetype of English legislation. The contribution which the barons had

---

(48) See letters to the sheriffs of 27 June 1215, *Rotuli Litterarum Patentium*, 145b, J.C. HOLT, *Magna Carta*, 347.

(49) The provision was added at the foot of the parchment in two of the originals of the Charter, Ci and Cii.

(50) *Foedera*, I, pt. i. 134, J.C. HOLT, *Magna Carta*, 348-9.

made has been examined elsewhere (51); it is too long a story
to be related in the present argument. The contribution which
government made was this. First, there was a negative achievement: the Charter was not rejected as something alien and inimical
to the effective operation of government. It was absorbed. Secondly, it was used to administrative advantage. It did not
simply survive. It is not enough to say that the Charter owed
its continued existence to papal blessing, a royal minority and
recurrent crises. The definitions of law required in the Articles
of the Barons were so clarified and extended that by 1217 they
underpinned the legal and financial relationships between the
Crown and the community, the working of the assizes, the sessions of shire and hundred and several important points of property law. The Charter of the Forest, even more obviously,
was now the basis on which the rights of landlords and com-
moners, the duties of officials and the functioning of the forest
courts would be determined. The Charters had become as essential to the working of government as they were to the defence
of baronial or communal privilege. Administrators had realised
the potential in the work of barons.

English historians may be tempted to accept this as an easy,
even inevitable, development. In some respects it was; barons
held office; officials held baronies; government and governed
were not at opposite poles of a sharply divided political structure.
But the English liberties were alone in this respect. None of
the continental charter of liberties, the Golden Bull of Hungary
of 1222 and 1231, the Imperial concessions of 1220 and 1231-2,
the Aragonese privileges of 1283 and 1287, the French provincial
charters of 1315, received similar attention. None survived as
the Great Charter did. Instead of being absorbed into the processes of government they contributed to a hardening antithesis
of royal power to feudal, local or communal privilege and to a
sharp distinction between legal enactment and chartered franchise. Royal authority overrode or by-passed them when and
where it could; some lived on only as distantly remembered apo-

---

(51) J.C. HOLT, *The Barons and the Great Charter* in *English Historical Review*, LXX
1955, 1-24. See above, 179-202.

crypha (52). The English Charters stand in striking contrast. English government could not do without them. Henry III, like his continental counterparts, sometimes tried to evade them. But from the earliest days of his majority he also intervened to enforce them. In the first of such instances, in 1225, he was concerned to ensure the equitable execution in Westmorland and Lancashire of the provisions for disafforestation (53). Nine years later, in August and October 1234, he issued letters to the sheriff of Lincolnshire, interpreting the arrangements of cap. 35 of the Charter for the session of the hundred courts. The letters of October were issued with the advice of archbishops, bishops, earls and barons. They were entered on the Close roll under the heading — " De interpretatione clausule contente in libertatibus, qualiter debeat intelligi " (54). Both these matters arose from the additional provisions of 1217.

Documents which were alike in form, did not necessarily spring from like situations or have similar effects. Magna Carta owed its longevity to its coincidence as a grant of liberties with a particular stage in the development of the royal courts, a stage which led barons into accepting and amending the procedures and administration of the law, and justices, administrators and clerks into taking baronial demands seriously by clarifying, amending or adding to them. This explains why Magna Carta survived and Henry I's charter did not; and why Magna Carta became a corner-stone of law, while the continental liberties did not. Magna Carta was not simply a grant of liberties. Its analogues also include the *Carta Caritatis* and the Statute of Pamiers. All three in different ways were founding statutes (55). All three

---

(52) On the apocryphal Aragonese liberties see Ralph A. GIESEY, *If Not, Not*, Princeton 1968.

(53) *Patent Rolls, 1216-25*, 575-6.

(54) *Close Rolls 1231-4*, 588-9.

(55) For the text of the Statute of Pamiers in which Simon de Montfort established laws in his conquests in southern France see C. DE VIC et J.J. VAISSETTE, *Histoire Générale de Languedoc* ed. E. DULAURIER, Toulouse 1872-94, viii. cols. 625-635. Both Simon and his barons swore to observe the provisions, and both the Statute and the shorter document in which Simon established the customs of Paris for his crusading companions who accepted fiefs, were sealed. But although these documents were similar to Magna Carta in these respects, they were not grants of liberties.

For the considerable literature on the *Carta Caritatis* see D.M. KNOWLES, *Great Historical*

demonstrate that, under varying pressures and with widely different objectives, men would legislate.

Hitherto in England legislation had been achieved by the use of royal letters directed to the sheriffs, or by " assizes " embodying instructions to the justices, or much more rarely by publishing written " constitutions ". The Charters combined the advantages of all these earlier methods. They embodied the consent of the great men of the land; through publication in the shire courts they became the best known of all legal enactments; they prescribed administrative and judicial procedures. They established the pattern for legislation by statute. The Provisions of Merton of 1236 were concerned to a great degree with elucidating matters first raised in the Charters (56). They approached the form of a grant of liberties — " it was provided by the aforesaid archbishop, bishops, earls and barons, and conceded by us " (57). Just as new material was added to the Charter in 1216 and 1217, so the Statute of Merton, as eventually enrolled, embodied six extra chapters, some authentic provisions from the years 1234-7, others less clearly so (58). The change was not sudden. The King might still legislate in effect by writ, as in the " statute " of mortmain (59), and lawyers might include documents like the Dictum de Kenilworth in their collections of statutes. Nevertheless, when men looked back, whether from the thirteenth or the seventeenth century, they were generally agreed that Magna Carta was the first statute (60). The consequences were

---

Enterprises, London 1962, 198-224; *The Monastic Order in England*, Cambridge 1963, 752-3. Even more than Magna Carta it underwent repeated revision and expansion.

(56) Caps. 1,2,5, i.e. three out of five chapters in all, refer to matters arising from the Charter, *Statutes of the Realm*, i. 1-4, *Close Rolls 1234-7*, 337-9.

(57) *Close Rolls 1234-7*, 337.

(58) H.G. RICHARDSON and G.O. SAYLES, *The Early Statutes* in *Law Quarterly Review*, L. 1934, 204; F.M. POWICKE, *op. cit.* 148-53, 760-71.

(59) For the miscellaneous methods of legislation employed in the thirteenth century see F. POLLOCK and F.W. MAITLAND, *op. cit.*, i. 180-1, and G.B. ADAMS, *Council and Courts in Anglo-Norman England*, Yale 1926, 324-32.

(60) Some seventeenth-century students of Magna Carta recognised that it was not initially a statute. " Neither was Magna Carta a law in the nineteenth of Henry the Third but simply a Charter; which he confirmed in the twenty-first year of his reign, and made it law in the twenty-fifth, according to Littleton's opinion ". *The Prerogative of Parliaments*, in *Harleian Miscellany*, London 1810, v. 196. The reference should properly be to 25 Edward I,

important. The Charter in its final form was legislation, but as legislation it was also a freely given grant in perpetuity. Hence in Maitland's words it was "the nearest approach to an irrepealable 'fundamental statute' that England has ever had" (61). It confused law and liberties (62). In the thirteenth century it provided lawyers with a vehicle for legislation. In the seventeenth century it gave them a platform for political protest. Each of these roles derived from the confluence of circumstances which determined the Charter's quality in the first decade of its history.

---

not 25 Henry III. I cannot trace the source of this in Littleton. Cf. EDWARD COKE, *First Institute*, section 108.

(61) F. POLLOCK and F.W. MAITLAND, *op. cit.*, i. 173.

(62) "And well may the Lawes of England be called *libertates, quia liberos faciunt*", EDWARD COKE, *First Institute*, section 108. For further study of this point and for the history of the Charter in England since the seventeenth century see ANNE PALLISTER, *The heritage of Liberty*, Oxford 1971.

INDEX

Aaron of Lincoln, 188, 195
Abbé, Ralph l', 43, 46
Abbeville, 59
Abingdon, abbey of, 185; Edmund of, 285
Acre, 248
Agen, bishop of, 31n.
Ainsty, wapentake of, 163
Albini, Philip de, 64; William de, 181n., 299;
    see also Arundel
Alemannus, William, 116n.
Alençon, 60, 61n., 247; John of, 80
Alexander the Mason, 184
Alfred, king, 68
aliens, political significance of, 106-8, 140
Almenesches, 247
Amiens, 56
Amiennois, 37, 60
Angers, 54
Angevin 'empire', revenues of, 35-8, 43-4, 65;
    structure of, 26-34, 39-42
Anglo-Saxons, laws and customs of, 5-13; see
    also Edward the Confessor
Angoulême, count of, 61n.,; Isabella of, 105
Anjou, 26-8, 30-1, 34-7, 40-1, 43-4, 46, 48,
    50, 61, 68, 127, 150, 153, 191n.; alleged
    exchequer of, 37n.; Geoffrey, count of,
    26, 28, 40-2; Henry, count of, 26, 68;
    Jocelin of Tours, seneschal of, 31;
    seneschalsy of, 43-4
Anstey, Richard of, 33n.
Appleby, 115
Aquitaine, 27, 30, 36n., 37n., 40n., 41, 52,
    68, 91, 153; see also Eleanor
Aragon, charters of liberties of, 304
Arflet of Northumberland, 53
Arques, 42n.
Arsuf, battle of, 81
Arthurian Legend, 7, 9, 53-4
Articles of the Barons, 217-20, 223-30, 236-
    7, 292-5, 301, 304,; cap. 25, 225-6, 228;
    cap. 48, 226; sealing of, 226-7
Artois, 37
Arundel, William, earl of, 182n., 299
Asterby, Roger of, 188, 193
Athée, Gerard d', 44n., 51
Aubrey see Louis VII
Aumale, 50, 60, 63
Auvergne, 50, 143

Bagot, Hervey, 75
Bardolf, Hugh, 52n.; Robert, 191; Thomas,
    181n.
Barewe, Thomas de, 222n.
Barfleur, 43
Barnwell Chronicler, 53, 99, 100, 185n.,
    187n., 192, 228, 229, 235n., 239

Bassingborn, John of, 223n.
Bath, Jocelin, bishop of, 243
Baudemont, 59; Joel de, 58
Bautr' (Beautr'), Benedict, 116n.; Hugh, 116n.;
    Thomas, 116n.
Bayonne, merchants of, 78
Beauchamp, Eudo de, 189
Beaumont, fee of, 247
Beaumont-le-Roger, 57, 60
Beauvais, 56
Beauvaisis, 60
Bec, abbey of, 56; Henry, 182n.
Bedford, 105; citizens of, 31n.; burgesses of, 72
Bedfordshire, 165, 262, 263
Bellême, 49
Berengaria, queen of England, 46n.
Berri, 142
Bertin, St, abbey of, 11
Berwick, John of, 11
Béthune, Baldwin de, 54, 63
Bigod see Norfolk
Bill of Rights, 291
Birkin, John de, 200
Blackstone, Sir William, 217, 219n., 227n., 259,
    265
Blanche of Castille, queen of France, 64, 65
Blois, Louis, count of, 59; Peter of, 29, 30, 246;
    Theobald VI, count of, 60
Bohun, see Hereford
Boissy-Mauvoisin, 57
Bologna, 184
Bordeaux, citizens of, 44n., 121
Born, Bertrand de, 51, 99, 139
Bosco, Arnold de, 62; Hugh de, 79
Boston, 117
Bouafle, church of St Martin, 56
Boulogne, Matthew, count of, 50
Bouvines, battle of, 23, 24, 63, 150, 159
Bovington, Walter de, 200
Brackley, 221; 'schedule', 220, 224n., 226
Bracton, Henry, 13, 17, 208, 214
Bréauté, Faulkes de, 105, 107, 152n., 222n.
Breteuil, 247
Brevia regis, 32-3, 70-3, 76-9; de ultra mare, 32-3
    76-7
Brionne, 57
Briouze (Braose), family of, 89; William de, 89,
    103, 137, 181n., 185, 186, 194, 195;
    Matilda, wife of, 88
Bristol, 242n.
Brittany, 26, 27, 36, 41, 48, 50, 54, 61, 152, 15!
    Arthur, duke of, 41, 53, 60n., 61, 89, 99,
    101, 105, 137n., 148; Constance, duchess
    of, 132
Briwerre, William, 52n., 198, 202, 223n., 232,
    244